2021
青岛统计年鉴
QINGDAO STATISTICAL YEARBOOK

（总　第42期　VOL.42）

青岛市统计局
国家统计局青岛调查队　编
QINGDAO MUNICIPAL BUREAU OF STATISTICS
NBS SURVEY OFFICE IN QINGDAO

中国统计出版社
China Statistics Press

© 中国统计出版社有限公司 2021
版权所有。未经许可，本书的任何部分不得以任何方式在世界任何地区以任何文字翻印、拷贝、仿制或转载。

© 2021 China Statistics Press Co.,Ltd.
All rights reserved. No part of the publication may be reproduced or transmitted in any form or by any means, electronic or mechanical, including photocopying, recording, or any information storage and retrieval system, without written permission from the publisher.

图书在版编目（CIP）数据

青岛统计年鉴 . 2021 = Qingdao Statistical Yearbook 2021 : 汉英对照 / 青岛市统计局，国家统计局青岛调查队编 . -- 北京 : 中国统计出版社，2021.8
ISBN 978-7-5037-9522-0

Ⅰ. ①青… Ⅱ. ①青… ②国… Ⅲ. ①统计资料－青岛－2021－年鉴－汉、英 Ⅳ. ① C832.523-54

中国版本图书馆 CIP 数据核字 (2021) 第 117261 号

青岛统计年鉴—2021

作　　者 / 青岛市统计局　国家统计局青岛调查队
责任编辑 / 钟　钰
装帧设计 / 青岛双福文化传播有限公司
出版发行 / 中国统计出版社有限公司
地　　址 / 北京市丰台区西三环南路甲 6 号
邮政编码 / 100073
电　　话 / 邮购（010）63376909　书店（010）68783171
网　　址 / http://www.zgtjcbs.com
印　　刷 / 青岛任缘印刷包装有限公司
经　　销 / 新华书店
开　　本 / 890mm × 1240mm　1/16
字　　数 / 1210 千字
印　　张 / 27.5　彩页 1.25
版　　别 / 2021 年 8 月第 1 版
版　　次 / 2021 年 8 月第 1 次印刷
定　　价 / 280.00 元　Price: 280.00yuan(RMB)

如有印装差错，由本社发行部调换。

全市生产总值构成（%）

Composition Of Gross Domestic Product (%)

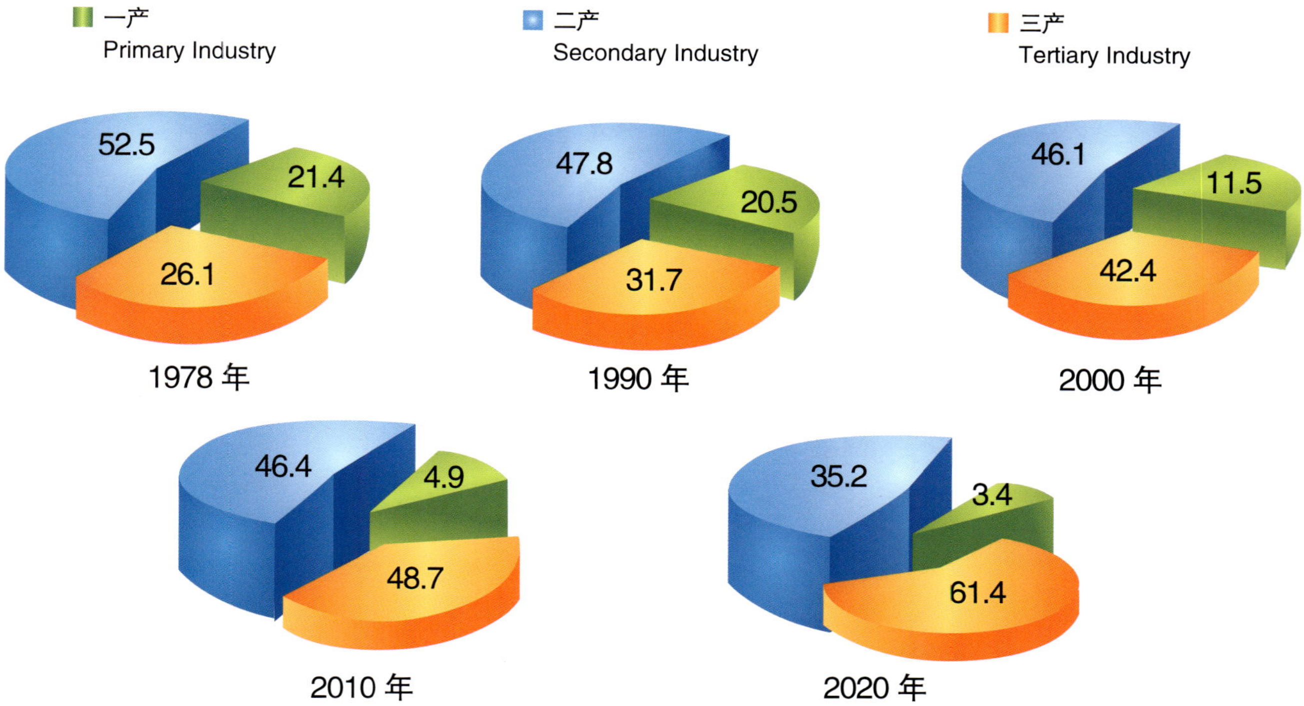

全市生产总值（亿元）

Gross Domestic Product (100 million yuan)

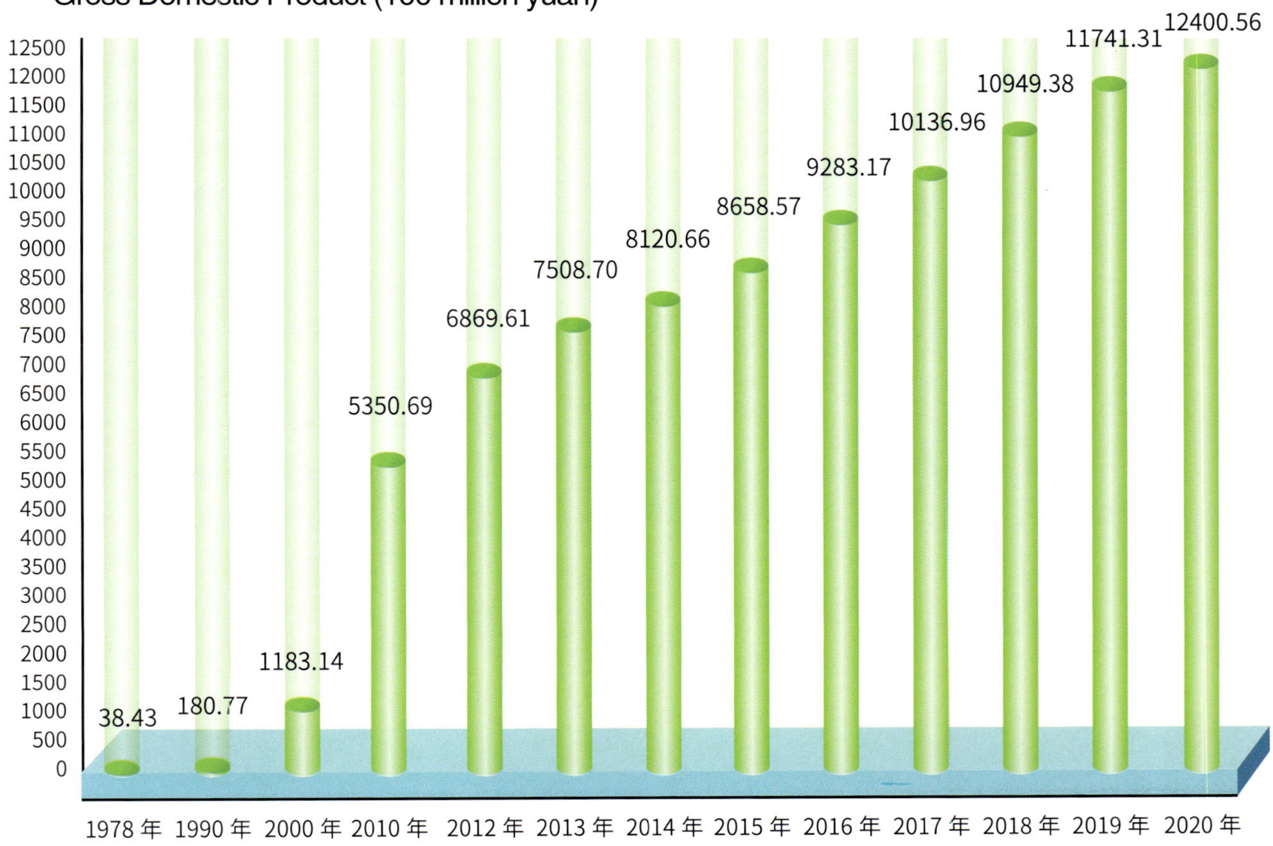

农林牧渔业总产值（亿元）

Gross Output Value Of Agriculture (100 million yuan)

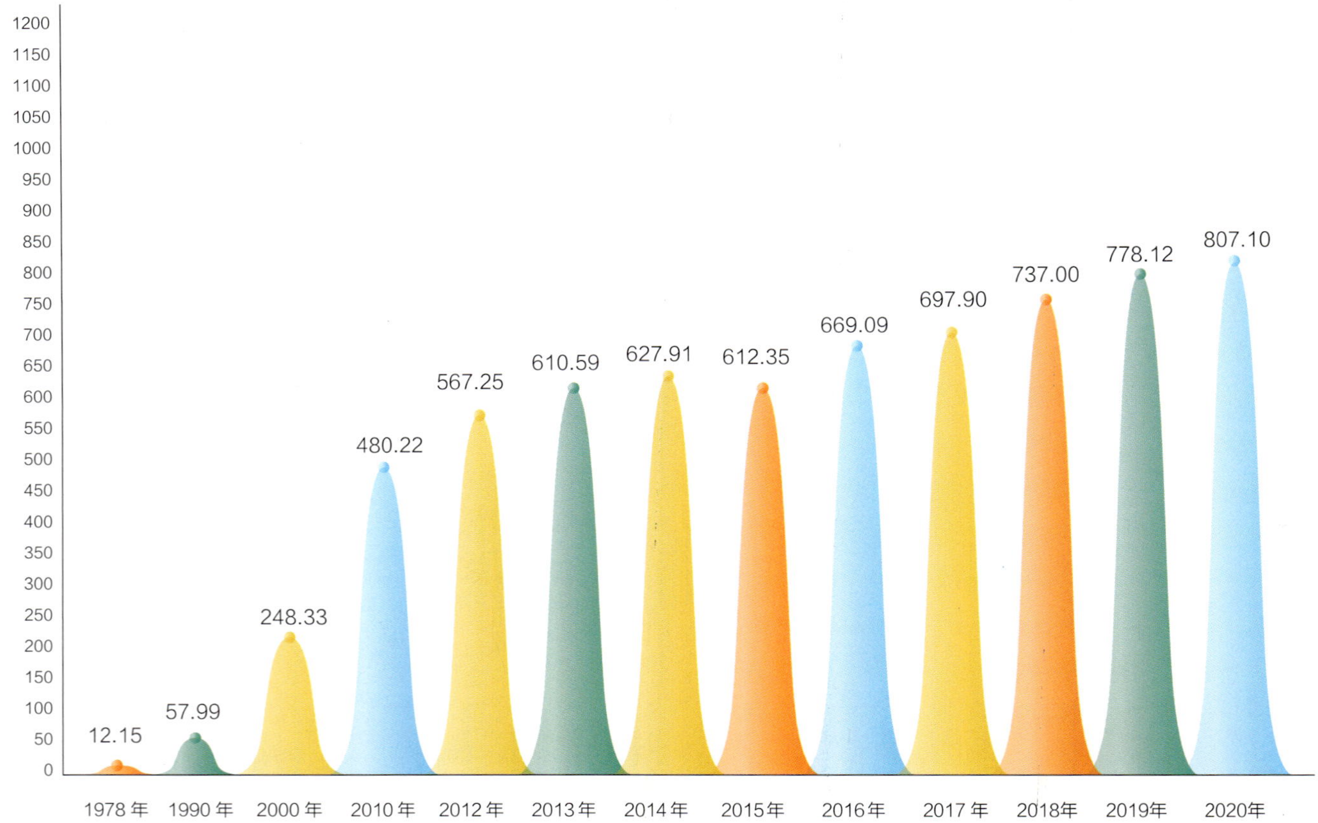

主要农产品产量（万吨）

Output Of Farm Products (10 000 tons)

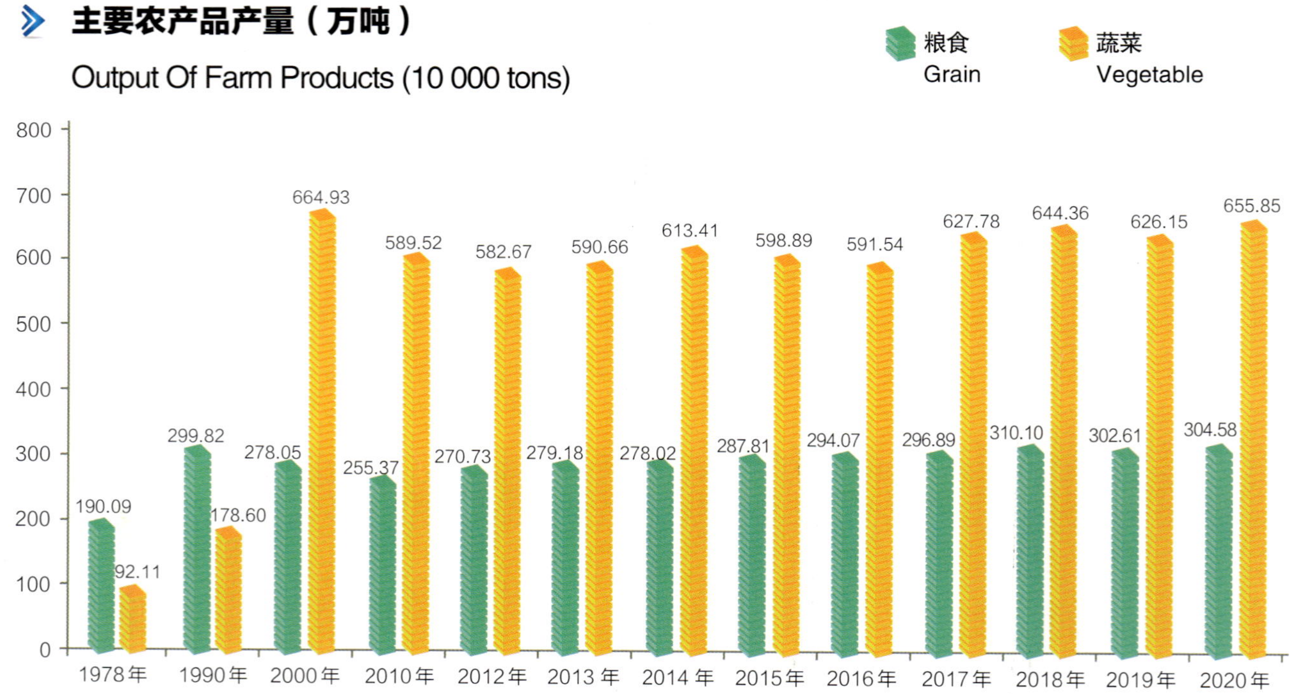

工业总产值（亿元）

Gross Industrial Output Value (100 million yuan)

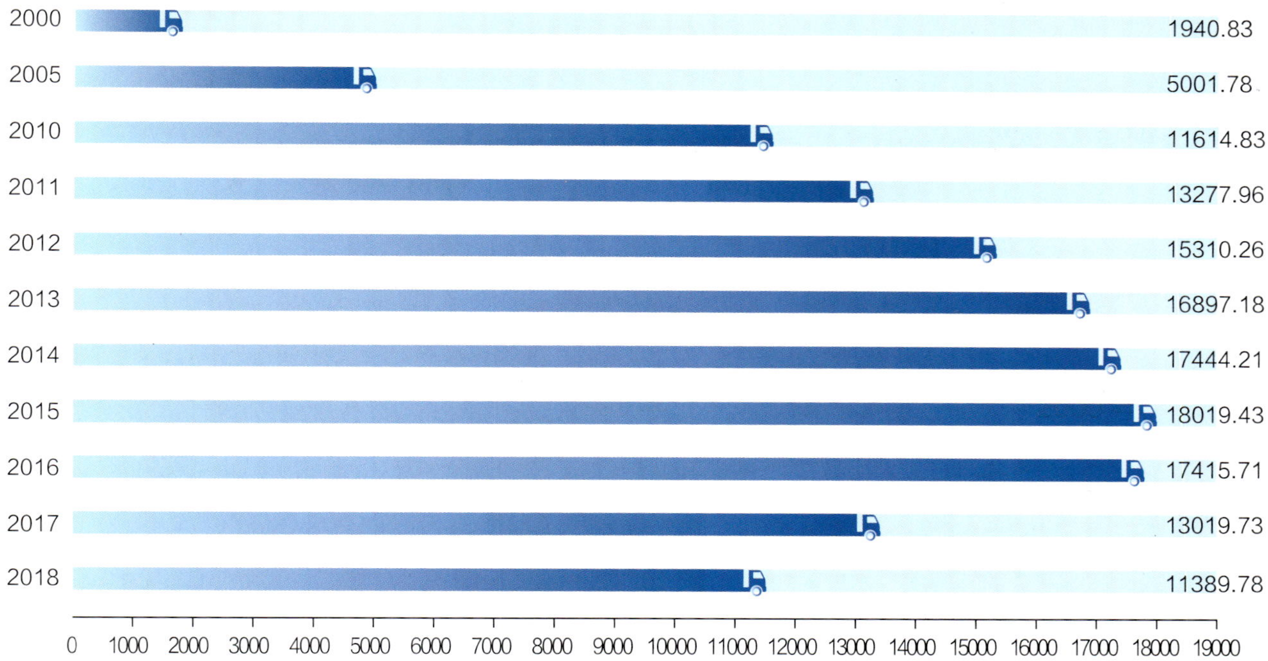

规模以上工业实现利润总额（亿元）

The Total Profits Made By The Industries Above The Designated Size (100 million yuan)

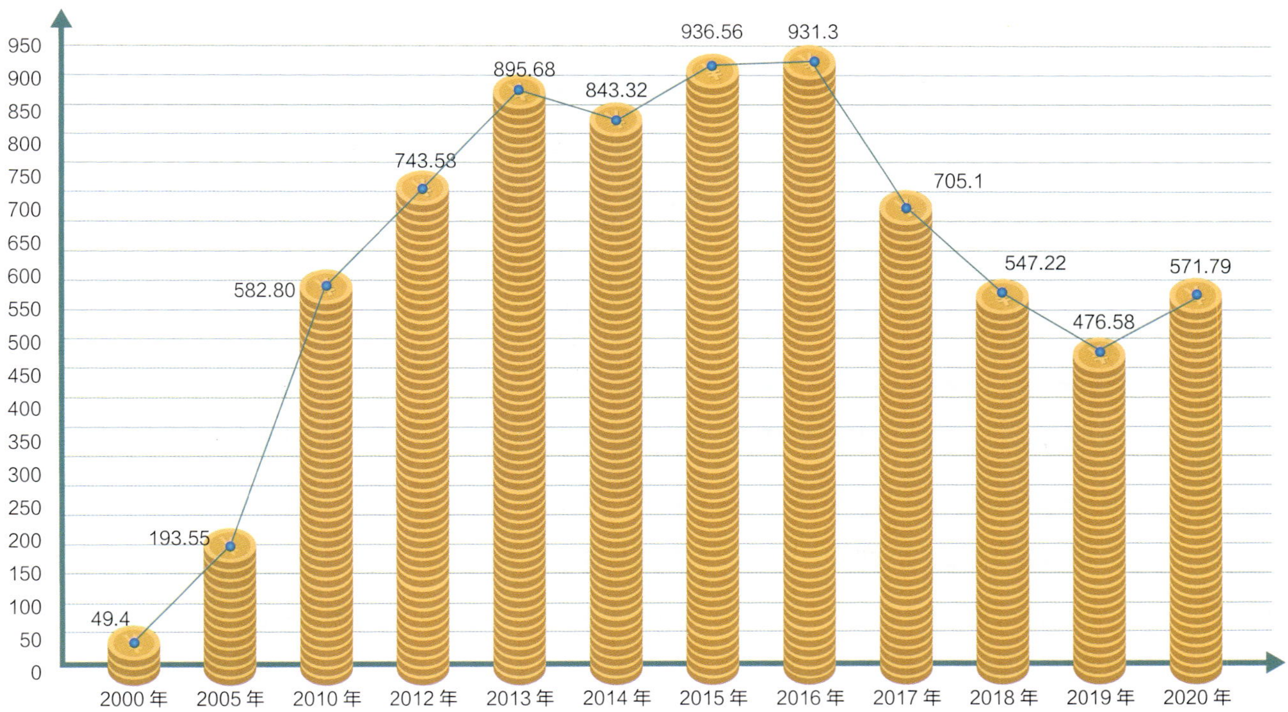

房地产开发投资（亿元）

Investment In Real Estate Development (100 million yuan)

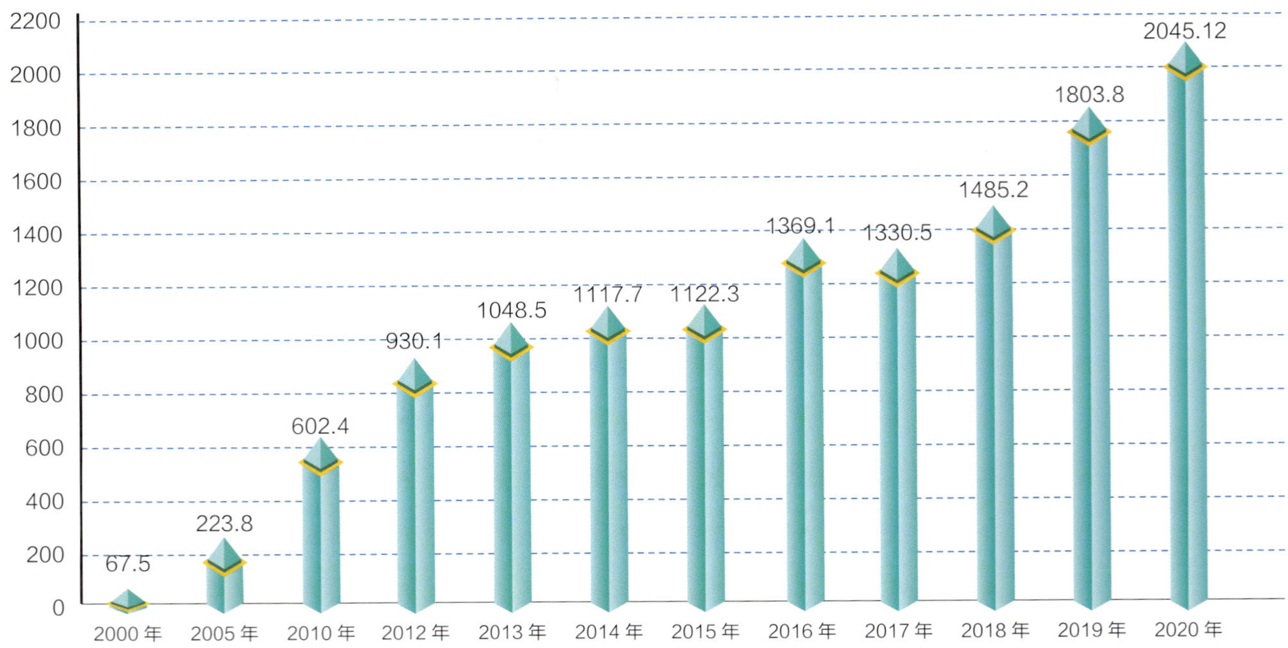

房屋销售面积（万平方米）

Floor Space Of Commercial Buildings Sold (10 000 sq.m)

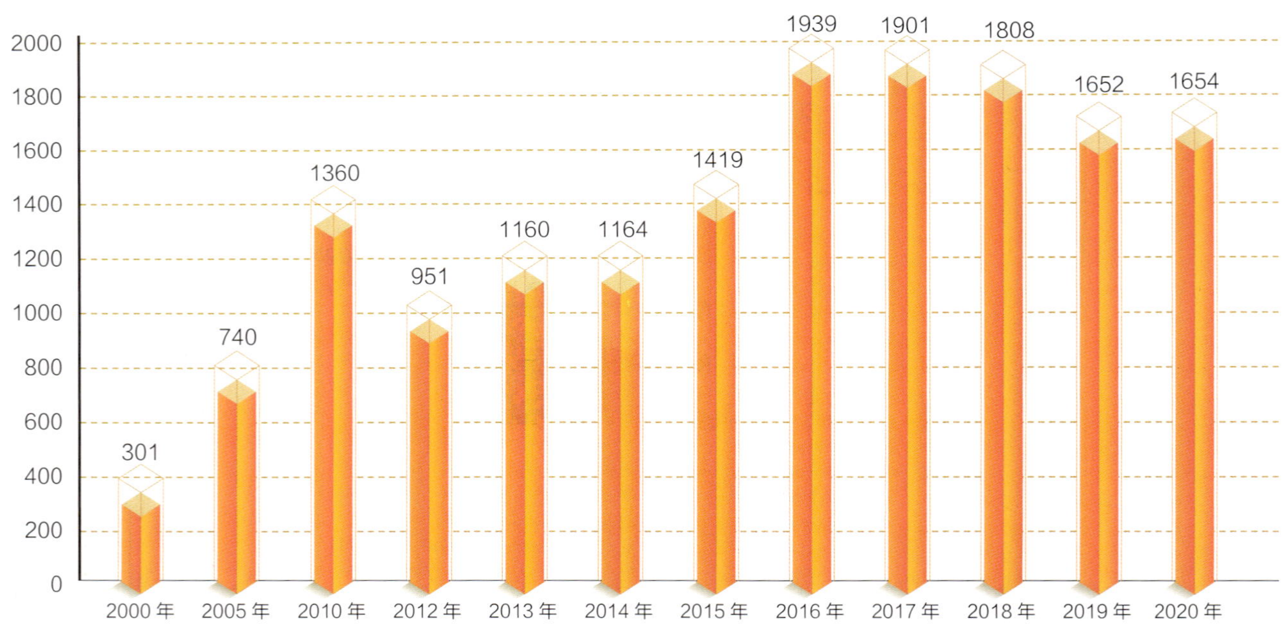

消费构成（%）（2020 年）

2020 Composition Of Consumption (%)

社会消费品零售总额（亿元）

Total Retail Sales Of Consumer Goods (100 million yuan)

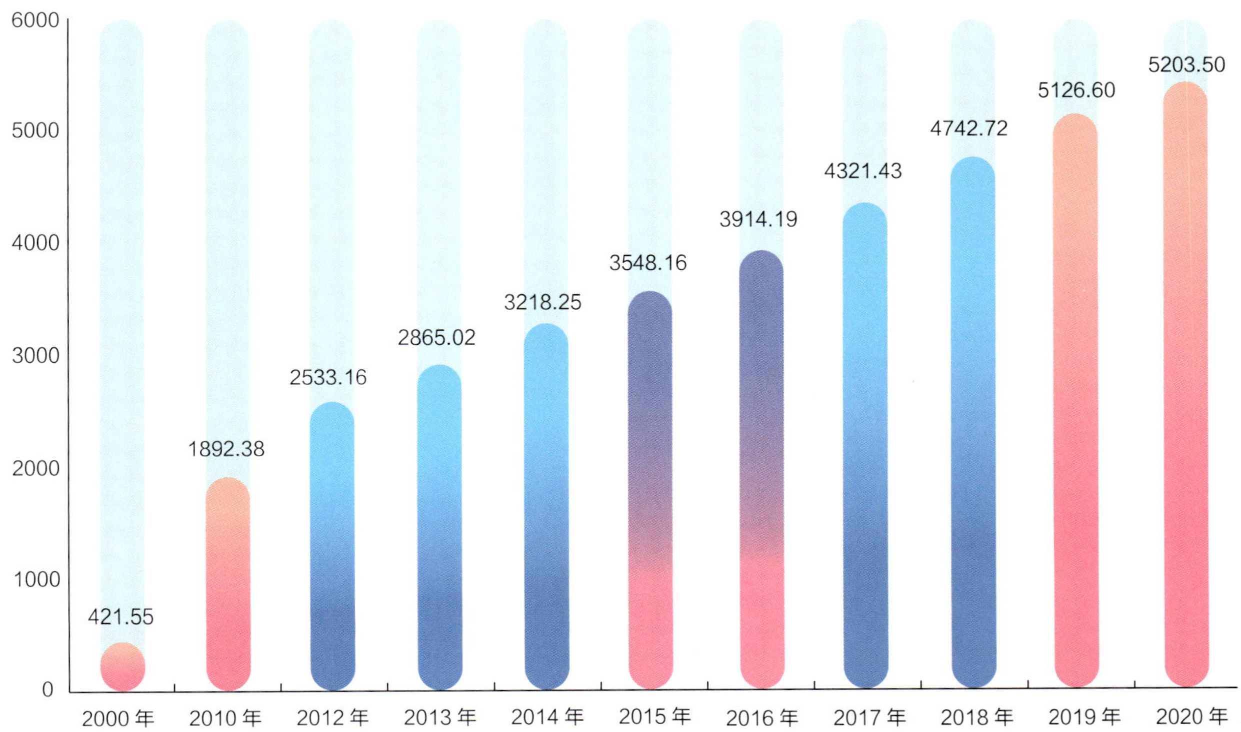

旅游人数（万人次）

Number Of Tourists (10 000 person–times)

国内旅游人数

Number Of Domestic Tourists

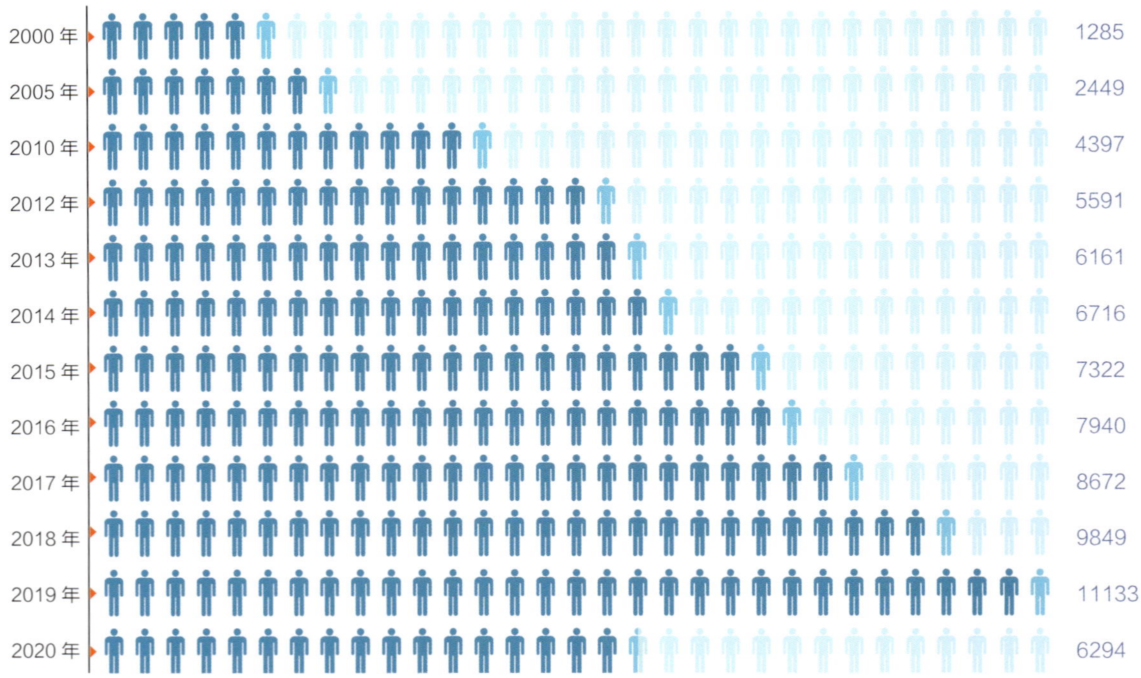

入境旅游人数

Number Of Oversea Visitor Arrivals

地方财政收入（亿元）

Revenue Of Local Government Finance (100 million yuan)

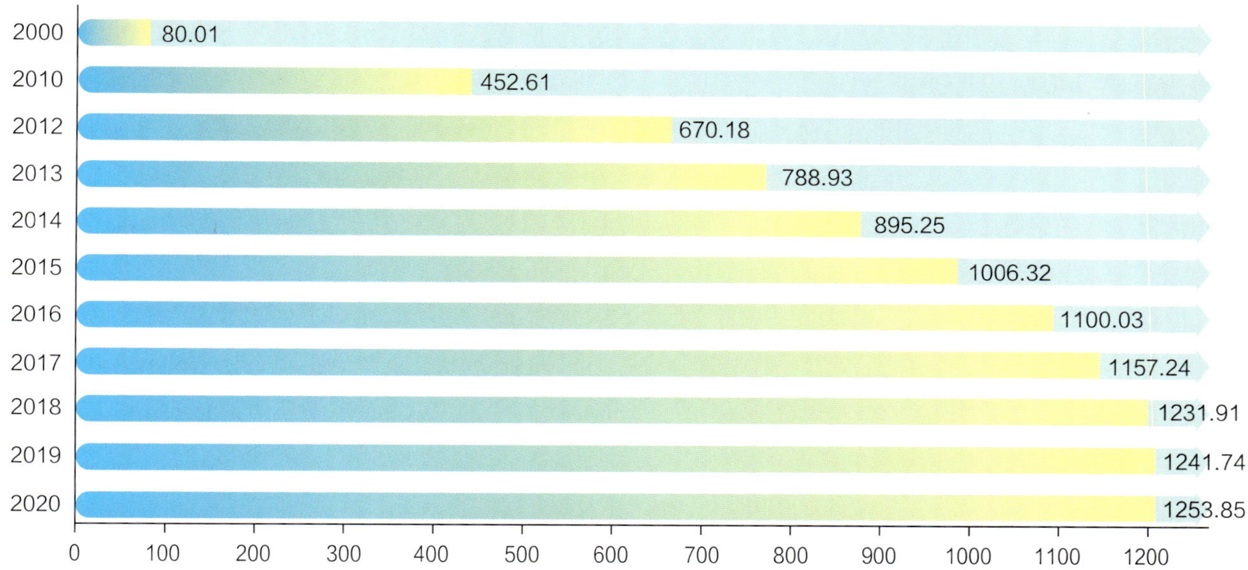

注：2002 年以后财政收入为一般预算收入数。

Note：Since 2002，revenue of government finance refers to general budgetary revenue.

金融机构年末人民币存贷款余额（亿元）

Year–end Savings Deposits And Loans Of Financial Institution (RMB) (100 million yuan)

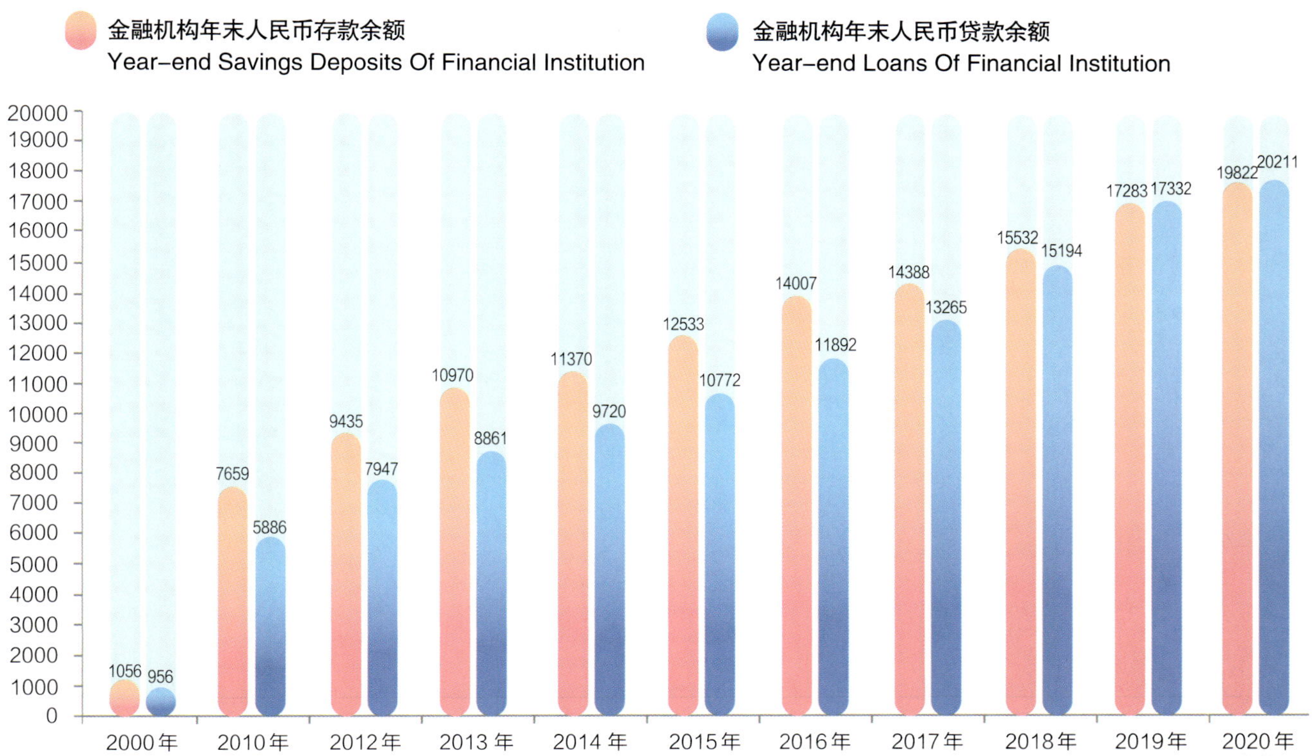

社会从业人数（万人）

Social Employment (10 000 persons)

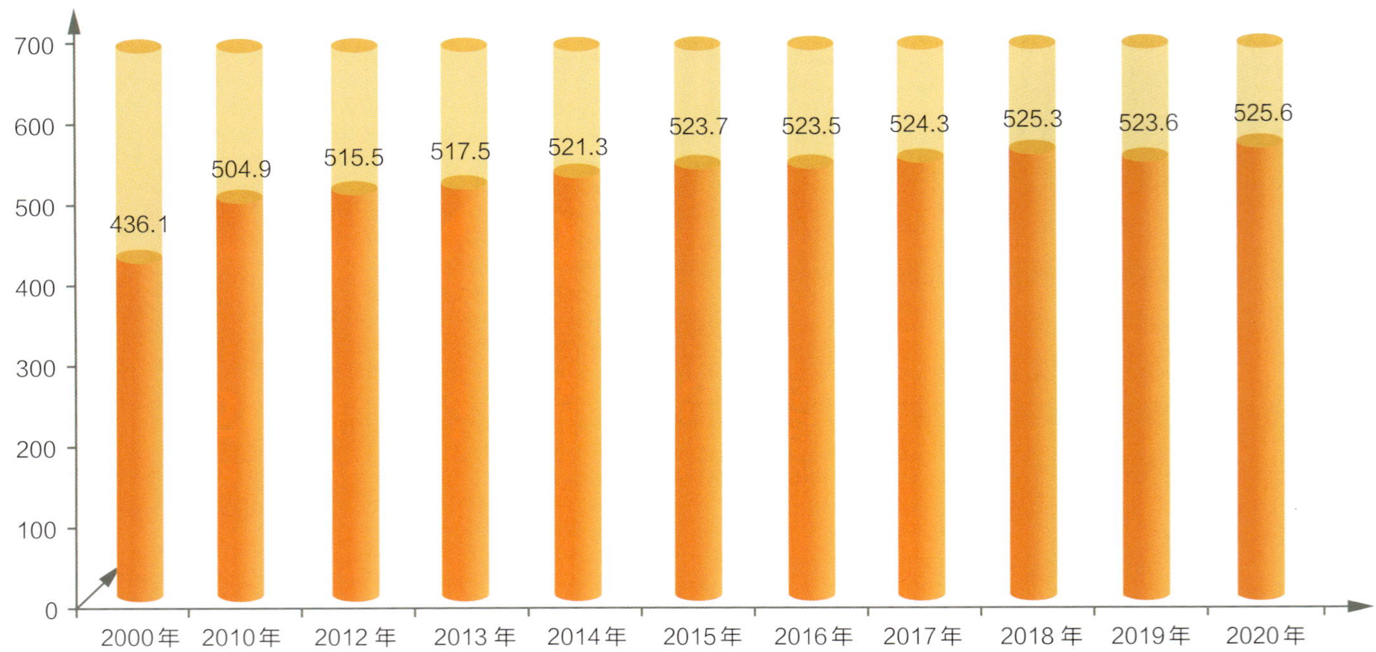

城镇非私营单位平均工资（元）

Average Salary Of Urban Non–Private Units (yuan)

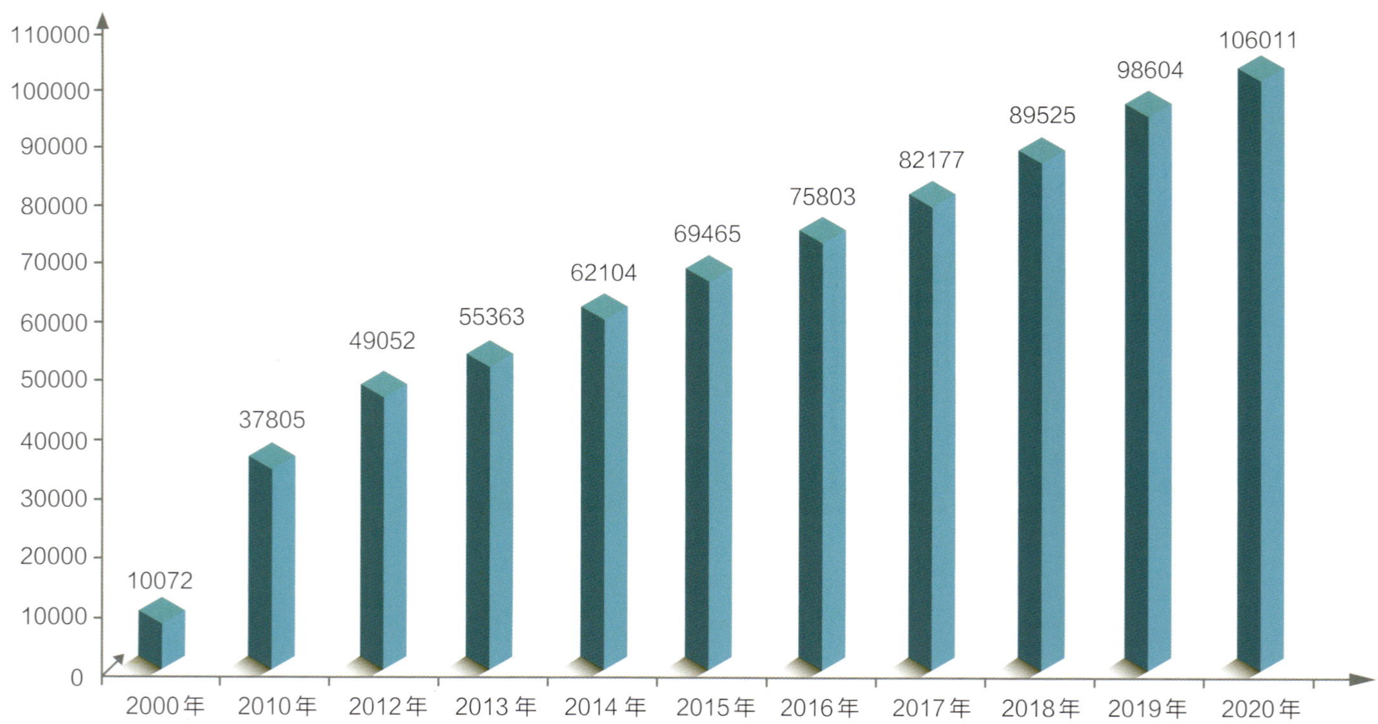

居民消费价格指数（上年＝100）

Consumer Price Indices (preceding year = 100)

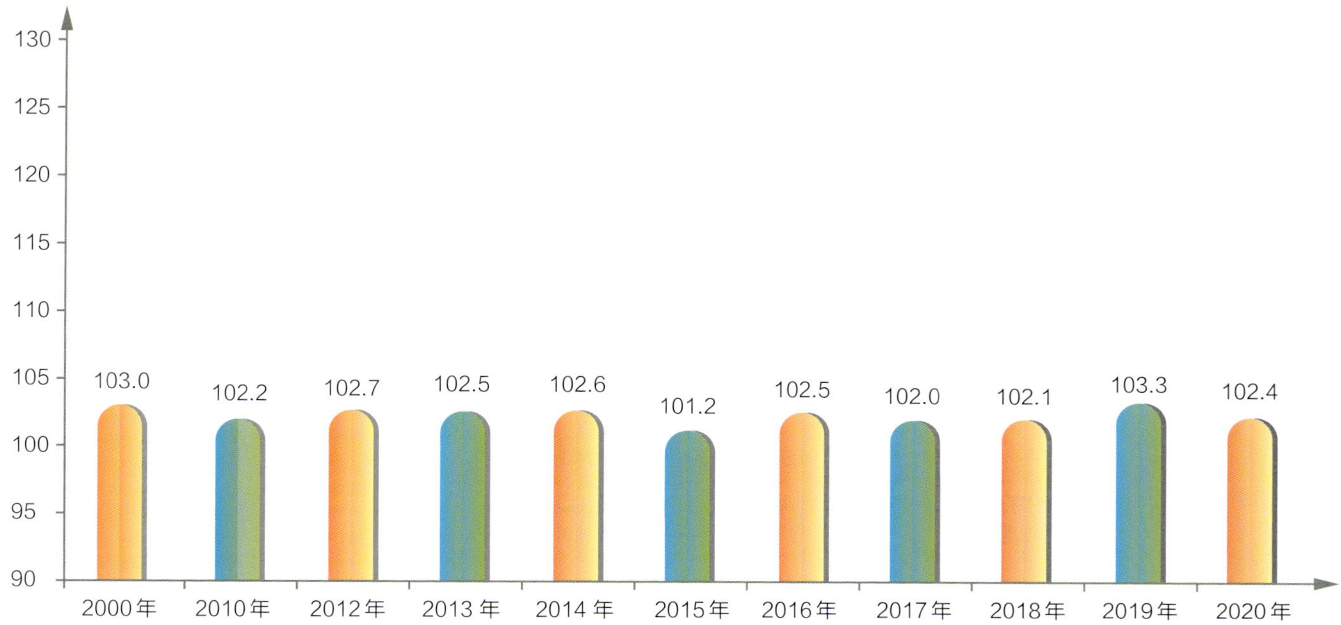

商品零售价格指数（上年＝100）

Retail Price Indices (preceding year = 100)

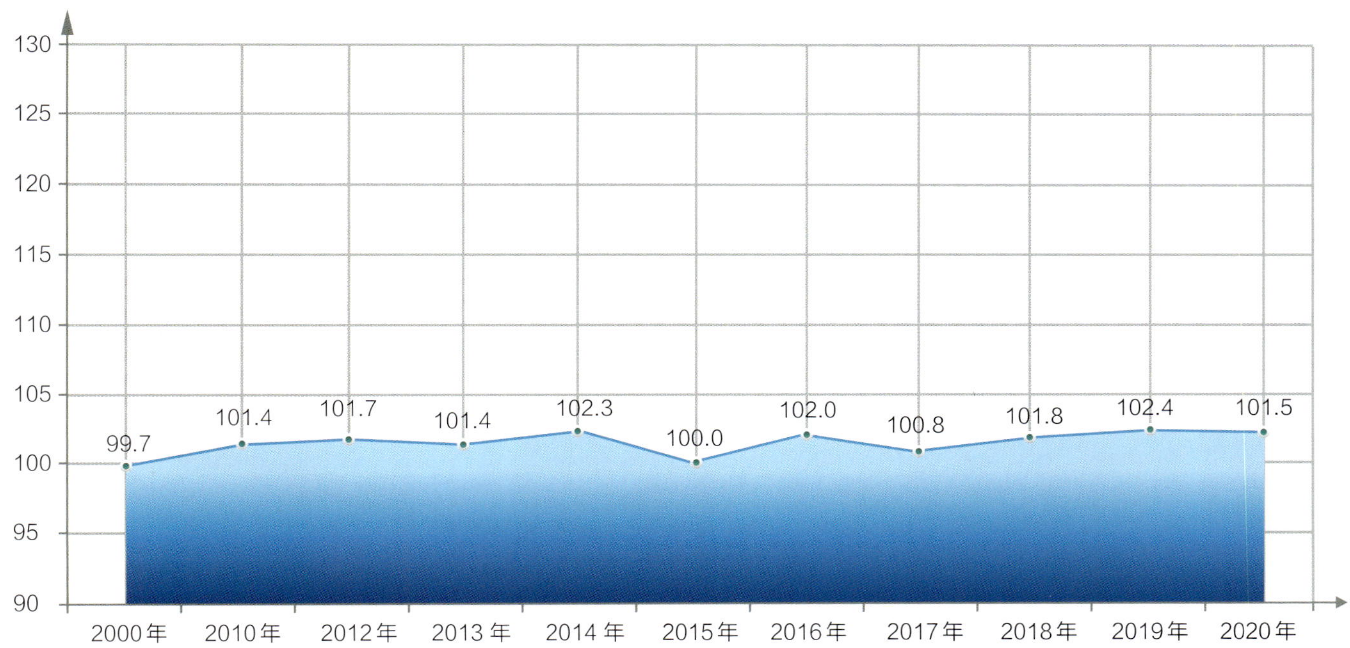

城市建成区面积（平方公里）

Developed Area Of the City (sq.km)

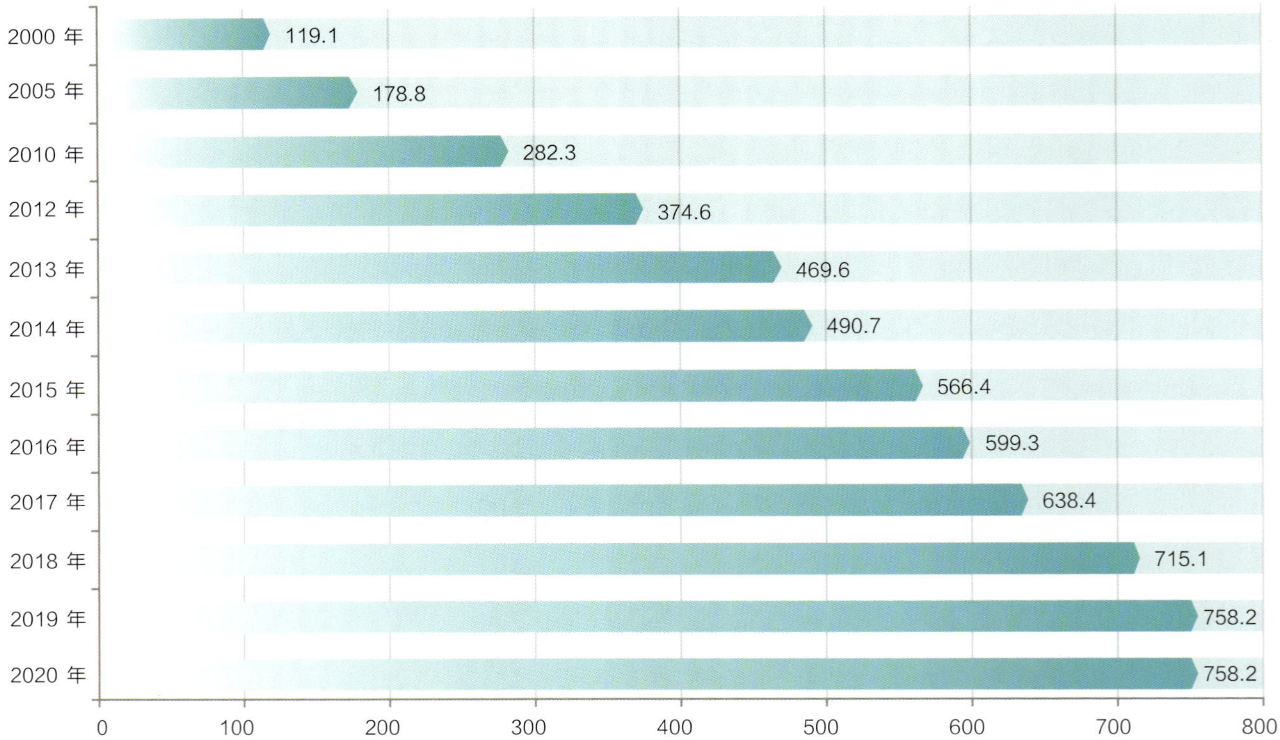

铺装道路面积（万平方米）

Area Of Roads (10 000 sq.m)

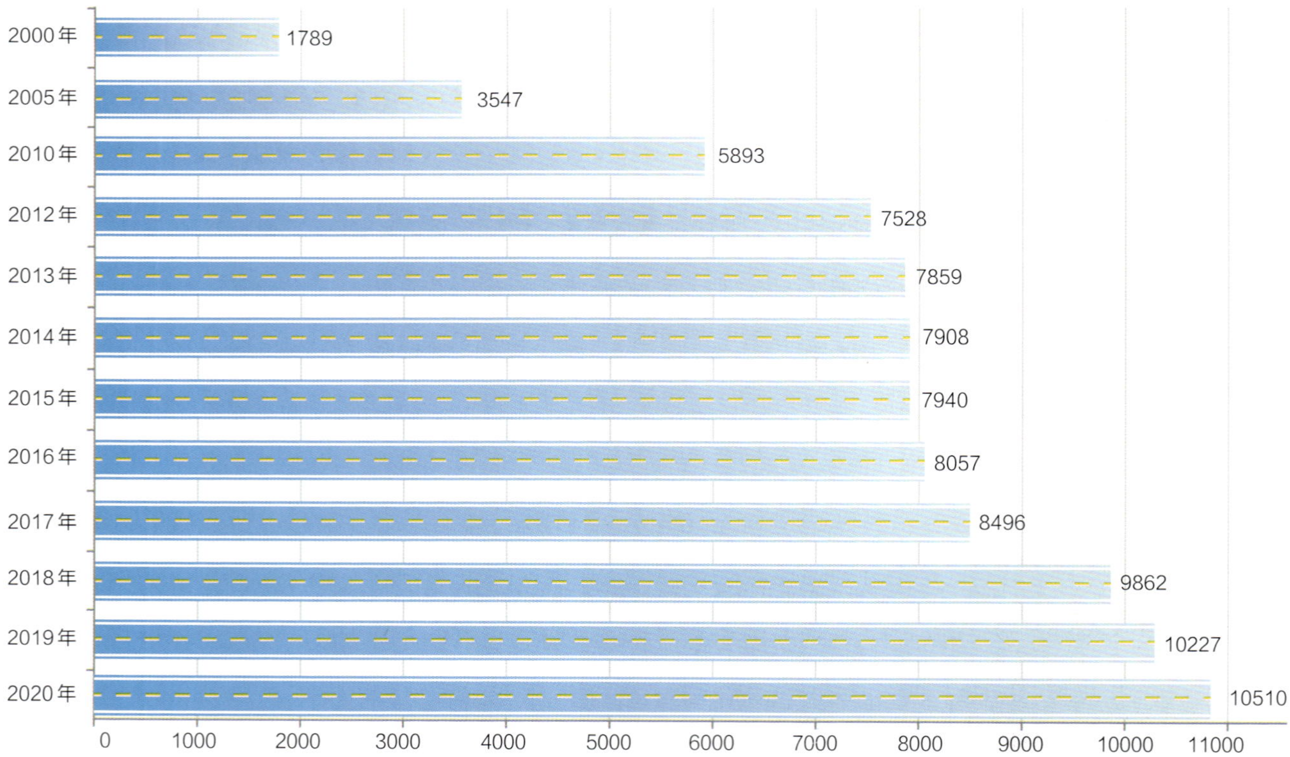

医疗卫生机构（个）

Health Care Institutions (unit)

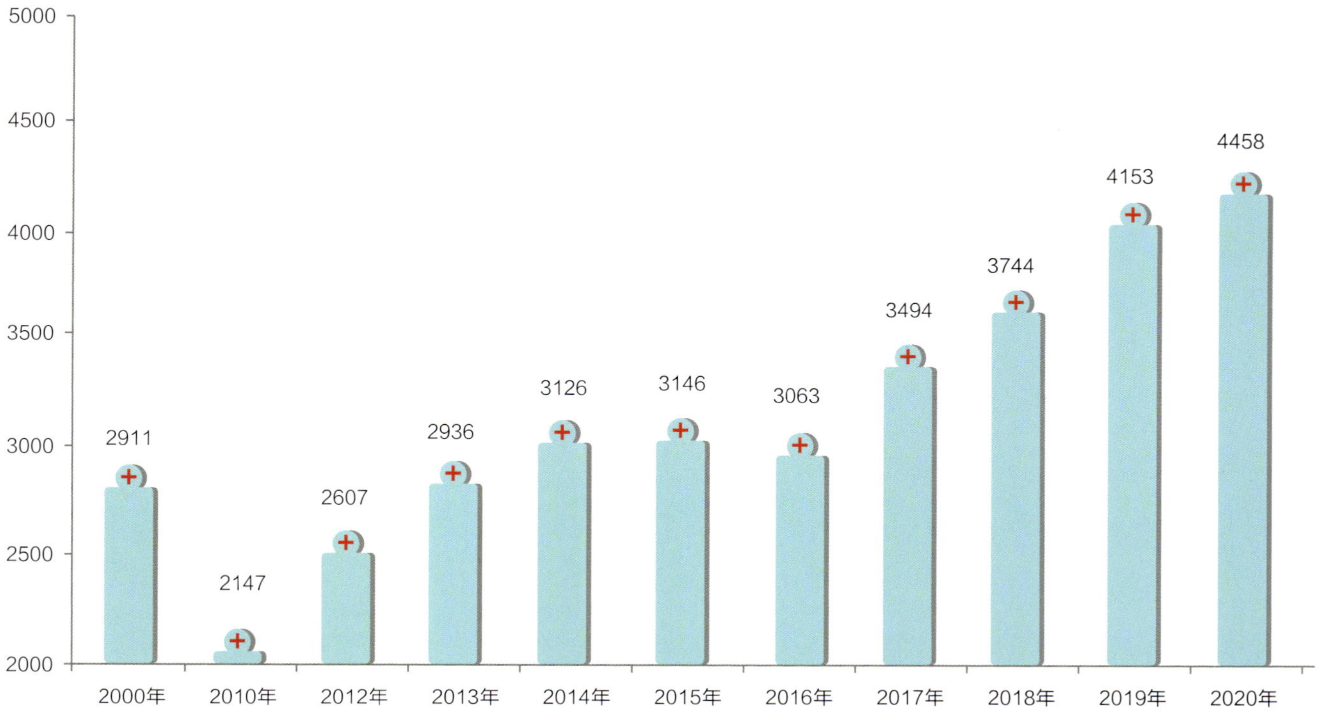

普通高校在校人数（万人）

Students Enrollment Of Regular Institutions Of Higher Education (10 000 persons)

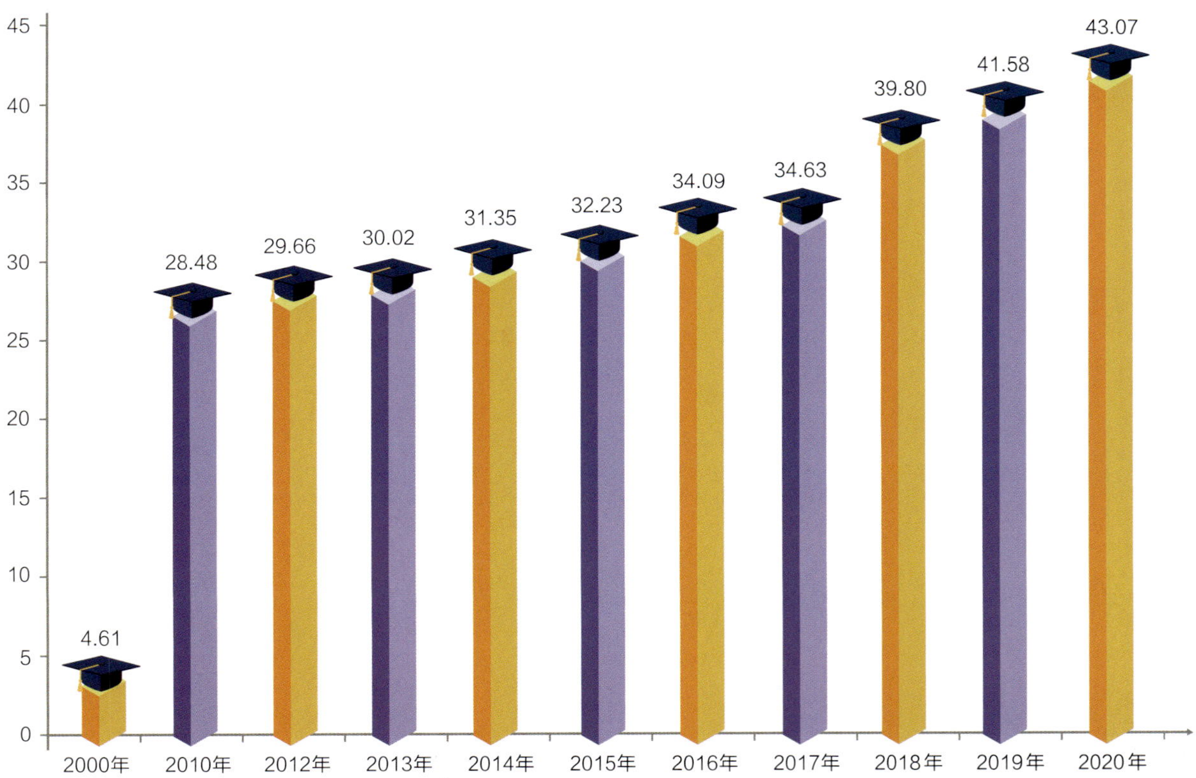

编辑委员会

◆ 主　　任：刘岐涛

◆ 副 主 任：黄成海　于春涛　李坤兴　刘　伟　张德祥　滕　涛
张茂海　胡宝良　侯　杰　徐凤霞　毛小美

◆ 委　　员：（以姓氏笔划为序）
于泳洋　于　洋　马　奇　王之钰　王维周　王　磊
左华卿　付增梁　李　勇　宋　波　张锦花　林玉森
周　巍　贾洪泰　钱孝高　韩君梁

◆ 主　　编：刘岐涛

◆ 常务副主编：刘　伟

◆ 副 主 编：马　奇　刘　斌　刘　芹

◆ 责任编辑：钟　钰

◆ 编　　辑：（以姓氏笔划为序）
于世涛　于安生　王　元　王　媛　尹正德　印春明
石　岩　史东姿　冯　健　乔　丹　刘连玫　刘俐娜
刘　斌　孙文斐　孙　辉　纪　琳　李守宝　李晓雯
杨雪雅　肖婷婷　何　帅　宋卫庆　宋天戈　张　进
张玮华　张砚惠　张翊钧　陈旭亮　陈　珊　陈骁聪
陈　菁　陈　强　林乐靖　林红云　周庆福　周　敏
徐凌云　盖　放　梁　莉　韩劭杰　窦　蕾　魏一杰

EDITORIAL BOARD

Director：Liu Qitao

Deputy Director：

Huang Chenghai	Yu Chuntao	Li Kunxing	Liu Wei	Zhang Dexiang	Teng Tao
Zhang Maohai	Hu Baoliang	Hou Jie	Xu Fengxia	Mao Xiaomei	

Board：(in order of strokes of Chinese Surname)

Yu Yongyang	Yu Yang	Ma Qi	Wang Zhiyu	Wang Weizhou	Wang Lei
Zuo Huaqing	Fu Zengliang	Li Yong	Song Bo	Zhang Jinhua	Lin Yusen
Zhou Wei	Jia Hongtai	Qian Xiaogao	Han Junliang		

Editor-in-chief：Liu Qitao

Managing Deputy Editor-in-chief：Liu Wei

Deputy Editor-in-chief：Ma Qi　Liu Bin　Liu Qin

Coordinator：Zhong Yu

Editorial Staff：(in order of strokes of Chinese Surname)

Yu Shitao	Yu Ansheng	Wang Yuan	Wang Yuan	Yin Zhengde	Yin Chunming
Shi Yan	Shi Dongzi	Feng Jian	Qiao Dan	Liu Lianmei	Liu Lina
Liu Bin	Sun Wenfei	Sun Hui	Ji Lin	Li Shoubao	Li Xiaowen
Yang Xueya	Xiao Tingting	He Shuai	Song Weiqing	Song Tiange	Zhang Jin
Zhang Weihua	Zhang Yanhui	Zhang Yijun	Chen Xuliang	Chen Shan	Chen Xiaocong
Chen Jing	Chen Qiang	Lin Lejing	Lin hongyun	Zhou Qingfu	Zhou Min
Xu Lingyun	Gai Fang	Liang Li	Han Shaojie	Dou Lei	Wei Yijie

编 者 说 明

一、《青岛统计年鉴—2021》是一部全面反映青岛市国民经济和社会发展情况、信息高度密集的资料工具书。

二、本年鉴共包括发展成果图、统计公报、统计表、附录四大部分。

统计表部分收录了 2020 年青岛市经济和社会等各方面的统计数据，以及中华人民共和国成立以来重要年份和改革开放以来的主要统计数据，包括：综合，人口，从业人员及职工工资，固定资产投资，对外经济贸易，城市建设、环境保护，能源消耗，财政金融和保险业，价格指数，人民生活，农业，工业，规模以上服务业，建筑业，运输、邮电，批发和零售业，住宿、餐饮业和旅游，教育、科技和文化，体育、卫生和民政、司法。

为方便读者正确地使用年鉴资料，各篇章前设有《简要说明》，概括介绍各篇主要内容和资料来源；篇末还附有《主要统计指标解释》。

三、本年鉴部分历史数据已根据经济普查、农业普查、人口普查数据进行了修订调整，在此之前公布的数据凡与本年鉴数字不符的一律以本年鉴为准。

四、部门分区市数据按照所属职能部门提供的区市名称范围划分。

五、本年鉴中的符号说明：年鉴各表中的“空格”表示该项统计指标数据不足本表最小单位数、数据不详或无该项数据；"#" 表示其中的主要项。

六、《青岛统计年鉴》自公开出版以来，受到社会各界的关心和支持，对于年鉴的内容和编辑工作提出了许多宝贵的意见，对此我们深表谢意。限于我们的水平，欢迎读者继续对年鉴的不足之处给予批评和指正，帮助我们进一步改进年鉴编辑工作，以期更好地为广大读者服务。

《青岛统计年鉴》编委会

2021 年 8 月

Editor's Note

Ⅰ. *Qingdao Statistical Yearbook 2021* is a very important reference book, which reflects various aspects of Qingdao's social and economic development and contains High-density information.

Ⅱ.The yearbook contains the following four parts: achievement graphs, statistic gazette, statistics and appendixes.

Statistics contains all kinds of data on Qingdao's social and economic development in 2020, and data in significant year or data since the beginning of reform and opening up, including: General Survey; Population; Employment and Wages; Investment in Fixed Assets; Foreign Trade; City Construction and Environment Protection; Consumption of Energy; Government Finance ,Financial Intermediation and Insurance; Price; People's Living Conditions; Agriculture; Industry; service industries above designated size; Construction; Transport, Postal and Telecommunication Services; Wholesale and Retail Trades; Hotels, Catering Services and Tourism; Education, Science and Culture; Sports, Public Health and Civil Affairs, Judicial Affairs; Enterprises Survey.

In brief introduction at the beginning of each chapter, main coverage, data sources and statistical coverage are concerned. Meanwhile explanatory notes on major statistical indicators have been attached for readers to use the data correctly.

Ⅲ. All of the data in the book are in accordance with new administrative division.

Some of the data have been adjusted on the basis of statistics of economic census. In any case the data of this book shall be deemed as the authentic ones.

Ⅳ. Departmental district city data is divided according to the range of district and city names provided by the functional department to which it belongs.

Ⅴ. Explanation of symbols in this yearbook: "blanks" in the tables in the yearbook indicate that the statistical indicator data is insufficient to the minimum unit number in this table, the data is unknown or there is no such data; "#" indicates the main item.

Ⅵ. Since the publication of the *"Qingdao Statistical Yearbook"*, it has received care and support from all walks of life, and has put forward many valuable opinions on the content and editing of the yearbook, for which we are deeply grateful. Limited to our level, readers are welcome to continue to criticize and correct the deficiencies of the yearbook, and to help us further improve the editing of the yearbook in order to better serve the readers.

Editorial Board

August,2021

目　录
CONTENTS

一、综　合
Chapter 1.　GENERAL SURVEY

二、人　口
Chapter 2.　POPULATION

三、从业人员及职工工资
Chapter 3.　EMPLOYMENT AND WAGES

四、固定资产投资
Chapter 4.　INVESTMENT IN FIXED ASSETS

五、对外经济贸易
Chapter 5.　FOREIGN TRADE

六、城市建设、环境保护
Chapter 6.　CITY CONSTRUCTION AND ENVIRONMENT PROTECTION

七、能源消耗
Chapter 7.　CONSUMPTION OF ENERGY

八、财政、金融和保险业
Chapter 8.　GOVERNMENT FINANCE, FINANCIAL AND INSURANCE

九、价格指数
Chapter 9.　PRICE INDEXES

十、人民生活
Chapter 10.　PEOPLE'S LIVING CONDITIONS

十一、农 业
Chapter 11. AGRICULTURE

十二、工　业
Chapter 12.　INDUSTRY

十三、规模以上服务业
Chapter 13.　SERVICE ENTERPRISES ABOVE DESIGNATED SIZE

十四、建　筑　业
Chapter 14.　CONSTRUCTION

十五、运输、邮电
Chapter 15. TRANSPORT, POSTAL AND TELECOMMUNICATION SERVICES

十六、批发和零售业
Chapter 16. WHOLESALE AND RETAIL TRADES

十七、住宿、餐饮业和旅游
Chapter 17. HOTELS, CATERING SERVICES AND TOURISM

十八、教育、科技和文化
Chapter 18.　EDUCATION SCIENCE & TECHNOLOGY AND CULTURE

十九、体育、卫生和民政、司法

Chapter 19.　SPORTS, PUBLIC HEALTH AND CIVIL AFFAIRS, JUDICIAL AFFAIRS

附　录
APPENDIX

2020 年
青岛市国民经济和社会发展
统 计 公 报[1]

青岛市统计局

国家统计局青岛调查队

（2021 年 3 月 16 日）

2020 年是青岛发展历程中极不平凡的一年，面对突如其来的疫情冲击和严峻复杂的形势，全市上下坚持以习近平新时代中国特色社会主义思想为指导，全面贯彻党的十九大和十九届二中、三中、四中、五中全会精神，深入落实习近平总书记对青岛工作的重要指示要求，在中央和省、市委的坚强领导下，科学把握新发展阶段，全面贯彻新发展理念，服务构建新发展格局，统筹疫情防控和经济社会发展，扎实做好“六稳”工作，全面落实“六保”任务，疫情防控取得阶段性成效，全市经济社会发展表现出强大韧性，高质量发展积厚成势，新旧动能转换初见成效，人民福祉水平持续提升，社会大局和谐稳定，“十三五”实现圆满收官，全面建成小康社会取得决定性进展和历史性成就，开放、现代、活力、时尚的国际大都市建设取得重大进展。

一、综 合

经济发展好于预期。统一核算结果显示，2020 年全市生产总值[2]12400.56 亿元，占全国生产总值的比重为 1.22%，按可比价格计算，增长 3.7%。其中，第一产业增加值 425.41 亿元，增长 2.6%；第二产业增加值 4361.56 亿元，增长 3.0%；第三产业增加值 7613.59 亿元，增长 4.1%。三次产业比例由 2019 年的 3.5 ：35.6 ：60.9 调整为 3.4 ：35.2 ：61.4。

图 1：2016-2020 年全市生产总值及增速

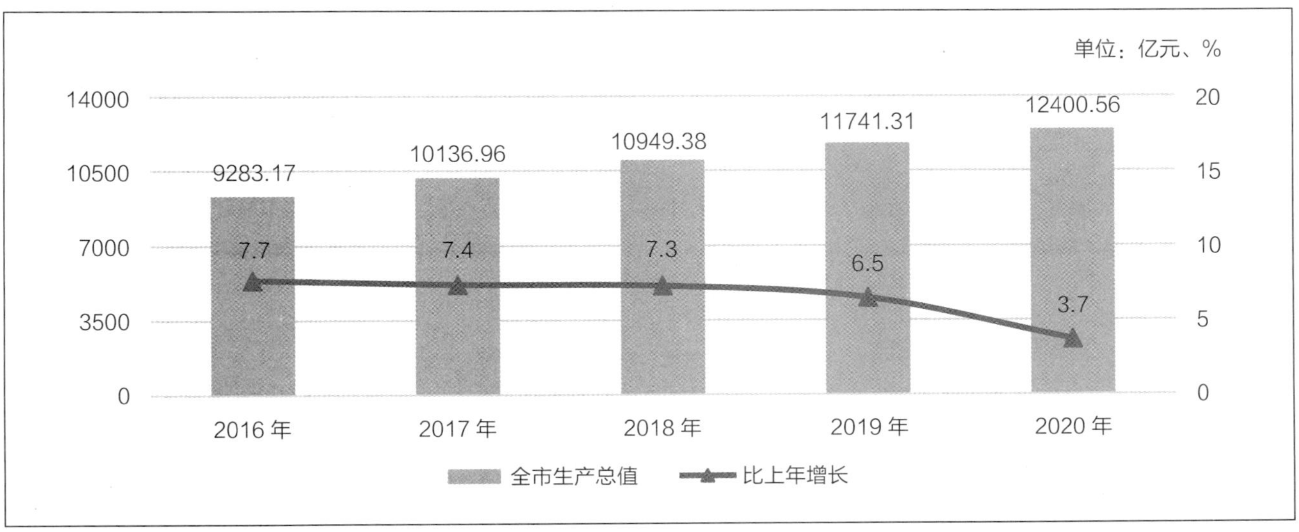

“六稳”“六保”落地见效。发挥政策调控作用，出台减税降费、稳岗就业、房租减免等政策，新增减税降费340亿元左右，帮助企业纾困解难，兜底基本民生。就业形势总体稳定，12月末，城镇登记失业率为3.03%，控制在较低水平。基本民生保障有力，2020年居民消费价格上涨2.4%；居民收入稳步提升，人均可支配收入47156元，增长3.7%[3]。市场主体活力增强，2020年规模以上工业[4]企业利润总额531.6亿元，增长12.4%，增速连续4个月保持两位数增长。粮食能源供给增加，粮食总产量连续3年保持在300万吨以上，能源生产量2589.1万吨标准煤，增长6.9%。产业链供应链保持稳定，规模以上工业35个大类行业中24个增长，增长面68.6%。财政支出兜底民生，公共卫生、住房保障、社会保障和就业等领域支出分别为31.0、30.7和223.0亿元，分别增长68.1%、29.7%和14.6%。

表1：2020年全市居民消费价格指数

指标名称	全年（上年同期=100）
居民消费价格总指数	102.4
非食品价格指数	100.4
服务价格指数	100.7
消费品价格指数	103.4
一、食品烟酒	108.0
食品	109.8
# 粮食	101.5
鲜菜	108.9
猪肉	153.0
鸡蛋	87.6
二、衣着	99.9
三、居住	100.5
四、生活用品及服务	99.4
五、交通和通信	94.5
六、教育文化和娱乐	102.1
七、医疗保健	102.0
八、其他用品和服务	102.7

三大攻坚战成效显著。全市不良贷款率降至 1.29%，较年初下降 0.14 个百分点。市级安排财政扶贫资金 6.6 亿元，全市 6 万多贫困人口和 200 个省定贫困村、310 个市定经济薄弱村、10 个市定经济薄弱镇全部脱贫摘帽。全市主要污染物细颗粒物（PM2.5）、二氧化硫、氮氧化物年均值分别为 31、7、31 微克 / 立方米，与上年相比，PM2.5 改善 16.2%，二氧化硫改善 12.5%，氮氧化物改善 3.1%。城市建成区基本消除黑臭水体，近岸海域水质优良比例达到 98.8%。

二、新动能与创新

“新经济”加快培育。全市围绕战略性新兴[5]产业、高技术[6]产业，推进新产业、新产品、新业态、新模式加快发展。“新经济”增加值占生产总值比重达 32.6%。2020 年，规模以上装备制造业增加值增长 9.7%，快于规模以上工业 4.2 个百分点；规模以上工业战略性新兴产业增加值占规模以上工业比重达 27.9%；直播带货、社区团购等新型消费业态蓬勃发展，限额以上单位网上零售额增长 9.5%，占社会消费品零售额的比重达到 8.1%；通过海关跨境电商管理平台进出口 54.2 亿元，增长 688.0%。全市规模以上软件和信息技术服务业营业收入 239.6 亿元，增长 11.4%；规模以上高技术服务业中，信息服务营业收入增长 12.2%，检验检测服务营业收入增长 15.3%，环境监测及治理服务营业收入增长 18.6%，知识产权及相关法律服务营业收入增长 15.5%。“新产品”产量增速较快，城市轨道车辆产量 1836 辆，增长 3.7%；智能电视产量 1681 万台，增长 15.6%；工业机器人产量 1702 套，增长 45.0%。

图 2：2017-2020 年“新经济”增加值占生产总值比重

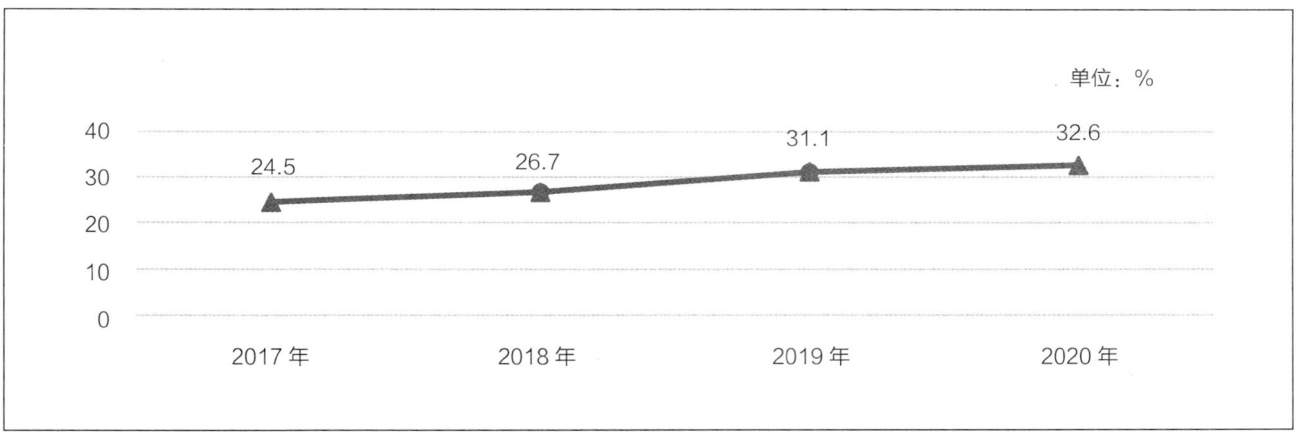

创新驱动战略全面推进。初步统计，全市共取得重要科技成果 428 项，获得国家级科技奖励 13 项。其中，技术发明奖 2 项，科技进步奖 11 项。获得省级科技奖励 92 项。其中，自然科学奖 11 项，技术发明奖 5 项，科技进步奖 74 项，最高奖项 1 项，国际合作奖 1 项。技术合同交易额 286.6 亿元，增长 68.0%。涉海技术合同成交额 28.4 亿元，增长 35.1%。全年有效发明专利 38549 件，增长 20.7%。每万人有效发明专利拥有量 41 件，比上年增加 6.6 件。PCT[7] 国际专利申请 1755 件，比上年增加 374 件。高新技术企业总数达到 4396 家，比上年增加 567 家。现有国家知识产权示范企业 12 家，国家知识产权优势企业 107 家，国家重点实验室 9 家，国家级工程技术研究中心 10 家，省级工程技术研究中心 82 家。

图 3：2016-2020 年高新技术企业数量及增幅

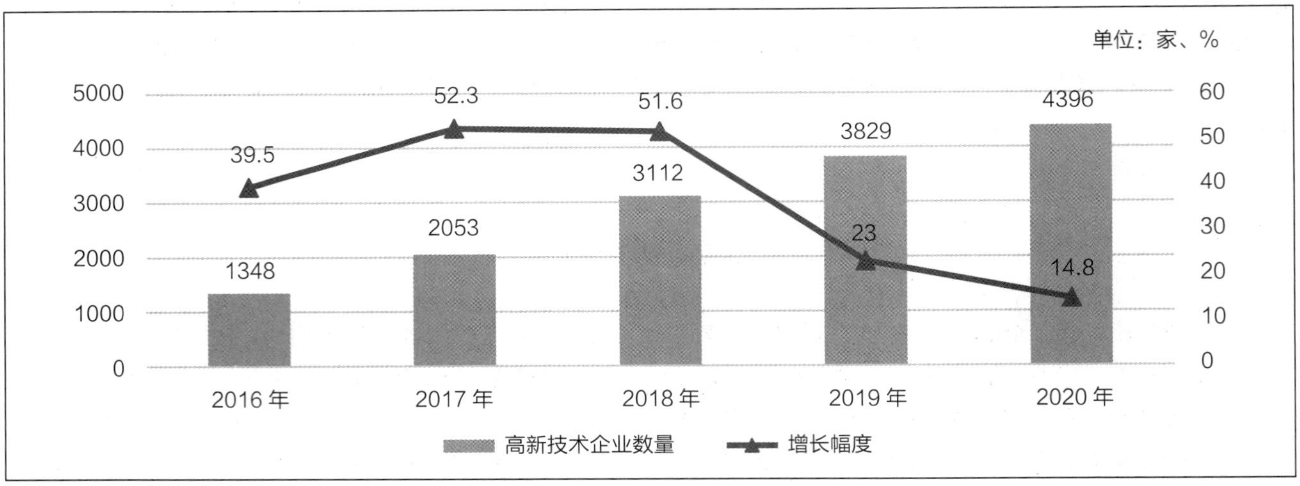

三、农　业

农林牧渔业发展稳中有进。全年农林牧渔业增加值 453.21 亿元，增长 2.7%。其中，农林牧渔服务业增加值 27.80 亿元，增长 4.5%。

种植业发展保持平稳。全年粮食播种面积 47.0 万公顷，蔬菜播种面积 10.9 万公顷，花生播种面积 7.5 万公顷。粮食产量 304.6 万吨，增长 0.7%；蔬菜及食用菌产量 655.8 万吨，增长 4.7%；花生产量 36.0 万吨，增长 5.1%；水果（含果用瓜）产量 116.5 万吨，下降 1.9%。

图 4：2016-2020 年粮食产量

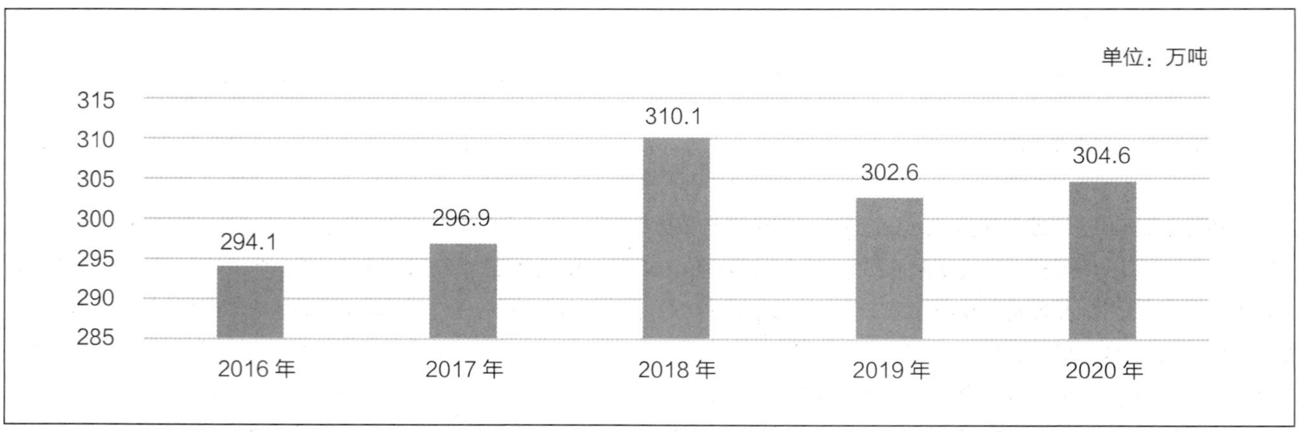

林牧渔业持续恢复。全年实际完成造林（更新）面积0.7万公顷。全年肉类产量48.0万吨，禽蛋产量24.7万吨，牛奶产量30.7万吨。全年水产品产量（不包括远洋捕捞）101.1万吨，增长0.2%。海、淡水养殖面积3.5万公顷，增长2.9%。远洋捕捞量14.7万吨，增长1.4%。

现代高效农业基础增强。现代高效农业增加值83.22亿元，增长16.9%。截至2020年，创建市级以上现代农业产业园10个，产业强镇12个；2020年新创建田园综合体13个、农业绿色园艺标准园48个、标准化示范场43家；"三品一标"（无公害农产品、绿色食品、有机农产品和农产品地理标志）产品805个，其中国家地理标志保护产品52个。农机总动力754.7万千瓦，比上年增加14.7万千瓦。农作物生产综合机械化水平达到89.3%。

表2：2020年主要种植业产品产量及增速

指标	单位	产量	增长（%）
粮食	万吨	304.6	0.7
夏粮	万吨	133.4	-6.5
秋粮	万吨	171.2	7.0
油料	万吨	36.0	5.1
蔬菜及食用菌	万吨	655.8	4.7
水果	万吨	116.5	-1.9
园林水果	万吨	75.0	0.6

四、工业与建筑业

工业生产企稳复苏。全市工业增加值3268.38亿元，增长2.8%。其中，规模以上工业增加值增长5.5%。分轻重工业看，轻工业增长4.7%，重工业增长5.8%。分经济类型看，国有控股企业增长6.7%，股份制企业增长7%，外商及港澳台商投资企业增长2.7%。分门类看，采矿业增长10.5%，制造业增长5.8%，电力、热力、燃气及水生产和供应业下降1.7%。分重点行业看，汽车制造业增长19.4%，电气机械和器材制造业增长14.8%，铁路、船舶、航空航天和其他运输设备制造业下降4.4%，石油、煤炭及其他燃料加工业增长0.1%，专用设备制造业增长11.5%。全年规模以上工业企业产销率达到99.5%。

表 3：2020 年规模以上工业主要产品产量及增速

产品名称	单位	产量	增长（%）
彩色电视机	万台	1774.9	15.3
其中：智能电视	万台	1681.0	15.6
家用电冰箱	万台	822.0	23.1
家用洗衣机	万台	575.4	54.9
房间空气调节器	万台	1478.3	10.0
智能手机	万台	502.4	-22.1
啤酒	万千升	176.1	1.4
橡胶轮胎外胎	万条	4563.3	4.3
平板玻璃	万重量箱	1004.0	8.9
粗钢	万吨	335.2	4.6
汽车	万辆	29.0	27.3
动车组	辆	996	-9.3
城市轨道车辆	辆	1836	3.7
金属集装箱	万立方米	1379.1	25.5

规模以上工业利润 531.6 亿元，增长 12.4%。其中，国有控股企业利润 177.8 亿元，增长 2.1%，股份制企业利润 353.7 亿元，增长 18.1%，外商及港澳台商投资企业利润 178.4 亿元，增长 3.3%。

表 4：2020 年规模以上工业利润增速

指标	增长（%）
规模以上工业利润	12.4
其中：国有控股	2.1
股份制企业	18.1
外商及港澳台商投资企业	3.3

建筑业不断发展壮大。全年资质内总承包、专业承包建筑业企业 820 家，实现增加值 1112.79 亿元，增长 4.0%。完成建筑业总产值 3000.2 亿元，增长 6.8%；上年结转合同额 2408.8 亿元，增长 6.4%。

五、服务业

服务业拉动作用明显。全市服务业实现增加值 7613.59 亿元，增长 4.1%，占 GDP 比重为 61.4%，比上年提高 0.5 个百分点；对经济增长贡献率为 65.7%。

图 5：2016-2020 年规模以上服务业营业收入及增速

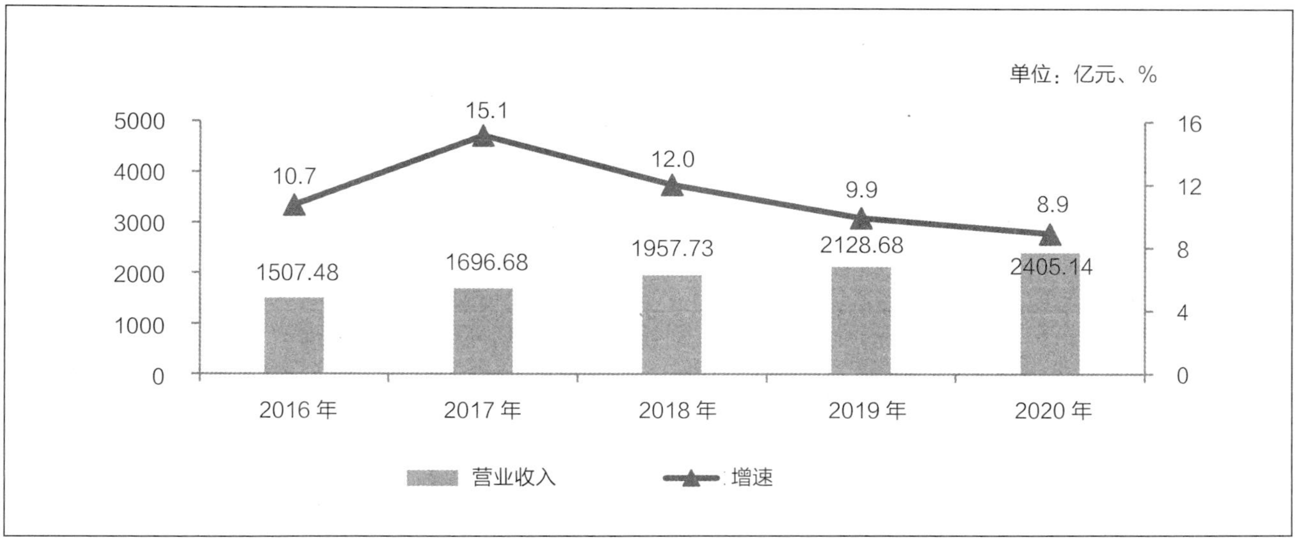

全市规模以上服务业[8]总体较快增长，实现营业收入 2405.1 亿元，增长 8.9%。生产性服务业中，规模以上互联网和相关服务营业收入增长 46.3%，软件和信息技术服务业营业收入增长 11.4%，商务服务业营业收入下降 4.3%。生活性服务业中，规模以上影视节目制作营业收入下降 7.5%，文艺创作与表演营业收入增长 23.7%，体育营业收入下降 15.6%，居民服务业营业收入增长 10.8%，机动车、电子产品和日用产品修理业营业收入下降 5.7%，其他服务业营业收入下降 1.5%。全市现代服务业实现增加值 3890.6 亿元，增长 3.4%，占全市 GDP 比重为 31.4%。

邮政电信业加快发展。全年完成邮电业务总量 1114.3 亿元，增长 21.7%。其中，邮政业务总量 130.8 亿元，增长 26.3%；电信业务总量 983.6 亿元，增长 21.1%。快递业务量 5.9 亿件，增长 29.5%。固定宽带互联网用户 464 万户，增长 11.0%。全市移动电话 1257 万户，增长 0.9%。累计建成并开通 5G 基站 10824 个。

旅游业逐渐复苏。2020 年，全市接待游客 6312.3 万人次，下降 44.2%，实现旅游总收入 1019.3 亿元，下降 49.2%。年末，拥有 A 级旅游景区 112 处。其中，5A 级旅游景区 1 处，4A 级旅游景区 26 处，3A 级旅游景区 69 处。拥有星级酒店 91 个。其中，5 星级酒店 9 个，4 星级酒店 23 个，3 星级酒店 56 个。拥有旅行社 599 个。其中，经营出境旅游业务旅行社 59 个，经营入境和国内旅游业务旅行社 540 个。

交通运输平稳回升。铁路、公路、水路共完成货运量 3.6 亿吨，增长 4.3%；完成旅客运量 3150 万人次，下降 56.5%。年末全市机动车保有量 314 万辆，增长 7.3%；其中，私人汽车 273 万辆，增长 7.8%。全年港口吞吐量 6.1 亿吨，增长 4.7%；外贸吞吐量 4.5 亿吨，增长 5.9%；集装箱吞吐量 2201 万标准箱，增长 4.7%。年末拥有国内航线 161 条，国际航线 9 条，港澳台地区航线 1 条；全年航空旅客吞吐量 1456 万人次，下降 43%；航空货邮吞吐量 21 万吨，下降 19.3%。

表 5：2020 年主要运输方式完成的运输量及增速

运输方式	单位	运输量	增长（%）
客运周转量	亿人公里	56.65	-56.9
铁路	亿人公里	31.92	-44.1
公路	亿人公里	24.66	-66.8
水运	亿人公里	0.07	-62.5
货运周转量	亿吨公里	1788.29	12.2
铁路	亿吨公里	71.93	20.7
公路	亿吨公里	568.22	1.4
水运	亿吨公里	1148.14	17.9

六、固定资产投资

投资实现平稳增长。全市固定资产投资增长 3.2%，在建项目 6907 个，比上年增加 1258 个。分产业看，第一产业投资增长 115.4%，第二产业投资增长 1.6%，第三产业投资增长 2.7%。装备制造业投资增长 12.5%，高技术制造业投资增长 14.5%，工业技改投资增 13.7%。医养健康等社会民生发展进一步提升，民生类投资增长 28.9%。

图 6：三次产业投资占固定资产投资比重

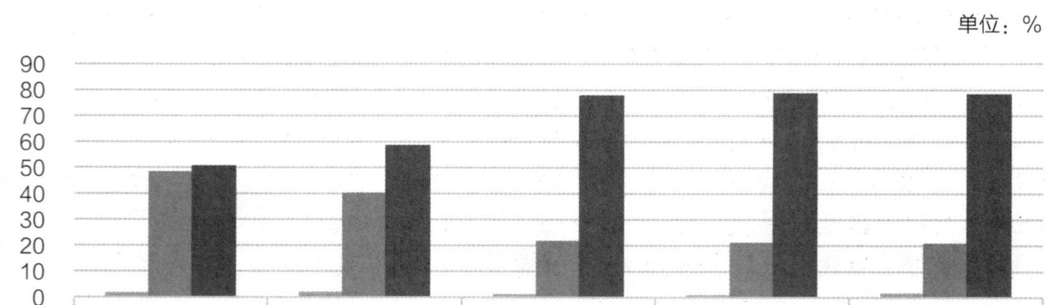

	2016 年	2017 年	2018 年	2019 年	2020 年
第一产业	1.5	1.7	0.8	0.6	1.3
第二产业	48.1	39.9	21.5	20.9	20.6
第三产业	50.4	58.4	77.6	78.4	78.1

15 个攻势[9]精准发力。产业空间进一步拓展，城市功能逐步完善，城市品质改善提升攻势投资增长 28.9%；区域协调发展进一步推动，突破平度莱西攻势投资增长 25.6%；美丽乡村、田园综合体建设进一步加快，乡村振兴攻势投资增长 15.1%；民营经济发展活力增强，民营经济攻势投资增长 13.0%。

13 条产业链[10]加速凝聚。现代金融服务投资增长 238.1%，商贸业投资增长 124.1%，现代高效农业投资增长 107.7%，新一代信息技术投资增长 50.0%，高端装备投资增长 28.3%，新能源新材料投资增长 11.7%，现代海洋投资增长 9.3%，高端化工及传统制造业投资增长 8.7%，现代物流投资增长 4.8%。

房地产市场健康运行。全年房地产开发完成投资 2045.1 亿元，增长 13.4%。其中，住宅投资 1479.2 亿元，增长 19.4%。商品房销售面积 1653.6 万平方米，增长 0.1%。其中，住宅销售面积 1430.4 万平方米，下降 3.1%。

表 6：2020 年全市房地产开发投资、商品房销售面积及增速

分 类	房地产开发投资（亿元）	增长（%）	商品房销售面积（万平方米）	增长（%）
总计	2045.1	13.4	1653.6	0.1
住宅	1479.2	19.4	1430.4	-3.1
办公楼	135.1	5.9	64.3	-9.6
商业营业用房	152.1	-14.8	48.0	-45.4
其他	278.7	7.8	110.9	543.7

全年开工建设公共租赁住房 3010 套，基本建成公共租赁住房 1193 套。截至 2020 年末，全市正在享受租赁补贴家庭共 12430 户，全年发放租赁补贴 8354.6 万元。

七、国内贸易

消费市场逐步回暖。全年实现社会消费品零售额 5203.5 亿元，增长 1.5%。按经营地统计，城镇消费品零售额 4294.4 亿元，增长 1.1%；乡村消费品零售额 909.1 亿元，增长 3.2%。分行业看，批发和零售业实现零售额 4683.7 亿元，增长 2.4%；住宿和餐饮业实现零售额 519.8 亿元，下降 5.7%。

图 7：2016-2020 年社会消费品零售总额及增速

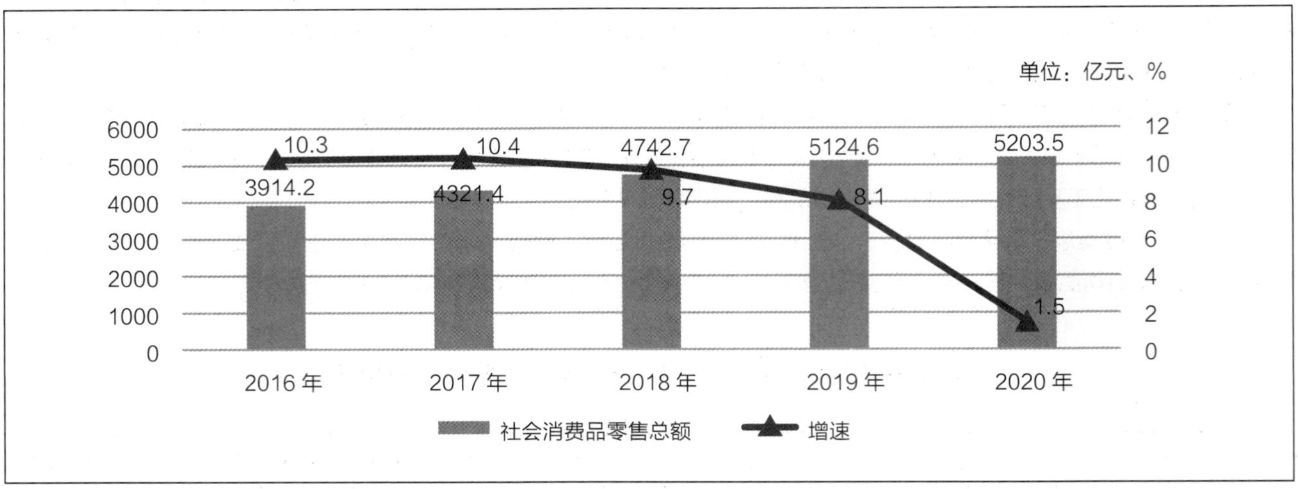

消费结构不断优化。在限额以上单位商品零售额中，粮油、食品类零售额增长 7.4%，饮料类增长 33.0%，烟酒类增长 13.9%，服装、鞋帽、针纺织品类下降 15.5%，化妆品类下降 4.0%，金银珠宝类下降 24.3%，日用品类下降 6.4%，家用电器和音像器材类下降 3.4%，中西药品类增长 4.9%，文化办公用品类增长 50.4%，电子出版物及音像制品类下降 41.8%，家具类下降 54.2%，通讯器材类下降 5.0%，智能手机类增长 0.7%，建筑及装潢材料类增长 18.8%，石油及制品类增长 4.4%，汽车类增长 3.6%。

网络交易迅速扩容。全市电子商务交易平台[11]实现交易额 1.17 万亿元，增长 4.2%；限额以上批发和零售业企业网络销售额 541.6 亿元，增长 22.9%。

八、对外经济

外贸进出口逆势上扬。全市实现货物进出口总额 6407 亿元，增长 8.2%。其中，出口额 3876.8 亿元，增长 13.7%；进口额 2530.2 亿元，增长 0.7%。对“一带一路”沿线国家进出口 1817.7 亿元，增长 16.3%。其中，出口 1099.8 亿元，增长 18.4%；进口 717.9 亿元，增长 13.2%。对上合组织国家进出口 448.4 亿元，增长 6.1%。其中，出口 278.2 亿元，增长 9.3%；进口 170.2 亿元，增长 1.2%。

图 8：2016-2020 年外贸货物进出口总额及增速

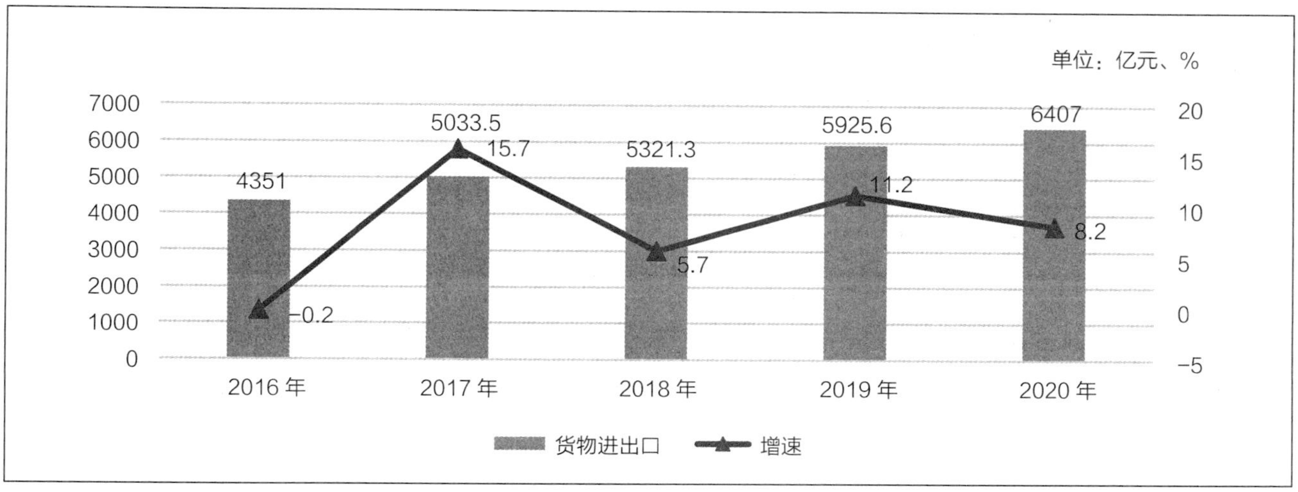

对外合作更加深入。全市承接服务外包合同 9318 份，增长 4.2%；合同额 70.1 亿美元，下降 1.9%；执行额 50.5 亿美元，增长 7.1%。其中，离岸服务外包合同 8007 份，增长 5.1%；合同额 62.6 亿美元，增长 1.8%；执行额 44.2 亿美元，增长 11.8%。青岛口岸对外贸易进出口总额 11672 亿元，下降 8.3%。其中，出口额 6615 亿元，下降 4.7%；进口额 5057 亿元，下降 12.5%。

表 7：2020 年全市主要商品进出口情况

项目	进出口		出 口		进 口	
	金 额（亿元）	增 长（%）	金 额（亿元）	增 长（%）	金 额（亿元）	增 长（%）
纺织服装	537.79	11.0	516.25	12.2	21.54	-12.8
农产品	967.58	3.9	393.74	-3.4	573.84	9.5
机电产品	2262.16	12.7	1813.94	18.1	448.22	-4.9
高新技术产品	543.17	4.3	314.96	12.9	228.21	-5.6

表 8：2020 年对主要国家和地区货物进出口额及增速

国别（地区）	出口额（亿美元）	增 长（%）	进口额（亿美元）	增 长（%）
亚洲	262.75	13.7	155.08	6.1
香港	20.52	40.4	0.68	−33.4
台湾	5.54	12.6	11.66	1.8
日本	59.52	2.7	19.25	4.3
韩国	46.08	6.5	31.47	−10.6
东盟	75.55	21.1	60.79	36.3
南亚	21.66	15.1	7.88	15.5
中东	29.51	14.3	18.49	−20.0
非洲	24.14	8.9	20.51	−24.0
南非	4.29	−5.3	2.90	50.2
欧洲	113.85	8.2	60.45	0.2
欧盟	82.70	8.6	37.31	11.2
英国	16.07	10.8	2.46	−66.3
德国	18.00	6.7	12.61	0.7
法国	8.25	−7.6	3.63	4.7
意大利	7.45	−4.0	2.68	10.0
独联体及东欧	21.95	10.8	16.93	−1.6
俄罗斯	10.24	3.8	14.09	−5.3
南美洲	17.19	10.2	66.13	−3.6
巴西	6.21	−2.0	50.31	−4.0
北美洲	104.08	16.9	28.09	5.7
美国	90.47	14.7	22.01	14.5
加拿大	13.61	34.4	5.61	−16.4
大洋洲	16.78	21.3	32.69	−1.5
澳大利亚	14.05	24.0	27.90	3.5

注：本表非全口径。

利用外资稳定增长。2020 年，全市新批外商投资项目 882 个，下降 7.6%；合同外资 178.5 亿美元，增长 33.7%。全市实际使用外资 58.5 亿美元，增长 0.2%。

“一带一路”融合发展。全市企业对“一带一路”沿线国家和地区投资项目 15 个，中方协议投资额 3.9 亿美元，下降 73.0%；中方实际投资额 1.2 亿美元，下降 49.2%。

对外投资更加广泛。全市对外承包工程业务新承揽项目 83 个，新签合同额 34.8 亿美元，增长 3.6%；完成营业额 28.8 亿美元，下降 31.2%。对外劳务合作业务派出各类劳务人员 10047 人。

九、财政金融

财政保障全面有力。全年财政总收入 3843.0 亿元，一般公共预算收入 1253.8 亿元，增长 1.0%。其中，税收收入 898.8 亿元，下降 0.3%；增值税 331.3 亿元，下降 8.3%；企业所得税 153.9 亿元，增长 3.6%；个人所得税 45.4 亿元，增长 29.3%；城市维护建设税 58.4 亿元，增长 2.2%。一般公共预算支出 1584.7 亿元，增长 0.6%。其中，一般公共服务支出 199.4 亿元，增长 8.1%；教育支出 288.6 亿元，增长 4.9%；科学技术支出 46.9 亿元，下降 29.9%；社会保障和就业支出 223.0 亿元，增长 14.6%；城乡社区事务支出 236.6 亿元，下降 15.4%。全年税务系统组织税收收入（含海关代征）2220.1 亿元，下降 9.1%。其中，国内税收 1708.7 亿元，下降 3.1%。

金融市场健康发展。截至 2020 年末，金融机构本外币存款余额 20507.1 亿元，比年初增加 2630.8 亿元；人民币存款余额 19821.8 亿元，比年初增加 2538.8 亿元。其中，住户存款 8030.9 亿元，比年初增加 1275.7 亿元。本外币贷款余额 21064.8 亿元，比年初增加 2854.9 亿元；人民币贷款余额 20211.0 亿元，比年初增加 2879.1 亿元，其中住户贷款 6644.7 亿元，比年初增加 953.2 亿元。保险业累计实现保费收入 511 亿元，增长 4.9%。其中，产险公司实现保费收入 148 亿元，增长 11.5%；寿险公司实现保费收入 363 亿元，增长 2.5%。证券分支机构证券交易额 59965 亿元，增长 53.9%，法人机构证券交易额 43698 亿元，增长 42.7%。在中基协登记的私募基金管理人 362 家，管理基金规模 1039.3 亿元，增长 26.6%。境内上市公司累计 44 家，比上年增加 5 家。

十、社会事业

教育事业健康发展。截至 2020 年末，全市共有各类大专院校（含民办高校）29 所。其中，普通高校 27 所。全年研究生招生 2.0 万人，在校研究生 5.3 万人，毕业生 1.3 万人（不含驻青科研院所研究生）。普通本专科招生 11.4 万人，在校生 37.7 万人，毕业生 9.4 万人；中等职业教育招生 3.0 万人，在校生 8.4 万人，毕业生 2.7 万人；普通高中招生 6.0 万人，在校生 14.4 万人，毕业生 3.9 万人；初中招生 9.7 万人，在校生 28.6 万人，毕业生 9.4 万人；普通小学招生 11.6 万人，在校生 60.4 万人，毕业生 9.8 万人；特殊教育招生 0.04 万人，在校生 0.2 万人，毕业生 0.03 万人；幼儿园在园幼儿 34.5 万人。

图 9：2016-2020 年各类学校招生人数

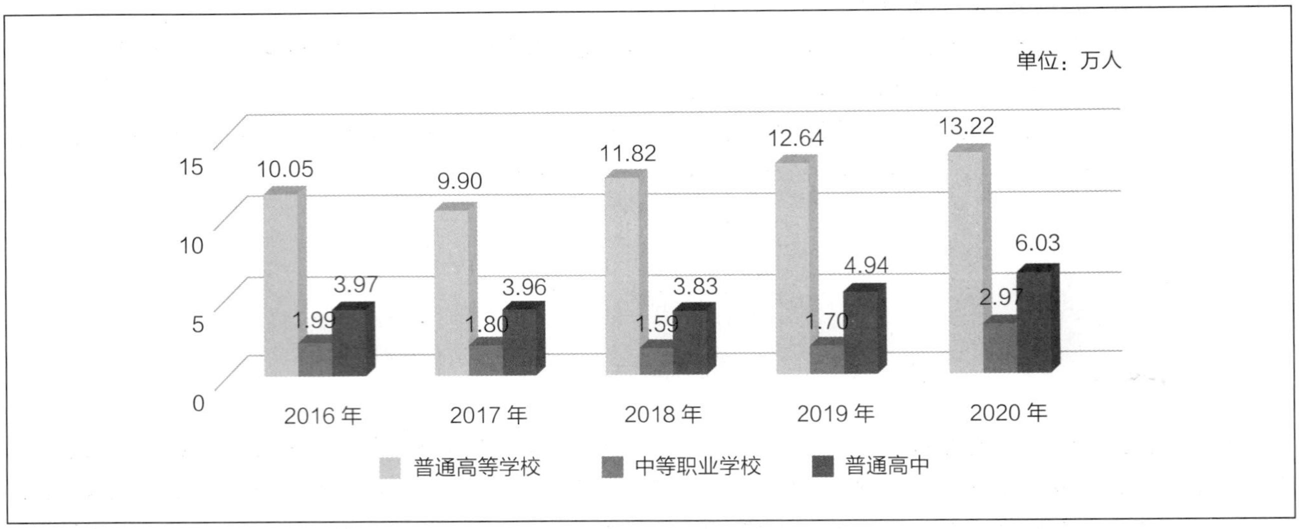

文化事业欣欣向荣。全市共有影剧院 91 处，文化馆（站）150 处，博物馆 104 处，公共图书馆 12 处，国有文艺院团 8 个，广播电台 6 座、11 套节目，电视台 6 座、17 套节目。全市共有档案馆 11 处。

卫生服务不断增强。截至 2020 年末，全市共有卫生机构（不含村卫生室）4459 处。其中，医院、卫生院 460 处，疾病预防控制中心 41 处，妇幼保健机构 12 处，门诊部（所）、诊所、卫生所、医务室 3573 处。各类卫生技术人员 9.49 万人。其中，医生 3.97 万人。全市拥有医疗床位 6.44 万张。其中，医院、卫生院床位 6.25 万张。

体育事业方兴未艾。全市运动员在各项比赛中共获得金牌 417.5 枚、银牌 254 枚、铜牌 267 枚。重点体校 1 所，学员 980 人；业余体校 10 所，学员 1807 人。

十一、城市建设

城市品质大幅提升。加快完善基础设施建设，胶东国际机场已建成，济青高铁、青连铁路、潍莱高铁开通，龙青高速、新机场高速一期等道路通车。年末，市区常规公交 8553 辆，线路 655 条，年客运量 65014 万人次，日均客运量 178 万人次。市区巡游出租汽车 10568 辆，年客运量 14720 万人次，日均客运量 40 万人次。地铁运营线路 6 条，年客运量 13975.3 万人次，日均客运量 38 万人次。全年地铁开行列车 46 万列次，总运营里程 1511 万列公里。

十二、能源、环境和安全生产

节能降耗成效明显。初步核算，全年能源消费总量 3187 万吨标准煤，下降 1.6%。全社会用电量 476.6 亿千瓦时，增长 2.5%。其中，工业用电量 258.8 亿千瓦时，增长 2.5%；服务业用电量 118.3 亿千瓦时，增长 2.4%；城乡居民生活用电量 81.4 亿千瓦时，增长 2.5%。全市规模以上工业综合能源消费量 1366.9 万吨标准煤，下降 3.8%。其中，煤炭消费量下降 4.5%；石油消费量增长 10.6%；天然气消费量增长 13.1%。全市万元生产总值能耗 0.27 吨标准煤，下降 5.1%。

图 10：2016-2020 年全社会用电量及增速

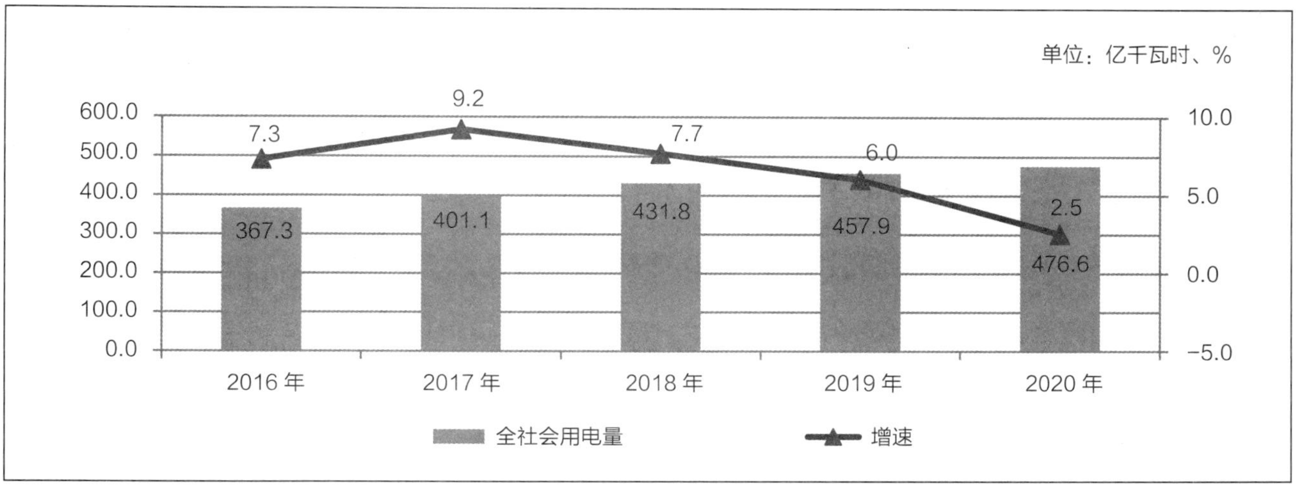

能源生产更加低碳清洁。全市能源生产量 2589.1 万吨标准煤，增长 6.9%。其中，原油加工量 1340.1 万吨，增长 11.7%；汽油生产量 370.8 万吨，增长 0.5%；柴油生产量 331.8 万吨，增长 11.5%。发电量 172.5 亿千瓦时，下降 4.7%。新能源发电量 20.5 亿千瓦时，增长 15.4%，占全市发电总量比重为 11.8%。其中，风力发电量增长 24.6%，垃圾焚烧发电量增长 26.1%。

环境治理效果显现。全市年平均气温 13.5℃，平均年降水量为 983.4 毫米。市区空气质量优良天数达 316 天，占全年的 86.3%。市区区域环境噪声平均值 58.7 分贝，市区交通干线噪声平均值 70.0 分贝。

平安青岛建设不断推进。全市共发生各类生产安全事故[12]82 起，死亡 59 人，分别下降 5.7% 和 6.3%。亿元 GDP 生产安全事故死亡率 0.0048，十万工矿商贸企业就业人员生产安全事故死亡率 0.55。

十三、人民生活和社会保障

居民生活质量提升。全年全市居民人均可支配收入 47156 元，增长 3.7%。按常住地分，城镇居民人均可支配收入 55905 元，增长 2.6%；农村居民人均可支配收入 23656 元，增长 4.8%。全市居民人均消费支出 30294 元，增长 2.7%，恩格尔系数为 28.1%。按常住地分，城镇居民人均消费支出 35936 元，增长 1.9%；农村居民人均消费支出 15138 元，增长 1.6%。据抽样调查，年末城镇居民人均现住房建筑面积 33.4 平方米，农村居民人均现住房建筑面积 38.0 平方米。

表 9：2020 年城乡居民人均可支配收入构成情况

指标名称	全体居民		城镇居民		农村居民	
	绝对值（元）	增长（%）	绝对值（元）	增长（%）	绝对值（元）	增长（%）
可支配收入	47156	3.7	55905	2.6	23656	4.8
工资性收入	28082	3.4	33641	2.2	13151	4.5
经营净收入	8816	1.5	8479	0.3	9720	4.8
财产净收入	4008	4.1	5365	2.5	365	6.0
转移净收入	6250	8.6	8420	6.9	421	10.9

表 10：2020 年城乡居民人均消费支出情况

指标名称	全体居民		城镇居民		农村居民	
	绝对值（元）	增长（%）	绝对值（元）	增长（%）	绝对值（元）	增长（%）
消费支出	30294	2.7	35936	1.9	15138	1.6
食品烟酒	8520	2.3	10025	1.5	4476	1.9
衣着	2706	1.8	3306	0.9	1096	0.5
居住	7173	2.9	8626	2.1	3269	1.4
生活用品及服务	1998	2.1	2365	1.4	1011	0.7
交通和通信	4477	2.5	5154	1.8	2659	1.8
教育文化娱乐	3012	3.7	3608	3.0	1412	1.7
医疗保健	1679	4.9	1977	4.4	880	2.7
其他用品和服务	729	1.3	876	0.3	336	1.0

表 11：2020 年每百户居民家庭主要耐用消费品拥有量

指标名称	单位	数量		
		全体居民	城镇居民	农村居民
家用汽车	辆	59	62	49
摩托车	辆	24	13	53
电冰箱（柜）	台	110	111	107
洗衣机	台	100	100	98
热水器	台	99	101	94
空调	台	119	127	97
彩色电视机	台	106	105	108
计算机	台	72	82	45
移动电话	部	234	235	231

民生保障更加有力。截至 2020 年末，全市城镇居民最低生活保障人数 18919 人，城镇居民最低生活保障资金支出 18335 万元；农村五保供养人数 10960 人，农村五保供养资金支出 15324.1 万元。全市城镇职工基本养老保险参保缴费人数为 312.1 万人，参加失业保险人数为 262.6 万人，全年累计领取失业保险金的人数为 7.8 万人。

图 11：2016-2020 年城镇职工基本养老保险参保缴费人数

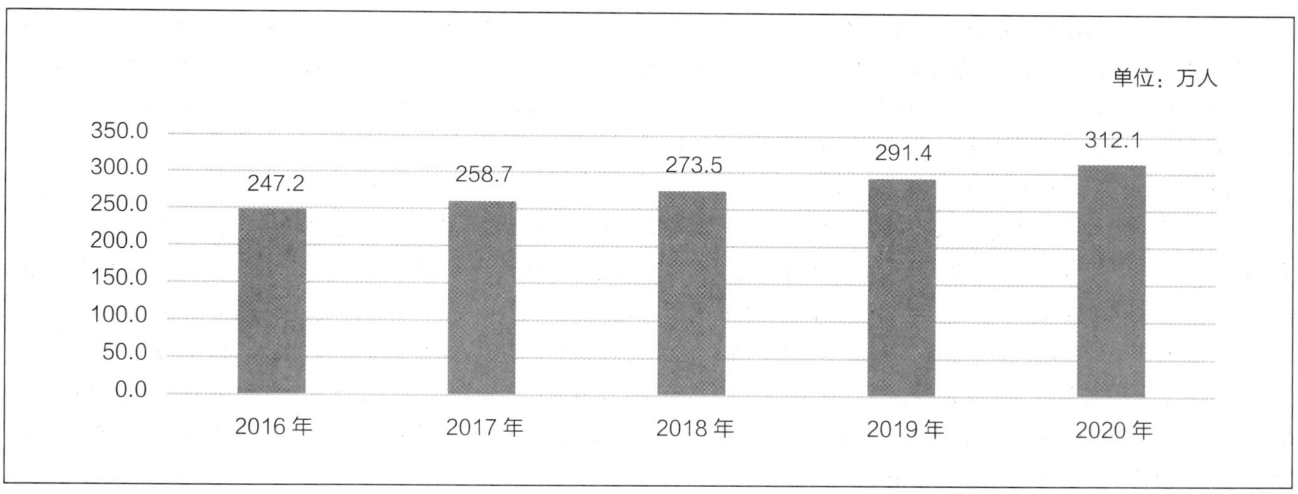

注：

[1] 公报中统计数据均为初步统计数，部分数据因四舍五入影响，存在总计与分项合计不等情况。2020 年开展第七次全国人口普查，人口数据将通过《青岛市 2020 年第七次全国人口普查主要数据公报》进行公布。

[2] 全市生产总值（GDP）及各产业增加值绝对数按现价计算，增长速度按可比价计算。

[3] 居民人均可支配收入比上年增长指名义增速，计算方法是：（当年居民人均可支配收入 / 上年居民人均可支配收入 −1）*100%；居民人均可支配收入实际增速 =（当年居民人均可支配收入 / 上年居民人均可支配收入 / 同期居民消费价格指数 −1）*100%。

[4] 规模以上工业企业为年主营业务收入 2000 万元及以上企业。限额以上贸易企业为批发业年主营业务收入在 2000 万元及以上、零售业 500 万元及以上、住宿和餐饮业 200 万元及以上的法人企业。固定资产投资项目统计的起点标准为计划总投资额 500 万元。

[5] 战略新兴产业指以重大技术突破和重大发展需求为基础，对经济社会全局和长远发展具有重大引领带动作用，知识技术密集、物质资源消耗少、成长潜力大、综合效益好的产业，包括：新一代信息技术产业、高端装备制造产业、新材料产业、生物产业、新能源汽车产业、新能源产业、节能环保产业、数字创意产业、相关服务业等 9 大领域。

[6] 按照《高技术产业（制造业）分类（2017）》，包括：医药制造，航空、航天器及设备制造，电子及通信设备制造，计算机及办公设备制造，医疗仪器设备及仪器仪表制造，信息化学品制造等 6 大类。按照《高技术产业（服务业）分类（2018）》，包括信息服务、电子商务服务、检验检测服务、专业技术服务业的高技术服务、研发与设计服务、科技成果转化服务、知识产权及相关法律服务、环境监测及治理服务和其他高技术服务等 9 大类。

[7] PCT(Patent Cooperation Treaty）是《专利合作条约》的英文缩写。PCT 国际专利是指我国专利申请人根据 PCT 规定，可以向中国专利局或向世界知识产权组织提交国际专利申请，是反映地区外向型经济发展水平和地区国际技术竞争能力的重要指标。

[8] 规模以上服务业企业，一是指年营业收入 2000 万元及以上服务业法人单位，包括：交通运输、仓储和邮政业，信息传输、软件和信息技术服务业，水利、环境和公共设施管理业三个门类和卫生行业大类；二是指年营业收入 1000 万元及以上服务业法人单位，包括：租赁和商务服务业，科学研究和技术服务业，教育三个门类，以及物业管理、房地产中介服务、房地产租赁经营活动和其他房地产业四个行业小类；三是指年营业收入 500 万元及以上服务业法人单位，包括：居民服务、修理和其他服务业，文化、体育和娱乐业两个门类，以及社会工作行业大类。

[9] 15 个攻势是经略海洋攻势、“双招双引”攻势、交通基础设施建设攻势、军民融合发展攻势、乡村振兴攻势、突破平度莱西攻势、国际航运贸易金融创新中心建设攻势、“高端制造业 + 人工智能”攻势、推进国有企业改革攻势、壮大民营经济攻势、科技引领城建设攻势、城市品质改善提升攻势、国际时尚城建设攻势、高效青岛建设攻势、平安青岛建设攻势。

[10] 13 条产业链包含新一代信息技术、新能源新材料、高端化工、高端装备、现代海洋、医养健康、现代高效农业、文化创意、精品旅游、现代金融服务等省“十强”产业，以及现代物流、商贸、商务服务等三个青岛特色产业。

[11] 电子商务交易平台统计范围：辖区内规模以上工业、有资质的建筑业、限额以上批发和零售业、限额以上住宿和餐饮业、有开发经营活动的全部房地产开发经营业、规模以上服务业法人单位拥有的电子商务交易平台，以及年交易额 1000 万元及以上的其他电子商务交易平台。

[12] 各类生产安全事故起数、死亡人数统计范围包括生产经营性道路交通、水上交通、铁路交通、民航飞行、农业机械、渔业船舶和工矿商贸七个行业（领域）发生的事故，不再包括森林火灾、火灾事故和非生产经营性道路交通。

资料来源：本公报中财政数据来自市财政局；税务数据来自市税务局；人才、登记失业率、社会保障数据来自市人力资源和社会保障局；银行数据来自人民银行青岛市中心支行；证券保险数据来自青岛证监局、青岛银保监局；水产品数据来自市海洋发展局；林业数据来自市园林和林业局；“三品一标”、农机等数据来自市农业农村局；灌溉面积数据来自市水务管理局；交通运输数据来自市交通运输局；邮政数据来自市邮政管理局；固定电话、宽带、移动电话等数据来自市通信管理局；进出口、外资、对外承包工程、对外劳务合作等数据来自市商务局；旅游数据来自市文化和旅游局；教育数据

来自市教育局；科技数据来自市科技局；专利数据来自市场监管局；低保数据来自市民政局；体育数据来自市体育局；卫生数据来自市卫生健康委；环境数据来自市生态环境局；用电量数据来自青岛供电公司；气象数据来自市气象局；安全生产数据来自市应急局；扶贫数据来自市扶贫开发办；汽车保有量来自市公安局；居民收支、价格、城乡居民住房面积等数据来自国家统计局青岛调查队；其他数据来自市统计局。

STATISTICS COMMUNIQUE QINGDAO'S ECONOMIC AND SOCIAL DEVELOPMENT IN THE YEAR OF 2020 [1]

QINGDAO MUNICIPAL STATISTICS BUREAU

NBS SURVEY OFFICE IN QINGDAO

(March 16, 2021)

2020 is an extraordinary year in the development of Qingdao. In the face of the sudden impact of the epidemic and the severe and complex situation, the whole city adheres to the guidance of Xi Jinping Thought on Socialism with Chinese Characteristics for a New Era, and fully implements the 19th National Congress of the Communist Party of China and the 19th National Congress of the Communist Party of China. The spirit of the Second, Third, Fourth and Fifth Plenary Sessions of the Second, Third, and Fifth Central Committees, in-depth implementation of General Secretary Jinping's important instructions for work in Qingdao, under the strong leadership of the central, provincial and municipal party committees, scientifically grasp the new development stage and fully implement the new development concept , Service to build a new development pattern, coordinate epidemic prevention and control and economic and social development, do a solid job of "six stability", fully implement the "six guarantees" task, epidemic prevention and control have achieved stage results, and the city's economic and social development has shown strong resilience. High-quality development accumulates momentum, the conversion of new and old kinetic energy has achieved initial results, the people's well-being has continued to improve, the overall social situation is harmonious and stable, the "13th Five-Year Plan" has achieved a successful conclusion, and the building of a moderately prosperous society has achieved decisive progress and historic achievements. Significant progress has been made in the construction of a modern, dynamic and fashionable international metropolis.2020 is an extraordinary year in the development of Qingdao. In the face of the sudden impact of the epidemic and the severe and complex situation, the whole city adheres to the guidance of Xi Jinping Thought on Socialism with Chinese Characteristics for a New Era, and fully implements the 19th National Congress of the Communist Party of China and the 19th National Congress of the Communist Party of China. The spirit of the Second, Third, Fourth and Fifth Plenary Sessions of the Second, Third, and Fifth Central Committees, in-depth implementation of General Secretary Jinping's important instructions for work in Qingdao, under the strong leadership of the central, provincial and municipal party committees, scientifically grasp the new development stage and fully implement the new development concept , Service to build a new development pattern, coordinate epidemic prevention and control and economic and social development, do a solid job of "six stability", fully implement the "six guarantees" task, epidemic prevention and control have achieved stage results, and the city's economic and social development has shown strong resilience. High-quality development accumulates momentum, the conversion of new and old kinetic energy has achieved initial results, the people's well-being has continued to improve, the overall social situation is harmonious and stable, the "13th Five-Year Plan" has achieved a successful conclusion, and the building of a moderately prosperous society has achieved decisive progress and historic achievements. Significant progress has been made in the construction of a modern, dynamic and fashionable international metropolis.

Ⅰ. General

Economic development is better than expected. The unified accounting results show that the city's GDP in 2020 [2]is 1,240.056 billion yuan, accounting for 1.22% of the country's GDP,calculated at comparable prices, an increase of 3.7%. Among them, the added value of the primary industry was 42.541 billion yuan, an increase of 2.6%; the added value of the secondary industry was 436.156 billion yuan, an increase of 3.0%;The added value of the tertiary industry was 761.359 billion yuan, an increase of 4.1%. The ratio of the three industries will be adjusted from 3.5 ∶ 35.6 ∶ 60.9 in 2019 to 3.4 ∶ 35.2 ∶ 61.4.

Figure 1: 2016–2020 GDP and growth rate of the city

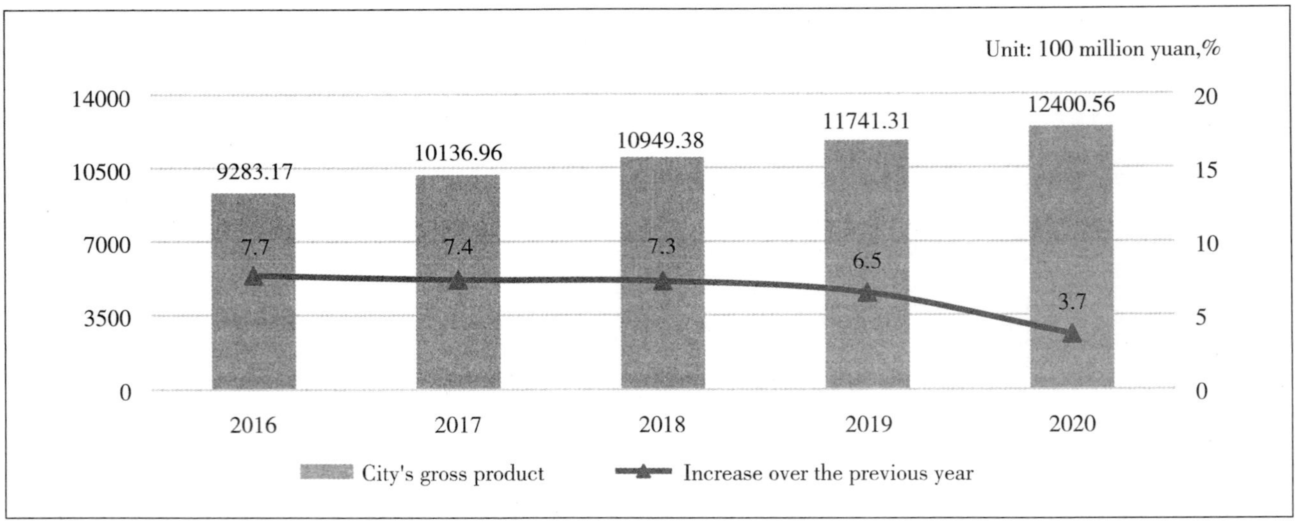

The implementation of "six stability" and "six guarantees" is effective. Give full play to the role of policy control, introduce policies such as tax reduction and fee reduction, job stabilization, rent reduction and exemption, and increase tax and fee reductions of about 34 billion yuan to help enterprises alleviate difficulties and solve basic people's livelihood. The employment situation is generally stable. At the end of December, the registered urban unemployment rate was 3.03%, which was kept at a low level. Basic people's livelihood protection is strong, and consumer prices will increase by 2.4% in 2020; residents' income will increase steadily, with per capita disposable income of 47,156 yuan, an increase of 3.7% [3]. The vitality of market entities has increased. In 2020, industrial enterprises above designated size [4] will have a total corporate profit of 53.16 billion yuan, an increase of 12.4%, and the growth rate has maintained double-digit growth for four consecutive months. Grain energy supply has increased. The total grain output has remained above 3 million tons for three consecutive years, and the energy production has been 25.891 million tons of standard coal, an increase of 6.9%. The supply chain of the industrial chain remained stable, and 24 of the 35 major industries above designated size increased by 68.6%. Fiscal expenditures cover people's livelihood. Expenditures in areas such as public health, housing security, social security and employment were 31.0, 30.7 and 22.30 billion yuan, an increase of 68.1%, 29.7% and 14.6% respectively.

Table 1: Consumer Price Index of the City in 2020

Indicator name	The whole year(the same period last year=100)
General Consumer Price Index	102.4
Non–Food Price Index	100.4
Service Price Index	100.7
Consumer Goods Price Index	103.4
1. Food, Tobacco and Liquor	108.0
Food	109.8
#Grain	101.5
Vegetables	108.9
Pork	153.0
Egg	87.6
2. Clothing	99.9
3. Residence	100.5

4. Supplies and Services	99.4
5. Transportation and Communication	94.5
6. Education, Culture and Recreation	102.1
7. Medical Care	102.0
8. Other supplies and services	102.7

The "three major battles" have achieved remarkable results. The city's non-performing loan ratio fell to 1.29%, a decrease of 0.14 percentage points from the beginning of the year. Municipal government arranged fiscal poverty alleviation funds of 660 million yuan, the city's more than 60,000 poor people, 200 provincially designated poor villages, 310 municipally designated economically weak villages, and 10 municipally designated economically weak towns have all been lifted out of poverty. City Lord the annual average values of major pollutants, fine particulate matter (PM2.5), sulfur dioxide, and nitrogen oxides were 31, 7, and 31 micrograms/m3, respectively. Compared with the previous year, PM2.5 changed good 16.2%, sulfur dioxide improved 12.5%, nitrogen oxides improved 3.1%. Black and smelly water bodies are basically eliminated in urban built-up areas, and the proportion of inshore waters with good water quality reaches 98.8%.

Ⅱ. New Kinetic Energy and Innovation

The "new economy" has accelerated its cultivation. Focusing on strategic emerging [5] industries, high-tech [6] industries, the city promotes the development of new industries, new products, new formats, and new models. The added value of the "new economy" accounted for 32.6% of the GDP. In 2020, the added value of the equipment manufacturing industry above designated size will grow by 9.7%, 4.2 percentage points faster than that of industries above designated size; the added value of strategic emerging industries above designated size will account for 27.9% of the proportion of industries above designated size; The business is booming. The online retail sales of units above designated size increased by 9.5%, accounting for 8.1% of the total retail sales of consumer goods; imports and exports through the customs cross-border e-commerce management platform were 5.42 billion yuan, an increase of 688.0%. The operating income of the software and information technology service industry above designated size in the city was 23.96 billion yuan, an increase of 11.4%; among the high-tech services above designated size, the operating income of information services increased by 12.2%, the operating income of inspection and testing services increased by 15.3%, and the environmental monitoring and governance services Revenue increased by 18.6%, intellectual property and The operating income of related legal services increased by 15.5%. The output of "new products" increased rapidly. The output of urban rail vehicles was 1,836, an increase of 3.7%; the output of smart TVs was 16.81 million, an increase of 15.6%; the output of industrial robots was 1,702, an increase of 45.0%.

Figure 2: The Proportion of the Added Value of the "New Economy" in the GDP from 2017 to 2020

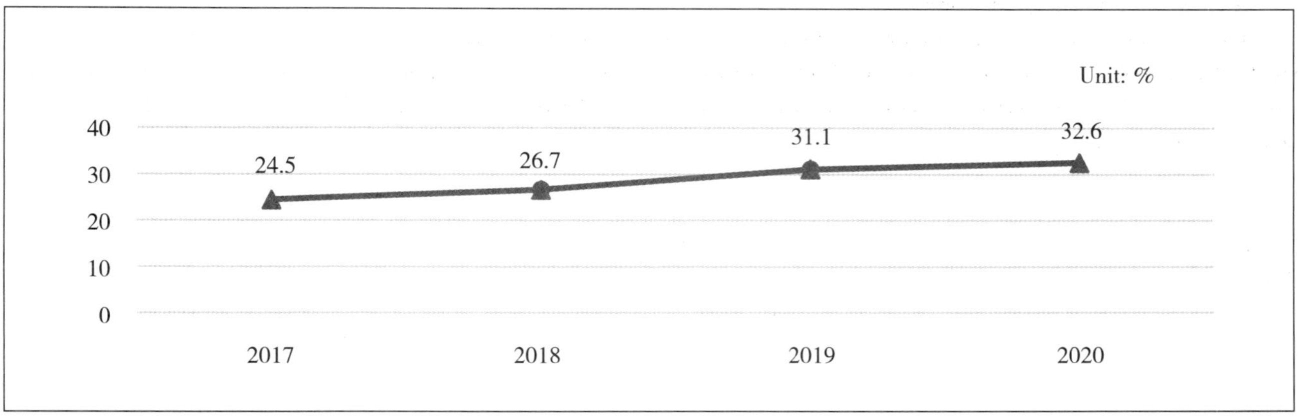

The innovation-driven strategy was comprehensively promoted. Preliminary statistics show that the city has achieved 428 important scientific and technological achievements, and won 13 national scientific and technological awards. Among them, there are 2 technological invention awards and 11 technological progress awards. Obtained 92 provincial science and technology awards. Among them, there are 11 natural science awards, 5 technological invention awards, 74 scientific and technological progress awards, 1 highest award, and 1 international cooperation award. The transaction volume of technology contracts was 28.66 billion yuan, an increase of 68.0%. The transaction volume of ocean-related technology contracts was 2.84 billion yuan, an increase of 35.1%. In the whole year, there were 38549 valid invention patents, an increase of 20.7%. There were 41 valid invention patents per 10,000 people, an increase of 6.6 over the previous year. There were 1,755 PCT[7] international patent applications, an increase of 374 over the previous year. The total number of high-tech enterprises reached 4,396, an increase of 567 over the previous year. There are 12 national intellectual property demonstration enterprises, 107 national intellectual property advantage enterprises, 9 state key laboratories, 10 national engineering technology research centers, and 82 provincial engineering technology research centers.

Figure 3: The Number and Growth Rate of High-tech Enterprises from 2016 to 2020

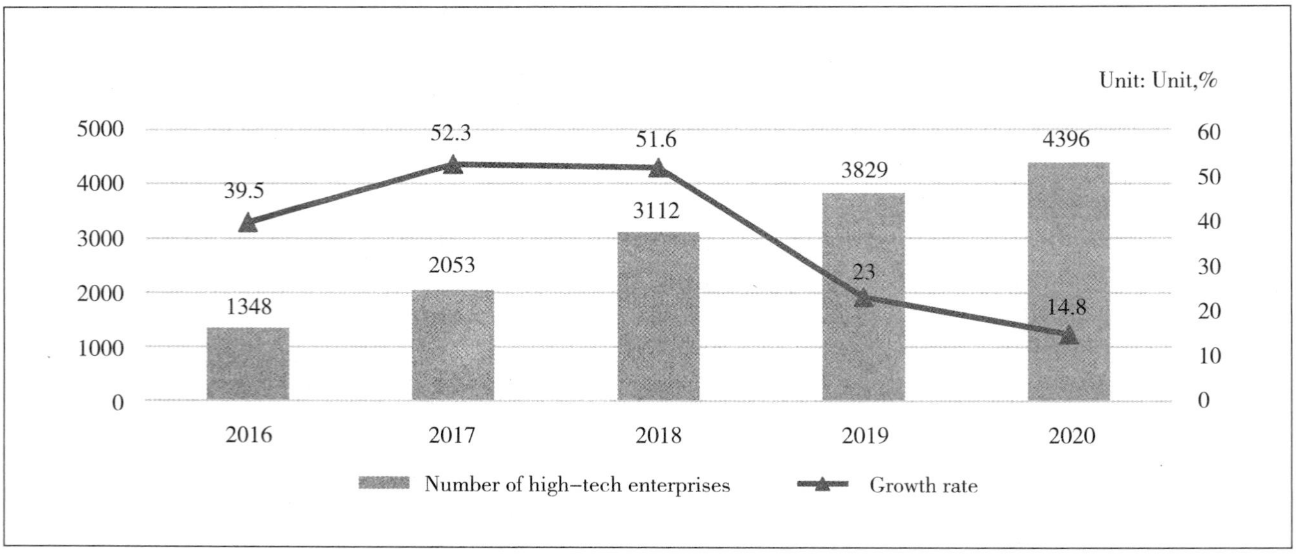

Ⅲ. Agriculture

The development of agriculture, forestry, animal husbandry and fishery is progressing steadily. The annual added value of agriculture, forestry, animal husbandry and fishery was 45.321 billion yuan, an increase of 2.7%. Among them, the added value of agriculture, forestry, animal husbandry and fishery services was 2.78 billion yuan, an increase of 4.5%.

The development of the planting industry remained stable. In the whole year, 470,000 hectares of grain were sown, 109,000 hectares of vegetable, and 75,000 hectares of peanut. The output of grain was 3.046 million tons, an increase of 0.7%; the output of vegetables and edible fungi was 6.558 million tons, an increase of 4.7%; the output of peanuts was 3.6 million tons, an increase of 5.1%; the output of fruits (including fruit melons) was 1.165 million tons, a decrease of 1.9%.

Figure 4: 2016–2020 Grain Production

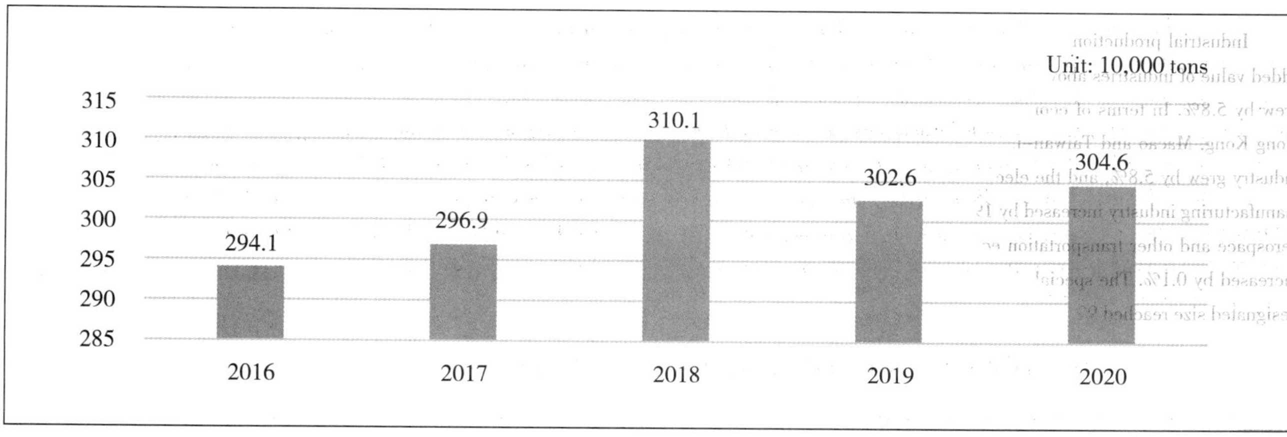

Forestry, animal husbandry and fishery continued to recover. The afforestation (renewal) area actually completed in the whole year was 0.7 thousand hectares. The annual output of meat was 480,000 tons, the output of poultry and eggs was 247,000 tons, and the output of milk was 307,000 tons. The annual output of aquatic products (excluding ocean fishing) was 1.011 million tons, an increase of 0.2%. The marine and freshwater aquaculture area was 35,000 hectares, an increase of 2.9%. The ocean fishing volume was 147,000 tons, an increase of 1.4%. The foundation of modern high–efficiency agriculture has been strengthened.

The added value of modern high–efficiency agriculture was 8.322 billion yuan, an increase of 16.9%. By 2020, 10 modern agricultural industrial parks above the municipal level and 12 strong industrial towns will be created; in 2020, 13 rural complexes, 48 agricultural green gardening standard parks, and 43 standardized demonstration sites will be created; There are 805 products (non–polluted agricultural products, green food, organic agricultural products, and geographical indications of agricultural products), including 52 products protected by national geographical indications. The total power of agricultural machinery was 7.547 million kilowatts, an increase of 147,000 kilowatts over the previous year. The comprehensive mechanization level of crop production reached 89.3%.

Table 2: Output and Growth Rate of Main Planting Products in 2020

Indicators	Unit	Yield	Growth(%)
Grain	10 000 tons	304.6	0.7
Summer grain	10 000 tons	133.4	-6.5
Autumn grain	10 000 tons	171.2	7.0
Oilseed	10 000 tons	36.0	5.1
Vegetable and edible fungi	10 000 tons	655.8	4.7
Fruit	10 000 tons	116.5	-1.9
Garden fruit	10 000 tons	75.0	0.6

Ⅳ. Industry and Construction

Industrial production stabilized and recovered. The city's industrial added value was 326.838 billion yuan, an increase of 2.8%. Among them, the added value of industries above designated size increased by 5.5%. In terms of light and heavy industries, light industry grew by 4.7%, and heavy industry grew by 5.8%. In terms of economic types, state-owned holding companies increased by 6.7%, joint-stock companies increased by 7%, and foreign, Hong Kong, Macao and Taiwan-invested companies increased by 2.7%. In terms of categories, the mining industry grew by 10.5%, the manufacturing industry grew by 5.8%, and the electricity, heat, gas and water production and supply industries fell by 1.7%. In terms of key industries, the automobile manufacturing industry increased by 19.4%, the electrical machinery and equipment manufacturing industry increased by 14.8%, the railway, shipbuilding, aerospace and other transportation equipment manufacturing industry decreased by 4.4%, and the petroleum, coal and other fuel processing industries increased by 0.1%. The special equipment manufacturing industry increased by 11.5%. Annual production and sales rate of industrial enterprises above designated size reached 99.5%.

Table 3: Output and Growth Rate of Main Products of Industries Above Designated Size in 2020

Description	Unit	Output	Growth(%)
Color TV sets	10 000 sets	1774.9	15.3
Of which: Smart TV	10 000 sets	1681.0	15.6
Household refrigerators	10 000 sets	822.0	23.1
Household washing machine	10 000 sets	575.4	54.9
Room air conditioners	10 000 sets	1478.3	10.0
Smart phone	10 000 sets	502.4	-22.1
Beer	10 000 KL	176.1	1.4
Rubber tire casing	10 000 tires	4563.3	4.3
Plate glass	10 000 weight cases	1004.0	8.9
Crude steel	10 000 tons	335.2	4.6
Automobile	10 000 vehicle	29.0	27.3
Motor train units	vehicle	996	-9.3
Urban rail vehicle	vehicle	1836	3.7
Metal shipping containers	10 000 cu.m	1379.1	25.5

The profit of industrial enterprises above designated size was 53.16 billion yuan, an increase of 12.4%. Among them, the profit of state-owned holding enterprises was 17.78 billion yuan, an increase of 2.1%, the profit of joint-stock enterprises was 35.37 billion yuan, an increase of 18.1%, and the profits of foreign, Hong Kong, Macao and Taiwan-invested enterprises were 17.84 billion yuan, an increase of 3.3%.

Table 4: The profit Growth Rate of Industrial Enterprises Above Designated Size in 2020

Indicators	Growth(%)
Industrial profits above designated size	12.4
Of which : State-owned holding	2.1
Shareholder businesses	18.1
Businesses invested by foreigner or by compatriots from Hong Kong , Macao and Taiwan	3.3

The construction industry continues to grow and develop. In the whole year, there were 820 general contracting and professional contracting construction enterprises within the qualifications, achieving an added value of 111.279 billion yuan, an increase of 4.0%. The total output value of the construction industry was 30.02 billion yuan, an increase of 6.8%; the contract value carried forward from the previous year was 240.88 billion yuan, an increase of 6.4%.

V . Service Industry

The service industry has an obvious pulling effect. The city's service industry achieved an added value of 761.359 billion yuan, an increase of 4.1%, accounting for 61.4% of GDP, an increase of 0.5% over the previous year; the contribution rate to economic growth was 65.7%.

Figure 5: 2016–2020 Operating Income and Growth Rate of Service Industries Above Designated Size

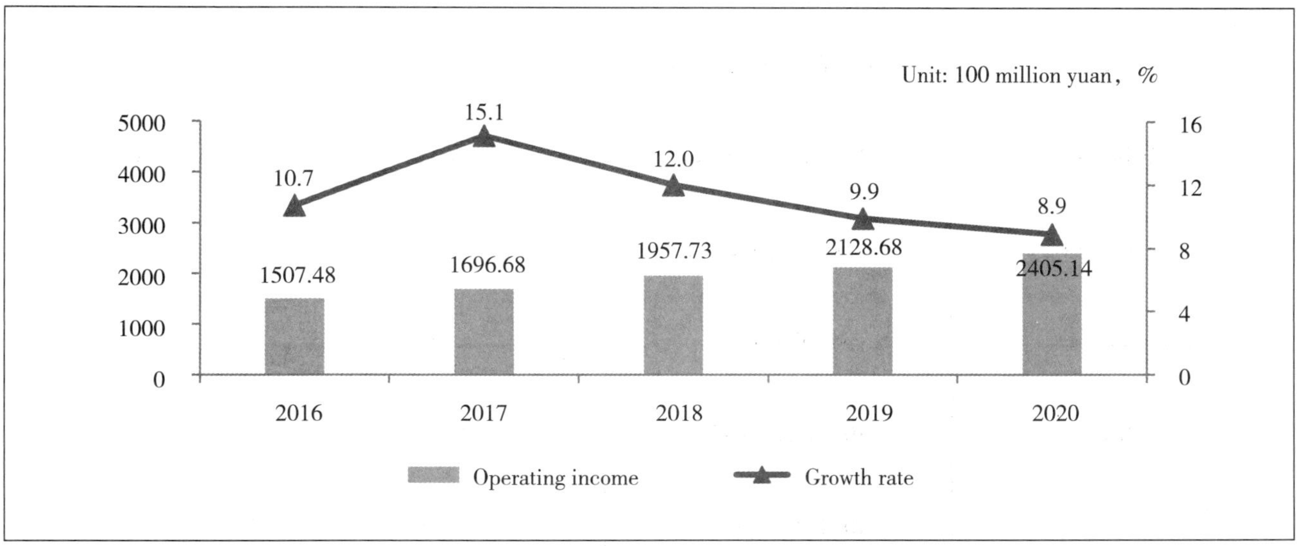

The city's service industry above designated size [8] grew rapidly overall, achieving an operating income of 240.51 billion yuan, an increase of 8.9%. In the producer service industry, the operating income of the Internet and related services above designated size increased by 46.3%, the operating income of the software and information technology service industry increased by 11.4%, and the operating income of the business service industry fell by 4.3%. In the life service industry, the operating income of film and television program production above designated size fell by 7.5%, the operating income of artistic creation and performance increased by 23.7%, the operating income of sports fell by 15.6%, the operating income of residential service industry increased by 10.8%, and the operating income of motor vehicles, electronic products and daily The operating income of the product repair industry fell by 5.7%, and the operating income of other service industries fell by 1.5%. The city's modern service industry achieved an added value of 389.06 billion yuan, an increase of 3.4%, accounting for 31.4% of the city's GDP.

The postal and telecommunications industry has accelerated development. The total volume of post and telecommunications services completed throughout the year was 111.43 billion yuan, an increase of 21.7%. Among them, the total postal business was 13.08 billion yuan, an increase of 26.3%; the total telecommunications business was 98.36 billion yuan, an increase of 21.1%. The express business volume was 590 million pieces, an increase of 29.5%. There were 4.64 million fixed broadband Internet users, an increase of 11.0%. There were 12.57 million mobile phone households in the city, an increase of 0.9%. A total of 10,824 5G base stations have been built and opened.

The tourism industry is gradually recovering. In 2020, the city received 63.123 million tourists, down 44.2%, and realized total tourism revenue of 101.93 billion yuan, down 49.2%. At the end of the year, there were 112 A-level tourist attractions. Among them, there are 1 5A-level tourist attractions, 26 4A-level tourist attractions, and 69 3A-level tourist attractions. Has 91 star-rated hotels. Among them, there are 9 5-star hotels, 23 4-star hotels, and 56 3-star hotels. There are 599 travel agencies. Among them, there are 59 travel agencies operating outbound tourism business, and 540 travel agencies operating inbound and domestic tourism business.

Transportation has picked up steadily. Railways, highways, and waterways completed a total of 360 million tons of freight, an increase of 4.3%; the completed passenger volume was 31.5 million, a decrease of 56.5%. At the end of the year, the number of motor vehicles in the city was 3.14 million, an increase of 7.3%; of which, 2.73 million were private cars, an increase of 7.8%. The annual port throughput was 610 million tons, an increase of 4.7%; the foreign trade throughput was 450 million tons, an increase of 5.9%; the container throughput was 22.01 million TEUs, an increase of 4.7%. At the end of the year, there were 161 domestic routes, 9 international routes, and 1 route from Hong Kong, Macao and Taiwan; the annual air passenger throughput was 14.56 million, a decrease of 43%; the air cargo and mail throughput was 210,000 tons, a decrease of 19.3%.

Table 5: Transportation Volume and Growth Rate Completed by Major Transportation Methods in 2020

Transportation	Unit	Traffic volume	Growth(%)
Passenger volume	100 billion person-km	56.65	-56.9
Railways	100 billion person-km	31.92	-44.1
Highways	100 billion person-km	24.66	-66.8
Waterways	100 billion person-km	0.07	-62.5
Cargo volumes	100 billion ton-km	1788.29	12.2
Railways	100 billion ton-km	71.93	20.7
Highways	100 billion ton-km	568.22	1.4
Waterways	100 billion ton-km	1148.14	17.9

Ⅵ. Investment in Fixed Assets

Investment achieved steady growth. The city's fixed asset investment increased by 3.2%, and 6,907 projects were under construction, an increase of 1,258 over the previous year. In terms of industries, investment in the primary industry increased by 115.4%, investment in the secondary industry increased by 1.6%, and investment in the tertiary industry increased by 2.7%. The investment in equipment manufacturing industry increased by 12.5%, the investment in high-tech manufacturing industry increased by 14.5%, and the investment in industrial technological transformation increased by 13.7%. The development of social and people' s livelihoods such as medical care and health was further improved, and investments in people' s livelihood increased by 28.9%.

Figure 6: The Proportion of Investment in Three Industries in Fixed Asset Investment

Unit: %

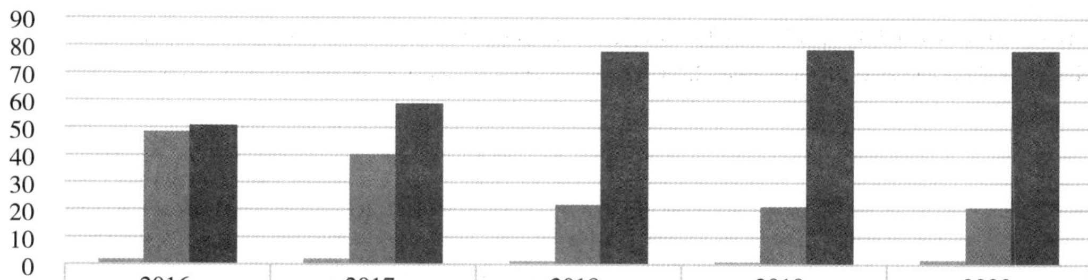

	2016	2017	2018	2019	2020
Primary Industry	1.5	1.7	0.8	0.6	1.3
Secondary Industry	48.1	39.9	21.5	20.9	20.6
Tertiary Industry	50.4	58.4	77.6	78.4	78.1

15 offensives [9] precise force. The industrial space is further expanded, the city function is gradually improved, the city quality is improved and the offensive investment increased by 28.9%; the regional coordinated development is further promoted, breaking through the Pingdu and Laixi offensive, the investment increased by 25.6%; the construction of beautiful villages and pastoral complexes is further accelerated, and the offensive of rural revitalization Investment increased by 15.1%; the vitality of the development of the private economy increased, and the offensive investment in the private economy increased by 13.0%.

13 industrial chains [10] accelerate cohesion. Investment in modern financial services increased by 238.1%, investment in commerce and trade increased by 124.1%, investment in modern and efficient agriculture increased by 107.7%, investment in new-generation information technology increased by 50.0%, investment in high-end equipment increased by 28.3%, investment in new energy and new materials increased by 11.7%, modern ocean Investment increased by 9.3%, investment in high-end chemicals and traditional manufacturing increased by 8.7%, and investment in modern logistics increased by 4.8%.

The real estate market is functioning healthily. In the whole year, real estate development completed investment of 204.51 billion yuan, an increase of 13.4%. Among them, residential investment was 147.92 billion yuan, an increase of 19.4%. The sales area of commercial housing was 16.536 million square meters, an increase of 0.1%. Among them, residential sales area was 14.304 million square meters, down 3.1%.

Table 6: The City's Real Estate Development Investment, Commercial Housing Sales Area and Growth Rate in 2020

Classification	Real Estate Development Investment (100 million yuan)	Growth (%)	Commercial Housing Sales Area (ten thousand square meters)	Increase (%)
Total	2045.1	13.4	1653.6	0.1
Residential	1479.2	19.4	1430.4	-3.1
Office Building	135.1	5.9	64.3	-9.6
Commercial Premises	152.1	-14.8	48.0	-45.4
Other	278.7	7.8	110.9	543.7

The construction of 3,010 public rental housing units was started throughout the year, and 1,193 public rental housing units were basically completed. As of the end of 2020, there were 12,430 households enjoying rental subsidies in the city, and the annual rental subsidy was 83.546 million yuan.

Ⅶ. Domestic Trade

The consumer market is gradually picking up. In the whole year, the retail sales of social consumer goods reached 520.35 billion yuan, an increase of 1.5%. According to the statistics of the place of operation, the retail sales of consumer goods in urban areas were 429.44 billion yuan, an increase of 1.1%; the retail sales of consumer goods in rural areas was 90.91 billion yuan, an increase of 3.2%. In terms of different industries, the wholesale and retail industry achieved retail sales of 468.37 billion yuan, an increase of 2.4%; the accommodation and catering industry achieved retail sales of 51.98 billion yuan, a decrease of 5.7%.

Figure 7: 2016–2020 Total Retail Sales of Consumer Goods and Growth Rate

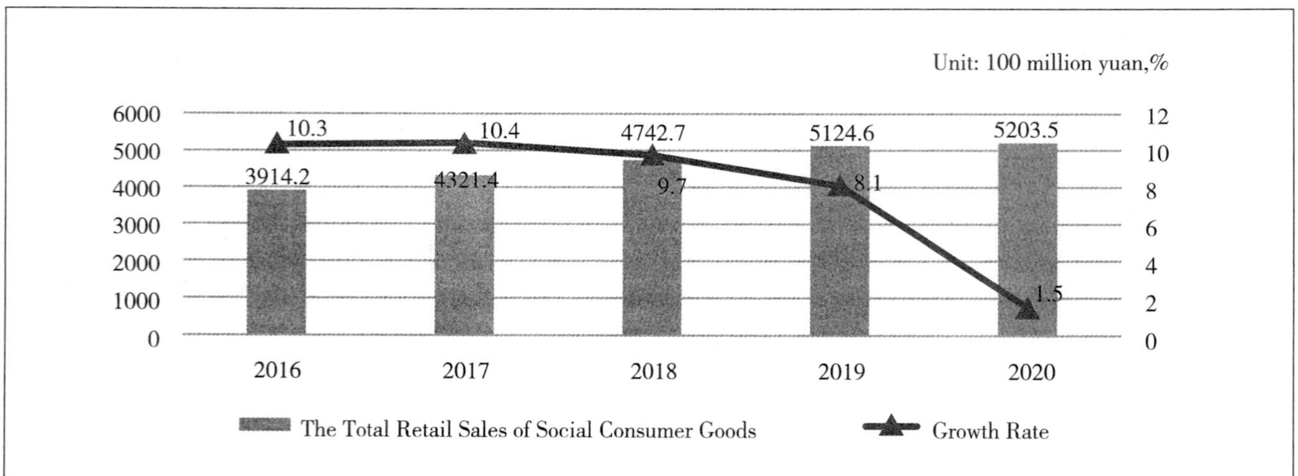

The consumption structure is continuously optimized. Among the retail sales of commodities above designated size, the retail sales of grain, oil and food increased by 7.4%, beverages increased by 33.0%, tobacco and alcohol increased by 13.9%, clothing, shoes and hats, knitted textiles decreased by 15.5%, and cosmetics decreased by 4.0%. Gold, silver and jewellery fell by 24.3%, daily necessities fell by 6.4%, household appliances and audio–visual equipment fell by 3.4%, Chinese and Western medicines rose by 4.9%, cultural office supplies rose by 50.4%, and electronic publications and audio–visual products fell by 41.8%. Furniture category fell by 54.2%, communication equipment category fell by 5.0%, smart phone category rose by 0.7%, construction and decoration materials category rose by 18.8%, petroleum and products category rose by 4.4%, and automotive category rose by 3.6%.

Network transactions expanded rapidly. The city's e-commerce trading platform[11] realized a transaction volume of 1.17 trillion yuan, an increase of 4.2%; the online sales of wholesale and retail enterprises above designated size was 54.16 billion yuan, an increase of 22.9%.

Ⅷ. Foreign Economy

Foreign trade imports and exports rose against the trend. The city's total import and export of goods reached 640.7 billion yuan, an increase of 8.2%. Among them, the export value was 387.68 billion yuan, an increase of 13.7%; the import value was 253.02 billion yuan, an increase of 0.7%. The import and export of countries along the "Belt and Road" was 181.77 billion yuan, an increase of 16.3%. Among them, exports were 109.98 billion yuan, an increase of 18.4%; imports were 71.79 billion yuan, an increase of 13.2%. Imports and exports to SCO countries were 44.84 billion yuan, an increase of 6.1%. Among them, exports were 27.82 billion yuan, an increase of 9.3%; imports were 17.02 billion yuan, an increase of 1.2%.

Figure 8: 2016–2020 total import and Export Volume and Growth Rate of Foreign Trade Goods

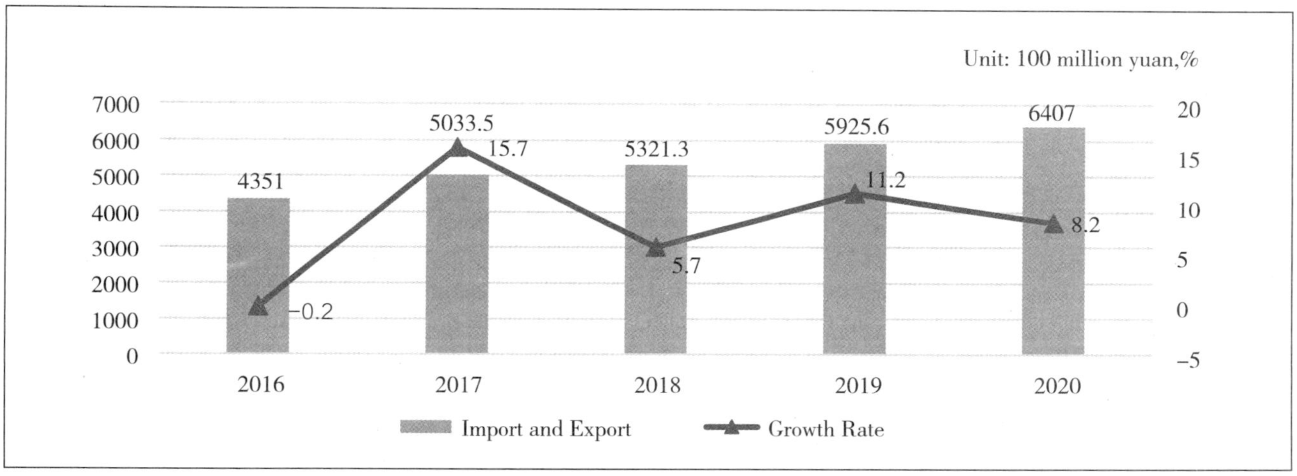

Foreign cooperation has become more in-depth. The city undertook 9,318 service outsourcing contracts, an increase of 4.2%; the contract value was US$7.01 billion, a decrease of 1.9%; the execution value was US$5.05 billion, an increase of 7.1%. Among them, there were 8,007 offshore service outsourcing contracts, an increase of 5.1%; the contract value was US$6.26 billion, an increase of 1.8%; the execution value was US$4.42 billion, an increase of 11.8%. The total import and export volume of foreign trade at Qingdao Port was 1,167.2 billion yuan, a decrease of 8.3%. Among them, the export value was 661.5 billion yuan, down 4.7%; the import value was 505.7 billion yuan, down 12.5%.

Table 7: Imports and Exports of Major Commodities in the City in 2020

Project	Import & Export		Export		Import	
	Amount (100 million yuan)	Growth (%)	Amount (100 million yuan)	Growth (%)	Amount (100 million yuan)	Growth (%)
Textile and Apparel	537.79	11.0	516.25	12.2	21.54	-12.8
Agricultural products	967.58	3.9	393.74	-3.4	573.84	9.5
Electronics	2262.16	12.7	1813.94	18.1	448.22	-4.9
High-tech products	543.17	4.3	314.96	12.9	228.21	-5.6

Table 8: Import and Export Volume and Growth Rate of Goods to Major Countries and Regions in 2020

Country (Region)	Export Amount (100 million USD)	Growth (%)	Import Amount (100 million USD)	Growth (%)
Asia	262.75	13.7	155.08	6.1
Hong Kong	20.52	40.4	0.68	–33.4
Taiwan	5.54	12.6	11.66	1.8
Japan	59.52	2.7	19.25	4.3
Korea	46.08	6.5	31.47	–10.6
ASEAN	75.55	21.1	60.79	36.3
South Asia	21.66	15.1	7.88	15.5
Middle East	29.51	14.3	18.49	–20.0
Africa	24.14	8.9	20.51	–24.0
South Africa	4.29	–5.3	2.90	50.2
Europe	113.85	8.2	60.45	0.2
EU	82.70	8.6	37.31	11.2
UK	16.07	10.8	2.46	–66.3
Germany	18.00	6.7	12.61	0.7
France	8.25	–7.6	3.63	4.7
Italy	7.45	–4.0	2.68	10.0
CIS and Eastern Europe	21.95	10.8	16.93	–1.6
Russia	10.24	3.8	14.09	–5.3
South America	17.19	10.2	66.13	–3.6
Brazil	6.21	–2.0	50.31	–4.0
North America	104.08	16.9	28.09	5.7
USA	90.47	14.7	22.01	14.5
Canada	13.61	34.4	5.61	–16.4
Oceania	16.78	21.3	32.69	–1.5
Australia	14.05	24.0	27.90	3.5

Note: This table is not full caliber.

The use of foreign capital has grown steadily. In 2020, there will be 882 new foreign investment projects approved in the city, a decrease of 7.6%; contractual foreign investment will be US$17.85 billion, an increase of 33.7%. The city's actual use of foreign capital was 5.85 billion US dollars, an increase of 0.2%.

"One Belt One Road" integrated development. The city's enterprises invested in 15 projects in countries and regions along the "Belt and Road". The agreed investment by China was US$390 million, a decrease of 73.0%; the actual investment by China was US$120 million, a decrease of 49.2%.

Foreign investment has become more extensive. The city's foreign contracted engineering business has newly contracted 83 projects, with a newly signed contract value of US$3.48 billion, an increase of 3.6%; and a completed turnover of US$2.88 billion, a decrease of 31.2%. The foreign labor service cooperation business dispatched 10047 various labor personnel.

Ⅸ. Finance

Financial security is comprehensive and strong. The total fiscal revenue for the year was 384.30 billion yuan, and the general public budget revenue was 125.38 billion yuan, an increase of 1.0%. Among them, tax revenue was 89.88 billion yuan, a decrease of 0.3%; value-added tax was 33.13 billion yuan, a decrease of 8.3%; corporate income tax was 15.39 billion yuan, an increase of 3.6%; personal income tax was 4.54 billion yuan, an increase of 29.3%; urban maintenance and construction tax was 5.84 billion yuan, An increase of 2.2%. The general public budget expenditure was 158.47 billion yuan, an increase of 0.6%. Among them, general public service expenditure was 19.94 billion yuan, an increase of 8.1%; education expenditure was 28.86 billion yuan, an increase of 4.9%; science and technology expenditure was 4.69 billion yuan, a decrease of 29.9%; social security and employment expenditure was 22.30 billion yuan, an increase of 14.6%; urban and rural communities Transaction expenditure was 23.66 billion yuan, a decrease of 15.4%. In the whole year, the tax revenue from the taxation system (including customs collection) was 222.01 billion yuan, a decrease of 9.1%. Among them, domestic tax revenue was 170.87 billion yuan, a decrease of 3.1%.

The healthy development of the financial market. As of the end of 2020, the balance of domestic and foreign currency deposits in financial institutions was 2050.71 billion yuan, an increase of 263.08 billion yuan from the beginning of the year; the balance of RMB deposits was 1982.18 billion yuan, an increase of 253.88 billion yuan from the beginning of the year. Among them, household deposits were 803.09 billion yuan, an increase of 127.57 billion yuan over the beginning of the year. The balance of domestic and foreign currency loans was 21.48 billion yuan, an increase of 285.49 billion yuan from the beginning of the year; the balance of RMB loans was 2021.10 billion yuan, an increase of 287.91 billion yuan from the beginning of the year, of which household loans were 664.47 billion yuan, an increase of 95.32 billion yuan from the beginning of the year. The insurance industry achieved a cumulative premium income of 51.1 billion yuan, an increase of 4.9%. Among them, property insurance companies realized premium income of 14.8 billion yuan, an increase of 11.5%; life insurance companies realized premium income of 36.3 billion yuan, an increase of 2.5%. The securities transaction volume of securities branches was 5,996.5 billion yuan, an increase of 53.9%, and the securities transaction volume of corporate institutions was 4,369.8 billion yuan, an increase of 42.7%. There are 362 private equity fund managers registered with China Foundation Association, and the scale of funds under management is 103.93 billion yuan, an increase of 26.6%. There are a total of 44 domestic listed companies, an increase of 5 over the previous year.

Ⅹ. Social enterprise

The career development in education is very impressive. As of the end of 2020, there are 29 colleges and universities of various types (including private colleges and universities) in the city. Among them, there are 27 colleges and universities. In the whole year, 20,000 graduate students were enrolled, 53,000 postgraduates were enrolled, and 13,000 graduates (excluding graduate students in research institutes). The general undergraduate and junior college enrolled 114,000 students, 377,000 students, and 94,000 graduates; secondary vocational education enrolled 30,000 students, 84,000 students, and 27,000 graduates; regular high schools recruited 60,000 students and 14.4 students. There are 10,000 students and 39,000 graduates; junior high school enrollment is 97,000, 286,000 students are enrolled, and 94,000 graduates; ordinary primary school enrollment is 116,000, 604,000 students are enrolled, and 98,000 graduates; special education enrollment is 0.04 There are 10,000 students, 2,000 students, and 30,000 graduates; there are 345,000 children in kindergartens.

Figure 9: The Number of Students Enrolled by Various Schools in 2016–2020

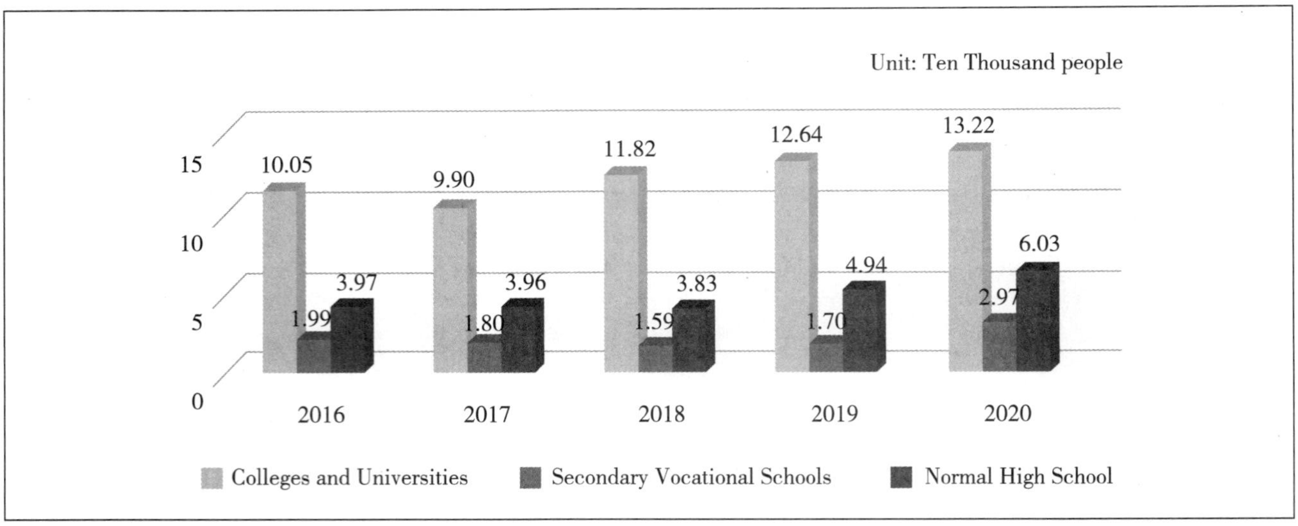

Cultural undertakings are thriving. The city has 91 theaters, 150 cultural centers (stations), 104 museums, 12 public libraries, 8 state–owned art troupes, 6 radio stations and 11 programs, and 6 TV stations and 17 programs. There are 11 archives in the city.

Health services have been continuously enhanced. As of the end of 2020, there are 4459 health institutions (excluding village clinics) in the city. Among them, there are 460 hospitals and health centers, 41 disease prevention and control centers, 12 maternal and child health care institutions, and 3573 outpatient departments (offices), clinics, health centers, and infirmaries. There are 94,900 various types of health technicians. Among them, there are 39,700 doctors. The city has 64,400 medical beds. Among them, there are 62,500 beds in hospitals and health centers.

Sports are in the ascendant. The city's athletes won 417.5 gold medals, 254 silver medals, and 267 bronze medals in all competitions. There is 1 key sports school with 980 students; 10 amateur sports schools with 1,807 students.

XI. Urban Construction

The quality of the city has been greatly improved. Speed up the improvement of infrastructure construction, Jiaodong International Airport has been completed, the Jinan–Qingdao High–speed Railway, Qinglian Railway, Wei–Lai High–speed Railway opened, and the Longqing Expressway, the first phase of the New Airport Expressway and other roads opened to traffic. At the end of the year, there were 8,553 conventional buses and 655 lines in the urban area, with an annual passenger volume of 650.14 million passengers and an average daily passenger volume of 1.78 million. There are 10,568 urban cruise taxis, with an annual passenger volume of 147.2 million person–times, and an average daily passenger volume of 400,000 person–times. There are 6 subway operating lines, with an annual passenger volume of 13.753 million passengers and an average daily passenger volume of 380,000 passengers. In the whole year, 460,000 subway trains were operated, with a total operating mileage of 15.11 million train kilometers.

Ⅻ. Energy, Environment and Safety Production

Obvious results have been achieved in energy saving and consumption reduction. According to preliminary calculations, the total energy consumption for the year was 31.87 million tons of standard coal, a decrease of 1.6%. The electricity consumption of the whole society was 47.66 billion kWh, an increase of 2.5%. Among them, industrial power consumption was 25.88 billion kWh, an increase of 2.5%; service industry power consumption was 11.83 billion kWh, an increase of 2.4%; urban and rural residents' domestic electricity consumption was 8.14 billion kWh, an increase of 2.5%. The city's industrial comprehensive energy consumption above designated size was 13.669 million tons of standard coal, a decrease of 3.8%. Among them, coal consumption decreased by 4.5%; oil consumption increased by 10.6%; natural gas consumption increased by 13.1%. The city's energy consumption per 10,000 yuan of GDP was 0.27 tons of standard coal, down 5.1%.

Figure 10: The Electricity Consumption and Growth Rate of the Whole Society from 2016 to 2020

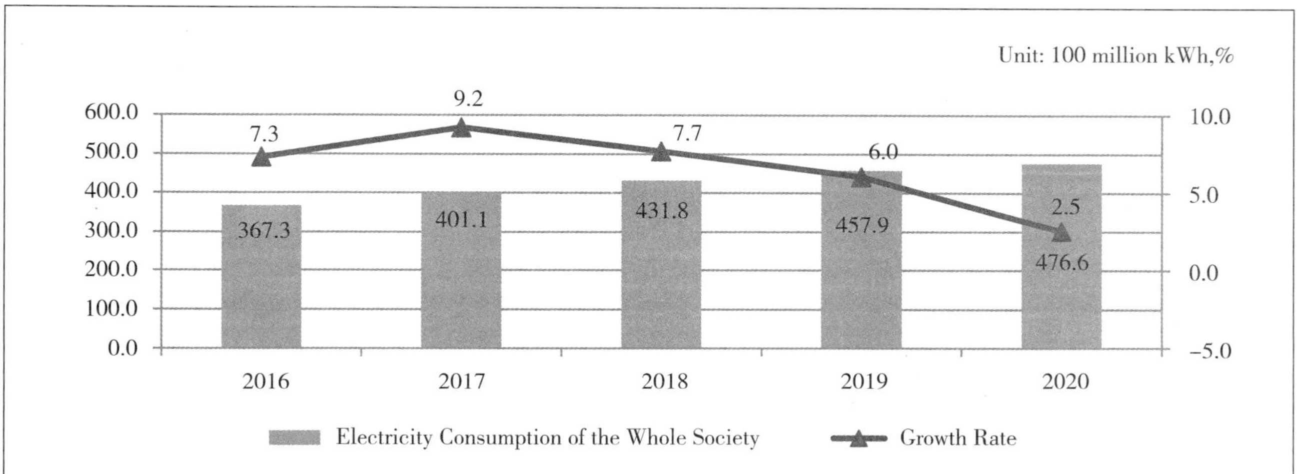

Energy production is more low-carbon and cleaner. The city's energy production was 25.891 million tons of standard coal, an increase of 6.9%. Among them, crude oil processing volume was 13.401 million tons, an increase of 11.7%; gasoline production volume was 3.708 million tons, an increase of 0.5%; diesel production volume was 3.318 million tons, an increase of 11.5%. The power generation was 17.25 billion kWh, a decrease of 4.7%. New energy power generation was 2.05 billion kWh, an increase of 15.4%, accounting for 11.8% of the city's total power generation. Among them, wind power generation increased by 24.6%, and waste incineration power generation increased by 26.1%.

The effect of environmental governance is apparent. The city's annual average temperature is 13.5 ℃, and the average annual precipitation is 983.4 mm. The number of days with good air quality in the urban area reached 316 days, accounting for 86.3% of the whole year. The average value of environmental noise in the urban area is 58.7 decibels, and the average value of urban traffic arterial noise is 70.0 decibels.

The construction of Safe Qingdao continues to advance. There were a total of 82 production safety accidents[12] in the city, with 59 deaths, a decrease of 5.7% and 6.3% respectively. The death rate of production safety accidents per 100 million yuan of GDP was 0.0048, and the death rate of production safety accidents for 100,000 employees in industrial, mining and commercial enterprises was 0.55.

XIII. People's Livelihood and Social Security

The quality of life of residents has improved. The annual per capita disposable income of residents in the city was 47,156 yuan, an increase of 3.7%. In terms of permanent residence, the per capita disposable income of urban residents was 55,905 yuan, an increase of 2.6%; the per capita disposable income of rural residents was 23,656 yuan, an increase of 4.8%. The per capita consumption expenditure of residents in the city was 30,294 yuan, an increase of 2.7%, and the Engel coefficient was 28.1%. By permanent residence, the per capita consumption expenditure of urban residents was 35,936 yuan, an increase of 1.9%; the per capita consumption expenditure of rural residents was 15,138 yuan, an increase of 1.6%. According to a sample survey, at the end of the year, the current housing area per capita of urban residents was 33.4 square meters, and that of rural residents was 38.0 square meters.

Table 9: The Composition of Per Capita Disposable Income of Urban and Rural Residents in 2020

Description of indicators	Residents		Urban Residents		Rural Residents	
	Absolute Value (yuan)	Growth (%)	Absolute Value (yuan)	Growth (%)	Absolute Value (yuan)	Growth (%)
Disposable income	47156	3.7	55905	2.6	23656	4.8
Salary income	28082	3.4	33641	2.2	13151	4.5
Operating net income	8816	1.5	8479	0.3	9720	4.8
Property net income	4008	4.1	5365	2.5	365	6.0
Transfer net income	6250	8.6	8420	6.9	421	10.9

Table 10: Per Capita Consumption Expenditure of Urban and Rural Residents in 2020

Description of indicators	Residents		Urban Residents		Rural Residents	
	Absolute Value (yuan)	Growth (%)	Absolute Value (yuan)	Growth (%)	Absolute Value (yuan)	Growth (%)
Expenditures	30294	2.7	35936	1.9	15138	1.6
Food, Tobacco and Liquor	8520	2.3	10025	1.5	4476	1.9
Clothing	2706	1.8	3306	0.9	1096	0.5
Residence	7173	2.9	8626	2.1	3269	1.4
Supplies and Services	1998	2.1	2365	1.4	1011	0.7
Transportation and Communication	4477	2.5	5154	1.8	2659	1.8
Education, Culture and Recreation	3012	3.7	3608	3.0	1412	1.7
Medical Care	1679	4.9	1977	4.4	880	2.7
Other supplies and services	729	1.3	876	0.3	336	1.0

Table 11: Ownership of Main Durable Consumer Goods Per 100 Households in 2020

Description of indicators	Unit	Quantity		
		Residents	Urban Residents	Rural Residents
Household automobiles	vehicle	59	62	49
Motorcycles	vehicle	24	13	53
Refrigerators	set	110	111	107
Washing machines	set	100	100	98
Water heaters	set	99	101	94
Air-conditioners	set	119	127	97
Color TV	set	106	105	108
Computers	set	72	82	45
Mobile telephones	set	234	235	231

The protection of people's livelihood is even stronger. As of the end of 2020, the city's urban residents have a minimum living guarantee of 18,919, and urban residents have spent 183.35 million in minimum living guarantee funds; 10,960 people have been supported by the five guarantees in rural areas and 153.241 million have been paid for rural five guarantees. The number of people participating in the basic pension insurance for urban employees in the city was 3.121 million, and the number of people participating in unemployment insurance was 2.626 million. The cumulative number of people receiving unemployment insurance benefits throughout the year was 78,000.

Figure 11: 2016–2020 Urban Employee Basic Pension Insurance Participation and Payment

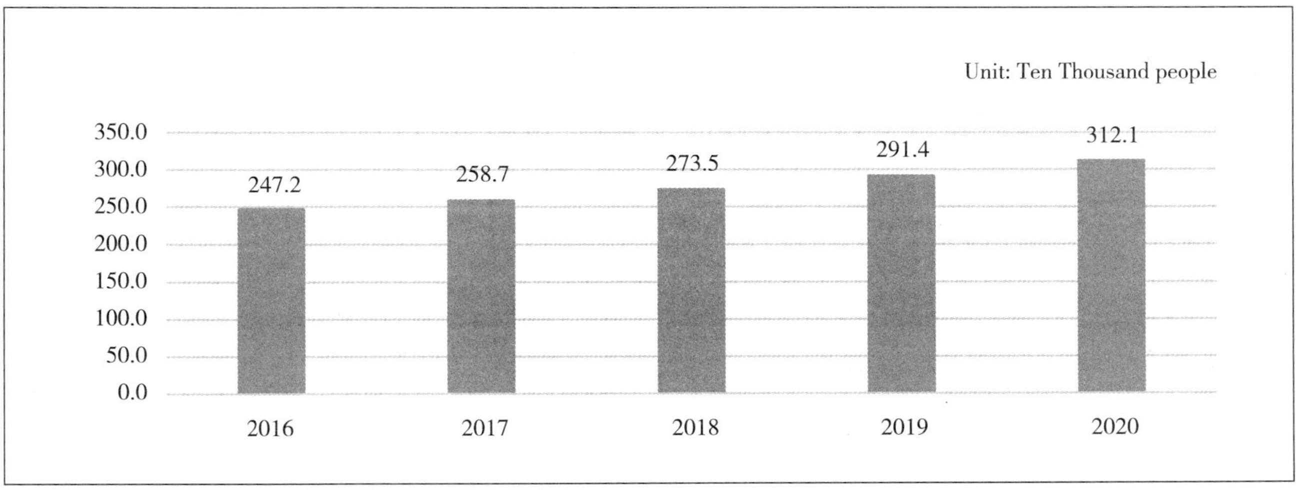

Note :

[1] The statistical data in the Bulletin are all preliminary statistics, and some data are affected by rounding, and there is a difference between the total and the sub-item total. The seventh national census will be launched in 2020, and population data will be announced through the "Qingdao 2020 Seventh National Census Major Data Bulletin".

[2] The city's gross product (GDP) and the absolute value of each industry's added value are calculated at current prices, and the growth rate is calculated at comparable prices.

[3] The increase in the per capita disposable income of residents over the previous year refers to the nominal growth rate. The calculation method is: (the current year's per capita disposable income of the residents / the last year's per capita disposable income of the residents −1) *100%; the actual increase in the per capita disposable income of residents Speed = (the current year's per capita disposable income of residents / the previous year's per capita disposable income of residents / the consumer price index of the same period−1) * 100%.

[4] Industrial enterprises above designated size are enterprises with annual main business income of 20 million yuan and above. Trading enterprises above designated size are legal entities with annual main business income of 20 million yuan and above in the wholesale industry, 5 million yuan and above in the retail industry, and 2 million yuan and above in the accommodation and catering industry. The starting standard for the statistics of fixed asset investment projects is the planned total investment of 5 million yuan.

[5] Strategic emerging industries refer to industries based on major technological breakthroughs and major development needs, which have a major leading and leading role in the overall economic and social and long-term development, with intensive knowledge and technology, low consumption of material resources, large growth potential, and good overall benefits. Including: new generation information technology industry, high-end equipment manufacturing industry, new material industry, bio-industry, new energy automobile industry, new energy industry, energy conservation and environmental protection industry, digital creative industry, and related service industries.

[6] According to the "High-tech Industry (Manufacturing) Classification (2017)", including: pharmaceutical manufacturing, aviation, spacecraft and equipment manufacturing, electronic and communication equipment manufacturing, computer and office equipment manufacturing, medical instrument equipment and instrumentation manufacturing , Information Chemical Manufacturing and other 6 categories. According to the "High-tech Industry (Service Industry) Classification (2018)", including information services, e-commerce services, inspection and testing services, high-tech services for professional technical services, R&D and design services, scientific and technological achievements transformation services, intellectual property rights and related services 9 categories including legal services, environmental monitoring and governance services, and other high-tech services.

[7] PCT (Patent Cooperation Treaty) is the abbreviation of "Patent Cooperation Treaty". PCT international patent refers to the fact that Chinese patent applicants can submit international patent applications to the Chinese Patent Office or to the World Intellectual Property Organization in accordance with the PCT regulations. It is an important indicator that reflects the development level of the region's export-oriented economy and the region's international technological competitiveness.

[8] Service industry enterprises above designated size, one refers to service industry legal entities with annual operating income of 20 million yuan and above, including: transportation, storage and postal industry, information transmission, software and information technology service industry, water conservancy, environment and public The three categories of facility management and the major categories of the sanitation industry; the second refers to the service industry legal entity with an annual operating income of 10 million yuan and above, including: leasing and business services, scientific research and technical services, three categories of education, and property Management, real estate intermediary services, real estate leasing business activities and other real estate industry four sub-categories; third refers to the service industry legal entity with an annual operating income of 5 million yuan and above, including: resident service, repair and other service industries, culture, sports And the entertainment industry, as well as the social work industry.

[9] The 15 offensives are the strategic marine offensive, the "double-stroke and double-lead" offensive, the transportation infrastructure construction offensive, the military-civilian integration development offensive, the rural revitalization offensive, the breakthrough of Pingdu and Laixi offensive, the international shipping trade financial innovation center offensive , "High-end manufacturing + artificial intelligence" offensive, advancing the offensive of state-owned enterprise reform, strengthening the offensive of private economy, technology leading the offensive of urban construction, urban quality improvement offensive, international fashion city construction offensive, efficient Qingdao construction offensive, safe Qingdao construction offensive.

[10] The 13 industrial chains include the "Top Ten" of the province, including new generation information technology, new energy and new materials, high-end chemicals, high-end equipment, modern oceans, medical care and health, modern and efficient agriculture, cultural creativity, boutique tourism, and modern financial services. Industry, as well as three Qingdao characteristic industries including modern logistics, commerce, and business services.

[11] Statistical scope of e-commerce trading platform: industries above designated size, qualified construction industry, wholesale and retail businesses above designated size, accommodation and catering industry above designated size, all real estate development and operation businesses with development and business activities, and services above designated size within the jurisdiction E-commerce transaction platforms owned by business

legal entities, and other e–commerce transaction platforms with an annual transaction volume of 10 million yuan and above.

[12] The scope of statistics on the number of various production safety accidents and deaths includes accidents in seven industries (fields) of production and business road traffic, water transportation, railway traffic, civil aviation, agricultural machinery, fishing vessels, and industrial, mining, and trade. It also includes forest fires, fire accidents and non–production and business road traffic.

Source: The fiscal data in this bulletin comes from the Municipal Finance Bureau; the tax data comes from the Municipal Tax Bureau; the talent, registered unemployment rate, and social security data come from the Municipal Human Resources and Social Security Bureau; the bank data comes from the Qingdao City Center Branch of the People's Bank of China; securities insurance Data comes from Qingdao Securities Regulatory Bureau and Qingdao Banking and Insurance Regulatory Bureau; aquatic product data comes from the Municipal Ocean Development Bureau; forestry data comes from the Municipal Gardens and Forestry Bureau; "three products and one standard", agricultural machinery and other data come from the Municipal Agriculture and Rural Bureau; irrigation area data comes from the city Water Affairs Administration; transportation data comes from the Municipal Transportation Bureau; postal data comes from the Municipal Postal Administration; fixed telephone, broadband, mobile phone and other data come from the Municipal Communications Administration; data on import and export, foreign investment, foreign contracted projects, foreign labor cooperation, etc. The tourism data comes from the Municipal Bureau of Commerce; the tourism data comes from the Municipal Bureau of Culture and Tourism; the education data comes from the Municipal Bureau of Education; the technological data comes from the Municipal Science and Technology Bureau; the patent data comes from the Market Supervision Bureau; the subsistence allowance data comes from the Civil Affairs Bureau; and the sports data comes from the Municipal Sports Bureau; Health data comes from the Municipal Health Commission; environmental data comes from the Municipal Ecological Environment Bureau; electricity consumption data comes from Qingdao Power Supply Company; meteorological data comes from the Municipal Meteorological Bureau; safety production data comes from the Municipal Emergency Bureau; poverty alleviation data comes from the Municipal Poverty Alleviation Development Office; car ownership The data comes from the Municipal Public Security Bureau; the data on residents' income and expenditure, prices, and the housing area of urban and rural residents come from the Qingdao Survey Team of the National Bureau of Statistics; other data comes from the Municipal Bureau of Statistics.

综 合 1

GENERAL SURVEY

简 要 说 明

一、本篇资料的主要内容

本篇资料是对我市行政区划、气象情况、分行业法人单位数、各部门机构数和国民经济、社会发展的综合反映，主要包括行政区划、气象情况、分行业法人单位数、各部门机构数、国民经济主要比例关系、国民经济和社会发展主要指标占全国全省比重、国民经济和社会发展主要指标及其增长速度等资料。

二、本篇资料的来源

1.“行政区划”主要包括2020年底各区（市）街道办事处（乡镇）、社区居委会（村民委员会）区划资料，数据来源于市民政局。

2.“气象情况”包括分区市、市区分月气象资料，数据来源于市气象局。

3.“全市生产总值”来源于国民经济核算统计报表，由市统计局国民经济核算处整理提供。

4. 国民经济和社会发展综合部分来源于本年鉴各篇章中的资料，由市统计局国民经济综合统计处加工整理。

Brief Introduction

I. Main Content

The information in this article is a comprehensive reflection of Qingdao's administrative divisions, meteorological conditions, the number of legal entities by industry, the number of various departments and institutions, and the national economic and social development, including administrative divisions, meteorological conditions, the number of legal entities by industry, the number of agencies, the main proportions of the national economy, the proportion of the main indicators of national economic and social development in the province, the main indicators of national economic and social development and their increase speed and other information.

II. Source of Data

1. "Administrative divisions" mainly include the division data of district (city) sub-district offices (townships) and community neighborhood committees (village committees) at the end of 2020. The data comes from Qingdao Civil Affairs Bureau.

2. "Meteorological conditions" includes monthly meteorological data of district cities and cities, and the data comes from Qingdao Meteorological Bureau.

3. The "Gross Product of the City" comes from the national economic accounting statistical report, which is compiled and provided by the National Economic Accounting Office of Qingdao Statistics Bureau.

4. The comprehensive part of the national economy and social development is derived from the data in each chapter of this yearbook, processed and compiled by the National Economic Comprehensive Statistics Division of Qingdao Bureau of Statistics.

1-1 行政区划（2020 年底）
ADMINISTRATIVE DIVISION (END OF 2020)

单位：个 (unit)

市区名称	Region	街道办事处 Street Offices	社区居委会 Community Residents' Committees	镇 Town	村民委员会 Villagers' Committees
全　市	**Whole Municipality**	**109**	**1154**	**36**	**697**
市南区	Shinan District	14	50		
市北区	Shibei District	30	137		
李沧区	Licang District	11	119		
崂山区	Laoshan District	5	163		
黄岛区	Huangdao District	14	231	8	145
城阳区	Chengyang District	8	250		
即墨区	Jimo District	11	42	4	1
胶州市	Jiaozhou	8	56	4	424
平度市	Pingdu	5	48	12	5
莱西市	Laixi	3	58	8	122

1-2 气象情况（2020 年）
METEOROLOGY (2020)

市区名称	Region	平均气温（摄氏度）Average Temperature (℃)	极端气温 Extreme Temperature (centigrade)		降水量（毫米/年）Precipitation (millimeter/year)	日照时数（小时/年）Sunshine Hours (hour/year)	平均气压（百帕）Average Atmospheric Pressure(100 pa)
			最高（摄氏度）Maximum(℃)	最低（摄氏度）Minimum(℃)			
市　区	Urban Area	13.9	32	-11.2	1093.8	2620	1008.2
崂山区	Laoshan District	13.7	31.1	-11.9	968.8	2012.7	1010.9
黄岛区	Huangdao District	13.9	34.7	-12.6	1213.7	2516.2	1016.3
即墨区	Jimo District	13.6	35.6	-14.3	1065.6	2191	1011.7
胶州市	Jiaozhou	13.7	34.4	-13.2	935.2	2197.3	1007.3
平度市	Pingdu	13.3	35.7	-11.9	827.5	3060	1010
莱西市	Laixi	12.7	35.1	-11.8	779.5	2253.3	1008.2

注：以上为 7 个国家基准站或基本站。
Note：These are 7 national reference or base stations.

1-3 市区分月气象情况（2020 年）
MONTHLY METEOROLOGY OF URBAN AREA (2020)

月　份	Month	平均气温（摄氏度）Average Temperature (℃)	降水量（毫米）Precipitation (millimeter)	日照时数（小时）Sunshine Hours (hour)
一月	Jan.	2.3	33.6	126.7
二月	Feb.	4.1	39.4	136
三月	Mar.	8.4	1.6	235.6
四月	Apr.	11.9	16.4	312.4
五月	May	17	132.4	308.9
六月	June	21.7	95.8	296.4
七月	July	23.2	297	299.5
八月	Aug.	25.6	378.5	207.9
九月	Sep.	23.1	32.3	220.2
十月	Oct.	16.4	2.7	166.3
十一月	Nov.	10.5	55.6	146.3
十二月	Dec.	2.1	8.5	163.8
全　年	Annual Total	13.9	1093.8	2620

1-4　各部门机构数(2020 年底)
GRASS-ROOTS UNITS IN VARIOUS SECTORS (END OF 2020)

项目	Item	单位	Unit	机构数 Grass-roots Units
农村基层单位	**Rural Grass-roots Units**			
镇政府	Town Governments	个	unit	36
乡村户数	Number of Rural Households	万户	10 000 households	126.6
规模以上工业企业单位	**Industrial enterprises above designated size**	个	**unit**	3856
#国有企业	State-owned Enterprises	个	unit	189
集体企业	Collective-owned Enterprises	个	unit	5
外商及港澳台商投资企业	Enterprises with Funds from Hong Kong, Macao, Taiwan and Foreign Countries	个	unit	825
交通运输业	**Transportation**			
铁路	Railway	个	unit	2
公路	Highway	个	unit	287
水运	Waterway	个	unit	20
邮电业	**Post and Telecommunication Services**			
邮政局(所)	Post Offices	处	unit	2376
电信营业网点(自有)	Telecom business outlets	个	unit	400
建筑业企业	**Construction Enterprises**	个	unit	806
国有企业	State-owned Enterprises	个	unit	19
集体企业	Collective-owned Enterprises	个	unit	6
其他	Others	个	unit	781
规模以上服务业企业单位	**Service industry enterprises above designated size**	个	unit	2229
内资企业	Domestic Funded Enterprises	个	unit	2102
港、澳、台商投资企业	Enterprises with Funds from Hong Kong, Macao and Taiwan	个	unit	46
外商投资企业	Foreign Funded Enterprises	个	unit	81
批发和零售业、住宿和餐饮业	Wholesale & Retail Trades, Hotels and Catering Services			
限额以上批发业	Wholesale Trade above Designated Size	个	unit	2431
限额以上零售业	Retail Trade above Designated Size	个	unit	764
限额以上住宿业	Hotel above Designated Size	个	unit	273
限额以上餐饮业	Catering Service above Designated Size	个	unit	339

1-4 续表
Continued

项目	Item	单位	Unit	机构数 Grass-roots Units
教育事业	Education			
普通高等学校	Regular Institutions of Higher Education	所	unit	27
中等专业学校	Specialized Secondary Schools	所	unit	6
普通中学	Regular Secondary Schools	所	unit	340
普通小学	Regular Primary Schools	所	unit	706
幼儿园	Kindergartens	所	unit	2527
文化及相关产业	Culture and Related Industry			
公共图书馆	Public Libraries	个	unit	12
影剧院	Theater	个	unit	91
卫生事业	Public Health			
#医院	Hospitals	个	unit	460
民政行政单位	Civil Affairs Departments			
#提供住宿的社会服务机构	Social service agencies that provide accommodation	个	unit	275

1-5 按行业分法人单位数

NUMBER OF CORPORATE UNITS BY SECTOR

单位：个 (unit)

行　业	Sector	2020年
总　计	Total	509255
农、林、牧、渔业	Agriculture, Forestry, Animal Husbandry and Fishery	0
采矿业	Mining	1107
制造业	Manufacturing	80935
电力、热力、燃气及水生产和供应业	Electricity, heat, gas, water production and supply industry	700
建筑业	Construction	40388
批发和零售业	Wholesale and Retail Trades	169355
交通运输、仓储和邮政业	Transport, Storage and Post	21465
住宿和餐饮业	Hotels and Catering Services	7977
信息传输、软件和信息技术服务业	Information Transmission, Computer Services and Software	24644
金融业	Financial Industry	3568
房地产业	Real Estate	13134
租赁和商务服务业	Leasing and Business Services	70299
科学研究和技术服务业	Scientific Research and Technical Services	29913
水利、环境和公共设施管理业	Management of Water, Conservancy Environment and Public Facilities	3512
居民服务、修理和其他服务业	Resident Services, Repairs and Other Services	10090
教育	Education	8421
卫生和社会工作	Health Social Security and Social Welfare	3492
文化、体育和娱乐业	Culture, Sports and Entertainment Industry	9269
公共管理、社会保障和社会组织	Public Administration, Social Security and Social Organization	10986

1-6　国民经济主要平均指标

AVERAGE INDICATORS ON NATIONAL ECONOMY

指　标	Indicator	单位	Unit	2000 年	2005 年
人口密度	Density of Population	人 / 平方公里	person/sq.km	664	695
每户年平均人口	Average Household Size	人	person	3.14	3.12
城镇非私营单位在岗职工年平均工资	The Average Annual Wage of Staff and Workers in the Post in Non-Private Units in Towns and Cities	元	yuan	10 072	19086
城市居民人均年可支配收入	Annual Per Capita Net Income of urban Households	元	yuan	7971	12725
农民人均年纯收入	Annual Per Capita Net Income of Rural Households	元	yuan	3534	5384
每一播亩平均粮食产量	Output of Grain Per Mu of Sowing Area	千克	kg	411	421
每亩蔬菜平均产量	Average Output of Vegetables Per Mu	千克	kg	2 735	2985
每亩茶叶平均产量	Average Output of tea Per Mu	千克	kg	8.1	16.5
每亩花生平均产量	Average Output of Peanut Per Mu	千克	kg	298	327
每亩棉花平均产量	Average Output of Cotton Per Mu	千克	kg	83	74
每台拖拉机负担耕地面积	Cultivated Area Ploughed by Per Tractor	亩 / 台	mu/unit	56	39
每亩耕地施用化肥量（折纯）	Chemical Fertilizer Consumption Per Mu (convert to pure amount)	千克	kg	45	52
每人平均消费品零售额	Per Capita Retail Sales of Consumer Goods	元	yuan	5965	11445
城市每天平均生活用水量	Daily Residential Consumption of Water	万吨	10 000 tons	33.33	34.35
城市每人平均公园绿地面积	Per Capita Public Green Areas	平方米	sq.m	8.50	11.82
每万人拥有医疗床位	Number of Hospital Beds Per 10000 Population	张	bed	34.5	41.3
每万人拥有医生数	Number of Doctors per 10000 Population	人	person	21.0	20.3
每万人中高等学校学生数	Students Enrollment of Institutions of Higher Education per 10000 Population	人	person	65	324
每万人中中等学校学生数	Students Enrollment of Secondary Schools per 10000 Population	人	person	704	768
每万人中小学学生数	Students Enrollment of primary Schools per 10000 Population	人	person	757	648

注：1. 自 2015 年开始，全市城乡住户调查统一使用一体化改革后的数据，与原数据相比，城乡居民收支指标的调查范围和口径均存较大变化。原“城市居民人均可支配收入”调整为“城镇居民人均可支配收入”；原“农民人均纯收入”调整为“农村居民人均可支配收入”。

2.2008 年 -2017 年农作物数据为根据第三次农业普查结果核定修正后数据。

Note: 1. Since 2015, the urban and rural households investigation unified the data after the integrated reform, compared with the original data, the investigation scope and the caliber of urban and rural residents' income and expenditure indicators have changed greatly.

The original "per capita disposable income of urban residents" is adjusted to be a "per capita disposable income of urban residents". The original "per capita net income of farmers" is adjusted to "per capita disposable income of rural residents".

2. Crop data from 2008 to 2017 are revised based on the results of the third agricultural census.

2008年	2009年	2010年	2012年	2013年	2014年	2015年	2016年	2017年	2018年	2019年	2020年
715	676	677	682								
3.13	3.12	3.10	3.09								
29404	32507	37501	49052	55363	62104	69465	76616	83539	90840	103108	116115
20034	21857	24380	31349	34356	37346	40370	43598	47176	50817	54484	55905
7666	8255	9326	12366	13905	15434	16730	17969	19364	20820	22573	23656
408	411	399	411	407	396	400	404	414	430	425	432
3551	3624	3689	3887	3957	3963	3889	3760	3931	3796	3883	3992
39	38	44	51	49	52	57	74	75	80	75	78
316	315	306	326	314	305	287	294	319	321	305	321
70	71	62	81	81	89	86	82	85	110	105	97
36	35	32			38	38	37	36	36	36	36
50	48	47			37	36	36	36	35	34	34
18982	21927	24781	32917	37032	41226	45309	49360	53722	57991	61862	62180
30.96	33.56	34.31	33.21	32.50	40.60	42.10	67.60	50.3	50.6	54.3	58.0
14.53	14.50	14.58	14.60	14.60	14.60	14.60	18.60	17.4	16.3	16.9	19.0
42.5	43.0	47.2	61.4	58.0	60.3	62.0	63.9	69.4	68.2	72.8	77.0
21.4	21.9	23.2	28.1	31.2	32.0	33.5	34.9	38.4	42.3	45.5	47.4
354	361	373	386	388	402	411.0	430.0	431.0	486.6	500.3	514.6
765	740	701	635	626	614	596.0	593.0	611.0	612.5	627.8	653.3
627	610	606	630	642	662	685.0	690.0	685.3	696.9	702.4	721.5

1-7 主要年份社会经济主要指标

MAJOR YEAR'S INDICATORS ON SOCIETY AND ECONOMY

指　标	Indicator	单位	Unit	2000 年	2005 年	2008 年
人口	**Population**					
总人口（年末）	Population at Year-end	万人	10 000 persons	706.65	740.91	761.56
男性人口	Male	万人	10 000 persons	357.74	374.03	382.46
女性人口	Female	万人	10 000 persons	348.91	366.87	379.10
市区人口	Urban Area	万人	10 000 persons	234.60	265.43	276.25
就业	**Employment**					
社会从业人员	Employment	万人	10 000 persons	436.1	467.4	484.8
#单位从业人员	Employed Persons in Units	万人	10 000 persons	118.3	224.3	254.1
经济总量	**Gross Economic Amount**					
全市生产总值（当年价）	GDP (at current price)	亿元	100 million yuan	1183.14	2576.95	4141.9
第一产业增加值	Primary Industry	亿元	100 million yuan	135.81	168.06	210.53
第二产业增加值	Secondary Industry	亿元	100 million yuan	546.12	1292.49	2007.89
第三产业增加值	Tertiary Industry	亿元	100 million yuan	501.21	1116.4	1923.49
人均生产总值	Per Capita GDP	元	yuan	15900	31725	49183
农林牧渔业总产值（当年价）	Gross Output Value of Farming, Forestry, Animal Husbandry and Fishery (at current price)	亿元	100 million yuan	248.33	320.51	399.5
工业总产值（当年价）	Gross Industrial Output Value (at current price)	亿元	100 million yuan	1940.83	5001.78	8946.73

注：1. 单位从业人员 2004 年以前为职工人数（不含私营企业）。
2. 规模以上固定资产投资数据 2003 年以前为城镇以上统计范围。
3. 2002 年以前地方财政一般预算收支数据为地方财政收支口径。
4. 2008 年 -2017 年农林牧渔业总产值为根据第三次农业普查结果核定修正后数据。
5. 全国第四次经济普查后，对 2000 年至 2018 年历年 GDP 数据进行了修订（以下相关表同）。

Note: 1. Before 2004, the data of employed persons in units refers to the number of staff and workers (excluding private enterprises) .
2. Before 2003, the data of investment in fixed assets above designated size refers to urban investment.
3. Before 2002, the data of general budgetary revenue and expenditure of local government finance refers to revenue and expenditure of local government finance.
4. Gross output value of farming, forestry, animal husbandry and fishery from 2008 to 2017 is revised according to the results of the third agricultural census.
5. After the fourth national economic census, the GDP data from 2000 to 2018 was revised (the following related tables are the same) .

2009年	2010年	2011年	2012年	2013年	2014年	2015年	2016年	2017年	2018年	2019年	2020年
762.92	763.64	766.36	769.56								
382.35	381.92	382.69	383.82								
380.56	381.72	383.67	385.74								
275.47	275.50	277.09	279.57								
489.3	504.9	510.8	515.5	517.5	521.3	523.7	523.5	524.3	525.3	523.6	525.6
260.5	269.4	275.9	283.2	293.7	303.0	309.2	315.6	321.4	330.4	146.6	147.7
4534.2	5350.69	6248.48	6869.61	7508.7	8120.66	8658.57	9283.17	10136.96	10949.38	11741.31	12400.56
216.99	261.03	288.73	305.72	332.1	341.68	356.19	357.4	367.71	386.91	409.98	425.41
2146.53	2482.6	2823.7	3010.6	3225.9	3389.1	3503.4	3592.80	3849.18	4033.33	4182.76	4361.56
2170.7	2607.08	3136.06	3553.33	3950.68	4389.87	4798.98	5332.96	5920.06	6529.14	7148.57	7613.59
53481	62148	70945	76636	82463	87677	92157	97430	104905	112129	118978	123828
407.1	480.2	534.6	567.3	610.6	627.9	612.4	669.1	697.9	737	778.1	807.1
10255.62	11614.83	13277.96	15306.32	16897.18	17444.21	18019.43	17416.71	13019.73	11389.78		

1-7 续表 1
Continued

指　标	Indicator	单位	Unit	2000 年	2005 年	2008 年
财政	**Government Finance**					
公共财政预算收入	Public Budget Revenue	亿元	100 million yuan	80.01	176.34	342.44
公共财政预算支出	Public Budget Expenditure	亿元	100 million yuan	87.87	203.06	369.41
规模以上固定资产投资额	**Investment in Fixed Assets above Designated Size**	亿元	**100 million yuan**	**242.68**	**1403.30**	**2019.01**
社会消费品零售额	**Total Retail Sales of Consumer Goods**	亿元	**100 million yuan**	**421.55**	**847.97**	**1445.62**
港口吞吐量	**Volume of Freight Handled in Ports**	万吨	**10 000 tons**	**8661**	**18727**	**30029**
集装箱吞吐量	**Volume of Containers Handled**	万标箱	**Ten Thousand TEUs**	**212.0**	**630.7**	**1037.7**
民航货邮吞吐量	**Civil Aviation Cargo and Mail Throughput**	万吨	**10 000 tons**	**3.44**	**8.91**	**13.05**
对外贸易	**Foreign Trade**					
外贸进出口总额	Imports and Exports（excluding central and provincial companies）	亿美元	100 million USD	108.31	304.55	521.59
#出口总额	Exports	亿美元	100 million USD	61.14	175.88	314.62
教育、卫生、文化	**Education, Public Health and Culture**					
小学在校学生数	Students Enrollment in Primary Schools	万人	10 000 persons	53.49	47.98	47.72
普通中学在校学生	Students Enrollment in Regular Secondary Schools	万人	10 000 persons	39.85	39.11	37.39

2009年	2010年	2011年	2012年	2013年	2014年	2015年	2016年	2017年	2018年	2019年	2020年
376.99	452.61	566.14	670.18	788.93	895.25	1006.26	1100.03	1157.24	1231.91	1241.74	1253.85
433.58	532.39	658.06	765.98	1014.23	1074.71	1222.87	1352.85	1403.03	1561.23	1575.97	1584.65
2458.89	**3022.48**	**3502.54**	**4153.91**	**5027.86**	**5766.03**	**6555.70**	**7454.70**	**7777.09**			
1672.88	**1892.38**	**2217.26**	**2533.16**	**2865.02**	**3218.25**	**3548.16**	**3914.19**	**4321.43**	**4742.72**	**5126.6**	**5203.5**
31668	**35012**	**37971**	**41465**	**45782**	**47701**	**49749**	**51463**	**51314**	**54250**	**57736**	**60459**
1027.7	**1201**	**1302**	**1450**	**1552**	**1658**	**1743**	**1805**	**1831**	**1932**	**2101**	**2201**
13.54	**16.37**	**16.65**	**17.19**	**18.62**	**20.44**	**20.81**	**23.69**	**23.21**	**22.45**	**25.63**	**20.7**
439.86	561.49	712.63	732.08	779.12	798.88	702.22	4350.67（亿元）	5033.50（亿元）	5321.26（亿元）	5925.58（亿元）	6407.01（亿元）
269.22	333.51	400.56	408.20	419.86	457.77	453.50	2821.91（亿元）	3031.81（亿元）	3172.22（亿元）	3411.90（亿元）	3876.76（亿元）
46.50	46.27	47.95	49.50	49.63	51.65	53.65	54.72	55.05	56.99	58.38	60.4
37.74	38.00	37.32	36.96	36.51	36.26	35.54	35.61	37.22	38.54	40.9	43.0

1-7 续表 2
Continued

指　标	Indicator	单位	Unit	2000 年	2005 年	2008 年
高等学校在校学生	Students Enrollment in Institutions of Higher Education	万人	10 000 persons	4.61	23.98	26.93
小学专任教师	Full-time Teachers in Primary Schools	万人	10 000 persons	3.17	3.17	3.24
普通中学专任教师	Full-time Teachers in Regular Secondary Schools	万人	10 000 persons	2.63	2.97	2.99
医生总数	Doctors	万人	10 000 persons	1.49	1.50	1.63
医院床位数	Hospital Beds	万张	10 000 beds	2.01	2.86	2.99
人民生活	**People's Living Conditions**					
就业人员工资总额	Total wages of Employed Persons	亿元	100 million yuan	120.4	359.5	578.7
城乡人民币储蓄存款余额	Savings Deposit of Urban and Rural Households	亿元	100 million yuan	535.32	1343.10	2123.36
物价指数	**Price Indexes**					
商品零售价格指数（以 1950 年价格为 100）	Retail Price Index（1950=100）	%	%	520.5	495.0	526.6
居民消费价格指数（以 1950 年价格为 100）	Consumer Price Index（1950=100）	%	%	711.9	753.1	831.4
#食品价格指数（以 1950 年价格为 100）	Food Price Index（1950=100）	%	%	800.1	871.8	1105.3

注：1. 就业人员工资总额 2005 年前统计范围为全部职工不含私营企业，2015 年及以前为在岗职工工资总额；自 2019 年统计口径变化，无全部单位数据；
2. 2015 年“城乡人民币储蓄存款余额”改为“住户存款”。

Note: 1. The total wages of employees before 2005 included all employees excluding private enterprises, and the total wages of employees in 2015 and before were the total wages of employees on the job; since the change in the statistical caliber in 2019, there is no data for all units;
2. In 2015, "balance of RMB deposits in urban and rural areas" changed to "household deposits."

2009年	2010年	2011年	2012年	2013年	2014年	2015年	2016年	2017年	2018年	2019年	2020年
27.52	28.49	29.15	29.66	30.02	31.35	32.23	34.09	34.62	39.8	41.58	43.1
3.22	3.20	3.16	3.17	3.28	3.22	3.45	3.42	3.47	3.69	3.53	3.52
3.06	3.08	3.14	3.20	3.18	3.20	3.29	3.39	3.47	3.60	3.98	4.15
1.67	1.77	1.83	2.16	2.41	2.50	2.63	2.76	3.09	3.46	3.78	3.97
3.05	3.34	3.56	4.12	3.97	4.30	4.51	4.73	4.63	5.08	5.85	6.23
638.1	738.0	877.5	1044.3	1251.7	1456.0	1644.4	1852.7	2034.7	2251.7		
2527.88	2912.33	3198.51	3757.60	4141	4436	5024	5326	5394	5914	6755	8031
519.2	526.5	550.2	559.6	567.4	580.5	580.5	592.1	596.8	607.6	622.2	631.5
835.6	854.0	896.7	920.9	943.9	968.4	980.0	1004.5	1024.6	1046.1	1080.6	1106.5
1123.0	1194.9	1327.5	1384.6	1458.0	1522.2	1548.1	1625.5	1619.0	1669.2	1862.8	2045.4

1-8 国民经济主要结构指标
COMPOSITION INDICATORS ON NATIONAL ECONOMY

指　标	Indicator	2000 年	2005 年	2008 年	2009 年	2010 年
社会从业人员	**Employment**					
产业结构	Industrial Composition					
第一产业	Primary Industry	36.4	22.2	19.9	20.1	19.5
第二产业	Secondary Industry	33.9	41.8	43.0	41.9	41.4
第三产业	Tertiary Industry	29.7	36.0	37.1	38.0	39.1
全市生产总值	**GDP**					
产业结构	Industrial Composition					
第一产业	Primary Industry	11.5	6.5	5.1	4.8	4.9
第二产业	Secondary Industry	46.1	50.2	48.5	47.3	46.4
第三产业	Tertiary Industry	42.4	43.3	46.4	47.9	48.7
农业	**Agriculture**					
农林牧渔业产值结构	Composition of Farming, Forestry, Animal Husbandry and Fishery					
#农业	Farming	45.0	39.5	43.2	43.5	45.8
林业	Forestry	0.8	0.8	0.6	0.5	0.4
畜牧业	Animal Husbandry	27.9	33.4	29.9	27.9	25.5
渔业	Fishery	26.4	26.3	22.7	24.1	24.6
工业	**Industy**					
轻重工业产值结构	Composition of Output Value of Light and Heavy Industry					
轻工业	Light Industry	64.1	49.4	42.3	41.7	38.7
重工业	Heavy Industry	35.9	50.6	57.7	58.3	61.3
固定资产投资	**Investment in Fixed Assets**					
投资结构	Composition of Investment					
生产性	Productive	54.0	65.4	61.6	56.3	53.6
非生产性	Non-productive	46.0	34.6	38.4	43.7	46.4

注：2008 年 -2017 年农业数据为根据第三次农业普查结果核定修正后数据。
Note: Agricultural data from 2008 to 2017 are revised according to the results of the third agricultural census.

2011 年	2012 年	2013 年	2014 年	2015 年	2016 年	2017 年	2018 年	2019 年	2020 年
19.2	18.8	18.8	18.4	18.1	17.8	16.9	16.2	15.7	15.6
41.2	41.0	40.6	39.0	38.6	38.0	37.8	36.4	38.3	31.9
39.6	40.2	40.6	42.6	43.3	44.2	45.3	47.4	46.0	52.5
4.6	4.5	4.4	4.2	4.1	3.9	3.6	3.5	3.5	3.4
45.2	43.8	43.0	41.7	40.5	38.7	38.0	36.9	35.6	35.2
50.2	51.7	52.6	54.1	55.4	57.4	58.4	59.6	60.9	61.4
40.9	40.0	41.7	42.1	40.3	42.5	43.0	44.7	46.3	46.2
0.4	0.4	0.4	0.4	0.4	0.4	0.4	0.5	0.6	0.6
28.1	26.6	25.5	24.8	25.0	24.2	23.8	22.1	21.5	22.3
26.7	28.8	28.0	27.7	29.6	26.6	26.2	26.1	24.9	24
38.3	39.5	39.5	38.8	39.5	39.4	37.6	34.3		
61.7	60.5	60.5	61.2	60.5	60.6	62.4	65.7		
53.2	58.4	61.65	57.08	63.16	59.81	53.64			
46.8	41.6	38.35	42.92	36.84	40.19	46.36			

1-9 平均每天主要社会经济活动
SELECTED INDICATORS ON AVERAGE DAILY SOCIAL AND ECONOMIC ACTIVITIES

指　标	Indicator	单位	Unit	2000 年	2005 年	2008 年	2009 年
全市生产总值	GDP	万元	10 000 yuan	32415	70601	113477	124225
工业总产值	Gross Industrial Output Value	万元	10 000 yuan	53174	137035	245116	280976
农林牧渔业总产值	Gross Output Value of Farming, Forestry, Animal Husbandry and Fishery	万元	10 000 yuan	6803	8781	10945	11153
主要工业产品产量	Output of Major Industrial Products						
发电量	Electricity	万千瓦时	10 000 kW · h	2489	2701	4509	4730
钢材	Rolled-steel	吨	ton	2558	9049	9593	9579
纱	Yarn	吨	ton	191	198	118	106
布	Cloth	万米	10 000 m	114	141	133	85
家用电冰箱	Refrigerator	台	unit	8523	24899	19813	22663
彩色电视机	Color TV set	台	unit	10395	36282	22922	29170
社会消费品零售总额	Total Retail Sales of Consumer Goods	万元	10 000 yuan	11549	23232	39606	45832
固定资产投资	Investment in Fixed Assets above Designated Size	万元	10 000 yuan	6649	38446	55315	67367
外贸进出口总额	Imports and Exports	万美元	10 000 USD	3707	9047	14695	12288
港口吞吐量	Volume of Freight Handled in Ports	万吨	10 000 tons	23.73	51.31	82.27	86.76

注：1. 固定资产投资包括城镇、农村 500 万元以上投资项目。
2. 一年按照 365 天计算。
3. 2008 年 -2017 年农林牧渔业总产值为根据第三次农业普查结果核定修正后数据。

Note :1. Investment in fixed assets includes construction projects involving an urban or rural investment of 5 million yuan and over.
2. A year is computed according to 365 days.
3. Gross output value of farming, forestry, animal husbandry and fishery from 2008 to 2017 is revised according to the results of the third agricultural census.

2010 年	2011 年	2012 年	2013 年	2014 年	2015 年	2016 年	2017 年	2018 年	2019 年	2020 年
146594	171191	188208	205718	222484	237221	254333	277725	299983	321680	339741
318215	363780	419351	462936	477924	493683	477143	356705	312048		
13157	14646	15541	16728	17203	16777	18331	19120	20192	21318	22112
4984	4759	4787	4935	4885	4754	4805	4981	5271	4947	4725
9136	9101	7525	6312	5830	3853	5243	7996	8764	9211	10663
97	53	53	92	89	76	92	73	79	111	83
48	120	134	141	122	77	68	65	127	31	44
21951	19686	15754	14366	16714	23893	24170	22429	24290	20050	22521
30444	31622	39452	41426	46984	37704	57855	46658	46443	43299	48626
51846	60747	69402	78494	88171	97210	107238	118395	129938	140455	142562
82808	95960	113806	137751	157973	179608	204238	213071			
15633	19768	20057	21346	21887	19239	119196（万元）	137904（万元）	145787（万元）	162345（万元）	175534（万元）
96	104	114	125	131	136	141	141	149	158	166

1-10　主要指标占全国全省比重（2020年）

PERCENTAGE OF MAIN INDICATORS TO CHINA AND SHANDONG (2020)

指　标	Indicator	单位	Unit
一、生产总值	**GDP**	亿元	100 million yuan
第一产业	Primary Industry	亿元	100 million yuan
第二产业	Secondary Industry	亿元	100 million yuan
第三产业	Tertiary Industry	亿元	100 million yuan
二、主要工业产品产量	**Output of Major Industrial Products**		
发电量	Electricity	亿千瓦小时	100 million kW・h
房间空气调节器	Air Conditioner	万台	10 000 units
家用电冰箱	Refrigerator	万台	10 000 units
彩色电视机	Color TV Set	万台	10 000 units
钢材	Rolled-steel	万吨	10 000 tons
水泥	Cement	万吨	10 000 tons
三、主要农产品产量	**Output of Major Farm Products**		
粮食	Grain	万吨	10 000 tons
油料	Oil Plants	万吨	10 000 tons
猪牛羊禽肉类产量	Output of Pork, Beef, Mutton And Poultry	万吨	10 000 tons
水产品	Aquatic Products	万吨	10 000 tons
四、房地产开发投资	**Investment In Real Estate Development**	亿元	100 million yuan
五、货物进出口总额	**Imports and Exports**	亿元	100 million yuan
其中：出口	Export	亿元	100 million yuan
进口	Import	亿元	100 million yuan

注：1. 本表全国、全省均为公报数。
　　2. 青岛市主要工业产品产量数据为本地口径。

Note： 1. The number of the country and province in the table are obtained from the statistical report.
　　2. The output of main industrial products of Qingdao are at local calibre.

全国 China	全省 Shandong	青岛市 Qingdao	青岛市占全国比重（%） Qingdao/China	青岛市占全省比重（%） Qingdao/Shandong
1015986	73129	12400.56	1.22	16.96
77754	5363.76	425.41	0.55	7.93
384255	28612.19	4361.56	1.14	15.24
553977	39153.05	7613.59	1.37	19.45
77790.6	5513.7	172.47	0.22	3.13
21035.3	1479.2	1478.3	7.03	99.94
9014.7	832.4	822.0	9.12	98.75
19626.2	1774.9	1774.9	9.04	100.00
132489.2	11269.3	389.2	0.29	3.45
240000	15768	414.0	0.17	2.63
66949	5446.81	304.58	0.45	5.59
3585	290.9	36.0	1.00	12.38
7639	721.8	48.0	0.63	6.65
6545	790.2	101.1	1.54	12.79
141443	9450.5	2045.1	1.45	21.64
321557	22009	6407	2.0	29.1
179326	13055	3877	2.2	29.7
142231	8955	2530	1.8	28.3

1-11 主要年份全市生产总值（按当年价格计算）

MAJOR YEAR'S GROSS DOMESTIC PRODUCT(AT CURRENT PRICE)

单位：亿元 (100 million yuan)

年份 Year	全市生产总值 GDP	第一产业 Primary Industry	第二产业 Secondary Industry	#工业 Industry	第三产业 Tertiary Industry	人均生产总值（元） Per Capita GDP (yuan)
1949	2.87	1.19	1.10		0.58	71
1952	6.74	1.76	3.25	2.95	1.73	163
1957	10.82	2.00	5.76	5.39	3.06	239
1962	9.69	1.11	4.68	4.27	3.90	205
1965	15.50	1.80	8.96	8.48	4.74	325
1970	23.23	3.15	14.46	13.86	5.62	451
1975	29.07	6.93	15.39	14.67	6.75	522
1978	38.43	8.23	20.16	19.15	10.04	663
1980	48.65	9.61	26.15	24.28	12.90	819
1985	82.28	20.06	37.37	34.03	24.84	1311
1988	142.87	30.84	69.99	63.42	42.04	2199
1990	180.77	37.00	86.36	78.94	57.41	2714
1991	205.65	40.56	98.48	89.64	66.61	3053
1992	261.35	41.39	129.67	117.61	90.29	3856
1993	371.90	58.62	182.50	164.35	130.79	5455
1994	510.81	80.21	243.17	218.87	187.43	7436
1995	631.45	106.04	293.07	263.98	232.34	9089
1996	713.60	125.59	320.84	289.87	267.17	10130
1997	802.59	110.71	376.50	342.80	315.39	11235
1998	901.19	132.56	407.70	369.89	360.93	12443
1999	1018.97	133.27	466.50	424.15	419.20	13884
2000	1183.14	135.81	546.12	497.34	501.21	15900

1-11 续表 1
Continued

单位：亿元 (100 million yuan)

年份 Year	全市生产总值 GDP	第一产业 Primary Industry	第二产业 Secondary Industry	#工　业 Industry	第三产业 Tertiary Industry	人均生产总值（元） Per Capita GDP (yuan)
2001	1349.98	139.14	625.59	566.71	585.24	17882
2002	1551.42	141.89	728.77	658.00	680.76	20236
2003	1819.03	143.51	877.95	786.49	797.58	23340
2004	2193.60	157.52	1080.95	961.94	955.13	27577
2005	2576.95	168.06	1292.49	1156.53	1116.40	31725
2006	3029.40	173.35	1528.60	1374.12	1327.45	36743
2007	3545.48	191.86	1752.63	1577.15	1600.99	42509
2008	4141.91	210.53	2007.89	1795.88	1923.49	49183
2009	4534.22	216.99	2146.53	1887.38	2170.70	53481
2010	5350.69	261.03	2482.57	2155.73	2607.08	62148
2011	6248.48	288.73	2823.69	2430.66	3136.06	70945
2012	6869.61	305.72	3010.56	2608.44	3553.33	76636
2013	7508.70	332.10	3225.92	2752.90	3950.68	82463
2014	8120.66	341.68	3389.11	2878.71	4389.87	87677
2015	8658.57	356.19	3503.40	2944.80	4798.98	92157
2016	9283.17	357.40	3592.80	2989.24	5332.96	97430
2017	10136.96	367.71	3849.18	3133.78	5920.06	104905
2018	10949.38	386.91	4033.33	3161.34	6529.14	112129
2019	11741.31	409.98	4182.76	3159.86	7148.57	118978
2020	12400.56	425.41	4361.56	3268.38	7613.59	123828

注：1. 人均生产总值按常住人口计算，2011—2020 年人均生产总值据根据第七次人口普查人口修订结果进行了修订（以下相关表同）。
2. 三次产业分类采用《国民经济行业分类》（GB/T 4754—2017）和《三次产业划分规定》（国统字 [2012]108 号），将农林牧渔业中的农、林、牧、渔专业及辅助性活动以及工业中的开采专业及辅助性活动和金属制品、机械和设备修理业归入第三产业。
3. 全国第四次经济普查后，对 2000 年至 2018 年历年 GDP 数据进行了修订（以下相关表同）。
4. 2020 年 GDP 数据为初步核算数（以下相关表同）。

Note: 1. The per capita GDP is calculated based on the permanent population, and the 2011-2020 per capita GDP has been revised according to the population revision results of the seventh census (the following related tables are the same).
2. The classification of the three industries adopts the "Classification of National Economic Industries" (GB/T 4754-2017) and the "Regulations on the Classification of the Three Industries" (Guo Tong Zi [2012] No. 108), which classifies the agricultural, forestry, animal husbandry and fishery Professional and ancillary activities, mining professional and ancillary activities in industry, and metal products, machinery and equipment repair businesses are included in the tertiary industry.
3. After the fourth national economic census, the GDP data from 2000 to 2018 was revised (the following related tables are the same).
4. GDP data for 2020 are preliminary accounting figures(The same applies to tables following).

1-12 主要年份全市生产总值构成（以全市生产总值为 100）
COMPOSITION OF MAJOR YEAR'S GROSS DOMESTIC PRODUCT
(GROSS DOMESTIC PRODUCT=100)

单位：%

年份 Year	全市生产总值 GDP	第一产业 Primary Industry	第二产业 Secondary Industry	#工 业 Industry	第三产业 Tertiary Industry
1952	100	26.1	48.2	43.8	25.7
1957	100	18.5	53.3	49.8	28.2
1962	100	11.4	48.3	44.1	40.3
1965	100	11.6	57.8	54.7	30.6
1970	100	13.6	62.2	59.7	24.2
1975	100	23.9	52.9	50.5	23.2
1978	100	21.4	52.5	49.8	26.1
1980	100	19.8	53.7	49.9	26.5
1985	100	24.4	45.4	41.4	30.2
1988	100	21.6	49.0	44.4	29.4
1990	100	20.5	47.8	43.7	31.7
1991	100	19.7	47.9	43.6	32.4
1992	100	15.8	49.6	45.0	34.6
1993	100	15.7	49.1	44.2	35.2
1994	100	15.7	47.6	42.8	36.7
1995	100	16.8	46.4	41.8	36.8
1996	100	17.6	45.0	40.6	37.4
1997	100	13.8	46.9	42.7	39.3
1998	100	14.7	45.2	41.0	40.1
1999	100	13.1	45.8	41.6	41.1
2000	100	11.5	46.1	42.0	42.4
2001	100	10.3	46.3	42.0	43.4
2002	100	9.1	47.0	42.4	43.9
2003	100	7.9	48.3	43.2	43.8
2004	100	7.2	49.3	43.9	43.5
2005	100	6.5	50.2	44.9	43.3
2006	100	5.7	50.5	45.4	43.8
2007	100	5.4	49.4	44.5	45.2
2008	100	5.1	48.5	43.4	46.4
2009	100	4.8	47.3	41.6	47.9
2010	100	4.9	46.4	40.3	48.7
2011	100	4.6	45.2	38.9	50.2
2012	100	4.5	43.8	38.0	51.7
2013	100	4.4	43.0	36.7	52.6
2014	100	4.2	41.7	35.4	54.1
2015	100	4.1	40.5	34.0	55.4
2016	100	3.9	38.7	32.2	57.4
2017	100	3.6	38.0	30.9	58.4
2018	100	3.5	36.9	28.9	59.6
2019	100	3.5	35.6	26.9	60.9
2020	100	3.4	35.2	26.4	61.4

1-13 主要年份全市生产总值增长速度（以上年为 100）

GROWTH RATE OF MAJOR YEAR 'S GROSS DOMESTIC PRODUCT (PRECEDING YEAR=100)

单位：%

年份 Year	全市生产总值 GDP	第一产业 Primary Industry	第二产业 Secondary Industry	第三产业 Tertiary Industry	人均生产总值（元） Per Capita GDP (yuan)
1979	12.0	10.6	12.9	11.4	10.4
1980	10.4	4.3	13.1	10.3	9.4
1981	-2.0	-3.6	-1.9	-1.0	-3.2
1982	4.1	5.5	-0.2	11.9	2.6
1983	16.9	42.8	9.3	12.7	15.3
1984	13.0	18.9	11.5	10.3	12.0
1985	9.9	5.4	5.8	21.3	9.3
1986	9.2	2.6	12.1	10.0	8.3
1987	12.0	3.6	16.0	12.0	10.6
1988	13.8	-0.3	21.5	11.2	12.1
1990	9.3	9.8	7.3	12.2	8.0
1991	10.6	16.6	11.6	5.4	9.4
1992	18.2	-1.6	22.9	24.7	17.4
1993	22.4	20.4	21.1	25.5	21.7
1994	14.4	3.7	14.7	19.7	13.5
1995	12.0	10.9	12.1	12.3	10.8
1996	7.2	7.6	7.6	6.5	5.7
1997	11.5	-10.7	16.8	14.1	9.9
1998	12.9	17.6	11.3	13.4	11.3
1999	13.9	4.0	15.5	15.2	12.4
2000	14.3	6.4	14.9	16.0	12.7
2001	13.0	1.8	14.9	13.9	11.3
2002	13.7	3.1	15.5	14.2	11.9

1-13 续表 1
Continued

单位：%

年份 Year	全市生产总值 GDP	第一产业 Primary Industry	第二产业 Secondary Industry	第三产业 Tertiary Industry	人均生产总值（元） Per Capita GDP (yuan)
2003	15.4	2.4	18.8	14.5	13.5
2004	15.8	2.7	18.8	14.9	13.5
2005	15.6	0.4	18.1	15.3	13.2
2006	14.5	0.5	15.3	15.6	12.8
2007	14.6	-2.6	13.8	17.8	13.3
2008	12.5	1.4	10.0	16.6	11.4
2009	11.3	3.0	11.3	12.0	10.5
2010	12.1	1.4	11.2	14.0	10.4
2011	11.0	4.5	11.0	11.8	8.5
2012	9.9	3.2	10.0	10.4	8.0
2013	9.4	2.1	8.5	10.9	7.7
2014	7.8	3.9	7.2	8.6	6.0
2015	7.9	3.6	7.0	9.0	6.3
2016	7.7	2.9	5.7	9.4	6.2
2017	7.4	3.1	5.8	8.7	5.9
2018	7.3	3.4	6.8	7.8	6.1
2019	6.5	1.6	4.7	8.0	5.3
2020	3.7	2.6	3.0	4.1	2.1
1978-2010 平均每年增长 1978-2010 Average Increase Rate	12.1	5.5	12.6	13.4	10.7
1991-2010 平均每年增长 1991-2010 Average Increase Rate	13.7	4.2	14.8	15.0	12.3
1996-2010 平均每年增长 1996-2010 Average Increase Rate	13.2	2.4	14.2	14.2	11.6
2001-2010 平均每年增长 2001-2010 Average Increase Rate	13.8	1.4	14.7	14.9	12.2
2006-2010 平均每年增长 2006-2010 Average Increase Rate	13.0	0.7	12.3	15.2	11.7
2011-2020 平均每年增长 2011-2020 Average Increase Rate	7.8	3.1	7.0	8.8	6.2
2016-2020 平均每年增长 2016-2020 Average Increase Rate	6.5	2.7	5.2	7.6	5.1

1-14 分市、区生产总值（2020 年）
GROSS DOMESTIC PRODUCT BY REGION (2020)

单位：亿元 (100 million yuan)

市、区名称	Region	地区生产总值 GDP	第一产业 Primary Industry	第二产业 Secondary Industry	第三产业 Tertiary Industry
市南区	Shinan District	1272.32		135.59	1136.73
市北区	Shibei District	962.18		176.54	785.64
李沧区	Licang District	545.88		155.92	389.96
崂山区	Laoshan District	886.42	5.94	264.19	616.29
西海岸新区	West Coast New Area	3721.68	82.25	1399.31	2240.12
黄岛区	Huangdao District	3584.02	82.25	1365.27	2136.50
保税港区	Qingdao Free Trade Port Area of China	137.66		34.04	103.62
城阳区	Chengyang District	1209.63	17.95	568.95	622.73
城阳区（不含高新区）	Chengyang District (Excluding High tech District)	1086.85	17.95	493.79	575.11
高新区	High tech District	122.78		75.16	47.62
即墨区	Jimo District	1278.36	76.97	630.19	571.20
胶州市	Jiaozhou	1225.86	57.79	567.80	600.27
平度市	Pingdu	715.69	113.44	254.62	347.63
莱西市	Laixi	551.87	68.91	199.12	283.84

1-15　全市生产总值构成（2020 年）

COMPOSITION OF GROSS DOMESTIC PRODUCT（2020）

指标	Indicator	增加值（亿元）Added Value (10 000 million yuan)	2020 年为 2019 年 % 2020/2019 (%)
地区生产总值	**GDP**	**12400.56**	**103.7**
农林牧渔业	Farming, Forestry, Animal Husbandry and Fishery	453.21	102.7
#农林牧渔服务业	Agriculture, Forestry, Animal Husbandry and Fishery Service Industry	27.80	104.5
工业	Industry	3268.38	102.8
#开采辅助活动	#Mining Auxiliary Activities	0.75	100.2
#金属制品、机械和设备修理业	#Metal Products, Machinery and Equipment Repair Industries	18.86	101.6
建筑业	Construction	1112.79	104.0
批发和零售业	Wholesale and Retail Trade	2010.22	106.3
批发业	Wholesale	1248.42	111.1
零售业	Retail Trade	761.80	99.3
交通运输、仓储和邮政业	Transport, Storage and Post	798.22	102.5
住宿和餐饮业	Hotels and Catering Services	222.49	92.5
住宿业	Hotels	28.21	106.2
餐饮业	Catering Services	194.28	89.9
金融业	Financial Industry	861.76	107.6
房地产业	Real Estate	870.40	102.0
房地产业（K 门类）	Real Estate (K category)	657.31	101.3
自有房地产经营活动	Self-Owned Real Estate Business Activities	213.09	105.0
其他服务业	Other Services	2803.09	103.4
营利性服务业	For-Profit Services	1461.26	100.1
非营利性服务业	Non-Profit Services	1341.83	107.2
第一产业	Primary Industry	425.41	102.6
第二产业	Secondary Industry	4361.56	103.0
第三产业	Tertiary Industry	7613.59	104.1

主要统计指标解释

国内生产总值（GDP）　指按市场价格计算的一个国家（或地区）所有常住单位在一定时期内生产活动的最终成果。国内生产总值有三种表现形态，即价值形态、收入形态和产品形态。从价值形态看，它是所有常住单位在一定时期内生产的全部货物和服务价值超过同期中间投入的全部非固定资产货物和服务价值的差额，即所有常住单位的增加值之和；从收入形态看，它是所有常住单位在一定时期内创造并分配给常住单位和非常住单位的初次收入分配之和；从产品形态看，它是所有常住单位在一定时期内最终使用的货物和服务价值与货物和服务净出口价值之和。在实际核算中，国内生产总值有三种计算方法，即生产法、收入法和支出法。三种方法分别从不同的方面反映国内生产总值及其构成。对于一个地区来说，称为地区生产总值或地区 GDP。

人均 GDP　人均 GDP 是一定时期内 GDP 与同期人口平均数的比值。按照国际标准，人口平均数应该是同期平均常住人口。我国在核算制度中也规定，无论是国家还是地区，人口数都采用常住人口。国家统计局规定从 2004 年开始，过去采用户籍人口计算人均 GDP 的地区，作为过渡性措施，可在两年内同时计算两种口径的人均 GDP（数据后面必须注明是什么口径），两年后取消按户籍人口计算的人均 GDP。我市采用常住人口计算人均 GDP。

三次产业　是根据社会生产活动历史发展的顺序对产业结构的划分，产品直接取自自然界的部门称为第一产业，对初级产品进行再加工的部门称为第二产业，为生产和消费提供各种服务的部门称为第三产业。它是世界上通用的产业结构分类，但各国的划分不尽一致。我国的三次产业划分是：

第一产业是指农、林、牧、渔业（不含农、林、牧、渔服务业）。

第二产业是指采矿业（不含开采辅助活动），制造业（不含金属制品、机械和设备修理业），电力、热力、燃气及水生产和供应业，建筑业。

第三产业即服务业，是指除第一产业、第二产业以外的其他行业。第三产业包括：批发和零售业，交通运输、仓储和邮政业，住宿和餐饮业，信息传输、软件和信息技术服务业，金融业，房地产业，租赁和商务服务业，科学研究和技术服务业，水利、环境和公共设施管理业，居民服务、修理和其他服务业，教育，卫生和社会工作，文化、体育和娱乐业，公共管理、社会保障和社会组织，国际组织，以及农、林、牧、渔业中的农、林、牧、渔服务业，采矿业中的开采辅助活动，制造业中的金属制品、机械和设备修理业。

气候　指地球与大气之间长期能量交换与质量交换所形成的一种自然环境状态，它是多种因素综合作用的结果。气候既是人类生活和生产的环境要素之一，又是供给人类生活和生产的重要资源。气温、降水、湿度等气象要素的多年平均值是用来描述一个地区气候状况的主要参数，而各种气象要素某年、某月的平均值（或总量）则可以反映出该时期天气气候状况的重要特征。

气温　指空气的温度，我国一般以摄氏度（℃）为单位表示。气象观测的温度表是放在离地面约 1.5 米处通风良好的百叶箱里测量的，因此，通常说的气温指的是离地面 1.5 米处百叶箱中的温度。其统计计算方法为：月平均气温是将全月各日的平均气温相加，除以该月的天数而得。

年平均气温　是将 12 个月的月平均气温累加后除以 12 而得。

降水量　指从天空降落到地面的液态或固态（经融化后）水，未经蒸发、渗透、流失而在地面上积聚的深度。其统计计算方法为：月降水量是将全月各日的降水量累加而得。年降水量是将 12 个月的月降水量累加而得。

Explanatory Notes on Main Statistical Indicators

Gross Domestic Product (GDP) refers to the final products at market prices produced by all resident units in a country(or a region)during a certain period of time.Gross domestic product is expressed in three different perspectives, namely value, income, and products respectively. GDP in its value perspective refers to the total value of all goods and services produced by all resident units during a certain period of time, minus the total value of input of goods and services of the nature of non–fixed assets, in other words, it is the sum of the value–added of all resident units. GDP from the perspective of products refers to the value of all goods and services for final consumption by all resident units minus the net exports of goods and services during a given period of time. In the practice of national accounting, gross domestic product is calculated from three approaches,namely production approach, income approach and expenditure approach, which reflect gross domestic product and its composition from different angles. For a certain region, it refers region gross product or region GDP.

Per Capita GDP refers to the ratio of GDP in a certain term and average population in the same term. According to the international standard, average population should be average permanent population in the same term.In the account regulation,population of both the country and the region should be permanent population.In the after two years since 2004, per capita GDP can be calculated at two coverage.i.e. at permanent population and household registered population(the note of coverage should follow the data). The per capita GDP calculated with household registered population will be abolished after two years. Per capita GDP of Qingdao is calculated at permanent population.

Three Strata of Industries has been classified according to the historical sequence of development. Primary industry refers to extraction of natural resources, secondary industry involves processing of primary products, and tertiary industry provides services of various kinds for production and consumption. The above classification is universal although it varies to some extent from country to country. In China economic activities are categorized into the following three strata of industry:

Primary industry refers to agriculture, forestry, animal husbandry, and fishery (excluding agriculture, forestry, animal husbandry, and fishery service industries).

The secondary industry refers to mining industry (excluding mining auxiliary activities), manufacturing industry (excluding metal products, machinery and equipment repair industry), electricity, heat, gas and water production and supply industry, and construction industry.

The tertiary industry is the service industry, which refers to industries other than the primary industry and the secondary industry. The tertiary industry includes: wholesale and retail industry, transportation, storage and postal industry, accommodation and catering industry, information transmission, software and information technology service industry, financial industry, real estate industry, leasing and business service industry, scientific research and technical service Industry, water conservancy, environment and public facilities management industry, resident service, repair and other service industry, education, health and social work, culture, sports and entertainment industry, public management, social security and social organization, international organization, and agriculture, forestry Agriculture, forestry, animal husbandry, and fishery services in agriculture, animal husbandry and fishery, mining auxiliary activities in mining, and metal products, machinery and equipment repair in manufacturing.

Climate refers to the natural environmental status formed by the long–term exchange of energy and mass between the earth and the air, and is the results of interaction of many factors. Climate is both one of the environment factors and the important resources for the living and production activities of the human being. The average values across several years of meteorological factors such as temperature, rainfall and humidity are used as important parameters to describe the climate of a region, while the average values (or total values) of a given year or month of meteorological factors reflect the key characteristics of climate for that period of time.

Temperature refers to the air temperature. China uses centigrade as the unit. The thermometry used for weather observation is put in a breezy shutter, which is 1.5 meters high from the ground. Therefore, the commonly used temperature refers to the temperature in the breezy shutter 1.5 meters away from the ground. The calculation method is as follows: Monthly average temperature is the summation of average daily temperature of one month divided by the actual days of that particular month.

Annual average temperature is the summation of monthly average of a year divided by 12 months.

Volume of Precipitation refers to the deepness of liquid state or solid state (thawed) water falling from the sky to the ground that has not been evaporated, infiltrated or run off. The calculation method is as follows: Monthly precipitation is the summation of daily precipitation of a month. Annual precipitation is the summation of 12 months precipitation of a year.

人　口 2

POPULATION

简要说明

一、本篇资料的主要内容

本篇资料主要反映了全市人口方面的基本情况，包括全市主要年份和区（市）的户数、人口数、人口密度、土地面积数据、人口出生率、死亡率、自然增长率、计划生育等数据。另外还对中华人民共和国成立以来开展的七次人口普查主要数据进行了比较。

二、本篇资料的来源

本篇资料分别来源于国家开展的人口普查、人口抽样调查和市公安局的户籍登记资料，由市统计局人口就业和社会科技文化统计处整理提供。

Brief Introduction

I. Main Content

The information in this article mainly reflects the basic demographic situation of the city, including the number of households, population, population density, land area data, birth rate, death rate, natural growth rate, family planning, etc. in main years and districts (cities) of the city data. In addition, the main data of the seven census conducted since the founding of the People's Republic of China were compared.

II. Source of Data

The data in this article are derived from the national population census, population sample survey and household registration data of Qingdao Public Security Bureau, compiled and provided by the Population Employment and Social Science, Technology and Culture Statistics Department of Qingdao Statistics Bureau.

2-1　主要年份全市户籍人口数
MAJOR YEAR´S TOTAL REGISTERED POPULATION

单位：人 (person)

年份 Year	总人口 Total Population	按性别分 Grouped by Gender		平均人口 Average Population
		男 Male	女 Female	
1949	4056550	1997293	2059257	4054431
1952	4233586	2125392	2108194	4203428
1957	4822756	2424729	2398027	4773862
1962	4627432	2319658	2307774	4578313
1965	4901670	2461629	2440041	4859712
1970	5391852	2720633	2671219	5337282
1975	5742206	2904347	2837859	5717456
1978	5853321	2959800	2893521	5841638
1980	5961129	3015357	2945772	5937187
1985	6267223	3185409	3081814	6253157
1988	6516920	3319534	3197386	6474541
1989	6571597	3348454	3223143	6544259
1990	6666482	3392253	3274229	6619040
1991	6709277	3411776	3297501	6687880
1992	6731072	3420886	3310186	6720175
1993	6753497	3431149	3322348	6742285
1994	6785291	3446019	3339272	6769394
1995	6846346	3476300	3370046	6815819
1996	6902677	3502600	3400077	6874512
1997	6954391	3527588	3426803	6928534
1998	6995666	3545403	3450263	6975029
1999	7029707	3561061	3468646	7012687
2000	7066481	3577367	3489114	7048094
2001	7104875	3595652	3509223	7085678
2002	7156537	3619778	3536759	7130706
2003	7206806	3644032	3562774	7181672
2004	7311228	3692991	3618237	7259017
2005	7409052	3740309	3668743	7360140
2006	7493812	3779891	3713921	7451432
2007	7579910	3816620	3763290	7536861
2008	7615647	3824665	3790982	7597779
2009	7629161	3823534	3805627	7622404
2010	7636392	3819240	3817152	7632777
2011	7663612	3826931	3836681	7650002
2012	7695585	3838205	3857380	7679599

注：截至出书前，未获得公安部门青岛市 2013-2020 年户籍人口信息。
Note：Data come from the Qingdao Municipal Public Security Bureau, and the data of 2013-2020 are absent.

2-2 主要年份全市户数、人口数、人口密度（户籍）
MAJOR YEAR´S HOUSEHOLDS, POPULATION AND DENSITY OF POPULATION (WITH PERMANENT RESIDENCE)

年份 Year	总户数（万户） Total Households (10000 households)		总人口（万人） Total Population (10000 persons)		平均每户人口（人） Average Persons Per Household(person)		人口密度（人/平方公里） Density of Population (person/sq.km)	
	全市 Whole Municipality	市区 Urban Area	全市 Whole Municipality	市区 Urban Area	全市 Whole Municipality	市区 Urban Area	全市 Whole Municipality	市区 Urban Area
1949	90.64	21.68	405.66	103.69	4.48	4.78	381	941
1952	93.96	22.70	423.36	107.62	4.51	4.74	397	977
1957	102.56	27.41	482.28	134.76	4.70	4.92	453	1223
1962	106.11	29.29	462.74	137.86	4.36	4.71	434	1251
1965	105.31	29.64	490.17	146.74	4.65	4.95	460	1332
1970	113.07	32.14	539.19	150.81	4.77	4.69	506	1369
1975	123.18	36.56	574.22	161.13	4.66	4.41	539	1462
1978	131.27	40.08	585.33	168.00	4.46	4.19	549	1525
1980	138.44	43.03	596.11	175.27	4.31	4.07	560	1591
1985	157.06	53.43	626.72	190.87	3.99	3.57	588	1732
1988	169.72	58.95	651.69	201.38	3.84	3.42	612	1827
1989	177.47	61.57	657.16	203.63	3.70	3.31	617	1848
1990	186.79	63.94	666.65	205.78	3.57	3.22	626	1867
1991	192.46	67.15	670.93	207.22	3.49	3.09	630	1880
1992	199.08	68.94	673.11	209.28	3.38	3.04	632	1899
1993	201.36	70.13	675.35	212.06	3.35	3.02	634	1924
1994	204.05	71.24	678.53	214.97	3.33	3.02	637	1951
1995	208.13	72.53	684.63	218.38	3.29	3.01	643	1982
1996	212.40	75.11	690.27	223.86	3.25	2.98	648	2032
1997	215.12	76.39	695.44	227.22	3.23	2.97	653	2062
1998	218.59	77.90	699.57	229.58	3.20	2.95	657	2084
1999	222.61	79.27	702.97	231.94	3.16	2.93	660	2105
2000	224.73	80.46	706.65	234.60	3.14	2.92	664	2129
2001	227.43	81.41	710.49	237.60	3.12	2.92	667	2156
2002	229.67	82.85	715.65	241.74	3.12	2.92	672	2194
2003	232.26	84.15	720.68	246.77	3.10	2.93	677	2240
2004	235.29	86.93	731.12	258.40	3.11	2.97	686	2229
2005	237.35	87.99	740.91	265.43	3.12	3.02	695	2290
2006	239.33	89.12	749.38	271	3.13	3.04	703	2338
2007	241.55	90.21	757.99	275.55	3.14	3.05	711	2377
2008	243.18	91.22	761.56	276.25	3.13	3.03	715	2384
2009	244.74	92.15	762.92	275.47	3.12	2.99	676	1873
2010	246.11	93.30	763.64	275.50	3.10	2.95	677	1873
2011	247.94	94.69	766.36	277.09	3.09	2.93	679	1884
2012	249.27	95.87	769.56	279.57	3.09	2.92	682	1901

2-3　主要年份全市常住人口数
MAJOR YESR´S TOTAL RESIDENT POPULATION

单位：万人 (10 000 persons)

年份 Year	总人口 Total population
2005	819.55
2006	829.42
2007	838.67
2008	845.61
2009	850.03
2010	871.51
2011	889.60
2012	903.20
2013	917.90
2014	934.50
2015	944.60
2016	961.00
2017	971.60
2018	981.40
2019	992.30
2020	1010.57

注：1.2011–2019 年为山东省统计局根据第七次人口普查结果修订反馈数据；
2.2020 年数据为山东省统计局反馈数据。

Note：1. From 2011 to 2019, the Shandong Provincial Statistics Bureau revised the feedback data based on the results of the seventh census;
2. The data for 2020 are feedback data from the Shandong Provincial Bureau of Statistics.

2-4　青岛市常住人口
TOTAL RESIDENT POPULATION

单位：万人 (10 000 person)

市、区名称	Region	2020 年	2019 年	2020 比 2019 年 ±% 2020/2019 ±%
全市	**Whole Municipality**	**1010.57**	**992.30**	**1.84**
市南区	Shinan District	48.60	49.68	–2.17
市北区	Shibei District	110.08	109.33	0.69
李沧区	Licang District	74.09	71.66	3.39
崂山区	Laoshan District	50.29	49.14	2.34
西海岸新区	West Coast New Area	191.37	185.31	3.27
城阳区（含高新区）	Chengyang District(Including High tech District)	111.59	107.22	4.07
即墨区	Jimo District	134.26	130.96	2.52
胶州市	Jiaozhou	99.25	97.04	2.28
平度市	Pingdu	119.07	119.64	–0.48
莱西市	Laixi	71.97	72.32	–0.48

注：1.2019 年数据为根据第七次人口普查结果修订数据；
2.2020 年数据为根据第七次人口普查结果年末推算数据。

Note：1. The data for 2019 are revised data based on the results of the seventh census;
2. The data for 2020 are extrapolated data based on the results of the seventh census at the end of the year.

2-5　主要年份常住人口城镇化率
THE URBANIZATION RATE OF THE MAIN YEAR PERMANENT RESIDENTS

单位：%(%)

年份 Year	城镇化率 Urbanization rate
2005	63.20
2006	63.59
2007	63.90
2008	64.31
2009	64.68
2010	65.81
2011	66.04
2012	66.09
2013	66.23
2014	66.31
2015	68.04
2016	70.54
2017	71.87
2018	74.20
2019	74.85
2020	76.34

注：1. 城镇化率为城镇区域常住人口数量与全市常住总人口的比值；
　　2.2011-2019 年为山东省统计局根据第七次人口普查结果修订反馈数据；
　　3.2020 年数据为山东省统计局反馈数据。

Note：1. Urbanization rate is the ratio of the number of permanent residents in urban areas to the total permanent population of the city;
　　2. From 2011 to 2019, the Shandong Provincial Statistics Bureau revised the feedback data based on the results of the seventh census;
　　3. The data for 2020 are feedback data from the Shandong Provincial Bureau of Statistics.

2-6　分市、区土地面积（2020 年底）
LAND AREA (END OF 2020)

市、区名称	Region	土地面积（平方公里）Land Area (aq.km)
全　市	**Whole Municipality**	**11293.36**
市南区	Shinan District	32.21
市北区	Shibei District	65.85
李沧区	Licang District	99.10
崂山区	Laoshan District	395.79
黄岛区	Huangdao District	2128.31
城阳区	Chengyang District	583.68
即墨区	Jimo District	1920.90
胶州市	Jiaozhou	1323.65
平度市	Pingdu	3175.65
莱西市	Laixi	1568.22

注：2018 年度土地变更调查结果。
Note：Survey results of land quality change in 2018.

2-7 第一、二、三、四、五、六、七次人口普查主要数据
MAIN DATA OF THE FIRST, SECOND, THIRD, FOURTH, FIFTH, SIXTH AND SEVENTH CENSUSES

项目	Item	第一次人口普查 1st National Population Census	第二次人口普查 2nd National Population Census	第三次人口普查 3rd National Population Census	第四次人口普查 4th National Population Census	第五次人口普查 5th National Population Census	第六次人口普查 6th National Population Census	第七次人口普查 7th National Population Census
一、总人口（万人）	**Total Population (10000 persons)**	**91.68**	**138.34**	**422.76**	**666.40**	**749.42**	**871.51**	**1007.17**
按性别分	By Gender							
男（万人）	Male(10000 persons)	48.44	69.64	214.09	338.86	375.74	439.18	513.22
女（万人）	Female(10000 persons)	43.24	68.71	208.67	327.54	373.68	432.33	493.95
二、总户数（万户）	**Total Household (10000 Household)**	**19.27**	**28.01**	**101.41**	**186.61**	**241.62**	**296.64**	**385.70**
家庭户（万户）	Family Household (10000 Household)			101.09	185.56	232.70	282.43	362.32
平均家庭户规模（人）	Average Family Household Size(person)			4.07	3.49	2.97	2.79	2.55
三、民　族	**Ethnicity**							
民族个数（个）	Number of Ethnic Groups (unit)	14	16	25	41	51	53	56
汉族人口（万人）	Population of Han (10000 persons)	91.33	137.76	422.09	665.58	746.12	863.84	995.39
少数民族人口（万人）	Population of Ethnic Minorities(10000 persons)	0.36	0.58	0.67	0.82	3.30	7.67	11.78
四、各种文化程度人口	**Population with Various Education Attainments**							
大　学（万人）	College(10000 persons)		1.51	3.62	12.39	41.64	129.54	227.12
高　中（万人）	Senior Secondary School (10000 persons)		4.86	34.82	68.42	111.40	150.82	176.69
初　中（万人）	Junior Secondary School (10000 persons)		13.72	102.28	195.10	281.91	334.22	323.79
小　学（万人）	Primary School (10000 persons)		51.25	144.52	236.34	206.91	170.77	187.26

2-8 计划生育情况（1978-2020年）
FAMILY PLANNING SITUATION (1978-2020)

年份 Year	已婚有生育能力的人数（人） Married and Fertile Persons (person)	节育人数（人） Persons under Birth Control (person)	节育率（%） Contraceptive Prevalence Rate (%)	四项手术人数（人） Persons Performed Four-operation (person)	#放环人数 Persons Set Rings
1978	694292	571077	82.25	125913	68475
1980	**763226**	**673069**	**88.19**	**180979**	**70927**
1985	1017649	929284	91.32	146742	67234
1990	**1258232**	**1165216**	**92.61**	**149327**	**70964**
1991	1319722	1219795	92.43	153970	77406
1992	1348503	1256271	93.16	90107	56226
1993	1380717	1271884	92.12	76783	45492
1994	1400425	1268378	90.57	73169	41482
1995	1427442	1285264	90.04	84099	52716
1996	1459465	1316516	90.21	84370	57648
1997	1482204	1340399	90.43	76579	55285
1998	1505499	1367648	90.84	74199	50526
1999	1523471	1378131	90.46	73663	44976
2000	**1521331**	**1371447**	**90.15**	**74285**	**45999**
2001	1514274	1360543	89.85	70205	43601
2002	1541855	1400145	90.81	50575	45453
2003	1518448	1354917	89.23	57458	47953
2004	1540706	1357703	88.04	52934	42859
2005	1590476	1417755	89.14	58097	49716
2006	1604665	1427785	88.98	51864	42457
2007	1595390	1426787	89.43	50074	41198
2008	1587344	1410426	88.85	120539	93291
2009	1623969	1418178	87.33	111084	100193
2010	**1591103**	**1377726**	**86.59**	**78721**	**51794**
2011	1581231	1355808	85.74	70823	48210
2012	1575996	1349572	85.63	62880	43021
2013	1527731	1293810	84.69	53252	30851
2014	1506274	1275142	84.66	34008	12827
2015	1475887	1226439	83.10	34879	9108
2016	1456953	1183221	81.21	36449	4474
2017	1439008	1188307	82.58	20905	4669
2018	1406047	1159775	82.48	17786	5097
2019	1375598	1141584	82.92	12582	3959
2020	**1310212**	**1109885**	**84.71**	**342553**	**339219**

2-9 分市、区计划生育情况（2020年）
FAMILY PLANNING SITUATION BY REGION (2020)

市、区名称	Region	计划生育率（%） Fertility Rate (%)	计划内出生（人） Birth within the Plan (person)		计划外出生（人） Birth without the Plan (person)		多胎（人） Third Birth and Above (person)
			一胎 First Birth	二胎 Second Birth	一胎 First Birth	二胎 Second Birth	
全市	**Whole Municipality**	**99.69**	**31253**	**31982**	**125**	**78**	**3065**
市南区	Shinan District	99.73	2346	1222	6	4	72
市北区	Shibei District	99.98	3552	2365	1	0	83
李沧区	Licang District	99.86	2518	2256	4	3	75
崂山区	Laoshan District	99.79	1324	1027	2	3	50
西海岸新区	West Coast New Area	99.71	5657	6582	19	18	630
城阳区	Chengyang District	99.87	2976	2878	3	5	201
即墨区	Jimo District	99.76	3887	4638	15	7	545
胶州市	Jiaozhou	99.56	2933	3490	18	13	554
平度市	Pingdu	99.59	3927	4996	28	11	555
莱西市	Laixi	99.14	2133	2528	29	14	300

主要统计指标解释

人口数　指一定时点、一定地区范围内有生命的个人总和。

出生率（又称粗出生率）　指在一定时期内（通常为一年）一定地区的出生人数与同期内平均人数（或期中人数）之比，用千分率表示。本资料中的出生率指年出生率，其计算公式为：

$$出生率=\frac{年出生人数}{年平均人数}\times 1000‰$$

式中：出生人数指活产婴儿，即胎儿脱离母体时（不管怀孕月数），有过呼吸或其他生命现象。

死亡率（又称粗死亡率）　指在一定时期内（通常为一年）一定地区的死亡人数与同期内平均人数（或期中人数）之比，用千分率表示。本资料中的死亡率指年死亡率，其计算公式为：

$$死亡率=\frac{年死亡人数}{年平均人数}\times 1000‰$$

人口自然增长率　指在一定时期内（通常为一年）人口自然增加数（出生人数减死亡人数）与该时期内平均人数（或期中人数）之比，用千分率表示。计算公式为：

$$人口自然增长率=\frac{本年出生人数-本年死亡人数}{年平均人数}\times 1000‰$$

$$=人口出生率-人口死亡率$$

Explanatory Notes on Main Statistical Indicators

Total Population to the total number of people alive at a certain point of time within a given area.

Birth Rate (or Crude Birth Rate) refers to the ratio of the number of births to the average population (or mid-period population) during a certain period of time (usually a year), expressed in ‰. Birth rate in the chapter refers to annual birth rate. The following formula is used:

Birth Rate=(Number of Births/Average Number of Population) × 1000‰

Number of births in the formula refers to live births, i.e. when a baby has breathed or showed any vital phenomena regardless of the length of pregnancy.

Death Rate (or Crude Death Rate) refers to the ratio of the number of deaths to the average population (or mid-period population) during a certain period of time (usually a year), expressed in ‰. Death rate in the chapter refers to annual death rate. The following formula is used:

Death Rate=(Number of Deaths/Annual Average Number of Population) × 1000‰

Natural Growth Rate of Population refers to the ratio of natural increase in population (number of births minus number of deaths) in a certain period of time (usually a year) to the average population (or mid-period population) of the same period, expressed in ‰. The following formula is applied:

Natural Growth Rate of Population=[(Number of Births−Number of Deaths)/Average Number of Population] × 1000‰

Natural Growth Rate of Population=Birth Rate−Death Rate

从业人员及职工工资 3

EMPLOYMENT AND WAGES

简要说明

一、本篇资料的主要内容

本篇资料主要反映了全市单位从业人员、工资总额和平均工资等方面的资料。

二、本篇资料的来源

全市单位从业人员、工资总额和平均工资来源于劳动工资统计年报，由市统计局人口就业和社会科技文化统计处整理提供。

Brief Introduction

I. Main Content

The data in this chapter mainly reflects the data on the employees, total wages and average wages of the city´s units.

II. Source of Data

The employees, total wages and average wages of the city´s units are derived from the annual labor wage statistics report, which is compiled and provided by the Population Employment and Social Science, Technology and Culture Statistics Department of Qingdao Statistics Bureau.

3-1 社会就业人数（1978-2020 年）
SOCIAL EMPLOYMENT (1978-2020)

单位：万人 (10 000 persons)

年份 Year	合计 Total	第一产业 Primary Industry	第二产业 Secondary Industry	第三产业 Tertiary Industry
1978	256.7	157.4	65.6	33.7
1979	265.6	156.1	72.2	37.3
1980	270.1	153.0	77.3	39.8
1981	278.9	153.6	82.1	43.2
1982	282.7	151.1	86.2	45.4
1983	289.6	156.4	85.0	48.1
1984	304.2	149.2	97.7	57.4
1985	315.3	149.2	104.5	61.7
1986	326.4	149.6	112.1	64.6
1987	334.8	149.9	120.2	64.7
1988	336.5	147.6	123.2	65.7
1989	344.2	152.5	122.1	69.6
1990	352.8	156.5	123.3	73.1
1991	361.2	161.9	124.3	74.9
1992	370.3	161.7	127.8	80.8
1993	365.7	160.5	128.8	76.4
1994	367.6	157.1	129.4	81.2
1995	374.2	155.4	132.4	86.4
1996	381.5	152.2	137.1	92.2
1997	388.7	155.2	138.1	95.3
1998	393.1	154.8	138.6	99.7
1999	396.1	150.3	142.0	103.8
2000	436.1	158.7	148.0	129.4
2001	439.5	146.9	156.2	136.4
2002	447.8	131.5	166.7	149.6
2003	450.8	123.1	168.4	159.3
2004	459.6	114.2	180.9	164.5
2005	467.4	103.7	195.3	168.4
2006	475.2	99.8	203.5	171.9
2007	481.5	97.4	207.3	176.8
2008	484.8	96.6	208.3	179.9
2009	489.3	98.3	205.1	185.9
2010	504.9	98.3	209.2	197.4
2011	510.8	98.2	210.4	202.2
2012	515.5	96.6	211.6	207.3
2013	517.5	97.4	210.3	209.8
2014	521.3	96.0	203.5	221.8
2015	523.7	94.9	201.8	227.0
2016	523.5	93.4	198.8	231.3
2017	524.3	88.4	198.1	237.8
2018	525.3	85.1	191.2	249.0
2019	523.6	82.2	200.5	240.9
2020	525.6	82.0	167.7	275.9

注：第七次全国人口普查后，对 2000 年至 2020 年历年社会就业人数进行修订。

Note: After the seventh national census, the number of social employment in the calendar years from 2000 to 2020 will be revised.

3-2 主要年份全市单位就业人员人数

MAJOR YEAR´S NUMBER OF EMPLOYEES IN THE CITY

单位：万人 (10 000 persons)

年份 Year	合计 Total	#市区 Urban Area	#国有单位 State-owned Units	#集体单位 Collective-owned Units	其他所有制单位 Other Ownership Units
1949	14.8	13.4	9.3	5.5	
1952	23.4	20.1	18.3	5.1	
1957	29.7	24.5	24.1	5.6	
1962	32.3	26.8	24.5	7.8	
1965	36.7	30.6	26.8	9.9	
1970	45.6	37.4	32.2	13.4	
1975	53.4	43.5	38.0	15.4	
1978	70.7	54.5	49.2	21.5	
1980	79.2	61.5	55.0	24.2	
1985	88.8	66.7	59.8	28.9	0.1
1988	98.2	70.0	66.7	31.2	0.3
1990	103.2	70.6	69.5	32.9	0.8
1991	105.4	78.4	71.5	32.5	1.4
1992	108.2	80.4	73.6	32.8	1.8
1993	109.4	80.8	75.3	29.5	4.6
1994	110.1	80.2	72.4	28.3	9.4
1995	111.6	80.2	72.4	27.5	11.7
1996	118.4	81.1	71.6	26.0	20.8
1997	117.1	78.1	69.0	22.6	25.5
1998	116.2	75.6	64.2	19.0	33.0
1999	119.0	78.3	60.4	16.6	42.0
2000	118.3	76.6	57.6	14.2	46.5
2001	117.5	75.1	53.2	12.2	52.1
2002	119.1	75.2	49.5	10.3	59.3
2003	118.0	74.3	47.2	8.9	61.9
2004	207.1	111.1	43.7	18.0	145.4
2005	224.3	122.3	43.9	18.2	162.2
2006	243.2	133.7	41.7	16.2	185.3
2007	249.8	137.3	45.1	17.9	186.8
2008	254.1	140.9	44.4	15.4	194.3
2009	260.5	145.6	44.4	14.6	201.5
2010	269.4	151.1	44.6	15.1	209.7
2011	275.9	156.5	44.3	14.7	216.9
2012	283.2	162.1	44.0	13.8	225.4
2013	293.7	184.1	37.8	5.4	250.5
2014	303.0	191.4	36.7	4.9	261.4
2015	309.2	192.4	35.8	4.6	268.8
2016	315.6	196.4	35.5	4.7	275.4
2017	321.4	249.1	35.1	4.6	281.7
2018	330.4	258.3	34.7	2.0	293.7
2019	146.6	118.5	34.1	1.1	111.4
2020	147.7				

注：1. 2004 年以前为城镇单位职工人数。
2. 2013 年统计口径变化，国有单位、集体单位数据与上年不可比。
3. 2019 年统计口径变化，全市单位就业人员人数为全市城镇非私营口径。
4. 2020 年劳动工资改革，单位就业人数不再分登记注册类型。

Note: 1. Before 2004, the data refer to number of staff and workers in urban units.
2. Because of the adjustment about the statistics system, the data of State-owned Units and Collective-owned Units since 2013 are not fully comparable with historical statistics.
3. The statistical caliber changes in 2019, the number of employees in the city's units is the city's urban non-private caliber.
4. In 2020, the labor and wage reform will no longer divide the number of employees into registration types.

3-3 全市城镇非私营单位国民经济各行业就业人员人数（2020 年）
NUMBER OF EMPLOYED PERSONS IN NON-PRIVATE UNITS OF THE CITY BY SECTOR (2020)

单位：万人 (10 000 persons)

		2020 年		2019 年	
		合计 Total	女性 Female	合计 Total	女性 Female
总计	**Total**	**147.7**	**60.2**	**146.6**	**60.8**
1. 农、林、牧、渔业	Farming, Forestry, Animal Husbandry and Fishery	0.0	0.0	0.0	0.0
2. 采矿业	Mining	0.0	0.0	0.0	0.0
3. 制造业	Manufacturing	44.5	15.7	43.7	16.2
4. 电力、热力、燃气及水生产和供应业	Electricity, Heat, Gas and Water Production and Supply Industry	2.1	0.5	2.0	0.5
5. 建筑业	Construction	15.8	2.1	16.3	2.1
6. 批发和零售业	Wholesale and Retail Trade	8.3	4.7	9.3	5.5
7. 交通运输、仓储和邮政业	Transport, Storage and Post	9.3	2.6	8.9	2.5
8. 住宿和餐饮业	Hotels and Catering Services	2.7	1.5	2.8	1.4
9. 信息传输、软件和信息技术服务业	Information Transmission Computer Services and Software	2.4	1.0	2.3	1.0
10. 金融业	Financial Industry	11.4	7.5	12.1	7.6
11. 房地产业	Real Estate	5.0	2.0	4.7	1.9
12. 租赁和商务服务业	Leasing and Business Services	3.5	1.4	3.6	1.5
13. 科学研究和技术服务业	Scientific Research and Technical Services	4.3	1.5	3.9	1.2
14. 水利、环境和公共设施管理业	Management of Water Conservancy, Environment and Public Facilities	2.4	0.8	1.7	0.6
15. 居民服务、修理和其他服务业	Residents Service, Repair and Other Services	0.5	0.2	0.6	0.3
16. 教育	Education	13.9	8.6	13.3	8.6
17. 卫生和社会工作	Health and Social Welfare	7.7	5.6	7.4	5.3
18. 文化、体育和娱乐业	Culture, Sports and Entertainment	1.2	0.5	1.2	0.5
19. 公共管理、社会保障和社会组织	Public Management, Social Security and Social Organization	12.6	3.7	12.9	4.1

3-4 全市就业人员工资总额、平均工资(1978-2020年)
TOTAL WAGES AND AVERAGE WAGE OF CITYWIDE FULL-TIME EMPLOYEES (1978-2020)

年份 Year	工资总额(亿元) Total Wage Bill (100 million yuan)		平均工资(元) Average Wage (yuan)	
	全社会单位 All Units	其中:非私营单位 of which : Non-private Units	全社会单位 All Units	其中:非私营单位 of which : Non-private Units
1978		4.0		584
1979		4.8		662
1980		6.0		782
1981		6.3		778
1982		6.6		785
1983		6.9		809
1984		9.0		1041
1985		9.6		1103
1986		11.8		1311
1987		14.2		1519
1988		18.0		1862
1989		20.7		2120
1990		24.4		2400
1991		26.4		2553
1992		31.8		2970
1993		40.4		3694
1994		59.5		5455
1995		68.3		6164
1996		78.2		6640
1997		82.5		7030
1998		87.2		7518
1999		100.1		8405
2000		120.4		10072
2001		135.8		11426
2002		153.8		12839
2003	225.6	160.3	12597	15335
2004	280.5	193.4	13932	17190
2005	359.5	242.8	16015	20022
2006	445.6	292.0	18574	23457
2007	518.1	338.6	21419	27083
2008	578.7	371.9	23296	30233
2009	638.1	393.2	25396	33258
2010	738.0	446.8	28549	37805
2011	877.5	522.0	32763	43077
2012	1044.3	613.1	37399	49052
2013	1251.7	785.7	42688	55363
2014	1456.0	890.5	48453	62104
2015	1644.4	993.0	53715	69465
2016	1852.7	1088.5	58551	75803
2017	2034.7	1193.6	63047	82177
2018	2251.7	1290.8	68197	89525
2019		1438.3		98604
2020		1560.4		106011

注:1. 2003年以前为职工工资总额、平均工资。
2. 2015年以前为在岗职工工资总额、平均工资。
3. 自2019年统计口径变化,无全部单位工资数据。

Note : 1. The data before 2003 refer to the total wage bill and average wage of stall and workers.
2. It was the total salary and average salary of the on-spot staff before 2015.
3. Since the statistical caliber change in 2019, there is no wage data for all units.

3-5 全市就业人员工资总额、平均工资指数（1978-2020年）
INDEXES OF TOTAL WAGES AND AVERAGE WAGE OF CITYWIDE FULL-TIME EMPLOYEES (1978-2020)

年份 Year	工资总额指数 Total Wage Bill Indexed		平均工资指数 Average Wage Indexes	
	全社会单位 All Units	其中：非私营单位 of which：Non-private Units	全社会单位 All Units	其中：非私营单位 of which：Non-private Units
1978		120.80		104.66
1979		119.53		113.36
1980		123.95		118.13
1981		106.71		99.49
1982		103.80		100.90
1983		104.14		103.06
1984		130.64		128.68
1985		107.11		105.96
1986		123.22		118.86
1987		120.10		115.87
1988		126.48		122.58
1989		115.29		113.86
1990		117.66		113.21
1991		108.28		106.38
1992		120.26		116.33
1993		127.09		124.38
1994		147.46		147.67
1995		114.76		113.00
1996		114.54		107.72
1997		105.50		105.87
1998		105.64		106.94
1999		114.81		111.80
2000		120.29		119.83
2001		112.77		113.44
2002		113.31		112.37
2003		108.84		110.30
2004	124.34	120.65	110.60	112.10
2005	128.16	125.54	114.95	116.47
2006	123.95	120.26	115.98	117.16
2007	116.27	115.96	115.32	115.46
2008	111.70	109.83	108.76	111.63
2009	110.26	105.73	109.01	110.01
2010	115.66	113.63	112.42	113.67
2011	118.90	116.83	114.76	113.95
2012	119.01	117.45	114.15	113.87
2013	119.86	128.15	114.14	112.87
2014	116.32	113.34	113.50	112.18
2015	112.94	111.51	110.86	111.85
2016	110.25	106.49	109.71	110.33
2017	109.82	109.66	107.68	108.41
2018	110.66	108.14	108.17	108.94
2019		111.43		110.14
2020		108.49		107.51

注：1. 2003 年以前为职工工资总额、平均工资。
2. 2015 年以前为在岗职工工资总额、平均工资。
3. 自 2019 年统计口径变化，无全部单位工资数据。

Note：1. The data before 2003 refer to the total wage bill and average wage of stall and workers.
2. It was the total salary and average salary of the on-spot staff before 2015.
3. Since the statistical caliber change in 2019, there is no wage data for all units.

3-6 城镇非私营和城镇私营单位分行业就业人员平均工资（2020 年）

AVERAGE WAGES OF EMPLOYED PERSONS IN URBAN NON-PRIVATE AND URBAN PRIVATE UNITS BY SECTOR (2020)

行业	Sector	非私营单位（元）Non-private Units (yuan)	私营单位（元）Private Units (yuan)
总计	**Total**	**106011**	**61761**
（一）农、林、牧、渔业	Farming, Forestry, Animal Husbandry and Fishery	69497	56638
（二）采矿业	Mining	53095	62621
（三）制造业	Manufacturing	85690	58905
（四）电力、热力、燃气及水生产和供应业	Electricity, Heat, Gas and Water Production and Supply Industry	100562	60803
（五）建筑业	Construction	95072	65710
（六）批发和零售业	Wholesale and Retail Trade	79865	56150
（七）交通运输、仓储和邮政业	Transport, Storage and Post	96712	61024
（八）住宿和餐饮业	Hotels and Catering Services	57880	48107
（九）信息传输、软件和信息技术服务业	Information Transmission, Computer Services and Software	137344	75357
（十）金融业	Financial Industry	101219	84597
（十一）房地产业	Real Estate	108896	68930
（十二）租赁和商务服务业	Leasing and Business Services	89117	71823
（十三）科学研究和技术服务业	Scientific Research and Technical Services	136204	77757
（十四）水利、环境和公共设施管理业	Management of Water Conservancy, Environment and Public Facilities	62512	38535
（十五）居民服务、修理和其他服务业	Residents Service, Repair and Other Services	75162	49527
（十六）教育	Education	147920	60825
（十七）卫生和社会工作	Health and Social Welfare	148064	63776
（十八）文化、体育和娱乐业	Culture, Sports and Entertainment	121320	63797
（十九）公共管理、社会保障和社会组织	Public Management, Social Security and Social Organization	156793	

主要统计指标解释

单位从业人员　指报告期末最后一日24时在本单位中工作，并取得工资或其他形式劳动报酬的人员数。该指标为时点指标，不包括最后一日当天及以前已经与单位解除劳动合同关系的人员，是在岗职工、劳务派遣人员及其他就业人员之和。就业人员不包括：

（1）离开本单位仍保留劳动关系，并定期领取生活费的人员；

（2）在本单位实习的各类在校学生；

（3）本单位因劳务外包而使用的人员。

在岗职工　指在本单位工作且与本单位签订劳动合同，并由单位支付各项工资和社会保险、住房公积金的人员，以及上述人员中由于学习、病伤、产假等原因暂未工作仍由单位支付工资的人员。在岗职工还包括：

（1）应订立劳动合同而未订立劳动合同人员（如使用的农村户籍人员）；

（2）处于试用期人员；

（3）编制外招用的人员；

（4）派往外单位工作，但工资仍由本单位发放的人员（如挂职锻炼、外派工作等情况）。

工资总额　指根据《关于工资总额组成的规定》（1990年1月1日国家统计局发布的一号令）进行修订，在报告期内（季度或年度）直接支付给本单位全部就业人员的劳动报酬总额。包括计时工资、计件工资、奖金、津贴和补贴、加班加点工资、特殊情况下支付的工资，是在岗职工工资总额、劳务派遣人员工资总额和其他就业人员工资总额之和。

工资总额是税前工资，包括单位从个人工资中直接为其代扣或代缴的房费、水费、电费、住房公积金和社会保险基金个人缴纳部分等。

工资总额不论是计入成本的还是不计入成本的，不论是以货币形式支付的还是以实物形式支付的，均应列入工资总额的计算范围。

平均工资　指单位就业人员在一定时期内平均每人所得的工资额。它表明一定时期工资收入的高低程度，是反映就业人员工资水平的主要指标。

Explanatory Notes on Main Statistical Indicators

Jobholders　refers to the number of employees who works in the institution or company and gets salary or other form of labor reward at 24:00 of the last day of the report period. This is a time–point indicator which is the total of on–spot staff, labor dispatched personnel and other employees, excluding persons that have released the employment contract with the institution or company on the last day or before. The following are not deemed as Jobholders:

1. Persons that keep the employment relations and get regular living expenses after leaving the institution or company.
2. All kinds of students who intern in our company.
3. Personnel that uses by the institution or company in labour outsourcing.

On–spot staff　refers to the employees that works for and signs the employment contract with the institution or company, and relevant salary, social insurance and house funding are paid by the institution or company, and the persons of the previous employees that are not working but still gets salary from the institution or company due to the reason of learning, injury, maternity leave, etc. It also includes the following:

1. Employees who shall sign the employment contract with institution or company but not signed (for example, employees of rural household registration).

2. Employees that are still in probation period.

3. Employees that are recruited outside the authorized size.

4. Employees that are sent to other institution or company but the salaries are still paid by the institution or company (such as onsite training and labour dispatching).

Total salary refers to total payment for labour made directly to all jobholders of the institution or company within the report period (quarterly or annually) revised according to Regulations on Constitution of Total Salary, Order No. 1 released by National Bureau of Statistics on January 1, 1990, including hourly wage, piece wage, bonus, allowance and subsidy, overtime wage, and wages paid under special situations. It is also the total volume of on–spot staff, labour dispatching staff and other employment.

Total salary is the pre–tax salary, including the expenses of housing, water, power and the personal part of house funding and social insurance funds, which has been withheld and paid by the institution or company from personal salaries.

No matter it is credited into cost or not, no matter it is paid in currency or in kind, all total salary shall be categorized as total salary.

Average salary refers to the total salary per capita of employees of the institution or company within the certain period, which is the major indicator of the salary level of employees and the level of salary income of the certain salary.

固定资产投资 4

INVESTMENT IN FIXED ASSETS

简 要 说 明

一、本篇资料的主要内容

本篇资料主要反映了全市固定资产投资及房地产开发方面的情况，主要包括固定资产投资的规模、结构、资金来源和房地产开发投资、施竣工及销售情况等方面的资料。

二、本篇资料的来源

本篇资料来源于固定资产投资及房地产开发投资统计年报，由市统计局固定资产投资统计处整理提供。

Brief Introduction

I. Main Content

Data in this chapter show the basic conditions of investment in fixed assets and real estate development of the whole city, mainly including the total investment in fixed assets, the structure of investment, the resources of investment and investment in real estate development, construction, completion and sales, etc.

II. Source of Data

Data in this chapter are based on the annual report on investment in fixed assets and real estate development, and provided by the Division of Investment and Construction Statistics of Qingdao Municipal Bureau of Statistics.

4-1　主要年份固定资产投资
MAJOR YEAR'S INVESTMENT IN FIXED ASSETS

单位：万元 (10 000 yuan)

年份 Year	规模以上固定资产投资总额 Investment in Fixed Assets above Designated Size	按用途分 Grouped by Use		
		生产性投资 Productive Investment	非生产性投资 Non-Productive Investment	#住宅投资 Investment in Residential Buildings
1949	16	12	4	3
1952	3097	1368	1729	1007
1957	5923	3947	1976	1151
1962	2747	2049	698	192
1965	5481	4155	1326	375
1970	6100	5813	287	154
1975	15839	13548	2381	1064
1978	29660	23499	6161	3203
1980	47499	33865	13634	9335
1985	107421	60643	73424	19058
1990	284576	210453	74123	38898
1991	349031	256633	92398	51898
1992	583068	420748	162320	83844
1993	953274	511684	441590	162419
1994	1329716	728532	601184	324094
1995	1648281	925194	723087	390206
1996	1610562	972398	638164	285412
1997	1611902	932207	679695	278951
1998	1909711	1125821	783890	316999
1999	2205891	1246328	959563	421151
2000	2426820	1311538	1115282	470963
2001	2934728	1487762	1446966	729181
2002	3683623	1962588	1721035	765030
2003	5475526	3023930	2451596	1038304
2004	9845646	6336279	3509367	1608738
2005	14032960	9172206	4860754	1841644
2006	14856894	9214578	5642316	2222733
2007	16353636	10231673	6121963	2720970
2008	20190098	12443179	7746919	3315538
2009	24588889	13852653	10736236	3831976
2010	30224785	16207885	14016900	5609189
2011	35025382	18622819	16402563	5707625
2012	41539146	24246803	17292343	6689114
2013	50278649	30996768	19281881	7220432
2014	57660308	32913906	24746402	7311090
2015	65556685	41402714	24153971	7569123
2016	74547006	44588200	29958806	9561782
2017	77770902	41719893	36051009	9255095

注：1. 规模以上固定资产投资数据 2003 年以前为城镇以上统计范围。
　　2. 因 2004 年以来数据有调整，故表中数据不可比。

Note：1. The data of investment above designated size refer to investment above city and town level before 2003.
　　2. The data since 2004 are not comparable with other data because of the adjustment.

4-1 续表
Continued

单位：万元 (10 000 yuan)

年份 Year	按构成分 Grouped by Composition of Funds			按资金来源分 Grouped by Sources of Funds			
	建筑安装工程 Construction and Installation	设备工器具购置 Purchase of Equipment and Instruments	其他费用 Others	国家投资 State Investment	国内贷款 Domestic Loans	利用外资 Foreign Investment	自筹及其他 Self-raising Fund and Others
1949	11	3	2	16			
1952	2146	870	81	1512			1585
1957	2853	2773	297	3816			2107
1962	1631	984	132	2205			542
1965	3346	1859	276	4451			1030
1970	3136	2835	129	2721			3379
1975	7489	8133	217	9378	1362		5099
1978	19968	9124	568	16828	1601		11231
1980	30993	15541	965	10371	12925	1420	22783
1985	64665	35100	7656	17377	35888	1136	53020
1990	167731	91305	25540	24687	91895	23688	144306
1991	196212	108929	43890	22615	131676	38325	156415
1992	304060	208384	70624	22660	213217	89130	258061
1993	600011	225555	127708	23736	208672	94469	626397
1994	842809	272126	214781	26062	318334	221265	764055
1995	1020484	385934	241863	25683	379198	328124	915276
1996	929735	458284	222543	35639	444443	310722	819758
1997	875057	485122	251723	27928	297089	363789	923096
1998	1034500	574852	300359	67762	491812	170709	1179428
1999	1456473	459596	289822	128603	584120	145589	1347579
2000	1476397	652640	297783	75978	489697	164175	1806238
2001	1781235	744549	408944	93491	620562	217526	2157787
2002	2328492	796685	558446	78775	719677	411704	2831288
2003	3544790	1133333	797403	127861	989178	722644	4237643
2004	6413046	2312139	1120461	85549	1100297	1016145	8245272
2005	8949231	3141732	1941997	136632	1250343	1850921	11540604
2006	8818614	3668191	2370089	391315	2126523	1662897	11856506
2007	9981666	4171878	2200092	215649	2427031	1788056	13109824
2008	11795435	5907195	2487468	322484	3309471	1951468	15855082
2009	14911874	5869214	3807801	778090	4217265	1593287	21555685
2010	18725922	6362880	5135983	1305737	5881886	2135736	27898294
2011	22865421	7521441	4638520	1640702	5871709	1766278	33579182
2012	26080239	8601282	6857625	1324159	5484459	1561597	37356847
2013	33237368	9969777	7071504	1959340	8154829	1528585	49552883
2014	39006113	11640126	7014069	1404667	7452983	1181541	55024776
2015	42893643	15972153	6690889	2067396	7249574	1098178	62458544
2016	45915827	16425993	8789790	1788103	14203650	903773	66069945
2017	55647641	10977494	11145767	2257927	14569701	641216	65055089

4-2 主要年份固定资产投资构成（以投资总额为 100）
COMPOSITION OF MAJOR YEAR´S INVESTMENT IN FIXED ASSETS (TOTAL INVESTMENT=100)

年份 Year	按用途分 Grouped by Use		
	生产性投资 Productive Investment	非生产性投资 Non-Productive Investment	#住宅投资占非生产性比重 Percentage of Investment in Residential Buildings to Non-Productive Investment
1949	75.00	25.00	75.00
1952	44.17	55.83	58.24
1957	66.64	33.36	58.25
1962	74.59	25.41	27.51
1965	75.81	24.19	28.28
1970	95.30	4.70	53.66
1975	84.97	15.03	44.69
1978	79.23	20.77	51.99
1980	71.30	28.70	68.47
1985	56.45	43.55	40.74
1990	73.95	26.05	52.50
1991	73.53	26.47	56.17
1992	72.16	27.84	51.65
1993	53.68	46.32	36.78
1994	54.79	45.21	53.91
1995	56.10	43.90	54.00
1996	60.40	39.60	44.70
1997	57.80	42.20	41.00
1998	59.00	41.00	16.60
1999	56.50	43.50	19.10
2000	54.00	46.00	19.40
2001	50.70	49.30	50.40
2002	53.30	46.70	44.50
2003	55.20	44.80	42.40
2004	64.40	35.60	45.80
2005	65.40	34.60	37.90
2006	62.00	38.00	39.40
2007	62.60	37.40	44.40
2008	61.60	38.40	42.80
2009	56.30	43.70	35.70
2010	53.62	46.38	40.02
2011	53.17	46.83	34.80
2012	58.37	41.63	38.68
2013	61.65	38.35	37.45
2014	57.08	42.92	29.54
2015	63.16	36.84	31.34
2016	59.81	40.19	31.92
2017	53.64	46.36	25.67

4-2 续表
Continued

年份 Year	按构成分 Grouped by Composition of Funds			按资金来源分 Grouped by Sources of Funds			
	建筑安装工程 Construction and Installation	设备工器具购置 Purchase of Equipment and Instruments	其他费用 Others	国家投资 State Investment	国内贷款 Domestic Loans	利用外资 Foreign Investment	自筹及其他 Self-raising Fund and Others
1949	68.75	18.75	12.5	100			
1952	69.29	28.09	2.62	48.82			51.18
1957	48.17	46.82	5.01	64.43			35.57
1962	59.37	35.82	4.81	80.27			19.73
1965	61.05	33.92	5.03	81.21			18.79
1970	51.41	46.48	2.11	44.61			55.39
1975	47.28	51.35	1.37	59.21	8.60		32.19
1978	67.32	30.76	1.92	56.74	5.40		37.86
1980	65.25	32.72	2.03	21.83	27.21	2.99	47.97
1985	60.2	32.68	7.12	16.18	33.41	1.06	49.35
1990	58.94	32.08	8.98	8.68	32.29	8.32	50.71
1991	56.22	31.21	12.57	6.48	37.73	10.98	44.81
1992	52.15	35.74	12.11	3.89	36.56	15.29	44.26
1993	62.94	23.66	13.4	2.49	21.89	9.91	65.71
1994	63.38	20.46	16.16	1.96	23.94	16.64	57.46
1995	61.9	23.4	14.7	1.6	23.0	19.9	55.5
1996	57.7	28.5	13.8	2.2	27.6	19.3	50.9
1997	54.3	30.1	15.6	1.7	18.4	22.6	57.3
1998	54.2	20.8	15.7	3.5	25.8	8.9	61.8
1999	66.0	20.8	13.2	5.8	26.5	6.6	61.1
2000	60.8	26.9	12.3	3.1	20.2	6.8	74.4
2001	60.7	25.4	13.9	3.0	20.1	7.0	69.9
2002	63.2	21.6	15.2	1.9	17.8	10.2	70.1
2003	64.7	20.7	14.6	2.1	16.3	11.9	69.7
2004	65.1	23.5	11.4	0.8	10.6	9.7	78.9
2005	63.8	22.4	13.8	0.9	8.5	12.5	78.1
2006	59.4	24.7	15.9	2.4	13.3	10.4	73.9
2007	61.0	25.5	13.5	1.2	13.8	10.2	74.8
2008	58.4	29.3	12.3	1.5	15.4	9.1	74.0
2009	60.6	23.9	15.5	2.8	15.0	5.6	76.6
2010	62.0	21.0	17.0	3.5	15.8	5.7	75.0
2011	65.3	21.5	13.3	3.8	13.7	4.1	78.4
2012	62.8	20.7	16.5	2.9	12.0	3.4	81.7
2013	66.1	19.8	14.1	3.2	13.3	2.5	81.0
2014	67.6	20.2	12.2	2.2	11.5	1.8	84.6
2015	65.4	24.4	10.2	2.8	10.0	1.5	85.7
2016	61.6	22.0	11.8	2.2	17.1	1.1	79.6
2017	71.6	14.1	14.3	2.7	17.7	0.8	78.8
2018	68.8	7.8	23.4	2.9	15.2	0.4	81.5
2019	65.3	7.0	27.7	1.8	16.2	1.3	80.7
2020	63.8	5.9	30.3	3.8	14.9	0.8	80.5

4-3 按三次产业分规模以上固定资产投资增速（2020年）
GROWTH RATE OF INVESTMENT IN FIXED ASSETS ABOVE DESIGNATED SIZE BY THREE STRATA OF INDUSTRY (2020)

单位：%

指标	Indicator	2020年
总　计	**Total**	**3.2**
第一产业	Primary Industry	115.4
第二产业	Secondary Industry	1.6
#工业	Industry	1.7
第三产业	Tertiary Industry	2.7

4-4 分市、区规模以上固定资产投资增速（2020年）
GROWTH RATE OF FIXED ASSET INVESTMENT ABOVE DESIGNATED SIZE BY CITY AND DISTRICT (2020)

单位：%

市、区名称	Region	规模以上固定资产投资增速 Growth Rate Of Investment In Fixed Assets Above Designated Size	#房地产开发投资增速 Real Estate Development Investment Growth Rate
全市		**3.2**	**13.4**
市南区	Shinan District	8.0	-18.7
市北区	Shibei District	8.0	-10.8
李沧区	Licang District	4.5	19.8
崂山区	Laoshan District	20.9	25.1
西海岸新区	West Coast New Area	1.5	20.3
黄岛区	Huangdao District	1.5	20.3
保税港区	Qingdao Free Trade Port Area of China	10.2	-
城阳区	Chengyang District	8.7	0.1
城阳区（不含高新区）	Chengyang District (Excluding High tech District)	7.0	-0.7
高新区	High tech District	17.8	2.9
即墨区	Jimo District	4.4	41.6
胶州市	Jiaozhou	4.5	17.5
平度市	Pingdu	21.5	-6.8
莱西市	Laixi	30.1	44.4

4-5 规模以上固定资产投资（2020 年）
INVESTMENT IN FIXED ASSETS ABOVE DESIGNATED SIZE (2020)

单位：%

项目	Item	合计 Total	# 房地产开发 Investment in Real Estate Development
一、本年施工项目（个）	**Projects Under Construction This Year (unit)**	**6907**	**1523**
# 本年新开工（个）	of which：Newly Started (unit)	3500	300
二、本年建成投产项目（个）	**Projects Completed and Put into Use This Year (unit)**	**2466**	
三、本年完成投资增速（%）	**Complete Investment Growth Rate This Year（%）**	**3.2**	**13.4**
1. 按构成分	**Grouped by Composition**		
# 建筑安装工程	Construction installation project	63.8	22.1
设备工器具购置	Purchase of Equipment and Instruments	5.9	-29.3
2. 按建设性质分	Grouped by Type of Construction		
# 新建	New Construction	-2.0	
扩建	Expansion	-0.3	
改建和技术改造	Reconstruction	-0.2	
3. 按国民经济行业分	Grouped by Economic Sector		
（1）农、林、牧、渔业	Farming, Forestry, Animal Husbandry and Fishery	111.0	
农业	Farming	138.6	
林业	Forestry	-58.0	
畜牧业	Animal Husbandry	214.5	
渔业	Fishery	86.0	
农、林、牧、渔服务业	Farming, Forestry, Animal Husbandry and Fishery Services	91.2	
（2）采矿业	Mining	-72.1	
煤炭开采和洗选业	Mining and Washing of Coal		
石油和天然气开采业	Extraction of Petroleum and Natural Gas	-100.0	
黑色金属矿采选业	Mining of Ferrous Metal Ores		
有色金属矿采选业	Mining of Non-ferrous Metal Ores	-85.5	
非金属矿采选业	Mining and Processing of Nonmetal Ores	-68.0	
开采辅助活动	Auxiliary Activities of Mining		
其他采矿业	Mining of Other Ores		

4-5 续表 1
Continued

单位：%

项目	Item	合计 Total	#房地产开发 Investment in Real Estate Development
（3）制造业	Manufacturing	4.9	
农副食品加工业	Processing of Food from Agricultural Products	-47.2	
食品制造业	Manufacture of Foods	57.6	
酒、饮料和精制茶制造业	Manufacture of Liquor, Beverage and Refined Tea	-11.9	
烟草制品业	Manufacture of Tobacco	-	
纺织业	Manufacture of Textile	-24.5	
纺织服装、服饰业	Manufacture of Textile Wearing Apparel	-15.0	
皮革、毛皮、羽毛及其制品和制鞋业	Manufacture of Leather, Fur, Feather & Its Products Footwear	21.6	
木材加工和木、竹、藤、棕、草制品业	Processing of Timbers, Manufacture of Wood, Bamboo, Rattan, Palm and Straw Products	25.8	
家具制造业	Manufacture of Furniture	25.0	
造纸和纸制品业	Manufacture of Paper and Paper Products	-24.4	
印刷和记录媒介复制业	Printing, Reproduction of Recording Media	-75.6	
文教、工美、体育和娱乐用品制造业	Manufacture of Articles for Culture, Arts & Crafts, Sports and Entertainment	-62.2	
石油加工、炼焦和核燃料加工业	Processing of Petroleum, Coking, Processing of Nucleus Fuel	27.9	
化学原料和化学制品制造业	Manufacture of Chemical Raw Material and Chemical Products	20.0	
医药制造业	Manufacture of Medicines	19.0	
化学纤维制造业	Manufacture of Chemical Fiber	-5.1	
橡胶和塑料制品业	Manufacture of Rubber and Plastic	15.9	
非金属矿物制品业	Manufacture of Non-metallic Mineral Products	-9.0	
黑色金属冶炼和压延加工业	Smelting and Pressing of Ferrous Metals	42.3	
有色金属冶炼和压延加工业	Smelting and Pressing of Non-ferrous Metals	-67.5	
金属制品业	Manufacture of Metal Products	0.7	
通用设备制造业	Manufacture of General Purpose Machinery	29.6	
专用设备制造业	Manufacture of Special Purpose Machinery	41.2	
汽车制造业	Manufacture of Vehicle	-21.6	
铁路、船舶、航空航天和其他运输设备制造业	Manufacture of Transport Equipment for Railway, Shipping, Aerospace and other uses	90.9	
电气机械和器材制造业	Manufacture of Electrical Machinery & Equipment	-23.4	
计算机、通信和其他电子设备制造业	Manufacture of Computer, Communication Equipment and Other Electronic Equipment	1.2	
仪器仪表制造业	Manufacture of Measuring Instrument	9.4	
其他制造业	Manufacture of Other Products	-60.9	
废弃资源综合利用业	Recycling and Disposal of Waste Resources	-26.1	
金属制品、机械和设备修理业	Maintenance of Metal Products, Machinery and Equipment	-100.0	

4-5 续表 2
Continued

单位：%

项目	Item	合计 Total	#房地产开发 Investment in Real Estate Development
（4）电力、燃气及水的生产和供应业	Electricity, Gas and Water Production and Supply Industry	-27.3	
电力、热力的生产和供应业	Electricity and Heat Production and Supply Industry	-36.0	
燃气生产和供应业	Gas Production and Supply Industry	1.6	
水的生产和供应业	Water Production and Supply Industry	-3.3	
（5）建筑业	Construction	-85.9	
（6）交通运输、仓储及邮政业	Transport Storage and Post	-19.9	
铁路运输业	Railway Transport	-58.2	
道路运输业	Road Transport	-33.7	
水上运输业	Water Transport	537.8	
航空运输业	Air Transport	-42.5	
管道运输业	Pipeline Transport	-81.0	
装卸搬运和运输代理业	Handing, Carrying and Transportation Agent	16.2	
仓储业	Ware houses and Storage	29.6	
邮政业	Post		
（7）信息传输、软件和信息技术服务业	Information Transmission, Software and Information Technology Service Industry	129.7	
（8）批发和零售业	Wholesale and Retail Trade	226.9	
（9）住宿和餐饮业	Hotels and Catering Services	31.8	
（10）金融业	Financial Industry	238.1	
（11）房地产业	Real Estate Industry	2.8	

4-5 续表 3
Continued

单位：%

项目	Item	合计 Total	#房地产开发 Investment in Real Estate Development
（12）租赁和商务服务业	Leasing and Business Services	-30.9	
（13）科学研究和技术服务业	Scientific Research, Technical Service and Geologic Prospecting	-10.6	
（14）水利、环境和公共设施管理业	Management of Water Conservancy, Environment and Pubic Facilities	16.9	
水利管理业	Management of Water Conservancy	2.4	
环境管理业	Environmental Management	32.5	
公共设施管理业	Management of Public Facilities	16.2	
（15）居民服务和其他服务业	Services to Households and Other Services	-12.5	
居民服务业	Services to Households	-26.5	
机动车、电子产品和日用产品修理业	Maintenance of Vehicle, Electronic Products and Daily Articles	-27.0	
其他服务业	Other Services		
（16）教育	Education	18.7	
（17）卫生和社会工作	Health and Social Work	81.4	
卫生	Health	80.0	
（18）文化、体育和娱乐业	Culture, Sports and Entertainment	27.3	
新闻出版业	Journalism and Publishing Activities	-100.0	
广播、电视、体育和音像业	Broadcasting, Movies, Televisions and Audiovisual Activities	40.0	
文化艺术业	Cultural and Art Activities	-7.6	
体育	Sports Activities	-15.4	
娱乐业	Entertainment	266.6	
（19）公共管理、社会保障和社会组织	Public Management, Social Security and Social Organization	-7.2	
中国共产党机关	Communist Party of China	-100.0	
国家机构	Government Agencies	17.7	
人民政协、民主党派	People' s Political Consultative Conference, Democratic Party		
社会保障	Social Security		
群众团体、社会团体和其他成员组织	Non-Governmental Institutions, Social Organizations and Other Organizations	-5.0	
基层群众自治组织	Local People Self-government Organization	-97.9	
（20）国际组织	International Organization	-	

4-5 续表 4
Continued

单位：%

项目	Item	合计 Total	#房地产开发 Investment in Real Estate Development
四、本年资金来源合计	**Total Funds This Year**	**-5.7**	**0.9**
上年末结余资金	Balance of Last Year	1.1	19.9
本年资金来源小计	Sub-total Funds This Year	-7.1	-5.9
国家预算内资金	State Budget	100.2	
国内贷款	Domestic Loans	-14.5	-11
债券	State Treasury Bond	-91.4	
利用外资	Foreign Investment	-46.6	-33.7
自筹资金	Self-raising Funds	-2.6	-7.5
其他资金来源	Others	-15.4	-2.3

4-6 主要年份房地产开发投资
MAJOR YEAR'S INVESTMENT IN REAL ESTATE DEVELOPMENT

单位：万元、万平方米 (10 000 yuan, 10 000 sq.m)

年份 Year	房地产开发投资额 Investment in Real Estate Development	房屋施工面积 Floor Space Under Construction	房屋竣工面积 Floor Space Completed	房屋实际销售面积 Floor Space of Buildings Sold	房屋实际销售额 Sale of Buildings
1995	562861	1008	240	103	185384
1996	455765	748	203	80	125150
1997	426570	675	237	113	216311
1998	438059	742	259	178	351805
1999	629717	900	474	240	430123
2000	675142	1047	352	301	550401
2001	925153	1374	532	406	802364
2002	1036476	1417	537	427	933031
2003	1277969	1765	552	469	1121885
2004	1626965	2101	635	516	1530964
2005	2238370	2363	811	740	2666738
2006	2683631	2751	654	719	3054907
2007	3223547	3224	641	833	4333566
2008	3805652	3773	672	770	3924175
2009	4594829	4310	814	1262	7036744
2010	6024387	5058	1020	1360	8952942
2011	7827193	5693	925	1026	7702379
2012	9301099	6474	1212	951	7660684
2013	10485229	7073	957	1160	9786176
2014	11177297	8171	1136	1164	9708984
2015	11223458	8971	1523	1419	12628568
2016	13691425	9101	1426	1939	17899532
2017	13305432	9533	1487	1901	19992012
2018	14852089	10390	1625	1808	22824618
2019	18038081	11580	1602	1652	22469992
2020	20451153	12528	1154	1654	22168506

4-7 房地产开发投资情况（2020年）
INVESTMENT IN REAL ESTATE DEVELOPMENT (2020)

单位：万元 (10 000 yuan)

指标名称	Indicator	合计 Total	按经济类型分 Grouped by Economic Types 国有经济 State-owned	集体经济 Collective-owned	其他经济 Others
本年完成投资额	**Investment Completed This Year**	**20451153**	**1449835**	**350383**	**18650935**
1. 住宅	Residential Buildings	14791719	909716	210902	13671101
2. 办公楼	Office Buildings	1351267	145487	5958	1199822
3. 商业营业用房	Houses for Business Use	1521119	86716	1483	1432920
4. 其他	Others	2787048	307916	132040	2347092

4-7 续表
Continued

单位：万元 (10 000 yuan)

指标名称	Indicator	按资质等级分 Grouped by Qualification Criteria 一级 First Grade	二级 Second Grade	三级 Third Grade	四级 Fourth Grade	暂定 Provisional	其他 Others
本年完成投资额	**Investment Completed This Year**	**512172**	**543149**	**454092**	**116444**	**14629229**	**4196067**
1. 住宅	Residential Buildings	436939	427345	384755	80273	10584686	2877721
2. 办公楼	Office Buildings	27532	16118	22538	2660	970442	311977
3. 商业营业用房	Houses for Business Use	16811	33744	24529	31295	1120261	294479
4. 其他	Others	30890	65942	22270	2216	1953840	711890

4-8 房地产施工、竣工面积及竣工价值（2020 年）
FLOOR SPACE UNDER CONSTRUCTION AND COMPLETED AND COMPLETED VALUE OF REAL ESTATE (2020)

单位：万平方米 (10 000 sq.m)

施工、竣工房屋面积及竣工价值	Construction and Completed Housing Area and Completed Value	施工面积 Floor Space Under Construction	#新开工 Newly Started	竣工房屋 Floor Space Completed	竣工房屋价值（万元） Completed Value（10 000 yuan）
房屋建筑面积总计	**Floor Space of Buildings**	**12528**	**3312**	**1154**	**4015762**
住宅	Residential Buildings	8242	2256	783	2847884
办公楼	Office Buildings	820	168	66	195400
商业营业用房	Houses for Business Use	974	177	117	444863
其他	Others	2492	711	188	527615

4-[illegible] 年）
BASIC STATISTICS ON SALES OF COMMERCIALIZED BUILDINGS (2020)

商品房屋销售情况	Sales and Rental of Commercialized Buildings	实际销售（万平方米） Actual Sales (10 000 sq.m)	实际销售额（万元） Actual Sales Volume (10 000 yuan)	待售面积（万平方米） Area for Sale（万平方米）
房屋面积总计	**Floor Space of Buildings**	**1654**	**22168506**	**510**
住宅	Residential Buildings	1431	20108187	189
办公楼	Office Buildings	64	849041	98
商业营业用房	Houses for Business Use	48	678501	170
其他	Others	111	532777	53

主要统计指标解释

固定资产投资 是以货币形式表现的在一定时期内建造和购置固定资产的工作量以及与此有关的费用的总称。

房地产开发投资 指各种登记注册类型的房地产开发法人单位统一开发的住宅、厂房、仓库、饭店、宾馆、度假村、写字楼、办公楼等房屋建筑物，配套的服务设施，土地开发工程（如道路、给水、排水、供电、供热、通讯、平整场地等基础设施工程）和土地购置的投资；不包括单纯的土地开发和交易活动。

固定资产投资的资金来源 根据固定资产投资的资金来源不同，分为国家预算资金、国内贷款、利用外资、自筹资金和其他资金。

固定资产投资 按建设性质分建设项目的性质一般分为新建、扩建、改建和技术改造、单纯建造生活设施、迁建、恢复、单纯购置。

固定资产投资 按构成分固定资产投资活动按其工作内容和实现方式分为建筑安装工程，设备、工具、器具购置，其他费用三个部分。

新增生产能力（或工程效益） 指建成投产项目或工程新增生产能力（或工程效益）的名称。

房屋施工面积 是指报告期内施工的全部房屋建筑面积。包括本期新开工的面积和上期开工跨入本期继续施工的房屋面积，以及上期已停缓建在本期恢复施工的房屋面积。本期竣工和本期施工后又停缓建的房屋，其建筑面积仍计入本期房屋施工面积中。

房屋竣工面积 是指在报告期内房屋建筑按照设计要求全部完工，达到住人和使用条件，经验收鉴定合格（或达到竣工验收标准），正式移交使用单位的各栋房屋建筑面积的总和。

本年新增固定资产 指在报告期已经完成建造和购置过程，并已交付生产或使用单位的固定资产的价值，包括已经建成投入生产或交付使用的工程投资和达到固定资产标准的设备、工具、器具的投资及有关应摊入的费用。

Explanatory Notes on Main Statistical Indicators

Fixed investment is a generic term of quantity of work from building and acquiring of fixed assets over a period of time and any relevant expenses incurred thereby in the form of currency.

Real estate development investment means investments in all kinds of registered housing & building, including residences, plants, warehouses, restaurants, hotels, resorts, office buildings and administrative buildings which are developed uniformly by real estate development corporation, supporting service facilities and land development projects (such as road, water supply & drainage, power supply, heat supply, telecommunication and ground leveling and other infrastructure projects) and land acquisition, excludes simple land development and transaction activities.

Source of funds for fixed-asset investment can be divided into national budget funds, domestic loans, utilization of foreign capital, self-raised funds and other funds in accordance with the different sources.

Construction items of fixed–asset investment can be divided into new construction, extension, reconstruction, technical reform, simply–constructed living facilities, relocation, restoration and simple acquisition by property of construction.

Fixed–asset investment activities can be divided into three parts, namely construction and installation project, acquisition of equipment, tools and appliances and other expenses by working content and method of achieving.

New productive capacity (or project benefit) means the completed projects or new productive capacity (or project benefit) of project.

Construction area means total areas of all buildings which are under construction in the report period, including the area which is newly constructed in this period and the areas of buildings which commence in the last period and carry forward to this period for continuing construction. and the areas of buildings which stop constructing in the last period and resume to be constructed in this period. The areas of the buildings which are completed in this period and stop constructing after this period' s construction are still reckoned in floor space under construction in this period.

Completed area means the sum total of areas of housings & buildings which are completed according to design requirements in the report period, reach conditions of living and using and are transferred to building users formally after checked and accepted (or reach the standards of completion and acceptance) .

New fixed assets in this year means the value of fixed assets which are completed and acquired in the report period and delivered for production or use, including investment in constructions which are put into production or service, investment in equipment, tools and appliances which reach the standards of fixed asset, and the expenses which should be added into fixed assets.

对外经济贸易 5

FOREIGN TRADE

简要说明

一、本篇资料的主要内容

本篇资料主要反映了全市外经外贸和外资企业的基本情况，主要包括外贸进出口、利用外资、对外投资与经济合作等方面的资料。

二、本篇资料的来源

1. 口岸进出口数据来源于青岛海关。

2. 进出口、利用外资等资料、对外投资与经济合作来源于市商务局。

本篇资料由市统计局外经贸易统计处整理提供。

Brief Introduction

I. Main Content

Data in this chapter show the basic conditions of foreign trade and foreign-funded enterprises, mainly including imports and exports, utilization of foreign capitals, production and operation condition of foreign-funded enterprises, etc.

II. Source of Data

1. Port import and export data comes from Qingdao Customs.

2. Data on imports & exports and utilization of foreign capitals are provided by Qingdao Municipal Commerce Bureau.

Data in this chapter are prepared and compiled by the Division of Trade and External Economic Relations Statistics of Qingdao Municipal Bureau of Statistics.

5-1 青岛口岸进出口总额(1985-2020年)

TOTAL VALUE OF IMPORTS AND EXPORTS OF QINGDAO PORT (1985-2020)

单位：万美元 (10 000 USD)、万元 (10 000 yuan)

年份 Year	青岛口岸进出口总额 Total Value of Imports and Exports Qingdao Port	出口 Exports	进口 Imports
1985	414448	234652	179796
1986	382840	191926	190914
1987	445090	259458	185632
1988	474516	259176	215340
1989	506152	268397	237755
1990	477117	304011	173106
1991	519273	332949	186324
1992	581495	350163	231332
1993	678013	360297	317716
1994	888574	510760	377814
1995	1307508	705245	602263
1996	1391323	760566	629757
1997	1542284	936142	609142
1998	1463718	933392	530326
1999	1696514	1063768	632746
2000	2520420	1423266	1097154
2001	2797085	1636888	1160197
2002	3128048	1889612	1238436
2003	4088096	2366046	1722050
2004	5677570	3197697	2479873
2005	6932944	3959947	2972997
2006	8019198	4495731	3523467
2007	9257099	5263539	3993560
2008	11558079	5953501	5604578
2009	9049699	4694832	4354867
2010	11912702	5988254	5924448
2011	15095088	7294226	7800862
2012	14888716	7120813	7767903
2013	15662732	7696141	7966591
2014	16489966	8736358	7753608
2015	14448349	8776286	5672063
2016	94927180	56513317	38413863
2017	111024375	63298062	47726314
2018	121968146	67385279	54582867
2019	127239314	69443761	57795553
2020	116719854	66149587	50570266

注：2016年起，统计单位为人民币万元。
Note : Statistic unit is RMB ten thousand Yuan as from 2016.

5-2 进出口总额（1988-2020 年）
TOTAL VALUE OF IMPORTS AND EXPORTS (1988-2020)

单位：万美元 (10 000 USD)、万元 (10 000 yuan)

年份 Year	进出口总额（含中央、省驻青公司） Total Value of Imports and Exports (including central and provincial companies)	出口 Exports	进口 Imports	进出口总额（不含中央、省驻青公司） Total Value of Imports and Exports (including central and provincial companies)	出口 Exports	进口 Imports
1988				28097	21731	6366
1989				39327	27797	11530
1990				41649	33529	8120
1991				54624	44746	9878
1992				88600	66291	22309
1993	517643	346288	171355	139048	100201	38847
1994	633213	434102	199111	234978	164135	70843
1995	858560	536386	322174	376372	245072	131300
1996	863521	516317	347204	461950	287123	174827
1997	916269	579261	377008	521967	338535	183432
1998	882042	573020	309022	595826	382657	213169
1999	1009885	631072	378813	775565	446260	329305
2000	1353222	826891	526331	1083133	611426	471707
2001	1541564	950160	591404	1235781	712024	523757
2002	1692567	1057141	635426	1409598	850420	559178
2003	2065912	1239199	826713	1784556	1035528	749028
2004	2698781	1578167	1120614	2433188	1391171	1042017
2005	3302230	1942242	1359988	3045542	1758834	1286708
2006	3911543	2346552	1564991	3655737	2164541	1491196
2007	4572534	2831004	1741530	4360499	2677596	1682903
2008	5363659	3262476	2101183	5215886	3146246	2069640
2009	4485115	2729865	1755250	4398639	2692197	1706442
2010	5705963	3391560	2314403	5614928	3335141	2279787
2011	7215217	4061309	3153908	7126310	4005572	3120738
2012				7320781	4081968	3238813
2013				7791217	4198605	3592612
2014				7988833	4577696	3411137
2015				7022243	4535015	2487228
2016				43506659	28219059	15287600
2017				50334973	30318103	20016870
2018				53212551	31722209	21490342
2019				59255880	34119000	25136880
2020				64070068	38767641	25302427

注：1. 2012 年起，中央、省驻青公司外贸统计划归青岛，取消含中央、省驻青公司统计口径；
2. 2016 年起，统计单位为人民币万元。

Note：1. Since 2012, the statistical calibre including central and provincial companies has been cancelled.
2. Statistic unit is RMB ten thousand Yuan as from 2016.

5-3 分国别外贸出口总额
TOTAL VALUE OF EXPORTS BY COUNTRIES OR REGIONS

单位：万美元 (10 000 USD)

国别（地区）	Country (Region)	2020 年	2020 年比 2019 年 ±% 2020/2019（±%）	占比 %
亚洲	Asia	2627468.0	13.7	46.8
香港	Hong Kong	205180	40.4	3.7
日本	Japan	595245	2.7	10.6
韩国	Korea	460785	6.5	8.2
东盟	ASEAN	755530	21.1	13.5
非洲	Africa	241448	8.9	4.3
南非	South Africa	42897	-5.3	0.8
欧洲	Europe	1138524	8.2	20.3
欧盟	EU	826995	8.6	14.7
南美洲	South America	171933	10.2	3.1
北美洲	North America	1040788	16.9	18.6
美国	USA	904680	14.7	16.1
大洋洲	Oceania	167799	21.3	3.0
澳大利亚	Australia	140450	24.0	2.5

5-4　外贸出口商品分类
EXPORT COMMODITIES BY CATEGORY

单位：万元 (10 000 yuan)

项目	Item	2020 年	2020 年比 2019 ± % 2020/2019(± %)	占比 %
合计	**Total**	**38767641**	**13.7**	**100.0**
按企业性质划分	By Enterprises Nature			
国有企业	State-owned Enterprises	2919654	-2.3	7.5
三资企业	Foreign-funded Enterprise	8815756	-5.3	22.7
其他企业	Other Enterprises	27032231	24.0	69.8
# 集体企业	#Collective-owned Enterprises	817966	-5.5	2.1
私营企业	Private Enterprises	26152756	25.2	67.5
按贸易方式划分	By Customs Regime			
一般贸易	Ordinary Trade	28953069	19.9	74.7
加工贸易	Processing Trade	8423317	-2.1	21.7
其他贸易	Others	1391255	3.3	3.6
按大类商品划分	By Category of Commodities			
纺织服装	Textile Garments	5162463	12.2	13.3
农产品	Agricultural Products	3937350	-3.4	10.2
机电产品	Mechanical and Electrical Products	18139379	18.1	46.8
高新技术产品	High-tech Products	3149601	12.9	8.1

5-5 外贸进口商品分类
IMPORT COMMODITIES BY CATEGORY

单位：万元（10 000 yuan）

项目	Item	2020 年	2020 年比 2019 ± % 2020/2019 (± %)	占比 %
合计	**Total**	**25302427**	**0.7**	**100.0**
按企业性质划分	By Enterprises Nature			
国有企业	State-owned Enterprises	3999208	-17.6	15.8
三资企业	Foreign-funded Enterprise	5893602	-9.7	23.3
其他企业	Other Enterprises	15409617	12.1	60.9
# 集体企业	#Collective-owned Enterprises	73035	19.9	0.3
私营企业	Private Enterprises	15164280	12.3	59.9
按贸易方式划分	By Customs Regime			0.0
一般贸易	Ordinary Trade	15438492	17.2	61.0
加工贸易	Processing Trade	2786732	-9.5	11.0
其他贸易	Others	7077203	-20.3	28.0
按大类商品划分	By Category of Commodities			0.0
纺织服装	Textile Garments	215439	-12.8	0.9
农产品	Agricultural Products	5738434	9.5	22.7
机电产品	Mechanical and Electrical Products	4482207	-4.9	17.7
高新技术产品	High-tech Products	2282090	-5.6	9.0

5-6 二十大出口商品出口情况
INFORMATION ON THE EXPORTATION OF TOP 20 PRODUCTS

单位：万美元 (10 000 USD)

商品名称	Name	2020 年	2020 年比 2019 年 ±% 2020/2019 (±%)	占比 %
合计	**Total**	**4789954**	**11.5**	**85.3**
机械设备	Machinery and Equipment	883239	18.1	15.7
电器及电子产品	Electric Appliance and Electronic Products	600756	20.5	10.7
运输工具	Transport Tools	453062	8.3	8.1
服装及衣着附件	Clothing and Clothing Accessories	388223	-6.6	6.9
纺织品	Textile Products	356597	41.8	6.4
金属制品	Metal Products	336764	25.3	6
化工产品	Chemical Products	315708	10.2	5.6
汽车零配件	Automobile Parts	218050	-13.2	3.9
塑料制品	Plastic Articles	199105	44.1	3.5
轮胎	Tyre	150475	-10.0	2.7
家具及其零件	Furniture	143158	33.2	2.6
钢材	Rolled Steel	128318	-0.9	2.3
水海产品	Aquatic and Seawater Products	126563	-20.9	2.3
蔬菜	Vegetables	94642	-11.6	1.7
鞋类	Shoes	88718	-11.3	1.6
陶瓷产品	Ceramic Products	75302	84.9	1.3
仪器仪表	Instrumentation	63499	14.6	1.1
箱包及类似容器	Bags and Similar Containers	58811	-6.2	1
鲜、干水果及坚果	Fresh and Dried Fruits and Nuts	57097	42.3	1
床垫、寝具及类似品	Mattresses, Bedding and Similar Products	51867	9.6	0.9

5-7 二十大进口商品进口情况
INFORMATION ON THE IMPORTATION OF TOP 20 PRODUCTS

单位：万美元 (10 000 USD)

商品名称	Name	2020 年	2020 年比 2019 年 ± % 2020/2019 (± %)	占比 %
合计	**Total**	**2881567**	**-2.9**	**78.7**
铁矿砂及其精矿	Iron Ore and Concentrate	496834	36.5	13.6
原油	Crude Oil	400916	-29.0	11
肉类	Meat	305557	40.7	8.3
电器及电子产品	Electric Appliance and Electronic Products	260025	5.0	7.1
机械设备	Machinery and Equipment	202610	-6.3	5.5
粮食	Grain	147107	2.0	4
仪器仪表	Instruments and Meters	134986	-1.7	3.7
水海产品	Aquatic and Seawater Products	130133	-22.9	3.6
合成橡胶	Synthetic Rubber	125683	6.1	3.4
集成电路	Integrated Circuits	116566	5.2	3.2
塑料原料	Plastic Raw Materials	115483	3.1	3.2
铜矿砂及其精矿	Copper Ore and Concentrate	74219	47.7	2
纸浆	Pulp	61356	-44.2	1.7
铝矿砂及其精矿	Aluminum Ore and Concentrate	60596	23.3	1.7
天然橡胶	Natural Rubber	57839	-37.9	1.6
成品油	Refined Petroleum Products	52413	-35.8	1.4
棉花	Cotton	44388	-35.6	1.2
钢材	Rolled Steel	38579	-1.7	1.1
纺织品	Textile Products	29050	-14.9	0.8
煤及褐煤	Coal and Lignite	27229	-32.1	0.7

5-8 利用外资情况（2000-2020年）
UTILIZATION OF FOREIGN CAPITAL（2000-2020）

项目	Item	单位	Unit	2000年	2005年
批准企业（项目）个数	**Number of Enterprises (Projects) Approved**	**个**	**unit**	**1132**	**2530**
一、外商直接投资	Foreign Direct Investments	个	unit	1128	2530
中外合资企业	Sino-foreign Joint Ventures	个	unit	303	274
中外合作企业	Sino-foreign Cooperative Enterprises	个	unit	57	18
外商独资企业	Foreign-owned Enterprises	个	unit	76	2236
外商投资股份制	Foreign-invested joint-stock system	个	unit	1	2
合伙企业	Partnership	个	unit		
二、外商其他投资	Other Foreign Investments	个	unit	4	
合同外资金额	**Total Amount of Contracted Foreign Investment**	**万美元**	**10000 USD**	**269081**	**954486**
一、外商直接投资	Foreign Direct Investments	万美元	10000 USD	266221	954486
中外合资企业	Sino-foreign Joint Ventures	万美元	10000 USD	69889	112777
中外合作企业	Sino-foreign Cooperative Enterprises	万美元	10000 USD	26835	17588
外商独资企业	Foreign-owned Enterprises	万美元	10000 USD	169370	813485
外商投资股份制	Foreign-invested joint-stock system	万美元	10000 USD	127	10636
合伙企业	Partnership	万美元	10000 USD		
二、外商其他投资	Other Foreign Investments	万美元	10000 USD	2860	
实际利用外资金额	**Total Amount of Foreign Investment Actually Utilized**	**万美元**	**10000 USD**	**128171**	**365625**
一、外商直接投资	Foreign Direct Investments	万美元	10000 USD	126132	365625
中外合资企业	Sino-foreign Joint Ventures	万美元	10000 USD	39224	77636
中外合作企业	Sino-foreign Cooperative Enterprises	万美元	10000 USD	3886	5654
外商独资企业	Foreign-owned Enterprises	万美元	10000 USD	82992	280130
外商投资股份制	Foreign-invested joint-stock system	万美元	10000 USD	30	2205
合伙企业	Partnership	万美元	10000 USD		
二、外商其他投资	Other Foreign Investments	万美元	10000 USD	2039	

单位：万美元 (10 000 USD)

2009 年	2010 年	2011 年	2012 年	2013 年	2014 年	2015 年	2016 年	2017 年	2018 年	2019 年	2020 年
647	**731**	**707**	**553**	**645**	**619**	**763**	**680**	**650**	**956**	**954**	**882**
647	731	707	553	645	619	763	680	650	956	954	882
99	153	158	113	165	140	162	154	188	294	358	190
2	4	4	2	2	1	2		1	8	1	
545	574	544	438	478	475	597	523	457	653	586	661
1		1			3	2	3	4	1	2	3
										7	25
271504	**475723**	**528501**	**600231**	**758063**	**638637**	**827357**	**769101**	**909629**	**980231**	**1335551**	**1785353**
271504	475723	528501	600231	758063	638637	827357	769101	909629	980231	1335551	1785353
61734	124148	142535	102252	191172	126878	116013	207933	246280	195336	415708	431250
4531	9179	15173	122	4765	−849	1731	28	327	34333	1010	
204187	341977	369425	490764	562208	506271	706172	554073	655377	756426	794686	1321040
1052	419	1368	7093	−82	6337	3441	7067	7645	−5864	93315	9547
										30832	23446
186397	**284281**	**363350**	**460027**	**552227**	**608100**	**669062**	**700273**	**773500**	**869257**	**584193**	**585297**
186397	284281	363350	460027	552227	608100	669062	700273	773500	869257	584193	585297
46856	84920	100699	169469	159424	172180	135671	171051	195189	191040	215914	230342
3971	3567	2759	6262	2355	128	1570	251	220	19032	68	
135026	194500	255763	275579	390210	435102	531544	520052	569461	658368	299610	352179
544	1294	4129	8717	238	690	277	8918	8325	817	68585	441
										16	1275

5-9 当年外商直接投资项目数和投资额（2020 年）

NUMBER OF PROJECTS AND TOTAL AMOUNT OF FOREIGN DIRECT INVESTMENT (2020)

单位：万美元 (10 000 USD)

项目	Item	批准企业项目数（个） Number of Projects Approved (unit)	实际利用外资金额（万美元） Total Amount of Foreign Investment Actually Utilized (10000 USD)
外商直接投资	**Foreign Direct Investments**	882	585297
一、按投资方式分	**Grouped by Investment Form**		
# 中外合资企业	Sino-foreign Joint Ventures	190	230342
中外合作企业	Sino-foreign Cooperative Enterprises		
外商独资企业	Foreign-owned Enterprises	661	352179
二、按主要行业分	**Grouped by Sector**		
# 农、林、牧、渔业	Farming, Forestry, Animal Husbandry and Fishery	4	6075
制造业	Manufacturing	101	49915
电力、燃气及水的生产和供应业	Production and Supply of Electricity, Gas and Water	6	1615
建筑业	Construction	11	13004
信息传输、计算机服务和软件业	Information transmission, computer services and software industry	66	58519
批发和零售业	Wholesale and Retail Trades	288	32358
房地产业	Real estate industry	51	162647
租赁和商务服务业	Leasing and Business Services	142	126369
科学研究、技术服务和地质勘查业	Scientific Research, Technical Service and Geological Survey	92	51079
三、按主要国别（地区）分	**Grouped by Countries (Regions)**		
# 香港	Hong Kong	346	506649
韩国	Korea	172	13080
美国	USA	46	10130
日本	Japan	26	6656
德国	Germany	17	2451
澳大利亚	Australia	18	2687
新加坡	Singapore	21	13848

5-10 对外投资与经济合作
OUTBOUND INVESTMENT AND INTERNATIONAL ECONOMIC COOPERATION

名称	Name	单位	Unit	2020 年	2020 年比 2019 年 ± % 2020/2019 (± %)
对外投资项目数	Number of Outbound Investment Projects	个	unit	63	-44.7
对外投资中方投资额	The Amount of Investment by Chinese Sides in Outbound Investment	万美元	10000 USD	118858.29	-55.4
对外承包工程新签合同额	The Amount of New Contracts for Foreign Contracted Projects	万美元	10000 USD	348234	3.6
对外承包工程完成营业额	The Completed Turnover of Foreign Contracted Projects	万美元	10000 USD	287779	-31.2
对外劳务合作	Number of Persons Sent Overseas for International Labor Service Cooperation	人	Person	10047	-47.6

5-11 对外投资分国别(地区)情况表(2020 年)
TABLE OF FOREIGN INVESTMENT BY COUNTRY (REGION) (2020)

国别(地区)	Country (Region)	项目数量(个) Number of Projects (unit)	2020 年比 2019 年 ± % 2020/2019 (± %)	中方投资额(万美元) Amount of Investment by Chinese Sides (10000 USD)	2020 年比 2019 年 ± % 2020/2019 (± %)
总计	**Total**	**63**	**-44.70**	**118858.29**	**-55.40**
亚洲	Asia	38	-47.95	34386.92	-71.19
中国香港	Hong Kong, China	23	130	1107.91	-6.3
新加坡	Singapore	3	-40	6859.62	-35.95
日本	Japan	2	-50	225.32	-84.48
泰国	Thailand	2	-71.43	17100.58	-38.56
韩国	Korea	2	-81.82	4043.22	-51.29
柬埔寨	Cambodia	1	-80.00	320.00	-95.73
马来西亚	Malaysia	1	-75.00	284.00	-88.34
哈萨克斯坦	Kazakhstan	1	-	7	-
土耳其	Turkey	1	0	30	-99.24
越南	Vietnam	1	-66.67	20.00	-99.91
印度尼西亚	Indonesia	增资	-100	5109.27	-56.29
孟加拉	Bengal	减资	-100	-720	-202.86

5-11 续表 4
Continued

国别（地区）	Country (Region)	项目数量（个）Number of Projects (unit)	2020 年比 2019 年 ± % 2020/2019 (± %)	中方投资额（万美元）Amount of Investment by Chinese Sides (10000 USD)	2020 年比 2019 年 ± % 2020/2019 (± %)
非洲	Africa	2	-66.67	128.57	-85.22
肯尼亚	Kenya	1	0	100	-50.00
南非	South Africa	1	-	28.57	-
欧洲	Europe	11	-21.43	12901.9	-68.78
西班牙	Spain	2	-	495.26	-
俄罗斯联邦	Russia	2	-33.33	5630	321.8
法国	France	2	-	1592.19	-
比利时	Belgium	1	-	307.33	-
德国	Germany	1	-85.71	1.48	-99.92
罗马尼亚	Romania	1	0	4232.00	284.73
瑞典	Sweden	1	-	393.71	-
斯洛文尼亚	Slovenia	1	0	249.93	-99.26
拉丁美洲	Latin America	7	75	7517.5	56.41
墨西哥	Mexico	2	100	7160	68.42
哥伦比亚	Colombia	1	-	7	-
阿根廷	Argentina	1	0	300	-45.45
巴西	Brazil	1	-	40	-
英属维尔京群岛	British Virgin Islands	1	0	0.5	-90
智利	Chile	1	-	10.0	-
北美洲	North America	5	-64.29	63770.11	734.03
美国	USA	5	-61.54	2077.47	-70.80
百慕大群岛	Bermuda	增资	-	61192.63	-
加拿大	Canada	增资	-100.00	500.00	-5.81
大洋洲	Oceania	增资	-100.00	153.29	-99.83
澳大利亚	Australia	增资	-100.00	153.29	-85.08

主要统计指标解释

批准企业（项目）个数 是指外商直接投资中批准设立的外商投资企业个数、批准的合作开发项目个数。

合同外资金额 是指批准外商投资企业的合同、章程中规定的外国投资者认缴的出资额和企业投资总额内的应由外方投资者以自己的境外自有资金直接向企业提供的贷款。包括新批准企业合同外资和原有企业的增资减资，增资减资不对企业（项目）个数进行调整。

实际使用外资金额 是指合同外资金额的实际执行金额。

外商直接投资 是指外国企业和经济组织或个人（包括华侨、港澳台胞以及我国在境外注册的企业）按我国有关政策、法规，用现汇、实物、技术等在我国境内开办外商独资企业、与我国境内的企业或经济组织共同举办中外合资经营企业、合作经营企业或合作开发资源的投资（包括外商投资收益的再投资）以及经政府有关部门批准的项目投资总额内，企业从境外借入的资金。

外商其它投资 是指除外商直接投资以外其他方式吸收的外资。

进出口总额 指实际进出我国国境的货物总金额。包括对外贸易实际进出口货物，来料加工装配进出口货物，国家间、联合国及国际组织无偿援助物资和赠送品，华侨、港澳台同胞和外籍华人捐赠品，租赁期满归承租人所有的租赁货物，进料加工进出口货物，边境地方贸易及边境地区小额贸易进出口货物（边民互市贸易除外），中外合资企业、中外合作经营企业、外商独资经营企业进出口货物和公用物品，到、离岸价格在规定限额以上的进出口货样和广告品（无商业价值、无使用价值和免费提供出口的除外），从保税仓库提取在中国境内销售的进口货物，以及其他进出口货物。

Explanatory Notes on Main Statistical Indicators

Enterprises (Projects) Permitted refers to number of foreign invested enterprises and developed projects under cooperation through the permission.

Contracted Foreign Investment refers to expenditure promised by the foreign investor and loan stemmed from broad innate fund of the foreign investor, according to the contract and regulation approved of enterprise invested by foreigner. Including the newly approved enterprise contract foreign investment and the capital increase and decrease of the original enterprise, the capital increase and decrease do not adjust the number of enterprises (projects) .

Actual Utilization of Foreign Investment refers to actual usage of contracted foreign investment, including cash, investment in kind and incorporeal agreed by the both sides as part of the investment, such as services and technology.

Foreign Direct Investment refers to the investments by foreign enterprises and economic organizations or individuals (including overseas Chinese, compatriots from Hong Kong, Macao and Taiwan and Chinese enterprises registered abroad) , following the relevant policies and laws of China, for the establishment of ventures and cooperative enterprises or cooperative exploration of resources with enterprises or economic organizations in China. It includes the reinvestment of the foreign entrepreneurs with the profits gained from the investment and the funds that enterprises borrow from aboard in the total investment of projects which are approved by the relevant department of the government.

Other Investment by Foreign Entrepreneurs refers to all forms of utilization of foreign capitals other than foreign direct investment.

Total Imports and Exports refers to the real value of commodities imported into and exported from the boundary of China. They include the actual imports and exports through foreign trade, imported and exported goods under the processing and assembling trades and materials, supplies and gifts as aid given gratis between governments and by the United Nations and other international organizations, and contributions donated by overseas Chinese, compatriots in Hong Kong, Macao and Chinese with foreign citizenship, leasing commodities owned by tenant at the expiration of leasing period, the imported and exported commodities processed with imported materials, commodities trading in border areas (excluding mutual exchange goods) , the imported and exported commodities and articles for public use of the Sino–foreign joint ventures, cooperative enterprises and ventures exclusively with foreign own investment. Also included are import or export of samples and advertising goods for whose CIF or FOB value are beyond the permitted ceiling (excluding goods of no trading or use value and free commodities for export) , imported goods sold in China from bonded warehouses and other imported or exported goods.

城市建设、环境保护 6

CITY CONSTRUCTION AND
ENVIRONMENT PROTECTION

简要说明

一、本篇资料的主要内容

本篇资料主要反映了全市城市基础设施基本情况，包括市政设施、供水、供电、公共交通、园林绿化、燃气供热、城市环卫、环境保护及工业“三废”排放情况等方面的资料。

二、本篇资料的来源

1. 本篇资料中市政设施、供水、公共交通、园林绿化、燃气供热、城市环卫相关资料来源于市住房和城乡建设局、市交通运输局，由市统计局固定资产投资统计处整理提供。

2. 本篇资料中供电资料来源于青岛供电公司，由市统计局能源统计处整理提供。

3. 本篇资料中环境保护、环境质量及工业“三废”排放情况来源于市生态环境局，由市统计局能源统计处整理提供。

Brief Introduction

I. Main Content

The data in this chapter mainly reflects the basic conditions of the city´s urban infrastructure, including information on municipal facilities, water supply, power supply, public transportation, landscaping, gas heating, urban sanitation, environmental protection, and industrial "three wastes" emissions.

II. Source of Data

1. The relevant information on municipal facilities, water supply, public transportation, landscaping, gas heating, and urban environmental sanitation in this article comes from the Municipal Housing and Urban-Rural Construction Bureau and the Municipal Transportation Bureau, and is provided by the Fixed Assets Investment Statistics Department of the Municipal Bureau of Statistics.

2. The power supply data in this data comes from Qingdao Power Supply Company, which is compiled and provided by the Energy Statistics Division of the Municipal Bureau of Statistics.

3. The environmental protection, environmental quality, and industrial "three wastes" emissions in this data come from the Municipal Ecological Environment Bureau and are compiled and provided by the Energy Statistics Division of the Municipal Bureau of Statistics.

6-1　主要年份城市建设和公用事业

MAJOR YEAR´S CITY CONSTRUCTION AND PUBLIC UTILITIES

年份 Year	建成区面积 （平方公里） Developed Areas (sq.km)	年末道路长度 （公里） Length of Roads at Year–end (km)	年末道路面积 （万平方米） Area of Roads at Year–end (10 000 sq.m)	公共汽车、电车线路网长度 （公里） Network Length of Bus and Trolley Bus (km)
1949	27	243	206	26.4
1952	29	245	213	124.4
1957	36	248	217	232.3
1962	55	266	235	252.8
1965	57	266	235	308.1
1970	59	374	346	358.5
1975	63	392	355	389.3
1978	66	408	368	422.1
1980	72	408	377	474.1
1985	79	462	464	611.3
1990	94.3	667	786	777
1991	94.7	673	826	922
1992	95.4	683	840	988
1993	99.9	764	944	1094
1994	103.9	811	985	1372
1995	106	936	1177	1101
1996	110	991	1339	1211
1997	112	1047	1436	1492
1998	114	1106	1436	1859
1999	116	1171	1698	2339
2000	119.1	1192	1789	2711
2001	123	1248	2169	2521
2002	133	1426	2594	896
2003	145.9	1595	2816	973
2004	154.8	1755	3254	1185
2005	178.8	1862	3547	1159
2006	227.5	3160	5218	1362
2007	250.7	3288	5411	1480
2008	267.1	3318	5596	1470
2009	272.9	3402	5763	1216
2010	282.3	3409	5893	1383
2011	291.5	3705	6605	1719
2012	374.6	4281	7528	1978
2013	469.6	4334	7859	2002
2014	490.7	4393	7908	2023
2015	566.4	4375	7940	2106
2016	599.3	4484	8057	2116
2017	638.4	4865	8496	2220
2018	715.1	5770	9862	2400
2019	758.2	6315	10227	3973
2020	758.2	6374	10510	4044

6-1 续表 1
Continued

年份 Year	自来水供水管道长度（公里）Length of Tap Water Pipelines (km)	全年供水总量（万立方米）Annual Volume of Tap Water Supply (10 000 cu.m)	#全年售水量（万立方米）Annual Volume of Tap Water Sale (10 000 cu.m)	#居民家庭用水 of which: Consumption for Residential Use	用水普及率（%）Coverage Rate of Population with Access to Tap Water (%)	排水管道长度（公里）Length of Sewage Pipes (km)	全年用电量（亿千瓦时）Annual Volume of Electricity Supply (100 million kW·h)	#居民生活用电 of which: Consumption for Residential Use
1949	308	721	456	331	89	200	0.88	0.14
1952	341	778	612	310	90	227	1.85	0.14
1957	412	1392	1 296	606	93	273	2.61	0.26
1962	483	2700	2 512	937	98	290	3.77	0.57
1965	500	3220	2 979	929	98	295	5.92	0.68
1970	521	4503	4106	1085	99	350	9.83	1.02
1975	564	6726	6302	1950	99	361	12.41	1.43
1978	572	5334	4975	1314	99	382	16.34	1.62
1980	588	8224	7874	2577	99	394	21.48	2.78
1985	685	7557	7038	2628	99.9	505	26.39	2.87
1990	873	11896	10211	4270	96.9	645	41.08	4.32
1991	908	13865	11760	4990	96.6	649	44.51	5.34
1992	1035	16385	13070	5931	96.5	672	51.78	6.84
1993	1123	16137	14027	6124	99.1	734	55.02	7.66
1994	1124	17367	14716	6405	100	811	60.74	8.78
1995	1046	22513	15810	7050	100	990	67.23	10.16
1996	1182	23277	16566	7731	100	1051	72.87	12.23
1997	1266	24130	17215	8787	100	1167	77.82	13.73
1998	1390	23845	17271	9115	100	1210	79.65	14.28
1999	1471	23849	18558	10032	100	1301	88.12	15.31
2000	1524	25414	20642	11405	100	1460	106.80	16
2001	1665	22225	18556	10555	100	1539	116.10	17.62
2002	1781	27662	21684	10129	100	1641	131.44	18.31
2003	2060	27594	21483	10142	100	1884	147.68	19.88
2004	2566	30877	23864	11695	100	2002	167.95	23.63
2005	2876	33265	25874	12536	100	2309	193.81	33.76
2006	3984	30524	25572	10682	100	3994	215.35	34.87
2007	4187	31533	26454	11408	100	4079	236.42	37.40
2008	4642	32675	27396	11301	100	4229	250.07	40.31
2009	4767	33490	28274	12250	100	4555	259.42	43.29
2010	4926	34909	29617	12524	100	4708	292.97	49.50
2011	5121	34109	28837	10049	100	5187	313.44	50.13
2012	5243	38945	33039	12121	100	6814	318.36	51.64
2013	5522	38331	32418	11851	100	6536	339.27	57.52
2014	6177	46649	40612	14834	100	6840	337.82	59.95
2015	6142	46203	40202	15381	100	6993	342.29	64.71
2016	6132	43033	36748	14430	100	7146	367.26	69.52
2017	6498	45991	38963	17439	100	7367	401.06	74.84
2018	7531	53235	43298	18473	100	8854	431.82	77.39
2019	7997	52203	44597	19809	100	9350	457.90	81.95
2020	8207	55352	48408	21166	100	9713	476.59	81.36

6-1　续表 2
Continued

年份 Year	公共汽车、电车营运车辆（辆） Number of Bus and Trolley Bus under Operation (unit)	全年客运量（万人次） Annual Passenger Traffic (10 000 person-times)	出租汽车（辆） Number of Taxi (unit)	使用液化气、煤气、天然气人数（万人） Population with Access to Gas (10 000 person)	液化气 Liquefied Petroleum	煤气 Coal Gas	天然气 Natural Gas	液化气供气量（吨） Volume of Liquefied Petroleum Supply (ton)
1949	32	298						
1952	76	932						
1957	112	4110						
1962	127	4747						
1965	173	6092						
1970	224	13002						
1975	324	14426		2	2			184.9
1978	409	27351		17	17			3246
1980	485	38981	48	24	24			4345
1985	621	48852	219	42.1	42.1			10619
1990	801	63495	832	75.0	57.4	17.6		17512
1991	1372	67552	1070	76.2	57.4	18.8		17963
1992	1470	73529	1828	82.8	62.0	20.8		19565
1993	1875	72427	4874	88.4	64.6	23.8		22224
1994	1850	78231	5806	103.6	77.4	26.2		24684
1995	1891	71867	5887	116.2	82.9	33.3		32443
1996	2012	49077	6660	126.0	88.0	38.0		4065
1997	2148	55642	6861	133.6	92.9	40.7		38717
1998	2184	51042	7469	146.8	97.8	49.0		45381
1999	2470	55414	7839	154.9	98.3	56.6		40537
2000	3141	59879	7933	164.1	93.3	70.8		46951
2001	3453	60167	8110	168.8	87.5	81.3		45295
2002	3681	61713	8376	224.2	133.8	90.4		60123
2003	3648	58792	8109	246.7	138.3	93.1	15.3	67803
2004	3848	66463	8144	258.4	140.6	78.8	39.0	58548
2005	4039	68776	8121	265.0	132.6	45.7	86.7	78000
2006	4167	73726	8146	271.0	112.5	49.5	109.0	97343
2007	4524	78702	8221	275.6	104.1	12.1	159.4	79715
2008	4701	82460	9241	276.3	91.9	10.5	173.9	81987
2009	4288	81768	9316	276.1	59.8	12.3	204.0	96721
2010	4664	85251	9539	276.3	36.7	12.6	227.0	80073
2011	5419	89614	9683	277.1	25.8	12.6	238.7	79812
2012	5640	97922	9693	313.7	36.7	13.1	263.9	54341
2013	6179	101108	9826	318.9	33.0	0.0	285.9	41302
2014	6515	105592	9720	325.4	33.0	0.0	292.4	39255
2015	6748	102402	10033	338.3	28.9	0.0	309.4	35255
2016	7210	99596	10048	441.6	29.0	0.0	412.6	32291
2017	7420	104898	10875	445.8	26.2	0.0	419.6	28309
2018	7795	104782	10867	512.7	29.9	0.0	482.8	30427
2019	8489	108339	10877	529.5	27.0	0.0	502.5	30210
2020	8553	65014	10877	550.1	23.8	0.0	526.3	29029

注：1990 年以前公共营运车辆不包括系统外及个体。

Note：Vehicles not belonging to system and individual vehicles are not contained in public operating vehicles before 1990.

6-1 续表 3

Continued

年份 Year	煤气供气量（万立方米） Volume of Coal Gas Supply (10 000 cu.m)	天然气供气量（万立方米） Volume of Natural Gas Supply (10 000 cu.m)	燃气普及率(%) Coverage Rate of Population with Access to Gas (%)	绿地面积（公顷） Area of Green Areas (hectare)	公园绿地面积（公顷） Park Green Areas (hectare)	人均公园绿地面积(平方米) Per Capita Park Green Areas (sq.m)	建成区绿化覆盖率(%) Green Coverage Rate of Developed Areas (%)	公园(个) Number of Parks and Zoos (unit)	公园面积（公顷） Area of Parks and Zoos (hectare)
1949				133	42	0.7	4.9	3	43
1952				134	43	0.7	4.4	4	45
1957				245	132	1.7	6.9	10	122
1962				771	184	2.2	14.0	12	174
1965				777	184	2.1	13.7	12	174
1970				772	184	2.1	13.0	6	117
1975			2.3	465	162	1.8	7.6	5	134
1978			18.6	469	162	1.7	7.6	6	165
1980			24.5	625	206	2.1	10.4	6	152
1985			36.3	1072	255	2.3	17.3	7	153
1990	3073		56.2	2120	492	3.7	22.8	26	404
1991	3439		56.5	2318	500	3.7	24.4	28	443
1992	3824		60.0	2471	515	3.7	25.9	28	417
1993	4215		63.1	2488	543	3.9	26.5	31	453
1994	4116		63.1	2866	572	4.0	27.9	31	463
1995	4734		79.2	4547	771	5.3	30.1	33	675
1996	5447		83.9	4679	836	5.6	30.4	33	675
1997	5920		87.3	4717	924	6.0	31.3	34	730
1998	5959		92.5	6812	1047	6.6	35.0	35	775
1999	7319		96.0	7007	1186	7.4	35.9	36	791
2000	9567		98.0	7439	1423	8.5	37.0	37	790
2001	11814		99.0	7688	1588	9.3	37.5	39	832
2002	13500		99.5	7967	1791	8.1	36.4	43	926
2003	14826	1181	100	8829	2305	9.3	37.5	45	1034
2004	15503	2710	100	10047	2842	11.0	38.0	48	1421
2005	16573	7456	100	11137	3132	11.8	38.8	47	1110
2006	9821	13876	100	11756	3198	11.8	39.2	47	1188
2007	9516	18103	100	15369	3661	13.3	37.8	73	1268
2008	8691	21780	100	15630	4014	14.5	41.5	77	1815
2009	7523	26948	100	16003	4003	14.5	43.4	71	1897
2010	9153	35681	100	16619	4027	14.6	43.4	72	1917
2011	9137	46147	100	18013	4041	14.6	44.7	74	1931
2012	8148	68397	100	21471	4573	14.6	44.7	78	2112
2013	0	70918	100	28007	4649	14.6	44.7	87	2698
2014	0	74823	100	28805	4741	14.6	44.7	91	2988
2015	0	70311	100	29117	4802	14.6	44.7	87	3163
2016	0	70586	100	34851	8194	18.6	38.6	151	4460
2017	0	91572	100	36209	7763	17.4	39.1	175	4727
2018	0	120089	100	39229	8587	16.3	39.2	191	5767
2019	0	131867	100	40844	8922	16.9	40.2	192	5773
2020	0	130745	100	41829	10508	19.0	41.0	212	8426

注：1. 自 2002 年起人均公共绿地面积按辖区内全部人口计算。

2. 2005 年以前所用园林绿地面积；公共绿地面积；人均公共绿地面积；公园、动物园个数；公园、动物园面积指标分别改为现在的绿地面积；公共绿地面积；人均公园绿地面积；公园个数；公园面积。

3. 由于城阳区绿化指标进行了调整，部分绿地属性发生变化。导致 2017 年公园绿地面积及人均公园绿地面积的数据小于 2016 年。

Note: 1. Per capita public green areas is calculated at total population in the area under jurisdiction since 2002.

2. Before 2005, the corresponding indicators of greenbelt area, public greenbelt area, public greenbelt area, per capita public greenbelt area, coverage rate of green, number of parks and zoos, area of parks and zoos.

3. As the green index of Chengyang District has been adjusted, some green space properties have changed. As a result, the data of park green area and per capita park green area in 2017 are smaller than 2016.

6-2 全年供电（2020 年）
ANNUAL ELECTRICITY SUPPLY (2020)

全年供电项目	Item	单位	Unit	2020 年
发电设备总容量	Total Capacity of Generation Equipment	万千瓦	10 000 kW	376.30
#青岛电厂	Qingdao Power Plant	万千瓦	10 000 kW	127.00
黄岛电厂	Huangdao Power Plant	万千瓦	10 000 kW	156.50
全年发电量	Annual Electricity Generation	亿千瓦时	100 million kw・h	172.47
#青岛电厂	Qingdao Power Plant	亿千瓦时	100 million kw・h	53.26
黄岛电厂	Huangdao Power Plant	亿千瓦时	100 million kw・h	60.06
全年实际用电量	Annual Electricity Consumption	亿千瓦时	100 million kw・h	476.59
#工业	Industrial Consumption	亿千瓦时	100 million kw・h	259.07
农业	Agricultural Consumption	亿千瓦时	100 million kw・h	9.95
生活	Residential Consumption	亿千瓦时	100 million kw・h	81.36
平均每日用电量	Average Daily Consumption	万千瓦时	10 000 kW・h	13057.2

6-3 分行业用电（2020 年）

ELECTRICITY CONSUMPTION BY SECTOR (2020)

单位：万千瓦时 (10 000 kW · h)

行业	Sector	2020 年	2020 年比 2019 年增长（%）Growth Rate in 2020 over 2019 (%)
全社会用电总计	**Total Electricity Consumption**	**4765867.94**	**3.08**
一、农、林、牧、渔业	Farming, Forestry, Animal Husbandry and Fishery	99470.62	3.07
二、工业	Industry	2590736.14	3.56
三、建筑业	Construction	102099.29	2.84
四、交通运输、仓储和邮政业	Transport, Storage and Post	221836.47	12.86
五、信息传输、计算机服务和软件业	Information Transmission, Computer Services and Software	77849.07	23.37
六、商业、住宿和餐饮业	Trade, Hotels and Catering Services	251624.97	-5.10
七、金融、房地产、商务及居民服务业	Finance, Real Estate, Business and Residential Services	265661.70	2.31
八、公共事业及管理组织	Public Management and Social Organization	342966.42	-1.26
九、城乡居民生活用电	Household Consumption	813623.24	2.45
城镇居民	Urban Area	514580.25	8.71
乡村居民	Rural Area	299043.00	-6.79

6-4 城市供水
URBAN WATER SUPPLY

项目	Item	单位	Unit	2020 年
自来水供水管道长度	Length of Tap Water Pipelines	公里	km	8207
综合生产能力	Synthesis Production Capacity	万立方米 / 日	10 000 cu.m/day	233
全年供水总量	Annual Volume of Tap Water Supply	万立方米	10 000 cu.m	55352
#售水量	Volume of Tap Water Supply	万立方米	10 000 cu.m	48408
#生产运营用水	Consumption for Production Use	万立方米	10 000 cu.m	18874
公共服务用水	Consumption for Public Services Use	万立方米	10 000 cu.m	7471
居民家庭用水	Consumption for Residential Use	万立方米	10 000 cu.m	21166
其他用水	Consumption for Other Uses	万立方米	10 000 cu.m	898
平均每日供水量	Daily Volume of Tap Water Supply	万立方米	10 000 cu.m	152
#生产用	Consumption for Production Use	万立方米	10 000 cu.m	52
生活用	Consumption for Residential Use	万立方米	10 000 cu.m	58
用水户数	Households with Access to Water	户	household	2042805
用水人口	Population with Access to water	万人	10 000 person	550
工业用水量重复利用率	Recycle Rate of water for Industrial Use	%	%	93

6-5 城市公共交通
URBAN PUBLIC TRAFFIC

项目	Item	单位	Unit	2020 年
公共汽车、电车线路网长度	Network Length of Bus and Trolley Bus	公里	km	4044
轨道交通线路长度	Rail Transit Line Length	公里	km	246
公共汽车、电车营运车辆	Number of Bus and Trolley Bus under Operation	辆	unit	8553
# 汽车	Bus	辆	unit	4648
电车	Trolley Bus	辆	unit	3905
公共汽车、电车全年客运量	Annual Passenger Traffic of Bus and Trolley Bus	万人次	10 000 person-times	65014
公共汽车、电车平均每日客运量	Daily Passenger Traffic of Bus and Trolley Bus	万人	10 000 person	180
出租汽车数	Number of Taxi	辆	unit	10877
轮渡运营船数	Number of Ferry Boat under Operation	艘	ship	—
轮渡客运总量	Passenger Traffic of Ferry Boat	万人次	10 000 person-times	—
轮渡平均每日客运量	Daily Passenger Traffic of Ferry Boat	万人	10 000 person	—
轨道交通客运总量	Total Passenger Traffic Of Rail Transit	万人次	10 000 person-times	13909
轨道交通平均每日客运量	Average Daily Passenger Volume of Rail Transit	万人	10 000 person	38

6-6　城市供气
URBAN GAS SUPPLY

项目	Item	单位	Unit	2020年
煤气供应总量	Volume of Coal Gas Supply	万立方米	10 000 cu.m	0
#家庭用量	Household Consumption	万立方米	10 000 cu.m	0
煤气用气户数	Households with Access to Coal Gas	户	household	0
#家庭用户	Household Users	户	household	0
液化石油气供应总量	Volume of Liquefied Petroleum Supply	吨	ton	29029
#家庭用量	Household Consumption	吨	ton	15750
液化石油气用气户数	Households with Access to Liquefied Petroleum	户	household	117780
#家庭用户	Household Users	户	household	109758
天然气供应总量	Volume of Natural Gas Supply	万立方米	10 000 cu.m	130745
#家庭用量	Household Consumption	万立方米	10 000 cu.m	33206
天然气用气户数	Households with Access to Natural Gas	户	household	2230023
#家庭用户	Household Users	户	household	2213100
燃气普及率	Coverage Rate of Population with Access to Gas	%	%	100

6-7 城市环境卫生
URBAN ENVIRONMENTAL SANITATION

项目	Item	单位	Unit	2020 年
市容环卫专用车辆总数	Number of Special Vehicles for Environmental Sanitation	辆	unit	6876
生活垃圾清运量	Volume of Garbage Disposal	万吨	10 000 ton	267
生活垃圾无害化处理厂（场）数	Number of Bio-safety Disposal Plant of Garbage	座	unit	7
生活垃圾无害化处理能力	Bio-safety Disposal Capacity of Garbage	吨 / 日	ton/day	7700
生活垃圾无害化处理量	Bio-safety Disposal Volume of Garbage	万吨	10 000 ton	267
道路清扫保洁面积	Area under Cleaning Program	万平方米	10 000 sq.m	7490
#机械化	of which：Mechanization	万平方米	10 000 sq.m	5920
公共厕所	Public Toilets	个	unit	1001

6-8　城市道路、下水道及绿化
URBAN ROAD, SEWAGE AND GREEN

项目	Item	单位	Unit	2020年
道路	**Road**			
年末道路长度	Length of Roads at Year-end	公里	km	6374
年末道路面积	Area of Roads at Year-end	万平方米	10 000 sq.m	10510
#人行道面积	Area of Pavements	万平方米	10 000 sq.m	2284
排水管道长度	Length of Sewage Pipes	公里	km	9713
园林绿化	**Greening**			
绿化覆盖面积	Area of Green Coverage Areas	公顷	hectare	45263
绿地面积	Area of Green Areas	公顷	hectare	41829
公园绿地面积	Area of Park Green Areas	公顷	hectare	10508
公园数	Number of Parks and Zoos	个	unit	212
公园面积	Area of Parks and Zoos	公顷	hectare	8426
城市每人平均公园绿地面积	Per Capita Park Green Area	平方米	sq.m	19
建成区绿化覆盖率	Green Coverage Rate of Developed Areas	%	%	41

6-9　环境保护基本情况
BASIC CONDITIONS OF ENVIRONMENTAL PROTECTION

项目	Item	单位	Unit	2020 年	2019 年
二氧化硫排放总量	Sulphur Dioxide Emission	吨	ton	4830.65	13916.78
氮氧化物排放总量	Discharge Amount of Nitrogen Oxides	吨	ton	10494.24	13923.01
烟（粉）尘排放总量	Soot (Dust) Emission	吨	ton	9948.21	12907.66
工业固体废物排放总量	Industrial Solid Wastes Discharged	吨	ton	0.00	0.00
化学需氧量排放总量	Discharge Amount of Chemical Oxygen Demand	吨	ton	40793.42	24414.40
氨氮排放总量	Discharge Amount of Ammonia and Nitrogen	吨	ton	2312.66	2391.09
废水排放总量	Waste Water Discharged	万吨	10 000 tons	30654.75	63363.91

注：2020 年核算方法与 2019 年不同，年际间数据变化较大。
Note： The accounting method in 2020 is different from that in 2019, and the inter-year data changes greatly.

6-10　环境质量状况
ENVIRONMENT CONDITION

项目	Item	单位	Unit	2020 年	2019 年	2020 年比 2019 年增（+）减（-）% 2020 Compared to 2019 (+/-)
市区空气质量优良率	Urban air quality good rate	%	%	86.30	78.60	7.70
一、二类海水水质面积比例	The proportion of Grade Ⅰ and Ⅱ waters	%	%	98.80	98.80	0.00
市区区域环境噪声平均等效声级	The Average Equivalent Sound Level of the Urban Regional Environmental Noise	分贝（A）	db(A)	58.70	56.50	3.89
市区道路交通噪声平均等效声级	The Average Equivalent Sound Level of the Urban Road Traffic Noise	分贝（A）	db(A)	70.00	68.30	2.49

6-11 工业“三废”排放情况
DISCHARGE CONDITIONS OF INDUSTRIAL WASTE WATER, WASTE GAS AND SOLID WASTE

项目	Item	单位	Unit	2020 年	2019 年	2020 年比 2019 年增（+）减（-）% 2020 Compared to 2019 (+/–)
工业废水排放总量	Industrial Waste Water Discharged	万吨	10 000 tons	5695.03	5779.99	-1.47
废水治理设施数	Number of Facilities for Treatment of Waste Water	套	set	458	424	8.02
废水治理设施处理能力	Capacity of Facilities for Treatment of Waste Water	万吨 / 日	10 000 tons/day	42.44	39.55	7.30
进入城市污水处理厂量	Volume Handled by Sewage Treatment Plant	万吨	10 000 tons	4956.96	5050.93	-1.86
化学需氧量排放量	Discharge Amount of Chemical Oxygen Demand	吨	ton	2710.47	1536.06	76.46
氨氮排放量	Discharge Amount of Ammonia and Nitrogen	吨	ton	75.96	73.44	3.42
工业废气排放总量	Industrial Waste Air Discharged	万标立方米	10 000 cu.m	42059494.51	42925879.90	-2.02
废气治理设施数	Number of Facilities for Treatment of Waste Air	套	set	2417	2794	-13.49
其中：脱硫设施数	of which ： Desulphurization Facilities	套	set	194	285	-31.93
废气治理设施处理能力	Capacity of Facilities for Treatment of Waste Air	万标立方米 / 时	10 000 cu.m/hr	34454.43	14535.82	137.03
二氧化硫去除量	Sulphur Dioxide Removed	吨	ton	205478.96	205242.55	0.12
二氧化硫排放量	Sulphur Dioxide Emission	吨	ton	3316.69	3511.58	-5.55
烟（粉）尘排放量	Soot (Dust) Emission	吨	ton	5857.54	4744.57	23.46
工业固体废物产生量	Industrial Solid Wastes Produced	万吨	10 000 tons	734.64	839.18	-12.46
其中：危险废物	of which: Hazardous Wastes	吨	ton	176946.66	176843.17	0.06
工业固体废物综合利用量	Industrial Solid Wastes Comprehensive Utilized	万吨	10 000 tons	643.62	719.09	-10.50
工业固体废物排放量	Industrial Solid Wastes Discharged	万吨	10 000 tons	0	0	0.00
其中：危险废物	of which: Hazardous Wastes	吨	ton	0	0	0.00

主要统计指标解释

供水综合生产能力　指按供水设施取水、净化、送水、出厂输水干管等环节设计能力计算的综合生产能力。

年末供水管道长度　指从送水泵至用户水表之间所有管道的长度。不包括新安装尚未使用的管道。

用水普及率　指城市用水人口数与城市人口总数的比率。计算公式：

$$用水普及率=\frac{城市用水人口数}{城市人口总数}\times 100\%$$

全年供水总量　指报告期供水企业（单位）供出的全部水量。包括有效供水量和漏损水量。

全年供气总量　指全年燃气企业（单位）向用户供应的燃气数量。包括销售量和损失量。

用气普及率　指报告期末使用燃气的城市人口数与城市人口总数的比率。计算公式为：

$$用气普及率=\frac{城市用气人口数}{城市人口总数}\times 100\%$$

年末道路长度　指年末道路长度和与道路相通的广场、桥梁、隧道的长度，按车行道中心线计算。在统计时只统计路面宽度在3.5米（含3.5米）以上的各种铺装道路，包括开放型工业区和住宅区道路在内。

工业废气排放量　指报告期内企业厂区内燃料燃烧和生产工艺过程中产生的各种排入大气的含有污染物的气体的总量，以标准状态（273K，101325Pa）计算。

工业废水排放量　指经过企业厂区所有排放口排到企业外部的工业废水量。包括生产废水、外排的直接冷却水、超标排放的矿井地下水和与工业废水混排的厂区生活污水，不包括外排的间接冷却水（清污不分流的间接冷却水应计算在内）。

工业废水排放达标量　指各项指标都达到国家或地方排放标准的外排工业废水量，包括未经处理外排达标的和经过处理后外排达标的和两部分。国家排放标准见GB8978–88。

工业固体废物产生量　指企业在生产过程中产生的固体状、半固体状和高浓度液体状废弃物的总量，包括危险废物、冶炼废渣、粉煤灰、炉渣、煤矸渣、尾矿、放射性废物和其他废物等；不包括矿山开采的剥离废石和掘进废石（煤矸石和呈酸性或碱性的废石除外）酸性或碱性废石是指采掘的废石其流经水、雨淋水的pH值小于4或pH值大于10.5者。

工业粉尘排放量　指企业在生产工艺过程中排放的能在空气中悬浮一定时间的固体颗粒物排放量。如钢铁企业的耐火材料粉尘、焦化企业的筛焦系统粉尘、烧结机的粉尘、石灰窑的粉尘、建材企业的水泥粉尘等。不包括电厂排入大气的烟尘。

化学需氧量（COD）　测量有机和无机物质化学分解所消耗氧的质量浓度的水污染指数。

Explanatory Notes on Main Statistical Indicators

Production Capacity of Water Supply　refers to the designed comprehensive production capacity of water facilities, covering the 4 links of water collection, purification, conveyance, and outflow through trunk pipelines.

Length of Water Supply Pipelines at the Year-end refers to the total length of all the pipelines between the water pumps and the user water meters, excluding pipelines newly installed but not used yet.

Coverage Rate of Urban Population with Access to Tap Water refers to the ratio of the urban population with access to tap water to the total urban population. The formula is:

Coverage rate of urban population with access to tap water= (Urban population with access to tap water) / (Urban population) × 100%

Annual Volume of Water Supply refers to the total volume of water supplied by water-works (units) during the reference period, including both the effective water supply and loss during the water supply.

Annual Volume of Gas Supply refers to the total volume of gas provided to users by gas-producing enterprises (units) in a year, including the volume sold and the volume lost.

Coverage Rate of Urban Population with Access to Gas refers to the ratio of the urban population with access to gas to the total urban population at the end of the reference period. The formula is:

Coverage rate of urban population with access to gas= (Urban population with access to gas / Urban population) × 100%

Length of Paved Roads at the Year-end refers to the length of roads with paved surface including squares bridges and tunnels connected with roads by the end of the year.Length of the roads is measured by the central lines for vehicles for paved roads with a width of 3.5 meters and over, including roads in open-ended factory compounds and residential quarters.

Industrial Waste Air Emission refers to discharge into atmosphere of waste air containing pollutants generated from fuel burning and production process in enterprises within a given period of time. It is calculated at standard status (273K, 101,325Pa) .

Waste Water Discharged by Industry refers to the volume of waste water discharged by industrial enterprises through all their outlets, including waste water from production process, directly cooled water, groundwater from mining wells which does not meet discharge standards and sewage from households mixed with waste water produced by industrial activities, but excluding indirectly cooled water discharged (It should be included if the discharge is not separated with waste water) .

Industrial Waste Water Meeting Discharge Standards refers to volume of industrial waste water discharge which, with or without treatment, reaches national or local standards with regard to all pollutants. National Discharge standards query GB8978-88.

Industrial Solid Wastes Produced refers to total volume of solid, semi-solid and high concentration liquid residues produced by industrial enterprises from production process in a given period of time, including hazardous wastes, slag, coal ash, gangue, tailings, radioactive residues and other wastes, but excluding stones stripped or dug out in mining (gangue and acid or alkaline stones not included). A stone is acid or alkaline depending on the pH value of the water below 4 or above 10.5 when the stone is in, or soaked by, the water.

Industrial Dust Emission refers to volume of dust emitted by production process of enterprises and suspended in the air for a given period of time, including dust from refractory material of iron and steel works, dust from coke-screening systems and sintering machines of coke plants, dust from lime kilns and dust from cement production in building material enterprises, but excluding soot and dust emitted from power plants.

Chemical Oxygen Demand (COD) refers to index of water pollution measuring the mass concentration of oxygen consumed by the chemical breakdown of organic and inorganic matter.

能源消耗 7

CONSUMPTION OF ENERGY

简 要 说 明

一、本篇资料的主要内容

本篇资料主要反映了全市规模以上工业主要能源消费与库存情况，主要包括规模以上工业主要能源消费与库存、规模以上工业主要能源分行业消费量、重点耗能工业企业能源加工转换、规模以上工业主要能源工业消费量等方面的资料。

二、本篇资料的来源

本篇资料来源于规模以上工业能源统计年报，由市统计局能源统计处整理提供。

Brief Introduction

I. Main Content

Data in this chapter show the consumption and stock of major energy of industry above designated size, including consumption and stock of major energy of industry above designated size, major energy consumption of industry above designated size grouped by sector, energy conversion of major energy-consuming industrial enterprises and major energy consumption of industry above designated size, etc.

II. Source of Data

Data in this chapter are based on the annual report of energy consumed by industrial enterprises above designated size. The data are provided by the Division of Energy Statistics of Qingdao Municipal Bureau of Statistics.

7-1 规模以上工业主要能源消费与库存（2020 年）

CONSUMPTION AND STOCK OF MAJOR ENERGY OF INDUSTRY ABOVE DESIGNATED SIZE (2020)

名称	Name	计算单位	Unit	年初库存 Stock at Year-beginning	本年消费 Consumption in the Year	#工业 Industry	非工业 Non-industry	年末库存 Stock at Year-end
原煤	Raw Coal	吨	ton	1307974.83	10691880.7	10691880.7		971468
焦炭	Coke	吨	ton	2843.00	1556166.8	1556166.8		43842
焦炉煤气	Coking Gas	万立方米	10 000 cu.m		28132.0	28132.0		
高炉煤气	Blast Furnace Gas	万立方米	10 000 cu.m		604060.9	604060.9		
原油	Crude Oil	吨	ton	462418.00	13405046.0	13405046.0		444293
汽油	Petrol	吨	ton	731.40	37787.3	37787.3		1040
煤油	Kerosene	吨	ton		72.3	72.3		
柴油	Diesel Oil	吨	ton	1905.20	92065.4	92065.4		787
燃料油	Fuel Oil	吨	ton	10996.24	59317.9	59317.9		13177
液化石油气	Liquefied Petroleum Gas	吨	ton	4.20	103995.6	103995.6		8
炼厂干气	Refinery Dry Gas	吨	ton		404779.0	404779.0		
热力	Heat	百万千焦	million kJ		25908707.5	25908707.5		
电力	Electricity	万千瓦时	10 000kW · h		1837096.7	1837096.7		

补充资料：2020 年综合能源消费量 1366.9 万吨标准煤。

Supplementary Information：The comprehensive energy consumption in 2020 will be 13.669 million tons of standard coal.

7-2 规模以上工业主要能源分行业消费量（2020年）
MAJOR ENERGY CONSUMPTION OF INDUSTRY ABOVE DESIGNATED SIZE BY SECTOR (2020)

名称	Name	原煤（吨） Raw Coal (ton)	焦炭（吨） Coke (ton)	焦炉煤气（万立方米） Coking Gas (10 000 cu.m)	原油（吨） Crude Oil (ton)	汽油（吨） Petrol (ton)
总　计	**Total**	**10691881**	**1556167**	**28132**	**13405046**	**19830**
采掘业	Mining					
制造业	Manufacturing	1601915	1524500	7563	13405046	19163
电力煤气及水生产供应业	Production and Supply of Electricity, Gas and Water	9089966	31667	20569		667

7-2 续表
Continued

名称	Name	煤油（吨） Kerosene (ton)	柴油（吨） Diesel Oil (ton)	燃料油（吨） Fuel Oil (ton)	液化石油气（吨） Liquefied Petroleum Gas (ton)	热力（百万千焦） Heat (million kJ)	电力（万千瓦时） Electricity (10 000kW・h)
总　计	**Total**	**70**	**54941**	**54172**	**103344**	**25908708**	**1832818**
采掘业	Mining		157				4873
制造业	Manufacturing	70	53569	50617	103344	21828080	1593553
电力煤气及水生产供应业	Production and Supply of Electricity, Gas and Water		1216	3555		4080628	234391

7-3 重点耗能工业企业能源加工转换（2020年）
ENERGY CONVERSION OF MAJOR ENERGY-CONSUMING INDUSTRIAL ENTERPRISES (2020)

名称	Name	单位	Unit	能源消费合计 Total Energy Consumption	#加工转换投入 Conversion Input	火电 Thermal Power	供热 Heating	炼油 Petroleum Refining	制气 Gas Production	能源加工转换产出 Conversion Output of Energy
原　煤	Raw Coal	吨	ton	10139262	9541898	4956092	4559250		26556	
洗精煤	Dressing Coal	吨	ton	1806717	1806717					
煤制品	Coal Products	吨	ton	66691	66691		66691			
焦　炭	Coke	吨	ton	1555180	31974	3176	28798			1289859
其他焦化产品	Other Coking Products	吨	ton	69182						80347
焦炉煤气	Coking Gas	万立方米	10 000 cn.m	20569	20569	20569				28132
高炉煤气	Blast Furnace GAS	万立方米	10 000 cn.m	591921	198194	198194				
原　油	Crude Oil	吨	ton	13405046	13400557			13400557		
汽　油	Petrol	吨	ton	316						3707811
煤　油	Kerosene	吨	ton							1231708
柴　油	Diesel Oil	吨	ton	1440	210	195	15			3317933
燃料油	Fuel Oil	吨	ton	6069	5954	709	2731	2514		1218588
液化石油气	Liquefied Petroleum Gas	吨	ton							1028898
炼厂干气	Refinery Dry Gas	吨	ton	404779	2417	242	2175			404779
其他石油制品	Other Petroleum Products	吨	ton	1076671	650078			650078		1026787
热　力	Heat	百万千焦	million kJ	10127405	2950039	2950039				87666620
电　力	Electricity	万千瓦时	10 000kW·h	543152						1593193
其他燃料	Other Fuel	吨标准煤	ton SCE	7400	7400	1947	5453			
能源合计	**Total**	**吨标准煤**	**ton SCE**	**36673809**	**30382669**	**4779350**	**3756916**	**20104985**	**25037**	**25891141**

7-4 规模以上工业主要能源工业消费量（2020 年）
MAJOR ENERGY CONSUMPTION OF INDUSTRY ABOVE DESIGNATED SIZE (2020)

行业	Sector
总　计	**Total**
煤炭开采和洗选业	Mining and Washing of Coal
石油和天然气开采业	Extraction of Petroleum and Natural Gas
黑色金属矿采选业	Mining of Ferrous Metal Ores
有色金属矿采选业	Mining of Non-ferrous Metal Ores
非金属矿采选业	Mining and Processing of Nonmetal Ores
开采辅助活动	Auxiliary Activities of Mining
其他采矿业	Mining of Other Ores
农副食品加工业	Processing of Food from Agricultural Products
食品制造业	Manufacture of Foods
酒、饮料和精制茶制造业	Manufacture of Liquor, Beverage and Refined Tea
烟草制品业	Manufacture of Tobacco
纺织业	Manufacture of Textile
纺织服装、服饰业	Manufacture of Textile Wearing Apparel
皮革、毛皮、羽毛及其制品和制鞋业	Manufacture of Leather, Fur, Feather &Its Products Footwear
木材加工和木、竹、藤、棕、草制品业	Processing of Timbers, Manufacture of Wood, Bamboo, Rattan, Palm and Straw Products
家具制造业	Manufacture of Furniture
造纸和纸制品业	Manufacture of Paper and Paper Products
印刷和记录媒介复制业	Printing, Reproduction of Recording Media
文教、工美、体育和娱乐用品制造业	Manufacture of Articles for Culture, Arts& Crafts, Sports and Entertainment
石油加工、炼焦和核燃料加工业	Processing of Petroleum, Coking, Processing of Nucleus Fuel
化学原料和化学制品制造业	Manufacture of Chemical Raw Material and Chemical Products
医药制造业	Manufacture of Medicines
化学纤维制造业	Manufacture of Chemical Fiber
橡胶和塑料制品业	Manufacture of Rubber and Plastic
非金属矿物制品业	Manufacture of Non-metallic Mineral Products
黑色金属冶炼和压延加工业	Smelting and Pressing of Ferrous Metals
有色金属冶炼和压延加工业	Smelting and Pressing of Non-ferrous Metals
金属制品业	Manufacture of Metal Products
通用设备制造业	Manufacture of General Purpose Machinery
专用设备制造业	Manufacture of Special Purpose Machinery
汽车制造业	Manufacture of Vehicle
铁路、船舶、航空航天和其他运输设备制造业	Manufacture of Transport Equipment for Railway, Shipping, Aerospace and other uses
电气机械和器材制造业	Manufacture of Electrical Machinery &Equipment
计算机、通信和其他电子设备制造业	Manufacture of Computer, Communication Equipment and Other Electronic Equipment
仪器仪表制造业	Manufacture of Measuring Instrument
其他制造业	Manufacture of Other Products
废弃资源综合利用业	Recycling and Disposal of Waste Resources
金属制品、机械和设备修理业	Manufacture of Metal Products, Machinery and Equipment
电力、热力生产和供应业	Production and Supply of Electric Power and Heat Power
燃气生产和供应业	Production and Supply of Gas
水的生产和供应业	Production and Supply of Water

原煤（吨）Raw Coal (ton)	洗精煤（吨）Dressing Coal (ton)	其他洗煤（吨）Other Dressing Coal (ton)	煤制品（吨）Coal Products (ton)	焦炭（吨）Coke (ton)
10691881	**1806717**	**41118**	**66691**	**1556167**
110160				1686
39509				
13442				
10				
8004				
21261				
510184		41118		
119718				307
185549				430
593577	1806717			1521520
36				557
12				
12				
428				
12				
9089966			66691	31667

7-4 续表 1
Continued

行业	Sector
总　　计	**Total**
煤炭开采和洗选业	Mining and Washing of Coal
石油和天然气开采业	Extraction of Petroleum and Natural Gas
黑色金属矿采选业	Mining of Ferrous Metal Ores
有色金属矿采选业	Mining of Non-ferrous Metal Ores
非金属矿采选业	Mining and Processing of Nonmetal Ores
开采辅助活动	Auxiliary Activities of Mining
其他采矿业	Mining of Other Ores
农副食品加工业	Processing of Food from Agricultural Products
食品制造业	Manufacture of Foods
酒、饮料和精制茶制造业	Manufacture of Liquor, Beverage and Refined Tea
烟草制品业	Manufacture of Tobacco
纺织业	Manufacture of Textile
纺织服装、服饰业	Manufacture of Textile Wearing Apparel
皮革、毛皮、羽毛及其制品和制鞋业	Manufacture of Leather, Fur, Feather &Its Products Footwear
木材加工和木、竹、藤、棕、草制品业	Processing of Timbers, Manufacture of Wood, Bamboo, Rattan, Palm and Straw Products
家具制造业	Manufacture of Furniture
造纸和纸制品业	Manufacture of Paper and Paper Products
印刷和记录媒介复制业	Printing, Reproduction of Recording Media
文教、工美、体育和娱乐用品制造业	Manufacture of Articles for Culture, Arts& Crafts, Sports and Entertainment
石油加工、炼焦和核燃料加工业	Processing of Petroleum, Coking, Processing of Nucleus Fuel
化学原料和化学制品制造业	Manufacture of Chemical Raw Material and Chemical Products
医药制造业	Manufacture of Medicines
化学纤维制造业	Manufacture of Chemical Fiber
橡胶和塑料制品业	Manufacture of Rubber and Plastic
非金属矿物制品业	Manufacture of Non-metallic Mineral Products
黑色金属冶炼和压延加工业	Smelting and Pressing of Ferrous Metals
有色金属冶炼和压延加工业	Smelting and Pressing of Non-ferrous Metals
金属制品业	Manufacture of Metal Products
通用设备制造业	Manufacture of General Purpose Machinery
专用设备制造业	Manufacture of Special Purpose Machinery
汽车制造业	Manufacture of Vehicle
铁路、船舶、航空航天和其他运输设备制造业	Manufacture of Transport Equipment for Railway, Shipping, Aerospace and other uses
电气机械和器材制造业	Manufacture of Electrical Machinery &Equipment
计算机、通信和其他电子设备制造业	Manufacture of Computer, Communication Equipment and Other Electronic Equipment
仪器仪表制造业	Manufacture of Measuring Instrument
其他制造业	Manufacture of Other Products
废弃资源综合利用业	Recycling and Disposal of Waste Resources
金属制品、机械和设备修理业	Manufacture of Metal Products, Machinery and Equipment
电力、热力生产和供应业	Production and Supply of Electric Power and Heat Power
燃气生产和供应业	Production and Supply of Gas
水的生产和供应业	Production and Supply of Water

焦炉煤气（万立方米）Coking Gas (10 000 cu.m)	高炉煤气（万立方米）Blast Furnace GAS (10 000 cu.m)	原油（吨）Crude Oil (ton)	汽油（吨）Petrol (ton)	煤油（吨）Kerosene (ton)
28132	**604061**	**13405046**	**19969**	**70**
			1357	
			472	
			98	
			553	
			611	
			165	
			9	
			97	
			185	
			857	
			419	
		13405046	57	
			893	
			271	
			11	
			1422	
7563	12140		656	
	393727		42	
			55	
			1283	6
			2104	60
			2017	
			1738	1
			1699	3
			901	
			493	
			773	
			63	
20569	198194		108	
			262	
			297	

7-4 续表 2
Continued

行业	Sector
总　计	**Total**
煤炭开采和洗选业	Mining and Washing of Coal
石油和天然气开采业	Extraction of Petroleum and Natural Gas
黑色金属矿采选业	Mining of Ferrous Metal Ores
有色金属矿采选业	Mining of Non-ferrous Metal Ores
非金属矿采选业	Mining and Processing of Nonmetal Ores
开采辅助活动	Auxiliary Activities of Mining
其他采矿业	Mining of Other Ores
农副食品加工业	Processing of Food from Agricultural Products
食品制造业	Manufacture of Foods
酒、饮料和精制茶制造业	Manufacture of Liquor, Beverage and Refined Tea
烟草制品业	Manufacture of Tobacco
纺织业	Manufacture of Textile
纺织服装、服饰业	Manufacture of Textile Wearing Apparel
皮革、毛皮、羽毛及其制品和制鞋业	Manufacture of Leather, Fur, Feather &Its Products Footwear
木材加工和木、竹、藤、棕、草制品业	Processing of Timbers, Manufacture of Wood, Bamboo, Rattan, Palm and Straw Products
家具制造业	Manufacture of Furniture
造纸和纸制品业	Manufacture of Paper and Paper Products
印刷和记录媒介复制业	Printing, Reproduction of Recording Media
文教、工美、体育和娱乐用品制造业	Manufacture of Articles for Culture, Arts& Crafts, Sports and Entertainment
石油加工、炼焦和核燃料加工业	Processing of Petroleum, Coking, Processing of Nucleus Fuel
化学原料和化学制品制造业	Manufacture of Chemical Raw Material and Chemical Products
医药制造业	Manufacture of Medicines
化学纤维制造业	Manufacture of Chemical Fiber
橡胶和塑料制品业	Manufacture of Rubber and Plastic
非金属矿物制品业	Manufacture of Non-metallic Mineral Products
黑色金属冶炼和压延加工业	Smelting and Pressing of Ferrous Metals
有色金属冶炼和压延加工业	Smelting and Pressing of Non-ferrous Metals
金属制品业	Manufacture of Metal Products
通用设备制造业	Manufacture of General Purpose Machinery
专用设备制造业	Manufacture of Special Purpose Machinery
汽车制造业	Manufacture of Vehicle
铁路、船舶、航空航天和其他运输设备制造业	Manufacture of Transport Equipment for Railway, Shipping, Aerospace and other uses
电气机械和器材制造业	Manufacture of Electrical Machinery &Equipment
计算机、通信和其他电子设备制造业	Manufacture of Computer, Communication Equipment and Other Electronic Equipment
仪器仪表制造业	Manufacture of Measuring Instrument
其他制造业	Manufacture of Other Products
废弃资源综合利用业	Recycling and Disposal of Waste Resources
金属制品、机械和设备修理业	Manufacture of Metal Products, Machinery and Equipment
电力、热力生产和供应业	Production and Supply of Electric Power and Heat Power
燃气生产和供应业	Production and Supply of Gas
水的生产和供应业	Production and Supply of Water

柴油 （吨） Diesel Oil (ton)	燃料油 （吨） Fuel Oil (ton)	液化石油气 （吨） Liquefied Petroleum Gas (ton)	炼厂干气 （吨） Refinery Dry Gas (ton)
55015	**54172**	**103344**	**404779**
157			
2072	545	607	
750		75	
168		262	
209		1035	
343		2	
293	395		
41			
175			
489			
1112	561		
346			
120	2514		404779
2216	506	99704	
126			
26			
1808	252	251	
29471	45156	731	
84		2	
530			
2063	62	352	
1222		44	
885			
3318		8	
4240	627	21	
616		229	
824		21	
17		1	
77			
1073	3555		
22			
121			

7-4 续表 3
Continued

行业	Sector
总　计	**Total**
煤炭开采和洗选业	Mining and Washing of Coal
石油和天然气开采业	Extraction of Petroleum and Natural Gas
黑色金属矿采选业	Mining of Ferrous Metal Ores
有色金属矿采选业	Mining of Non-ferrous Metal Ores
非金属矿采选业	Mining and Processing of Nonmetal Ores
开采辅助活动	Auxiliary Activities of Mining
其他采矿业	Mining of Other Ores
农副食品加工业	Processing of Food from Agricultural Products
食品制造业	Manufacture of Foods
酒、饮料和精制茶制造业	Manufacture of Liquor, Beverage and Refind Tea
烟草制品业	Manufacture of Tobacco
纺织业	Manufacture of Textile
纺织服装、服饰业	Manufacture of Textil Wearing Apparel
皮革、毛皮、羽毛及其制品和制鞋业	Manufacture of Leather, Fur, Feathre&Its Products Footwear
木材加工和木、竹、藤、棕、草制品业	Processing of Timbers, Manufacture of Wood, Bamboo, Rattan, Palm and Straw Products
家具制造业	Manufacture of Furniture
造纸和纸制品业	Manufacture of Paper and Paper Products
印刷和记录媒介复制业	Printing, Reproduction of Recording Media
文教、工美、体育和娱乐用品制造业	Manufacture of Articles for Culture, Arts& Crafts, Sports and Entertainment
石油加工、炼焦和核燃料加工业	Processing of Petroleum, Coking, Processing of Nucleus Fuel
化学原料和化学制品制造业	Manufacture of Chemical Raw Material and Chemical Products
医药制造业	Manufacture of Medicines
化学纤维制造业	Manufacture of Chemical Fiber
橡胶和塑料制品业	Manufacture of Rubber and Plastic
非金属矿物制品业	Manufacture of Non-metallic Mineral Products
黑色金属冶炼和压延加工业	Smelting and Pressing of Ferrous Metals
有色金属冶炼和压延加工业	Smelting and Pressing of Non-ferrous Metals
金属制品业	Manufacture of Metal Products
通用设备制造业	Manufacture of General Purpose Machinery
专用设备制造业	Manufacture of Special Purpose Machinery
汽车制造业	Manufacture of Vehicle
铁路、船舶、航空航天和其他运输设备制造业	Manufacture of Transport Equipment for Railway, Shipping, Aerospace and other uses
电气机械和器材制造业	Manufacture of Electrical Machinery &Equipment
计算机、通信和其他电子设备制造业	Manufacture of Computer, Communication Equipment and Other Electronic Equipment
仪器仪表制造业	Manufacture of Measuring Instrument
其他制造业	Manufacture of Other Products
废弃资源综合利用业	Recycling and Disposal of Waste Resources
金属制品、机械和设备修理业	Manufacture of Metal Products, Machinery and Equipment
电力、热力生产和供应业	Production and Supply of Electric Power and Heat Power
燃气生产和供应业	Production and Supply of Gas
水的生产和供应业	Production and Supply of Water

其他油制品 （吨） Other Petroleum Products (ton)	热力 （百万千焦） Heat (million kJ)	电力 （万千瓦时） Electricity (10 000kW · h)	其他燃料 （吨标准煤） Other Fuel (ton SCE)
1082631	**25908708**	**1833699**	**10147**
		3145	
		1728	
	2753759	83131	8981
	478298	37328	
	2070546	19882	
	1667600	38102	2
	337406	11781	874
	50361	8049	133
		2853	
		7544	
	538301	10231	
	52368	13239	
	2210	16359	
1048678	2539	115180	
33863	6444051	214225	
	334246	17601	
	14228	4657	
	3184140	177374	
	58633	100769	
	1952042	202760	
	33492	21341	
11	63528	77374	126
69	82819	70124	4
	95872	31875	26
	549783	116666	
12	780378	61649	
	270874	69340	
	10607	57556	
		3437	
		2769	
		534	
		730	
	3980553	178827	
	100074	11148	
		44391	

主要统计指标解释

工业企业能源消费量　工业企业能源消费包括工业企业在生产过程中作为燃料、动力、原料、辅助材料使用的能源以及工艺用能、非生产用能；作为能源加工转换企业，还要包括能源加工转换的投入量。工业企业能源消费量具体包括：

（1）用于本企业产品生产、工业性作业和其他生产性活动的能源。

（2）用于技术更新改造措施、新技术研究和新产品试制以及科学试验等方面的能源。

（3）用于经营维修、建筑及设备大修理、机电设备和交通运输工具等方面的能源。

（4）用于劳动保护的能源。

（5）其他非生产消费的能源。

不包括：

（1）由仓库发到车间，但在报告期最后一天没有消费的能源。这部分能源应在办理假退料手续后计入库存量。

（2）拨到外单位，委托外单位加工用的能源。

（3）调出本单位或借给外单位的能源。

工业生产能源消费　是指工业企业为进行工业生产活动所使用的能源。主要包括：

1. 用于本企业产品生产、工业性作业的能源，包括用作原料、材料、燃料、动力：作为能源加工转换企业，还包括用作加工转换的能源。

2. 产品生产过程中作为辅助材料使用的能源。

3. 生产工艺过程使用的能源。

4. 新技术研究、新产品试制、科学试验使用的能源。

5. 为了工业生产活动而在进行的各种修理过程中使用的能源。

6. 生产区内的劳动保护用能等。

Explanatory Notes on Main Statistical Indicators

Energy Consumption of Industrial Enterprises　include energy in the production process as fuel, power, raw materials, supplementary materials, and for use of technology and non–production. As energy processing and conversion enterprises, also include energy processing and conversion of inputs. These specifically include：1. Energy for the enterprise product, industrial production operations and other activities. 2. Energy for technical upgrading measures and new technology research and new product production and scientific experiments. 3. Energy for operation maintenance, construction and equipment overhaul, electrical and mechanical equipment and transport, and other aspects. 4. Energy for the protection of labor. 5. Energy for Other non–production and consumption. And these exclude: 1. Energy from the warehouse to the workshop, but out of consumption on the last day of the reporting period. This part of the energy should leave retreat materials handling procedures included stock. 2. Energy transferred to other units, entrusted with the processing. 3. Energy transferred out of the unit or loans to other units.

Energy Consumption for Industrial Production　refers to energy for industrial enterprises in industrial production activities. These mainly include: 1. Energy for the enterprise products, industrial operations, including energy as raw materials, materials, fuels, and power. As energy processing and conversion enterprises, also include energy for processing and conversion. 2. Energy as supplementary material in product process. 3. Energy used in production process. 4. Energy for new technologies, new product production, and scientific experiment. 5. Energy in process of repairing for industrial production activities. 6. Energy for labor protection in production areas and so on.

8 财政、金融和保险业

GOVERNMENT FINANCE, FINANCIAL AND INSURANCE

简要说明

一、本篇资料的主要内容

本篇资料主要反映了全市财政收支、金融和保险方面的情况，主要包括财政收入、财政支出、金融机构存贷款、保险业务开展等方面的资料。

二、本篇资料的来源

1. 财政部分的资料来源于市财政局。

2. 金融方面的资料来源于中国人民银行青岛市中心支行。

3. 保险方面的资料来源于中国银行保险监督管理委员会青岛监管局。

本篇资料由市统计局国民经济核算处整理提供。

Brief Introduction

I. Main Content

Data in this chapter mainly reflects the city´s fiscal revenue and expenditure, finance and insurance, mainly including fiscal revenue, fiscal expenditure, deposits and loans of financial institutions, and insurance business development.

II. Source of Data

1. The financial information comes from the Qingdao Municipal Finance Bureau.

2. The financial information comes from the Qingdao City Center Branch of the People´s Bank of China.

3. The insurance information comes from the Qingdao Supervision Bureau of the China Banking and Insurance Regulatory Commission.

The data in this article is compiled and provided by the National Economic Accounting Office of Qingdao Statistics Bureau.

8-1 主要年份地方财政收支

MAJOR YEAR´S REVENUE AND EXPENDITURE OF LOCAL GOVERNMENT FINANCE

单位：万元 (10 000 yuan)

年份 Year	财政收入 Revenue of Government Finance	财政支出 Expenditure of Government Finance
1949	1527	306
1952	19809	2226
1957	29875	3556
1962	32869	4327
1965	47682	6280
1970	95778	7825
1975	90220	11966
1978	130749	19427
1980	124835	20064
1985	165155	41996
1988	201206	93931
1990	242303	133875
1991	259377	137716
1992	275589	155696
1993	182348	211938
1994	227490	277331
1995	294771	376982
1996	379674	469569
1997	476804	564787
1998	580434	678575
1999	680089	740937
2000	800120	878702
2001	987080	1097848
2002	1006616	1243880
2003	1201398	1471747
2004	1305136	1646214
2005	1763412	2030622
2006	2257663	2367875
2007	2925798	3211777
2008	3424359	3694111
2009	3769896	4335754
2010	4526138	5323888
2011	5661400	6580605
2012	6701820	7659801
2013	7889313	10142273
2014	8952450	10747138
2015	10063220	12228664
2016	11000303	13528516
2017	11572389	14030252
2018	12319138	15597764
2019	12417359	15759729
2020	12538548	15846485

注：1. 1993 年以后实行新制度，财政收入数与历年不可比。
2. 2002 年以后，财政收入、支出为一般预算数。

Note：1. Since 1993, new regulations have been adopted in calculating revenue of government finance, the figures are not comparable with those over the years.
2. Since 2002, revenue of government finance and expenditure of government finance refer to general budgetary revenue and expenditure.

8-2 分市、区公共财政预算收入（2020年）
PUBLIC FINANCE BUDGET REVENUE BY CITY AND DISTRICT (2020)

单位：万元 (10 000 yuan)

市、区名称	Region	一般公共预算收入 Public Finance Budget Revenue	#增值税 Value-added Tax	#营业税 Business Tax	#企业所得税 Enterprise Income Tax
全　市	**Whole Municipality**	**12538548**	**3312788**		**1539747**
市南区	Shinan District	856962	269209		131791
市北区	Shibei District	920506	249642		134423
李沧区	Licang District	1005120	150405		58891
崂山区	Laoshan District	1618049	420412		333017
西海岸新区	West Coast New Area	2672048	753185		362417
黄岛区	Huangdao District	2570155	722727		324836
保税港区	Qingdao Free Trade Port Area of China	101893	30458		37581
城阳区	Chengyang District	1552146	470828		192707
城阳区（不含高新区）	Chengyang District (Excluding High tech District)	1209567	377528		138633
高新区	High tech District	342579	93300		54074
即墨区	Jimo District	1120246	293702		93618
胶州市	Jiaozhou	1031557	282642		88380
平度市	Pingdu	609592	138962		37026
莱西市	Laixi	545041	248901		41370

8-2 续表
Continued

单位：万元 (10 000 yuan)

市、区名称	Region	# 个人所得税 Personal Income Tax	# 城市维护建设税 Urban Maintenance and Development Tax	# 基金预算收入 Funds Budgetary Revenue
全　市	**Whole Municipality**	**453663**	**583943**	**11699068**
市南区	Shinan District	74182	40142	
市北区	Shibei District	34572	50154	
李沧区	Licang District	17055	26821	
崂山区	Laoshan District	100564	108035	1309282
西海岸新区	West Coast New Area	85839	138967	2389534
黄岛区	Huangdao District	82338	133739	2380525
保税港区	Qingdao Free Trade Port Area of China	3501	5228	9009
城阳区	Chengyang District	43283	69569	1335407
城阳区（不含高新区）	Chengyang District (Excluding High tech District)	32394	53951	1101727
高新区	High tech District	10889	15618	233680
即墨区	Jimo District	18395	47917	1652793
胶州市	Jiaozhou	28997	42664	1352852
平度市	Pingdu	8853	21749	343731
莱西市	Laixi	41923	37925	284767

8-3 分市、区公共财政预算支出（2020年）
PUBLIC FINANCE BUDGET REVENUE BY CITY AND DISTRICT (2020)

单位：万元 (10 000 yuan)

市、区名称	Region	一般公共预算支出 Public Finance Budget Revenue	#一般公共服务支出 General Public Services	#公共安全 Public Security	#教育 Education	#科学技术 Science and Technology	#文化体育与传媒 Culture, Sport and Media
全　市	**Whole Municipality**	**15846485**	**1993899**	**959049**	**2885546**	**468514**	**284622**
市南区	Shinan District	511823	56196	20745	109010	9840	2942
市北区	Shibei District	669046	129876	25472	173106	35621	5573
李沧区	Licang District	755600	84582	19214	148588	17501	6414
崂山区	Laoshan District	1147455	118143	39952	171207	85090	6682
西海岸新区	West Coast New Area	2281233	473149	82942	524594	84577	36262
黄岛区	Huangdao District	2223449	433990	82671	524578	83031	36262
保税港区	Qingdao Free Trade Port Area of China	57784	39159	271	16	1546	0
城阳区	Chengyang District	1318772	162593	41477	283146	93150	11309
城阳区（不含高新区）	Chengyang District (Excluding High tech District)	1005717	131142	37748	260528	57978	11116
高新区	High tech District	313055	31451	3729	22618	35172	193
即墨区	Jimo District	1282052	178910	41361	318139	14161	20859
胶州市	Jiaozhou	1231048	175630	67106	291435	20485	19518
平度市	Pingdu	1157299	107832	40007	294765	11231	9153
莱西市	Laixi	813356	79362	27870	135174	2409	8338

8-3 续表
Continued

单位：万元 (10 000 yuan)

市、区名称	Region	#社会保障和就业 Social Security and Employment	#医疗卫生 Health Care	#节能环保 Environment Protection	#城乡社区事务 Urban and Rural Community Affairs	#农林水事务 Affairs of Agriculture Forest and Irrigation	#基金预算支出 Funds Budgetary Expenditure
全　市	**Whole Municipality**	**2230004**	**1039257**	**209024**	**2365875**	**829448**	**15202243**
市南区	Shinan District	83834	33969	9466	124785	5130	216819
市北区	Shibei District	120494	35178	7304	95783	2430	452287
李沧区	Licang District	73942	29623	8465	333262	4288	416878
崂山区	Laoshan District	64297	45149	5244	276704	66609	1126764
西海岸新区	West Coast New Area	315460	148754	30574	127438	116551	3186191
黄岛区	Huangdao District	311737	148669	30521	125909	116551	3178636
保税港区	Qingdao Free Trade Port Area of China	3723	85	53	1529		7555
城阳区	Chengyang District	104307	82761	7704	193998	53250	1768520
城阳区（不含高新区）	Chengyang District (Excluding High tech District)	88067	76311	6779	152620	49258	1417238
高新区	High tech District	16240	6450	925	41378	3992	351282
即墨区	Jimo District	202249	84297	11693	169212	86472	2006266
胶州市	Jiaozhou	136709	99471	30166	158089	85543	2111471
平度市	Pingdu	225252	109043	11731	80435	170109	481514
莱西市	Laixi	169292	71302	12736	60051	67980	524995

8-4 主要年份金融系统人民币存贷款（年末余额）

MAJOR YEAR'S DEPOSITS AND LOANS OF FINANCIAL INSTITUTIONS (YEAR-END BALANCE)

单位：万元 (10 000 yuan)

年份 Year	存款合计 Total Deposits	#企业存款 Deposits by Enterprises	#储蓄存款 Savings Deposits	贷款合计 Total Loans
1949	693	239	28	278
1952	9093	4308	1838	3322
1957	10372	3359	4037	30690
1962	20040	8579	3279	73601
1965	27331	11830	6347	64555
1970	38264	13024	7576	126382
1975	60622	22568	15637	207006
1978	66523	21004	21455	297184
1980	120644	38105	38609	379666
1985	344760	99736	155604	452142
1990	1235562	321542	655895	1535751
1991	1553564	411417	824428	1871462
1992	2076667	612868	1044165	2352449
1993	2747294	835617	1372239	2940658
1994	3769019	1399110	1918734	3610564
1995	5324026	2030382	2687888	4777864
1996	6991289	2630958	3499219	5941281
1997	7385092	2885632	4060259	6508776
1998	8183471	3018063	4591012	7239231
1999	9160001	3454570	4978045	8945730
2000	10560624	4386316	5353215	9564293
2001	12323942	4955336	6187409	10798871
2002	15225733	5819655	7449408	13044792
2003	18920868	7027227	9084693	16783917
2004	22462592	7924690	10894941	18472613
2005	26975372	8226661	13431016	20394792
2006	32453583	10144296	15676197	25779442
2007	38915882	13213434	17020383	30970553
2008	47353803	14641948	21233637	37483209
2009	63019764	21001185	25278658	48735326
2010	76592065	27271963	29123256	58862263
2011	86384994	49189415	31985099	69477500
2012	94348924	50978985	37576007	79465532
2013	109695588	60367185	41405946	88607439
2014	113703085	60791933	44358964	97200532
2015	125330268	45526577	50235905	107718528
2016	140071344	50912759	53263262	118916821
2017	143877550	53835435	53941843	132647913
2018	155321863	57270448	59137089	151941934
2019	172829678	66873600	67552370	173318261
2020	198218001	76209031	80309469	202109625

注：本表数据来源于人民银行，自2015年起，人民银行报表指标变化，企业存款指标暂用非金融企业存款，储蓄存款指标暂用住户存款，口径与以前年度不一致。

Note: The data in this table comes from the People' s Bank of China. Since 2015, the report index of the People's Bank of China has changed, the enterprise deposit index is temporarily used as the deposit of the enterprise, the savings deposit index is temporarily used for household deposit, the caliber is not consistent with the previous year.

8-5　金融系统人民币存贷款（年末余额）
DEPOSITS AND LOANS OF FINANCIAL INSTITUTIONS (YEAR-END BALANCE)

单位：万元 (10 000 yuan)

项目	Item	2020 年	比年初增减数 Incremental/Reductions Compared to the Beginning of the Year
一、存款总计	Total Deposits	198218001	25388323
住户存款	Household Deposits	80309469	12757099
非金融企业存款	Non-Financial Corporate Deposits	76209031	9335431
广义政府存款	General Government Deposits	30870969	-209922
非银行业金融机构存款	Non-Banking Financial Institutions' s Deposits	10317001	3461321
二、贷款总计	Total Loans	202109625	28791364
住户贷款	Household Loans	66447003	9532000
# 短期贷款	Short-Term Loans	7844517	2325929
中长期贷款	Medium And Long-Term Loans	58602486	7206071
非金融企业及机关团体贷款	Non-Financial Enterprises And Institutions/ Organizations' Loans	135450447	19332506
# 短期贷款	Short-Term Loans	41308176	5577051
中长期贷款	Medium&Long-term Loans	84836166	12426534
票据融资	Notes Financing	7889098	1184158
非银行业金融机构贷款	Non-Banking Financial Institution' s Loans		-19852

注：自 2015 年起，人民银行报表中指标发生变化，本表数据按照新指标提供。

Note: Since 2015, the indexes in the People' s Bank of China' s statements have changed, the data in the table are provided according to the new indexes.

8-6 国内保险业务（2000-2020 年）
DOMESTIC INSURANCE BUSINESS (2000-2020)

项目	Item	2000 年	2005 年	2009 年	2010 年	2011 年
风险保障金额	**Total domestic insurance Value**	**38357485**	**91691581**	**293519697**	**309244255**	**380829634**
国内业务收入	**Domestic Business Income**	**220780**	**495701**	**1153101**	**1538526**	**1457269**
1. 保费收入	Premium Income	218714	495701	1153101	1538526	1457269
# 财产险	Property Insurance	85161	159746	339314	492190	556257
农业险	Agriculture Insurance	18	12	4066	3261	3587
人身险	Personal Insurance	133535	335943	809721	1043075	897425
国内业务支出	**Domestic Business Expenditure**	**94877**	**214148**	**476377**	**497832**	**463751**
1 . 赔款支出	Indemnity Expenditure	62275	111385	219546	279019	307564
# 财产险	Property Insurance	58361	92700	188723	250966	286214
农业险	Agriculture Insurance	5	11	3452	2808	1087
人身险	Personal Insurance	3909	18674	27371	25245	20263
2 . 给付支出	Mature Payment	27955	32739	123056	109318	156188
3 . 退保	Surrender	4647	70024	133775	109496	69275

注：本表由青岛银保监局提供，风险保障金额 2012 年之前为国内保险总值。

Note: This table is provided by Qingdao Banking and Insurance Regulatory Bureau. The amount of risk protection before 2012 is the total value of domestic insurance.

单位：万元 (10 000 yuan)

2012 年	2013 年	2014 年	2015 年	2016 年	2017 年	2018 年	2019 年	2020 年
447476690	**491953749**	**611632799**	**836499657**	**1687559828**	**2232390824**	**2337365406**	**2759993215**	**3149621411**
1602881	**1789854**	**2031421**	**2441172**	**3359013**	**3967170**	**4393970**	**4868673**	**5183142**
1602881	1789854	2031421	2441172	3359013	3967170	4393970	4868673	5183142
644269	744470	872805	920229	1046908	1062116	1269489	1243160	1451301
5046	6824	8395	12100	12734	15670	18043	24523	28263
953566	1038560	1150220	1508843	2299371	2889384	3106438	3600989	3703578
592167	**757404**	**1031415**	**1236281**	**1522375**	**1704218**	**1919252**	**1882881**	**1788966**
360085	432494	492693	539320	681211	733493	917964	937025	1045920
328877	392860	442168	492573	526586	554513	756987	706639	831317
1833	3820	5519	9724	16337	18232	10985	14019	24474
29375	35814	45006	37023	138288	160749	149992	216368	190129
154922	194592	274790	340786	455300	470266	493511	498555	379492
77159	130318	263932	356175	376777	500459	507777	447301	363553

主要统计指标解释

财政收入 指国家财政参与社会产品分配所取得的收入，是实现国家职能的财力保证。财政收入所包括的内容几经变化，目前主要包括：

（1）税收收入：包括增值税、营业税、企业所得税、个人所得税、资源税、城市维护建设税、房产税、印花税、城镇土地使用税、土地增值税、车船税、耕地占用税、契税、烟叶税、其他税收收入。

（2）非税收入：包括专项收入、行政事业性收费收入、罚没收入、国有资本经营收入、国有资源有偿使用收入、捐赠收入、政府住房基金收入、其他收入。

财政支出 国家财政将筹集起来的资金进行分配使用，以满足经济建设和各项事业的需要，主要包括：

（1）一般公共服务支出：反映政府提供一般公共服务的支出。

（2）公共安全：反映政府维护社会公共安全方面的支出，有关事务包括武装警察、公安、国家安全、检察、法院、司法行政、监狱、劳教、国家保密、缉私警察等。

（3）教育支出：反映政府教育事务支出。有关具体教育事务包括教育行政管理、学前教育、小学教育、初中教育、普通高中教育、普通高等教育、初等职业教育、中专教育、技校教育、职业高中教育、高等职业教育、广播电视教育、留学生教育、特殊教育、干部继续教育、教育机关服务等。

（4）科学技术：反映政府用于科学技术方面的支出。

（5）文化体育与传媒：反映政府在文化、文物、体育、广播电视、新闻出版等方面的支出。

（6）社会保障和就业：反映政府在社会保障与就业方面的支出。有关事项包括社会保障与就业管理事务、民政管理事务、财政对社会保险基金的补助、补充全国社会保障基金、行政事业单位离退休、企业改革补助、就业补助、抚恤、退役安置、社会福利、残疾人事业、城市居民最低生活保障、其他城镇社会救济、农村社会救济、自然灾害生活补助、红十字事务等。

（7）医疗卫生支出：反映政府医疗卫生方面的支出。具体包括医疗卫生管理事务支出、医疗服务支出、医疗保障支出、疾病预防控制支出、卫生监督支出、妇幼保健支出、农村卫生支出等。

（8）环境保护：反映政府环境保护支出。具体包括：环境保护管理事务支出、环境监测与监察支出、污染治理支出、自然生态保护支出、天然林保护工程支出、退耕还林支出、风沙荒漠治理支出、退牧还草支出、已垦草原退耕还草支出。

（9）城乡社区事务：反映政府城乡社区事务支出。具体包括：城乡社区管理事务支出、城乡社区规划与管理支出、城乡社区公共设施支出、城乡社区住宅支出、城乡社区环境卫生支出、建设市场管理与监督支出等。

（10）农林水事务：反映政府农林水事务方面的支出。具体包括农业、林业、水利、扶贫支出、农业综合开发支出等。

存款 指企业、机关、团体或居民根据资金必须收回的原则，把货币资金存入银行或其他信贷机构保管并取得一定利息的一种信用活动形式。根据存款对象或性质的不同可划分为住户存款、非金融企业存款、财政性存款、机关团体存款、非银行业金融机构存款等科目。它是银行信贷资金的主要来源。

贷款 指银行或其他信贷机构根据资金必须归还的原则，按一定利率，为企业、个人等提供资金的一种信用活动形式。我国银行贷款分为短期贷款、中长期贷款、融资租赁、票据融资、各项垫款等。

保费 指投保人为取得保险人在约定范围内所承担赔偿责任而支付给保险人的费用。

Explanatory Notes on Main Statistical Indicators

Government Revenue refers to the revenue of the government finance by means of participating in the distribution of the social products, which is the financial resources for ensuring the government to function. The contents of government revenue have been changed several times. Now it includes the following main items:

1. Various tax revenues: including value added tax, business tax, enterprise income tax, personal income tax, resources tax, fixed assets investment direction regulating tax, tax on city maintenance and construction, real estate tax, stamp tax, tax on use of urban land, land value added tax, vehicle and vessel tax, tax on occupancy of cultivated land, property tax, tobacco leaf tax, and other tax revenues.

2. Non–tax income: including special income, administrative fee income, fine and confiscated income, state–owned capital operating income, income from the paid use of state–owned resources, donation income, government housing fund income, and other income.

Government Expenditure refers to the distribution and use of the funds the government finance has raised, so as to meet the needs of economic construction and various causes. It includes the following main items:

1. Expenditure for general public services: It reflects the expenditure from the government for general public services.

2. Expenditure on public security: It reflects the expenditure from the government towards safeguarding the public security, including the related affairs of armed police, public security, state security, procuratorial administration, law court, judicial administration, jail, reeducation through labor, state confidentiality, anti–smuggling patrol, etc.

3. Expenditure on education: It reflects the expenditure from the government on education, including the related affairs of educational administration management, preschool education, primary education, junior secondary educate, regular senior secondary educate, regular higher education, primary vocational education, specialized secondary educate, technical educate, vocational senior secondary educate, vocational higher education, radio and television education, foreign student educate, special education, cadre continuing education, education institution services, etc.

4. Expenditure on science and technology: It reflects the expenditure from the government on science and technology.

5. Expenditure on culture, sport and media: It reflects the expenditure from the government on culture, cultural relics, sport, radio and television, publication, etc.

6. Expenditure on social security and employment: It reflects the expenditure from the government on social security and employment, including the related affairs of management of social security and employment, civil administration, subsidies to social insurance funds, supplement to national social security funds, retirees of government agencies and institutions, subsidies to enterprises reform, subsidies to employment, pension, settling down demobilized servicemen, social security, disabled person administration, minimum living allowance in urban area, other social relief in urban area, social relief in rural area, subsidies to natural disaster, Red Cross business, etc.

7. Expenditure on health care: It reflects the expenditure from the government on health care, including expenditure on management of health care, medical services, medical security, disease control and prevention, public health supervision, rural health care, etc.

8. Expenditure on environment protection: It reflects the expenditure from the government on environment protection, including expenditure on management of environment protection, environment monitoring and supervisory, pollution government, natural ecological protection, project of natural forest protection, returning farmland to forest, sandstorm and wilderness government, returning grazing land to grassland, returning cultivated grassland to grassland, etc.

9. Expenditure on urban and rural community affairs: It reflects the expenditure from the government on urban and rural community affairs, including expenditure on management of urban and rural community affairs, plan and management of urban and rural community, public utility of urban and rural community, residential buildings of urban and rural community, environmental sanitation of urban and rural community, management and supervision of markets construction, etc.

10. Expenditure on agriculture, forest and irrigation: It reflects the expenditure from the government on agriculture, forest and irrigation, including expenditure on agriculture, forest, irrigation, poverty alleviation, comprehensive development of agriculture, etc.

Deposit refers to a form of credit activity in which enterprises, agencies, organizations or residents deposit monetary funds in banks or other credit institutions for safekeeping and obtain a certain amount of interest based on the principle that funds must be recovered. According to the different deposit objects or nature, it can be divided into accounts such as household deposits, non–financial enterprise deposits, fiscal deposits, government agency deposits, and non–banking financial institutions deposits. It is the main source of bank credit funds.

Loan refers to a form of credit activity in which banks or other credit institutions provide funds for enterprises and individuals at a certain interest rate based on the principle that funds must be returned. Bank loans in my country are divided into short–term loans, medium and long–term loans, financial leasing, bill financing, and various advances.

Premium is the fee paid by the insurant to the insurer to obtain the obligation of compensation from the insurance within the agreed terms.

价格指数 9

PRICE INDEXES

简要说明

一、本篇资料的主要内容

本篇资料主要包括工业生产者出厂、工业生产者购进、固定资产投资、房地产、居民消费、商品零售等价格指数。

二、本篇资料的来源

1. 工业生产者出厂、工业生产者购进、固定资产投资、房地产价格指数分别来源于生产、投资、房地产价格统计调查月报，由国家统计局青岛调查队生产价格调查处整理提供。

2. 居民消费、商品零售价格指数来源于消费价格统计调查月报，由国家统计局青岛调查队消费价格调查处整理提供。

Brief Introduction

I. Main Content

Data in this chapter mainly include producer price indices for manufactured goods, purchasing price indices for industrial producers, price indices of investment in fixed assets, real estate price indices, consumer price indices and retail price indices.

II. Source of Data

1. Data on producer price indices for manufactured goods, purchasing price indices for industrial producers, price indices of investment in fixed assets, real estate price indices are based on monthly report of price survey on production, investment, real estate, and provided by the Division of Production Price Survey of Survey Office of the National Bureau of Statistics in Qingdao.

2. Data on consumer price indices and retail price indices are based on monthly report of consumer price survey, and provided by the Division of Consumer Price Survey of Survey Office of the National Bureau of Statistics in Qingdao.

9-1 主要年份居民消费和商品零售价格指数（以上年价格为 100）
MAJOR YEAR'S CONSUMER AND RETAIL PRICE INDEXES (PRECEDING YEAR=100)

年份 Year	居民消费价格指数 Consumer Price Index	#食品类 Food	#衣着类 Clothing	#服务项目价格指数 Services Price Index	商品零售价格指数 Retail Price Index
1951	110.5	105.2	112.4		110.5
1952	99.8	99.6	98.7		99.8
1957	101.4	101.3	101.4	99.3	101.4
1962	102.6	102.0	100.2	99.9	102.6
1965	101.2	101.3	98.8	96.9	101.2
1970	98.9	99.7	100.0	99.5	98.9
1975	100.3	100.1	100.0	100.0	100.3
1978	100.5	100.2	99.8	100.0	100.5
1980	105.2	108.5	100.3	100.6	105.5
1985	110.4	115.2	102.3	102.7	110.9
1988	120.7	125.2	117.3	118.3	120.9
1990	104.5	103.4	103.4	118.8	103.6
1991	107.0	107.0	112.1	109.6	106.8
1992	111.4	115.1	108.6	119.9	110.8
1993	123.9	120.9	119.0	158.5	119.8
1994	126.9	135.2	130.1	117.9	122.8
1995	116.2	118.1	122.8	123.2	114.2
1996	112.6	110.1	104.3	130.4	106.0
1997	104.0	101.2	102.3	120.8	100.2
1998	100.0	93.7	94.5	136.2	94.9
1999	100.2	96.7	97.1	115.6	96.6
2000	103.3	100.0	108.3	112.0	99.7
2001	101.0	100.6	98.0	108.7	98.9
2002	98.9	97.8	100.2	101.0	99.5
2003	101.4	104.3	98.4	101.7	98.3
2004	102.1	104.0	103.6	104.7	99.0
2005	102.3	102.1	108.3	101.4	99.3
2006	100.9	101.7	99.4	100.8	99.7
2007	104.5	111.6	99.4	102.4	102.7
2008	104.7	111.7	103.9	99.8	103.9
2009	100.5	101.6	101.4	100.6	98.6
2010	102.2	106.4	101.0	100.4	101.4
2011	105.0	111.1	108.2	103.1	104.5
2012	102.7	104.3	106.3	102.1	101.7
2013	102.5	105.3	104.9	100.7	101.4
2014	102.6	104.4	103.2	101.9	102.3
2015	101.2	101.7	102.8	101.3	100.0
2016	102.5	105.0	100.3	101.8	102.0
2017	102.0	99.6	100.5	103.4	100.8
2018	102.1	103.1	103.8	101.6	101.8
2019	103.3	111.6	100.6	101.7	102.4
2020	102.4	109.8	99.9	100.7	101.5

注：1. 2016 年起，食品类统计口径有变化，不包括“茶及饮料”和“在外餐饮”两项内容。
2. 2016 年起，统计分类“服务项目价格指数”改为“服务价格指数”，增加“养老服务”和“金融服务”两项内容。

Note: 1. Statistical caliber of food category has changed since 2016. The two sections of "Tea and Drinks" and "Catering Service" are not included.
2. The statistical category of "Price Index of Service Item" has been revised to "Price Index of Service" as of 2016 with two additional sections of "Elderly Care Service" and "Financial Service".

9-2 主要年份居民消费和商品零售价格指数（以 1950 年价格为 100）
MAJOR YEAR´S CONSUMER AND RETAIL PRICE INDEXES (1950=100)

年份 Year	居民消费价格指数 Consumer Price Index	#食品类 Food	#衣着类 Clothing	#服务项目价格指数 Services Price Index	商品零售价格指数 Retail Price Index
1951	110.5	105.2	112.4		110.5
1952	110.3	104.8	110.9		110.3
1957	119.5	120.7	115.3	91.6	119.5
1962	127.4	128.8	115.1	94.2	127.4
1965	133.3	138.7	108.4	81.5	133.3
1970	129.0	137.6	110.3	76.8	129.0
1975	128.8	138.2	110.0	75.7	128.8
1978	129.1	138.7	109.8	75.7	129.1
1980	137.6	154.1	109.3	76.1	138.1
1985	160.8	196.1	103.8	80.5	162.5
1988	223.8	295.2	133.2	100.8	227.6
1990	269.7	333.3	166.8	155.9	269.7
1991	288.6	356.7	187.0	170.9	288.1
1992	321.5	410.5	203.1	204.9	319.2
1993	398.3	496.3	241.7	324.8	382.4
1994	505.4	671.1	314.4	382.9	469.5
1995	587.3	792.5	386.1	471.8	536.2
1996	661.3	872.6	402.7	615.2	568.4
1997	687.8	883.0	412.0	743.1	569.5
1998	687.8	827.4	389.3	1012.1	540.5
1999	689.2	800.1	378.0	1170.0	522.1
2000	711.9	800.1	409.4	1310.4	520.5
2001	719.0	804.9	401.2	1424.4	514.8
2002	711.1	787.2	402.0	1438.7	512.2
2003	721.1	821.0	395.6	1463.1	503.5
2004	736.2	853.9	409.8	1531.9	498.5
2005	753.1	871.8	443.8	1553.4	495.0
2006	759.9	886.6	441.2	1565.8	493.5
2007	794.1	989.5	438.5	1603.4	506.8
2008	831.4	1105.3	455.6	1600.2	526.6
2009	835.6	1123.0	462.0	1609.8	519.2
2010	854.0	1194.9	466.6	1616.2	526.5
2011	896.7	1327.5	504.9	1666.3	550.2
2012	920.9	1384.6	536.7	1701.3	559.6
2013	943.9	1458.0	563.0	1713.2	567.4
2014	968.4	1522.2	581.0	1745.8	580.5
2015	980.0	1548.1	597.3	1768.5	580.5
2016	1004.5	1625.5	599.1	1800.3	592.1
2017	1024.6	1619.0	602.1	1861.5	596.8
2018	1046.1	1669.2	625.0	1891.3	607.6
2019	1080.6	1862.8	628.7	1923.4	622.2
2020	1106.5	2045.4	628.1	1936.9	631.5

注：1. 2016 年起，食品类统计口径有变化，不包括“茶及饮料”和“在外餐饮”两项内容。
　　2. 2016 年起，统计分类“服务项目价格指数”改为“服务价格指数”，增加“养老服务”和“金融服务”两项内容。

Note: 1. Statistical caliber of food category has changed since 2016. The two sections of "Tea and Drinks" and "Catering Service" are not included.
　　2. The statistical category of "Price Index of Service Item" has been revised to "Price Index of Service" of 2016 with two additional sections of "Elderly Care Service" and "Financial Service" .

9-3 主要年份生产投资价格指数（以上年价格为 100）

MAJOR YEAR´S PRICE INDEXES FOR PRODUCTION AND INVESTMENT (PRECEDING YEAR=100)

年份 Year	工业生产者出厂价格指数 Producer Price Indexes for Industrial Producers	工业生产者购进价格指数 Purchasing Price Indexes for Industrial Producers	房屋销售价格指数 Sales Price Indexes of Houses	房屋租赁价格指数 Renting Price Indexes of Houses	物业管理价格指数 Property Management Price Indexes	固定资产投资价格指数 Price Indexes for Investment in Fixed Assets
1990	104.33	108.64				
1991	101.68	108.10				
1992	105.46	107.13				
1993	115.49	126.91				
1994	121.62	120.30				
1995	112.70	114.25				
1996	103.81	103.25				
1997	100.22	101.93				
1998	94.96	92.77	100.1	94.0		
1999	96.93	95.88	103.7	104.3		
2000	101.89	106.81	102.3	95.8		
2001	98.00	97.81	104.1	107.0		
2002	97.37	96.78	107.6	94.4		
2003	100.97	106.51	114.6	99.4		
2004	102.92	113.62	115.2	98.6		105.8
2005	101.39	106.52	110.9	103.3	100.2	103.1
2006	101.08	105.80	106.9	110.1	99.8	102.6
2007	101.50	106.69	106.5	108.3	100.4	104.1
2008	105.33	115.91	105.1	106.5	102.1	111.0
2009	95.78	90.35	100.3	103.5	100.4	94.6
2010	103.75	112.21		103.0	100.5	104.9
2011	104.90	109.39				107.0
2012	98.61	97.00				100.0
2013	98.82	96.53				100.1
2014	99.20	97.40				99.9
2015	97.04	94.24				97.1
2016	98.77	97.28				99.8
2017	104.40	110.73				107.3
2018	104.22	105.22				106.6
2019	100.0	98.4				

说明：2010 年之前工业生产者出厂价格为工业品出厂价格；工业生产者购进价格为主要原材料、燃料、动力购进价格；根据国家制度规定 2019 年起不编制固定资产投资价格指数；根据国家有关规定 2020 年起不再编制工业生产者价格指数。

Explanation: Producers Prices at works were the prices of industrial products at words before 2010. Producers purchasing price refers to the purchasing price of main raw materials, fuels and power.According to the national system, the fixed asset investment price index will not be compiled from 2019; according to the relevant national regulations, the industrial producer price index will no longer be compiled from 2020.

9-4 工业生产者出厂价格指数（以上年价格为 100）

PRODUCER PRICE INDEXES FOR INDUSTRIAL PRODUCERS (PRECEDING YEAR=100)

类别	Item	2000 年	2005 年	2009 年	2010 年
总指数	**General Index**	**101.89**	**101.39**	**95.78**	**103.75**
其中：轻工业	Light Industry	98.50	99.78	97.21	100.80
重工业	Heavy Industry	105.62	104.32	93.45	107.57
其中：生产资料	**Means of Production**	**105.03**	**103.24**	**94.25**	**106.43**
采掘	Excavation	95.67	114.74	93.44	130.94
原料	Raw Materials	113.82	106.91	90.67	115.24
加工	Processing	97.58	101.45	95.34	103.50
生活资料	**Means of Livelihood**	**98.25**	**99.13**	**97.45**	**99.61**
食品	Food	96.59	98.80	98.21	105.06
衣着	Clothing	99.37	101.48	102.03	101.56
一般日用品	Articles for Daily Use	104.52	101.97	99.39	99.96
耐用消费品	Durable Consumer Goods	97.70	97.43	94.52	93.23

注：根据国家有关规定 2020 年起不再编制工业生产者价格指数。

Note : According to relevant national regulations, the industrial producer price index will no longer be compiled from 2020.

2011年	2012年	2013年	2014年	2015年	2016年	2017年	2018年	2019年
104.90	**98.61**	**98.82**	**99.20**	**97.04**	**98.77**	**104.40**	**104.22**	**100.0**
103.46	99.70	99.11	99.62	99.85	98.74	101.13	101.27	101.6
105.89	97.87	98.62	98.91	95.10	98.79	106.46	106.01	98.9
105.54	**97.55**	**98.58**	**98.87**	**95.23**	**98.60**	**106.34**	**105.86**	**99.0**
132.07	93.35	91.72	100.65	95.12				
111.52	99.05	99.26	98.87	88.59	93.92	112.92	114.50	95.8
103.49	97.20	98.50	98.84	97.06	99.60	104.96	103.95	99.8
103.82	**100.42**	**99.21**	**99.76**	**100.07**	**99.12**	**100.69**	**100.95**	**101.8**
109.71	99.91	95.34	98.34	102.53	102.59	100.55	100.55	104.8
107.44	102.03	102.74	100.34	100.39	100.93	101.54	100.14	101.6
108.02	101.64	101.42	101.01	99.59	100.12	101.63	101.54	100.3
94.34	98.79	98.41	99.65	98.26	94.58	99.78	101.32	100.3

9-5 工业生产者购进价格指数（以上年价格为 100）

PURCHASING PRICE INDEXES FOR INDUSTRIAL PRODUCERS (PRECEDING YEAR=100)

类别	Item	2000 年	2005 年	2009 年	2010 年
总指数	**General Index**	**106.81**	**106.52**	**90.35**	**112.21**
燃料、动力类	Fuel and Power	113.82	117.34	90.53	115.43
黑色金属材料类	Ferrous Metals	102.66	107.84	82.38	111.97
#钢材	Rolled-steel	105.44	106.57	85.25	108.67
其他	Others	101.1	112.88	72.73	122.64
有色金属材料及电线类	Nonferrous Metals and Electric Wire	106.75	108.06	86.24	122.65
化工原料类	Raw Chemical Materials	106.9	112.47	87.66	111.04
木材及纸浆类	Timber and Paper Pulp	108.98	103.8	89.16	117.06
建筑材料及非金属矿类	Building Materials and Nonmetals	99.5	115.54	100.98	107.61
其他工业原材料及半成品	Other Industrial Raw Materials and Semi-finished Goods	105.32	97.87	92.70	106.41
农副产品	Agricultural Products	92.73	101.55	88.60	121.30
纺织原料类	Textile Materials	104.03	98.15	98.69	112.90

注：根据国家有关规定 2020 年起不再编制工业生产者价格指数。

Note：According to relevant national regulations, the industrial producer price index will no longer be compiled from 2020.

2011年	2012年	2013年	2014年	2015年	2016年	2017年	2018年	2019年
109.39	**97.00**	**96.53**	**97.40**	**94.24**	**97.28**	**110.73**	**105.22**	**98.4**
111.29	100.64	95.18	97.65	88.51	89.94	112.91	112.55	95.3
113.08	93.20	93.76	95.81	87.26	97.23	117.41	104.02	100.0
107.95	92.33	92.87	96.87	89.99	96.89	119.10	108.75	99.1
129.01	94.64	96.57	92.49	78.70	98.41	110.30	86.82	103.4
108.45	93.64	96.23	96.24	92.34	96.29	114.82	103.94	97.7
113.79	96.72	96.47	99.51	96.44	101.00	107.63	101.55	94.2
103.78	93.12	98.79	102.42	98.33	99.93	125.23	111.21	89.3
116.71	102.48	100.13	97.36	95.52	100.91	115.06	115.97	107.8
103.31	98.05	96.65	96.25	96.95	97.50	106.42	102.41	100.5
115.04	98.21	98.54	97.62	99.75	101.53	105.92	99.70	103.6
111.11	95.61	99.60	97.38	95.86	99.81	110.09	105.80	97.1

9-6 按工业行业分工业生产者出厂价格指数

PRODUCER PRICE INDEXES FOR INDUSTRIAL PRODUCERS BY SECTOR

（上年价格 =100）

行业	Sector
工业生产者出厂价格指数	**Producer Price Indexes for Manufactured Manufactured Goods**
黑色金属矿采选业	Mining of Ferrous Metal Ores
有色金属矿采选业	Mining of Non-ferrous Metal Ores
非金属矿采选业	Mining and Processing of Nonmetal Ores
农副食品加工业	Processing of Food from Agricultural Products
食品制造业	Manufacture of Foods
酒、饮料和精制茶制造业	Manufacturing Industry of Alcohol, Beverage and Refined Tea
纺织业	Manufacture of Textile
纺织服装、服饰业	Industry of Textile and Garment, and Apparel
皮革、毛皮、羽毛及其制品和制鞋业	Industry of Leather, Furs, Down and Related Products, and Shoes Making
木材加工和木、竹、藤、棕、草制品业	Processing of Timbers, Manufacture of Wood, Bamboo, Rattan, Palm, and Staw Products
家具制造业	Manufacture of Furniture
造纸和纸制品业	Manufacture of Paper and Paper Products
印刷和记录媒介复制业	Printing, Reproduction of Recording Media
文教、工美、体育和娱乐用品制造业	Industry of Culture and Education, Arts and Crafts, and Entertainment Products Manufacturing
石油、煤炭及其他燃料加工业	Processing of Petroleum, Coking, Processing of Nucleus Fuel
化学原料和化学制品制造业	Manufacture of Chemical Raw Material and Chemical Products
医药制造业	Manufacture of Medicines
化学纤维制造业	Manufacture of Chemical Fiber
橡胶和塑料制品业	Industry of Rubber and Plastic Products
非金属矿物制品业	Manufacture of Non-metallic Mineral Products
黑色金属冶炼和压延加工业	Smelting and Pressing of Ferrous Metals
有色金属冶炼和压延加工业	Smelting and Pressing of Non-ferrous Metals
金属制品业	Manufacture of Metal Products
通用设备制造业	Manufacture of General Purpose Machinery
专用设备制造业	Manufacture of Special Purpose Machinery
汽车制造业	Vehicle Manufacturing Industry
铁路、船舶、航空航天和其他运输设备制造业	Manufacturing Industry of Railroads. Vessels, Aerospace and Other Transportation Equipment
电气机械和器材制造业	Manufacture of Electrical Machinery&Equipment
计算机、通信和其他电子设备制造业	Computer. Communications and Other Electronic Equipment Manufacturing
仪器仪表制造业	Instruments Manufacturing Industry
其他制造业	Other Manufacturing Industry
金属制品、机械和设备修理业	Industry of Metal Products, and Repair of Machinery and Equipment
电力、热力生产和供应业	Production and Supply of Electric Power and Heat Power
燃气生产和供应业	Production and Supply of Gas
水的生产和供应业	Production and Supply of Water

注：2019 年国民经济行业分类调整，本表中 2011 年— 2019 年数据采用新国民经济行业分类 GB/T 4754-2017。
根据国家有关规定 2020 年起不再编制工业生产者价格指数。

Note: Classification of national economic industries was adjusted in 2019. The new national economic industries classification by GB/T 4754-2017 applies to data from 2011 to 2019 in this table.
According to relevant national regulations, the industrial producer price index will no longer be compiled from 2020.

(preceding year=100)

2011年	2012年	2013年	2014年	2015年	2016年	2017年	2018年	2019年
104.90	**98.61**	**98.82**	**99.20**	**97.04**	**98.77**	**104.40**	**104.22**	**100.0**
104.33	99.93	100.00	99.86	100.00				
111.39	102.48	98.72	95.57	89.94				
145.13	89.33	87.06	102.14	94.85				
111.34	98.69	93.46	97.58	102.47	102.80	101.12	101.41	104.8
112.52	103.11	103.08	101.78	100.66	100.30	101.40	98.67	99.4
104.14	105.89	100.48	98.76	99.01	99.97	99.54	100.85	107.2
105.09	96.15	100.18	100.27	99.41	97.60	103.84	103.58	101.0
105.43	101.66	104.17	101.74	100.84	100.83	102.17	100.28	102.5
104.79	102.59	101.83	98.56	99.72	99.81	100.15	99.82	99.6
108.13	103.21	99.67	100.96	100.35				
101.11	102.00	100.02	100.00	99.91	98.46	98.72	100.48	99.3
105.71	95.59	96.13	101.96	99.78	99.58	115.83	104.86	96.7
110.06	107.10	108.65	96.97	95.96	98.45	101.11	102.77	97.5
100.61	101.47	100.47	100.00	99.96	99.88	101.90	100.54	101.2
114.95	104.26	99.49	97.38	76.03	91.60	114.48	121.44	97.8
114.60	89.61	98.04	99.70	96.53	95.20	119.17	113.72	94.2
107.33	95.05	105.08	127.56	100.73	104.83	101.06	100.95	102.6
123.72	92.56	95.65	96.69	90.31	89.56	117.03	98.53	96.4
114.68	99.67	95.40	95.50	94.93	97.60	100.62	100.10	99.4
108.19	98.39	99.82	100.91	101.62	99.08	114.14	120.19	100.1
111.00	86.47	93.52	94.45	83.44	99.13	117.16	108.23	99.7
108.26	89.14	93.87	94.43	87.95	95.29	125.17	102.35	98.0
99.79	99.82	104.14	96.62	96.59	103.64	106.15	105.34	99.4
101.39	100.07	103.87	101.02	100.37	98.78	103.45	104.80	103.4
101.69	101.26	99.99	99.81	99.72	98.36	100.00	101.23	101.0
99.27	98.97	98.59	102.49	101.04	101.46	100.93	99.83	100.9
99.17	99.66	97.65	100.96	100.03	99.29	100.16	99.79	97.3
103.10	98.40	98.82	99.24	98.61	98.96	102.82	102.36	99.8
84.65	95.43	94.31	98.88	96.31	90.16	102.17	100.06	97.7
102.01	98.72	98.01	98.43	97.05	100.00	100.09	100.15	100.2
95.16	98.52	99.94	100.12	99.89	100.87	104.20	105.84	108.8
102.17	98.43	88.75	91.69	90.21				
101.49	104.36	99.81	99.15	98.10	97.59	97.05	97.83	96.6
107.34	103.32	102.54	109.38	98.88	101.26	96.32	108.74	104.7
100.15	100.25	100.05	100.34	103.46	108.78	100.00	113.81	100.0

9-7 固定资产投资价格指数（以上年价格为 100）
PRICE INDEXES FOR INVESTMENT IN FIXED ASSETS (PRECEDING YEAR=100)

项目名称	Item	2005	2009	2010	2011	2012	2013	2014	2015	2016	2017	2018
总计	**Total**	**103.1**	**94.6**	**104.9**	**107.0**	**100.0**	**100.1**	**99.9**	**97.1**	**99.8**	**107.3**	**106.6**
建筑安装、装饰工程	Construction and Installation Project	103.7	92.1	107.5	110.1	99.8	100.0	99.6	95.5	99.6	110.7	109.5
其中：人工费	Of which : Labor Cost	112.7	104.9	112.0	115.9	110.4	107.8	104.8	103.1	101.6	103.0	104.9
材料费	Materials Expenses	101.0	87.5	107.0	109.6	96.7	97.6	97.7	92	98.8	114.9	112.4
机械使用费	Expenses on Machinery Use	104.2	100.0	104.3	105.0	102.3	101.0	100.8	100.9	100.1	101.2	102.0
设备、工器具购置	Purchase of Equipment, Tools and Instruments	99.7	98.0	100.2	101.8	99.2	99.3	99.9	99.2	98.7	100.6	101.5
其他费用	Others	105.5	98.5	102.2	103.0	102.0	101.4	101.4	101.2	102.2	102.0	99.9

注：根据国家制度规定 2019 年起不编制固定资产投资价格指数。

Note: According to national regulations, starting from 2019, no fixed asset investment price index will be compiled.

9-8 住宅销售价格指数（2020 年）（上年同期 =100）
SALES PRICE INDEXES FOR RESIDENCE（2020）(PRECEDING YEAR=100)

项目	Item	
新建住宅销售价格指数	**Sales Price Indexes for Newly Constucted Residence**	
一月	January	103.7
二月	February	103.3
三月	March	102.3
四月	April	102.4
五月	May	101.9
六月	June	102.5
七月	July	102.3
八月	August	102.5
九月	September	102.9
十月	October	102.9
十一月	November	102.8
十二月	December	102.8
二手住宅销售价格指数	**Sales Price Indexes for Second-hand Residence**	
一月	January	94.5
二月	February	94.2
三月	March	94.1
四月	April	94.3
五月	May	94.5
六月	June	95.4
七月	July	95.8
八月	August	96.6
九月	September	97.0
十月	October	97.2
十一月	November	97.7
十二月	December	97.9

9-9 居民消费价格分类指数（2020年）（上年=100）
CONSUMER PRICE INDEXES BY CATEGORY (2020) (PRECEDING YEAR=100)

项目	Item	指数 Indexes
居民消费价格总指数	**Consumer Price Index**	**102.4**
非食品烟酒价格指数	Price index of non-food cigarettes and alcohol	99.9
服务价格指数	Price index of services	100.7
鲜活食品价格指数	Price index of fresh food	112.1
消费品价格指数	Consumer Goods Price Index	103.4
扣除鲜菜鲜果价格指数	Price Index Without Fresh Vegetables and Fresh Fruits	102.6
一、食品烟酒	**Food, cigarettes and liquor**	**108.0**
1. 食品	Food	109.8
（1）粮食	Grain	101.5
（2）薯类	Potatoes	106.7
（3）豆类	Beans	110.3
（4）食用油	Cooking Oil	103.1
（5）菜	Vegetables	108.2
（6）畜肉类	Livestock Products	138.3
（7）禽肉类	Poultry Products	100.5
（8）水产品	Aquatic Products	102.9
（9）蛋类	Eggs	89.9
（10）奶类	Dairy Products	103.1
（11）干鲜瓜果类	Dried and Fresh Melons and Fruits	89.6
（12）糖果糕点类	Candy and Pastry	100.8
（13）调味品	Flavoring	103.7
（14）其他食品类	Other foods	102.4
2. 茶及饮料	Tea and Beverages	101.3
3. 烟酒	Tobacco Liquor	102.6
4. 在外餐饮	Catering service	105.3

注：2016年起，居民消费价格调查目录进行了调整，新调查目录与国际标准更为接近。

Note: Since 2016, the consumption price investigation directory has been adjusted, and the new investigation directory is basically consistent with the household consumption expenditure catalogue.

9-9 续表
Continued

项目	Item	指数 Indexes
二、衣着	**Clothing**	**99.9**
1. 服装	Garments	100.4
2. 服装材料	Clothing material	100.2
3. 其他衣着及配件	Other clothing an accessories	97.4
4. 衣着加工服务费	Service charge of clothing processing	100.9
5. 鞋类	Shoes	98.3
三、居住	**Residence**	**100.5**
1. 租赁房房租	Rents	101.1
2. 住房保养维修及管理	Maintenance and management of house	99.1
3. 水电燃料	Water, Electricity and Fuels	100.5
4. 自有住房	Private Housing	100.7
四、生活用品及服务	**Article of daily use and service**	**99.4**
1. 家具及室内装饰品	Furniture and interior decoration	99.9
2. 家用器具	Home appliances	95.4
3. 家用纺织品	Home textile	101.7
4. 家庭日用杂品	Daily Use Household Articles	98.4
5. 个人护理用品	Personal-care supply	100.0
6. 家庭服务	Household Services	107.4
五、交通和通信	**Transportation and Communication**	**94.5**
1. 交通	Transportation	92.5
2. 通信	Communication	98.7
六、教育文化和娱乐	**Education, culture and entertainment**	**102.1**
1. 教育	Education	105.2
2. 文化娱乐	Culture and Entertainment	99.1
七、医疗保健	**Health Care**	**102.0**
1. 药品及医疗器具	Medicine and medical apparatus	103.4
2. 医疗服务	Medical service	100.3
八、其他用品和服务	**Other articles and services**	**102.7**
1. 其他用品类	Other articles	108.7
2. 其他服务类	Other services	98.8

9-10 商品零售价格分类指数（2020 年）（上年 =100）
RETAIL PRICE INDEXES BY CATEGORY (2020) (PRECEDING YEAR=100)

项目	Item	指数 Indexes
商品零售价格总指数	**Retail Price Indexes**	**101.5**
一、食品	**Food**	**109.2**
1. 粮食	Grain	101.5
2. 薯类	Potatoes	106.7
3. 豆类	Beans	110.3
4. 食用油	Edible oil	103.1
5. 菜	Vegetables	108.2
6. 畜肉类	Stock meat	138.3
7. 禽肉类	Poultry meat	100.5
8. 水产品	Aquatic Products	102.9
9. 蛋类	Eggs	89.9
10. 奶类	Dairy	103.1
11. 干鲜瓜果类	Dried and Fresh Melon, and Fruits	89.6
12. 糖果糕点类	Sweets and cakes	100.8
13. 调味品	Flavoring	103.7
14. 其他食品类	Other food	102.4
15. 在外餐饮	Catering service	105.3
二、饮料、烟酒	**Beverages, Tobacco and Liquor**	**101.9**
1. 茶及饮料	Tea and Beverages	101.3
2. 烟草	Tobacco	100.2
3. 酒类	Liquor	104.7
三、服装、鞋帽	**Clothing**	**99.9**
1. 服装	Garments	100.5
2. 鞋帽袜	Footgear and Hats	98.1
3. 其他衣着配件	Other clothing and accessories	100.1
四、纺织品	**Textiles**	**102.1**
1. 服装材料	Clothing material	100.2
2. 床上用品	Blend Cloth	102.4
五、家用电器及音像器材	**Household Appliances, Music and Video Equipment**	**96.2**
1. 家庭设备	Household Facilities	95.4
2. 文娱用耐用消费品	Durable Consumer Goods for Cultural and Recreational Use and Services	97.5
3. 专业音像器材	Professional Audio and Video Equipment	98.9

注：2016 年起，商品零售价格调查目录进行了微调。
Note: Since 2016, the retail price survey catalogue has been fine-tuned.

9-10 续表
Continued

项目	Item	指数 Indexes
六、文化办公用品	**Culture and office Articles**	**98.8**
七、日用品	**Articles for Daily Use**	**99.4**
1. 日用百货	General Merchandise for Daily Use	100.1
2. 厨具餐具茶具	Kitchen ware, tableware, tea set	99.6
3. 清洗用品	Cleaning Products	98.4
4. 其他日用品	Other Articles for Daily Use	99.1
八、体育娱乐用品	**Sports and Recreation Articles**	**99.3**
1. 体育户外用品	Sports and outdoors	100.2
2. 娱乐用品	Recreation Articles	98.8
九、交通、通信用品	**Transportation and Communication Appliances**	**98.0**
1. 交通运输机械	Transportation Machines	97.8
2. 通信器材	Communication Equipment	98.8
十、家具	**Furniture**	**100.5**
十一、化妆品	**Cosmetics**	**100.1**
十二、金银饰品	**Gold, Silver and Jewelry**	**113.9**
十三、中西药品及医疗保健用品	**Traditional Chinese and Western Medicals and Health Care Articles**	**103.5**
1. 医疗卫生器具	Medical apparatus	99.9
2. 中药	Herbal medicine	100.2
3. 西药	Western Medicines	105.7
4. 保健器具及用品	Health Care Articles	102.7
十四、书报杂志及电子出版物	**Books, Newspapers, Magazines and Electronic Publications**	**107.0**
1. 教材及参考书	Teaching Material and Reference Books	114.0
2. 书报杂志	Books, Newspapers and Magazines	100.0
3. 计算机办公软件	Computer office software	96.3
十五、燃料	**Fuels**	**89.9**
1. 煤炭及制品	Coal and Its Products	105.3
2. 石油及制品	Petroleum and Its Products	89.7
十六、建筑材料及五金电料	**Building Materials and Hardware**	**99.4**
1. 建筑装璜材料	Building Decoration Materials	99.5
2. 五金水暖	Hardware	99.1

主要统计指标解释

居民消费价格指数 是反映一定时期内城乡居民所购买的生活消费品价格和服务项目价格变动趋势和程度的相对数，是对城市居民消费价格指数和农村居民消费价格指数进行综合汇总计算的结果。该指数可以观察和分析消费品的零售价格和服务价格变动对城乡居民实际生活费支出的影响程度。

商品零售价格指数 是反映一定时期内城乡商品零售价格变动趋势和程度的相对数。商品零售价格的变动直接影响到城乡居民的生活支出和国家的财政收入，影响居民购买力和市场供需的平衡，影响到消费与积累的比例关系。因此，该指数可以从一个侧面对上述经济活动进行观察和分析。

工业生产者出厂价格指数 是反映一定时期内全部工业产品出厂价格总水平的变动趋势和程度的相对数，包括工业企业售给本企业以外所有单位的各种产品和直接售给居民用于生活消费的产品。该指数可以观察出厂价格变动对工业总产值及增加值的影响。

工业生产者购进价格指数 是反映工业企业作为生产投入，而从物资交易市场和能源、原材料生产企业购买原材料、燃料和动力产品时，所支付的价格水平变动趋势和程度的统计指标，是扣除工业企业物质消耗成本中的价格变动影响的重要依据。

房地产价格指数 是反映一定时期内房地产价格变动趋势和程度的相对数，包括新建住宅销售价格指数、二手住宅销售价格指数。

Explanatory Notes on Main Statistical Indicators

Consumer Price Indices reflect the trend and degree of changes in prices of consumer goods and services purchased by urban and rural households during a given period. They are obtained by combining the Urban Consumer Price Indices and the Rural Consumer Price Indices. The Indices enable the observation and analysis of the degree of impact of the changes in the prices of retailed goods and services on the actual living expenses of urban and rural residents.

Retail Price Indices reflect the trend and degree of change in retail prices of commodities during a given period. The change in retail prices of commodities directly affect the living expenditure of urban and rural residents, government revenue, purchasing power of residents and the equilibrium of market supply and demand, and the ratio of consumption to accumulation. Therefore, the retail price indices are useful to analyze the changes of the above economic activities.

Producer Price Indices for Industrial Producers reflect the trend and degree of changes in general ex-factory prices of all industrial products during a given period, including sales of industrial products by an industrial enterprise to all units outside the enterprise, as well as sales of consumer goods to residents. It can be used to analyze the impact of ex-factory prices on gross output value and value-added of the industrial sector.

Purchasing Price Indices for Industrial Producers reflect changes in the level and degree of prices paid by industrial enterprises when they purchase production input such as raw materials, fuels and power from the market or from other energy or raw materials producing enterprises. These indices provide important basis for measuring the material consumption of industrial enterprises after removing influence of price changes.

Price Indices for Real Estate reflect the trend and degree of changes in prices of real estate during a given period, including sales price indices for newly constructed residential buildings and secondhand residential buildings.

人民生活 10

PEOPLE'S LIVING CONDITIONS

简要说明

一、本篇资料的主要内容

本篇资料主要反映了全市居民的家庭收支、居住、家庭消费构成、耐用消费品拥有量等方面的情况。

二、本篇资料的来源

本篇资料中相关数据来源于住户收支与生活状况调查年报，由国家统计局青岛调查队住户调查处整理提供。

Brief Introduction

I. Main Content

This section mainly reflects the residents´ household income and expenditure, housing, household consumption structure, quantity of durable consumer goods possessed and other information.

II. Source of Data

The relevant data in this article comes from the annual survey of household income and expenditure and living conditions, compiled and provided by the Household Survey Division of the Qingdao Survey Team of the National Bureau of Statistics.

10-1 城镇居民收支（1978-2014 年）
INCOME AND EXPENDITURE OF URBAN RESIDENTS (1978-2014)

年份 Year	城镇居民人均可支配收入（元） Annual Per Capita Disposable Income of Urban Households (yuan)	城镇居民人均消费支出（元） Per Capita Consumption Expenditure of Urban Households (yuan)	城镇居民恩格尔系数（%） Engel Coefficient of Urban Residents (%)
1978	336	321	
1979	380	360	
1980	537	495	53.5
1981	500	490	57.8
1982	528	484	61.5
1983	549	510	63.7
1984	665	580	62.8
1985	733	681	58.6
1986	882	806	59.2
1987	1089	996	58.1
1988	1225	1278	55.9
1989	1455	1439	57.8
1990	1624	1507	58.4
1991	1856	1767	57.4
1992	2138	1956	57.0
1993	2668	2445	51.8
1994	3880	3479	53.2
1995	5357	4606	52.5
1996	5602	5079	51.8
1997	6222	5525	48.2
1998	6542	5567	46.4
1999	7255	5985	44.3
2000	7971	6684	42.1
2001	8665	6858	41.5
2002	8641	7356	39.8
2003	9962	8072	38.4
2004	10944	9023	36.7
2005	12725	9909	35.9
2006	15066	11981	33.9
2007	17516	13421	33.7
2008	20034	15055	33.4
2009	21857	16145	33.7
2010	24380	17608	30.9
2011	27861	19382	31.1
2012	31349	20481	30.4
2013	34356	22157	30.8
2014	37346	24122	30.2

注：自 2015 年开始，全市城乡住户调查统一使用一体化改革后的数据，与原数据相比，城乡居民收支指标的调查范围和口径均存较大变化。原“城市居民人均可支配收入”调整为“城镇居民人均可支配收入”；原“农民人均纯收入”调整为“农村居民人均可支配收入”。

Note: Since 2015, the city's urban and rural household surveys have uniformly used the data after the integration reform. Compared with the original data, the survey scope and caliber of the income indicators of urban and rural residents have changed significantly. The"per capita disposable income of residents in cities was changed to" per capita disposable income of urban residents" , the "per capita net income of farmers" was changed to "per capita disposable income of rural residents.

10-2 农村居民收支（1978-2014年）

INCOME AND EXPENDITURE OF RURAL RESIDENTS (1978-2014)

年份 Year	农村居民人均可支配收入（元） Per Capita Disposable Income of Rural Residents (yuan)	农村居民人均消费支出（元） Per Capita Consumption Expenditure of Rural Households (yuan)	农村居民恩格尔系数（%） Engel Coefficient of Rural Residents(%)
1978	146	109	59.2
1979	153	129	58.3
1980	209	142	55.0
1981	218	163	44.2
1982	273	199	53.0
1983	399	277	52.8
1984	452	304	50.0
1985	567	376	47.8
1986	647	474	46.4
1987	730	462	42.9
1988	820	439	38.8
1989	876	510	38.9
1990	952	494	41.5
1991	1021	546	41.3
1992	1029	572	41.7
1993	1255	743	42.7
1994	1694	1384	54.5
1995	2225	1641	55.7
1996	2625	2173	50.5
1997	2599	2150	52.9
1998	3144	2112	49.5
1999	3349	2135	47.2
2000	3534	2354	42.9
2001	3756	2579	40.8
2002	4003	2768	38.3
2003	4283	2921	37.0
2004	4757	3266	37.6
2005	5384	3625	36.3
2006	6013	4061	35.2
2007	6801	4557	35.6
2008	7666	5083	35.9
2009	8255	5568	34.4
2010	9326	6335	32.8
2011	10934	7285	33.7
2012	12366	8228	33.3
2013	13905	9305	32.1
2014	15434	10277	31.0

注：自2015年开始，全市城乡住户调查统一使用一体化改革后的数据，与原数据相比，城乡居民收支指标的调查范围和口径均存较大变化。原“城市居民人均可支配收入”调整为“城镇居民人均可支配收入”；原“农民人均纯收入”调整为“农村居民人均可支配收入”。

Note: Since 2015, the city's urban and rural household surveys have uniformly used the data after the integration reform. Compared with the original data, the survey scope and caliber of the income indicators of urban and rural residents have changed significantly. The"per capita disposable income of residents in cities was changed to" per capita disposable income of urban residents" , the "per capita net income of farmers" was changed to "per capita disposable income of rural residents.

10-3 城乡居民住房面积（1990-2014年）
HOUSING AREA OF URBAN AND RURAL RESIDENTS (1990-2014)

年份 Year	城市居民人均现住房建筑面积（平方米） Per Capita Home Floor Area of Urban Residents (square meter)	农村居民人均居住面积（平方米） Per Capita Housing Area of Rural Residents (square meter)
1990	14.16	19.60
1995	17.12	23.03
2000	20.76	25.88
2001	21.86	26.59
2002	22.76	27.00
2003	23.73	27.00
2004	24.22	27.99
2005	22.96	29.54
2006	23.73	30.82
2007	23.72	30.95
2008	26.83	30.73
2009	26.71	31.39
2010	27.42	30.97
2011	27.67	31.73
2012	27.86	32.32
2013	29.12	33.50
2014	29.80	34.20

10-4 全体居民家庭基本情况（2015年）

BASIC INFORMATION ON ALL HOUSEHOLDS (2015)

指标名称	Name	单位	Unit	2015年	2014年	2015年比2014年增长（±%） 2015/2014（±%）
人均可支配收入	**Per Capita Disposable Income**	**元**	**yuan**	**32885**	**30273**	**8.6**
（一）工资性收入	Income from Wages and Salaries	元	yuan	20068	18348	9.4
（二）经营净收入	Net Income from Household Operations	元	yuan	6480	6035	7.4
（三）财产净收入	Income from Properties	元	yuan	2522	2396	5.2
（四）转移净收入	Income from Transfers	元	yuan	3815	3494	9.2
人均消费支出	**Per Capita Consumption Expenditure**	**元**	**yuan**	**21326**	**19653**	**8.5**
（一）食品烟酒	Food, Tobacco and Liquor	元	yuan	6459	5970	8.2
（二）衣着	Clothing	元	yuan	2096	1944	7.8
（三）居住	Residence	元	yuan	4584	4316	6.2
（四）生活用品及服务	Household Facilities, Articles and Services	元	yuan	1485	1374	8.1
（五）交通通信	Transportation and Communication	元	yuan	3226	2905	11.0
（六）教育文化娱乐	Education, Cultural and Recreation Services	元	yuan	1830	1654	10.6
（七）医疗保健	Health Care and Medical Services	元	yuan	1115	1002	11.2
（八）其他用品和服务	Other Goods and Services	元	yuan	531	488	8.8
城镇居民人均现住房建筑面积	**Per Capita Building Space in Urban Areas**	**平方米**	**sq.m**	**31.5**		
农村居民人均现住房建筑面积	**Per Capita Living Space in Rural Areas**	**平方米**	**sq.m**	**32.4**		

注：自2015年开始，全市城乡住户调查统一使用一体化改革后的数据，与原数据相比，城乡居民收支指标的调查范围和口径均存较大变化。原“城市居民人均可支配收入”调整为“城镇居民人均可支配收入”；原“农民人均纯收入”调整为“农村居民人均可支配收入”。2014年数据也为新口径，与2015年年鉴数据不一致。2014年农村居民住房为拥有面积，2015年为现住房建筑面积。

Note: Since 2015, the city's urban and rural household surveys have uniformly used the data after the integration reform. Compared with the original data, the survey scope and caliber of the income indicators of urban and rural residents have changed significantly. The"per capita disposable income of residents in cities was changed to" per capita disposable income of urban residents" , the "per capita net income of farmers" was changed to "per capita disposable income of rural residents. Data in 2014 were counted by new gauge and they are different from the data in last year' s yearbook. As for the statistics of rural resident homes, the owned house area was taken in 2014, but in 2015, the construction area was counted.

10-5 全体居民家庭基本情况（2016 年）
BASIC INFORMATION ON ALL HOUSEHOLDS (2016)

指标名称	Name	单位	Unit	2016 年	2015 年	2016 年比 2015 年增长（±%）2016/2015 (±%)
人均可支配收入	**Per Capita Disposable Income**	**元**	**yuan**	**35680**	**32885**	**8.5**
（一）工资性收入	Income from Wages and Salaries	元	yuan	21700	20068	8.1
（二）经营净收入	Net Income from Household Operations	元	yuan	7011	6480	8.2
（三）财产净收入	Income from Properties	元	yuan	2781	2522	10.3
（四）转移净收入	Income from Transfers	元	yuan	4188	3815	9.8
人均消费支出	**Per Capita Consumption Expenditure**	**元**	**yuan**	**23256**	**21326**	**9.0**
（一）食品烟酒	Food, Tobacco and Liquor	元	yuan	6983	6459	8.1
（二）衣着	Clothing	元	yuan	2271	2096	8.4
（三）居住	Residence	元	yuan	5018	4584	9.5
（四）生活用品及服务	Household Facilities, Articles and Services	元	yuan	1607	1485	8.2
（五）交通通信	Transportation and Communication	元	yuan	3479	3226	7.8
（六）教育文化娱乐	Education, Cultural and Recreation Services	元	yuan	2075	1830	13.4
（七）医疗保健	Health Care and Medical Services	元	yuan	1233	1115	10.6
（八）其他用品和服务	Other Goods and Services	元	yuan	590	531	11.2
城镇居民人均现住房建筑面积	**Per Capita Building Space in Urban Areas**	**平方米**	**sq.m**	**31.7**	**31.5**	**0.6**
农村居民人均现住房建筑面积	**Per Capita Living Space in Rural Areas**	**平方米**	**sq.m**	**33.2**	**32.4**	**2.5**

10-6 全体居民家庭基本情况（2017 年）
BASIC INFORMATION ON ALL HOUSEHOLDS (2017)

指标名称	Name	单位	Unit	2017 年	2016 年	2017 年比 2016 年增长（±%）2017/2016 (±%)
人均可支配收入	**Per Capita Disposable Income**	**元**	**yuan**	**38763**	**35680**	**8.6**
（一）工资性收入	Income from Wages and Salaries	元	yuan	23514	21700	8.4
（二）经营净收入	Net Income from Household Operations	元	yuan	7485	7011	6.8
（三）财产净收入	Income from Properties	元	yuan	3082	2781	10.8
（四）转移净收入	Income from Transfers	元	yuan	4682	4188	11.8
人均消费支出	**Per Capita Consumption Expenditure**	**元**	**yuan**	**25232**	**23256**	**8.5**
（一）食品烟酒	Food, Tobacco and Liquor	元	yuan	7489	6983	7.2
（二）衣着	Clothing	元	yuan	2467	2271	8.6
（三）居住	Residence	元	yuan	5454	5018	8.7
（四）生活用品及服务	Household Facilities, Articles and Services	元	yuan	1747	1607	8.7
（五）交通通信	Transportation and Communication	元	yuan	3753	3479	7.9
（六）教育文化娱乐	Education, Cultural and Recreation Services	元	yuan	2347	2075	13.1
（七）医疗保健	Health Care and Medical Services	元	yuan	1350	1233	9.5
（八）其他用品和服务	Other Goods and Services	元	yuan	625	590	6.0
城镇居民人均现住房建筑面积	**Per Capita Building Space in Urban Areas**	**平方米**	**sq.m**	**32.7**	**31.7**	**3.2**
农村居民人均现住房建筑面积	**Per Capita Living Space in Rural Areas**	**平方米**	**sq.m**	**34.8**	**33.2**	**4.8**

10-7 全体居民家庭基本情况（2018 年）
BASIC INFORMATION ON ALL HOUSEHOLDS (2018)

指标名称	Name	单位	Unit	2018 年	2017 年	2018 年比 2017 年增长（±%）2018/2017 (±%)
人均可支配收入	**Per Capita Disposable Income**	**元**	**yuan**	**42019**	**38763**	**8.4**
（一）工资性收入	Income from Wages and Salaries	元	yuan	25303	23514	7.6
（二）经营净收入	Net Income from Household Operations	元	yuan	8027	7485	7.3
（三）财产净收入	Income from Properties	元	yuan	3475	3082	12.8
（四）转移净收入	Income from Transfers	元	yuan	5214	4682	11.3
人均消费支出	**Per Capita Consumption Expenditure**	**元**	**yuan**	**27316**	**25232**	**8.3**
（一）食品烟酒	Food, Tobacco and Liquor	元	yuan	7787	7489	4.0
（二）衣着	Clothing	元	yuan	2538	2467	2.9
（三）居住	Residence	元	yuan	6365	5454	16.7
（四）生活用品及服务	Household Facilities, Articles and Services	元	yuan	1837	1747	5.1
（五）交通通信	Transportation and Communication	元	yuan	4084	3753	8.8
（六）教育文化娱乐	Education, Cultural and Recreation Services	元	yuan	2571	2347	9.5
（七）医疗保健	Health Care and Medical Services	元	yuan	1480	1350	9.6
（八）其他用品和服务	Other Goods and Services	元	yuan	654	625	4.6
城镇居民人均现住房建筑面积	**Per Capita Building Space in Urban Areas**	**平方米**	**sq.m**	**32.9**	**32.7**	**0.8**
农村居民人均现住房建筑面积	**Per Capita Living Space in Rural Areas**	**平方米**	**sq.m**	**35.9**	**34.8**	**3.1**

10-8 全体居民家庭基本情况（2019 年）
BASIC INFORMATION ON ALL HOUSEHOLDS (2019)

指标名称	Name	单位	Unit	2019 年	2018 年	2019 年比 2018 年增长（±%）2019/2018 (±%)
人均可支配收入	**Per Capita Disposable Income**	**元**	**yuan**	**45452**	**42019**	**8.2**
（一）工资性收入	Income from Wages and Salaries	元	yuan	27164	25303	7.4
（二）经营净收入	Net Income from Household Operations	元	yuan	8685	8027	8.2
（三）财产净收入	Income from Properties	元	yuan	3850	3475	10.8
（四）转移净收入	Income from Transfers	元	yuan	5753	5214	10.3
人均消费支出	**Per Capita Consumption Expenditure**	**元**	**yuan**	**29501**	**27316**	**8.0**
（一）食品烟酒	Food, Tobacco and Liquor	元	yuan	8325	7787	6.9
（二）衣着	Clothing	元	yuan	2657	2538	4.7
（三）居住	Residence	元	yuan	6969	6365	9.5
（四）生活用品及服务	Household Facilities, Articles and Services	元	yuan	1957	1837	6.5
（五）交通通信	Transportation and Communication	元	yuan	4369	4084	7.0
（六）教育文化娱乐	Education, Cultural and Recreation Services	元	yuan	2904	2571	12.9
（七）医疗保健	Health Care and Medical Services	元	yuan	1600	1480	8.1
（八）其他用品和服务	Other Goods and Services	元	yuan	720	654	10.2
城镇居民人均现住房建筑面积	**Per Capita Building Space in Urban Areas**	**平方米**	**sq.m**	**31.9**	**32.9**	**-3.3**
农村居民人均现住房建筑面积	**Per Capita Living Space in Rural Areas**	**平方米**	**sq.m**	**37.0**	**35.9**	**3.1**

10-9 全体居民家庭基本情况（2020 年）
BASIC INFORMATION ON ALL HOUSEHOLDS (2020)

指标名称	Name	单位	Unit	2020 年	2019 年	2020 年比 2019 年增长（±%）2020/2019 (±%)
人均可支配收入	**Per Capita Disposable Income**	**元**	**yuan**	**47156**	**45452**	**3.7**
（一）工资性收入	Income from Wages and Salaries	元	yuan	28082	27164	3.4
（二）经营净收入	Net Income from Household Operations	元	yuan	8816	8685	1.5
（三）财产净收入	Income from Properties	元	yuan	4008	3850	4.1
（四）转移净收入	Income from Transfers	元	yuan	6250	5753	8.6
人均消费支出	**Per Capita Consumption Expenditure**	**元**	**yuan**	**30294**	**29501**	**2.7**
（一）食品烟酒	Food, Tobacco and Liquor	元	yuan	8520	8325	2.3
（二）衣着	Clothing	元	yuan	2706	2657	1.8
（三）居住	Residence	元	yuan	7173	6969	2.9
（四）生活用品及服务	Household Facilities, Articles and Services	元	yuan	1998	1957	2.1
（五）交通通信	Transportation and Communication	元	yuan	4477	4369	2.5
（六）教育文化娱乐	Education, Cultural and Recreation Services	元	yuan	3012	2904	3.7
（七）医疗保健	Health Care and Medical Services	元	yuan	1679	1600	4.9
（八）其他用品和服务	Other Goods and Services	元	yuan	729	720	1.3
城镇居民人均现住房建筑面积	**Per Capita Building Space in Urban Areas**	**平方米**	**sq.m**	**33.4**	**31.9**	**4.8**
农村居民人均现住房建筑面积	**Per Capita Living Space in Rural Areas**	**平方米**	**sq.m**	**38.0**	**37.0**	**2.7**

10-10 城镇居民家庭基本情况（2015 年）
BASIC CONDITIONS OF URBAN HOUSEHOLDS (2015)

指标名称	Name	单位	Unit	2015 年	2014 年	2015 年比 2014 年增长（±%） 2015/2014 (±%)
人均可支配收入	**Per Capita Disposable Income**	**元**	**yuan**	**40370**	**37346**	**8.1**
（一）工资性收入	Income from Wages and Salaries	元	yuan	25040	23034	8.7
（二）经营净收入	Net Income from Household Operations	元	yuan	6277	5818	7.9
（三）财产净收入	Income from Properties	元	yuan	3580	3436	4.2
（四）转移净收入	Income from Transfers	元	yuan	5473	5058	8.2
人均消费支出	**Per Capita Consumption Expenditure**	**元**	**yuan**	**26052**	**24122**	**8.0**
（一）食品烟酒	Food, Tobacco and Liquor	元	yuan	7856	7295	7.7
（二）衣着	Clothing	元	yuan	2685	2497	7.5
（三）居住	Residence	元	yuan	5607	5302	5.8
（四）生活用品及服务	Household Facilities, Articles and Services	元	yuan	1819	1686	7.9
（五）交通通信	Transportation and Communication	元	yuan	3810	3455	10.3
（六）教育文化娱乐	Education, Cultural and Recreation Services	元	yuan	2264	2057	10.0
（七）医疗保健	Health Care and Medical Services	元	yuan	1352	1227	10.2
（八）其他用品和服务	Other Goods and Services	元	yuan	659	603	9.3

注：本表数据为新口径，2014 年数据与 2015 年年鉴数据不一致。

Note: The data in this sheet is in line with new statistic caliber, which leads to the inconsistency between the data of 2014 and of 2015.

10-11 城镇居民家庭基本情况（2016年）
BASIC CONDITIONS OF URBAN HOUSEHOLDS (2016)

指标名称	Name	单位	Unit	2016年	2015年	2016年比2015年增长（±%）2016/2015（±%）
人均可支配收入	**Per Capita Disposable Income**	**元**	**yuan**	**43598**	**40370**	**8.0**
（一）工资性收入	Income from Wages and Salaries	元	yuan	26898	25040	7.4
（二）经营净收入	Net Income from Household Operations	元	yuan	6846	6277	9.1
（三）财产净收入	Income from Properties	元	yuan	3909	3580	9.2
（四）转移净收入	Income from Transfers	元	yuan	5945	5473	8.6
人均消费支出	**Per Capita Consumption Expenditure**	**元**	**yuan**	**28285**	**26052**	**8.6**
（一）食品烟酒	Food, Tobacco and Liquor	元	yuan	8473	7856	7.9
（二）衣着	Clothing	元	yuan	2882	2685	7.4
（三）居住	Residence	元	yuan	6105	5607	8.9
（四）生活用品及服务	Household Facilities, Articles and Services	元	yuan	1962	1819	7.8
（五）交通通信	Transportation and Communication	元	yuan	4089	3810	7.3
（六）教育文化娱乐	Education, Cultural and Recreation Services	元	yuan	2553	2264	12.8
（七）医疗保健	Health Care and Medical Services	元	yuan	1490	1352	10.2
（八）其他用品和服务	Other Goods and Services	元	yuan	731	659	10.8

10-12 城镇居民家庭基本情况（2017 年）
BASIC CONDITIONS OF URBAN HOUSEHOLDS (2017)

指标名称	Name	单位	Unit	2017 年	2016 年	2017 年比 2016 年增长（±%）2017/2016 (±%)
人均可支配收入	**Per Capita Disposable Income**	元	**yuan**	**47176**	**43598**	**8.2**
（一）工资性收入	Income from Wages and Salaries	元	yuan	28992	26898	7.8
（二）经营净收入	Net Income from Household Operations	元	yuan	7299	6846	6.6
（三）财产净收入	Income from Properties	元	yuan	4297	3909	9.9
（四）转移净收入	Income from Transfers	元	yuan	6588	5945	10.8
人均消费支出	**Per Capita Consumption Expenditure**	元	**yuan**	**30569**	**28285**	**8.1**
（一）食品烟酒	Food, Tobacco and Liquor	元	yuan	9059	8473	6.9
（二）衣着	Clothing	元	yuan	3117	2882	8.1
（三）居住	Residence	元	yuan	6605	6105	8.2
（四）生活用品及服务	Household Facilities, Articles and Services	元	yuan	2121	1962	8.1
（五）交通通信	Transportation and Communication	元	yuan	4399	4089	7.6
（六）教育文化娱乐	Education, Cultural and Recreation Services	元	yuan	2875	2553	12.6
（七）医疗保健	Health Care and Medical Services	元	yuan	1624	1490	9.0
（八）其他用品和服务	Other Goods and Services	元	yuan	769	731	5.2

10-13 城镇居民家庭基本情况（2018 年）
BASIC CONDITIONS OF URBAN HOUSEHOLDS (2018)

指标名称	Name	单位	Unit	2018 年	2017 年	2018 年比 2017 年增长（±%）2018/2017 (±%)
人均可支配收入	**Per Capita Disposable Income**	元	**yuan**	**50817**	**47176**	**7.7**
（一）工资性收入	Income from Wages and Salaries	元	yuan	30955	28992	6.8
（二）经营净收入	Net Income from Household Operations	元	yuan	7836	7299	7.4
（三）财产净收入	Income from Properties	元	yuan	4789	4297	11.4
（四）转移净收入	Income from Transfers	元	yuan	7237	6588	9.9
人均消费支出	**Per Capita Consumption Expenditure**	元	**yuan**	**32890**	**30569**	**7.6**
（一）食品烟酒	Food, Tobacco and Liquor	元	yuan	9318	9059	2.9
（二）衣着	Clothing	元	yuan	3168	3117	1.7
（三）居住	Residence	元	yuan	7751	6605	17.3
（四）生活用品及服务	Household Facilities, Articles and Services	元	yuan	2207	2121	4.0
（五）交通通信	Transportation and Communication	元	yuan	4765	4399	8.3
（六）教育文化娱乐	Education, Cultural and Recreation Services	元	yuan	3122	2875	8.6
（七）医疗保健	Health Care and Medical Services	元	yuan	1764	1624	8.6
（八）其他用品和服务	Other Goods and Services	元	yuan	795	769	3.4

10-14 城镇居民家庭基本情况（2019年）
BASIC CONDITIONS OF URBAN HOUSEHOLDS (2019)

指标名称	Name	单位	Unit	2019年	2018年	2019年比2018年增长（±%）2019/2018（±%）
人均可支配收入	**Per Capita Disposable Income**	**元**	**yuan**	**54484**	**50817**	**7.2**
（一）工资性收入	Income from Wages and Salaries	元	yuan	32921	30955	6.4
（二）经营净收入	Net Income from Household Operations	元	yuan	8455	7836	7.9
（三）财产净收入	Income from Properties	元	yuan	5234	4789	9.3
（四）转移净收入	Income from Transfers	元	yuan	7874	7237	8.8
人均消费支出	**Per Capita Consumption Expenditure**	**元**	**yuan**	**35266**	**32890**	**7.2**
（一）食品烟酒	Food, Tobacco and Liquor	元	yuan	9877	9318	6.0
（二）衣着	Clothing	元	yuan	3276	3168	3.4
（三）居住	Residence	元	yuan	8449	7751	9.0
（四）生活用品及服务	Household Facilities, Articles and Services	元	yuan	2333	2207	5.7
（五）交通通信	Transportation and Communication	元	yuan	5062	4765	6.3
（六）教育文化娱乐	Education, Cultural and Recreation Services	元	yuan	3503	3122	12.2
（七）医疗保健	Health Care and Medical Services	元	yuan	1893	1764	7.3
（八）其他用品和服务	Other Goods and Services	元	yuan	873	795	9.9

10-15 城镇居民家庭基本情况（2020 年）
BASIC CONDITIONS OF URBAN HOUSEHOLDS (2020)

指标名称	Name	单位	Unit	2020 年	2019 年	2020 年比 2019 年增长（±%）2020/2019（±%）
人均可支配收入	**Per Capita Disposable Income**	元	**yuan**	**55905**	**54484**	**2.6**
（一）工资性收入	Income from Wages and Salaries	元	yuan	33641	32921	2.2
（二）经营净收入	Net Income from Household Operations	元	yuan	8479	8455	0.3
（三）财产净收入	Income from Properties	元	yuan	5365	5234	2.5
（四）转移净收入	Income from Transfers	元	yuan	8420	7874	6.9
人均消费支出	**Per Capita Consumption Expenditure**	元	**yuan**	**35936**	**35266**	**1.9**
（一）食品烟酒	Food, Tobacco and Liquor	元	yuan	10025	9877	1.5
（二）衣着	Clothing	元	yuan	3306	3276	0.9
（三）居住	Residence	元	yuan	8626	8449	2.1
（四）生活用品及服务	Household Facilities, Articles and Services	元	yuan	2365	2333	1.4
（五）交通通信	Transportation and Communication	元	yuan	5154	5062	1.8
（六）教育文化娱乐	Education, Cultural and Recreation Services	元	yuan	3608	3503	3.0
（七）医疗保健	Health Care and Medical Services	元	yuan	1977	1893	4.4
（八）其他用品和服务	Other Goods and Services	元	yuan	876	873	0.3

10-16 农村居民家庭基本情况（2015 年）
BASIC CONDITIONS OF RURAL HOUSEHOLDS (2015)

指标名称	Name	单位	Unit	2015 年	2014 年	2015 年比 2014 年增长（±%）2015/2014（±%）
人均可支配收入	**Per Capita Disposable Income**	**元**	**yuan**	**16730**	**15434**	**8.4**
（一）工资性收入	Income from Wages and Salaries	元	yuan	9337	8517	9.6
（二）经营净收入	Net Income from Household Operations	元	yuan	6919	6489	6.6
（三）财产净收入	Income from Properties	元	yuan	236	216	9.3
（四）转移净收入	Income from Transfers	元	yuan	238	212	12.4
人均消费支出	**Per Capita Consumption Expenditure**	**元**	**yuan**	**11127**	**10277**	**8.3**
（一）食品烟酒	Food, Tobacco and Liquor	元	yuan	3442	3188	8.0
（二）衣着	Clothing	元	yuan	826	784	5.3
（三）居住	Residence	元	yuan	2377	2248	5.8
（四）生活用品及服务	Household Facilities, Articles and Services	元	yuan	765	720	6.2
（五）交通通信	Transportation and Communication	元	yuan	1965	1751	12.2
（六）教育文化娱乐	Education, Cultural and Recreation Services	元	yuan	895	809	10.6
（七）医疗保健	Health Care and Medical Services	元	yuan	604	532	13.5
（八）其他用品和服务	Other Goods and Services	元	yuan	253	245	3.3

注：本表数据为新口径，2014 年与去年年鉴数据不一致。

Note: The data in this table is a new caliber, and the data in 2014 and last year's yearbook are inconsistent.

10-17 农村居民家庭基本情况（2016 年）
BASIC CONDITIONS OF RURAL HOUSEHOLDS (2016)

指标名称	Name	单位	Unit	2016 年	2015 年	2016 年比 2015 年增长（±%）2016/2015 (±%)
人均可支配收入	**Per Capita Disposable Income**	元	**yuan**	**17969**	**16730**	**7.4**
（一）工资性收入	Income from Wages and Salaries	元	yuan	10074	9337	7.9
（二）经营净收入	Net Income from Household Operations	元	yuan	7381	6919	6.7
（三）财产净收入	Income from Properties	元	yuan	256	236	8.6
（四）转移净收入	Income from Transfers	元	yuan	258	238	8.2
人均消费支出	**Per Capita Consumption Expenditure**	元	**yuan**	**12006**	**11127**	**7.9**
（一）食品烟酒	Food, Tobacco and Liquor	元	yuan	3651	3442	6.1
（二）衣着	Clothing	元	yuan	905	826	9.5
（三）居住	Residence	元	yuan	2586	2377	8.8
（四）生活用品及服务	Household Facilities, Articles and Services	元	yuan	814	765	6.4
（五）交通通信	Transportation and Communication	元	yuan	2113	1965	7.5
（六）教育文化娱乐	Education, Cultural and Recreation Services	元	yuan	1004	895	12.2
（七）医疗保健	Health Care and Medical Services	元	yuan	658	604	9.0
（八）其他用品和服务	Other Goods and Services	元	yuan	275	253	8.8

10-18 农村居民家庭基本情况（2017年）
BASIC CONDITIONS OF RURAL HOUSEHOLDS (2017)

指标名称	Name	单位	Unit	2017年	2016年	2017年比2016年增长（±%）2017/2016（±%）
人均可支配收入	**Per Capita Disposable Income**	**元**	**yuan**	**19364**	**17969**	**7.8**
（一）工资性收入	Income from Wages and Salaries	元	yuan	10882	10074	8.0
（二）经营净收入	Net Income from Household Operations	元	yuan	7913	7381	7.2
（三）财产净收入	Income from Properties	元	yuan	280	256	9.0
（四）转移净收入	Income from Transfers	元	yuan	289	258	12.2
人均消费支出	**Per Capita Consumption Expenditure**	**元**	**yuan**	**12928**	**12006**	**7.7**
（一）食品烟酒	Food, Tobacco and Liquor	元	yuan	3869	3651	6.0
（二）衣着	Clothing	元	yuan	971	905	7.3
（三）居住	Residence	元	yuan	2801	2586	8.3
（四）生活用品及服务	Household Facilities, Articles and Services	元	yuan	885	814	8.8
（五）交通通信	Transportation and Communication	元	yuan	2262	2113	7.0
（六）教育文化娱乐	Education, Cultural and Recreation Services	元	yuan	1129	1004	12.4
（七）医疗保健	Health Care and Medical Services	元	yuan	717	658	9.0
（八）其他用品和服务	Other Goods and Services	元	yuan	294	275	6.8

10-19 农村居民家庭基本情况（2018年）
BASIC CONDITIONS OF RURAL HOUSEHOLDS (2018)

指标名称	Name	单位	Unit	2018年	2017年	2018年比2017年增长（±%）2018/2017(±%)
人均可支配收入	**Per Capita Disposable Income**	元	**yuan**	**20820**	**19364**	**7.5**
（一）工资性收入	Income from Wages and Salaries	元	yuan	11684	10882	7.4
（二）经营净收入	Net Income from Household Operations	元	yuan	8487	7913	7.3
（三）财产净收入	Income from Properties	元	yuan	310	280	10.8
（四）转移净收入	Income from Transfers	元	yuan	339	289	17.1
人均消费支出	**Per Capita Consumption Expenditure**	元	**yuan**	**13885**	**12928**	**7.4**
（一）食品烟酒	Food, Tobacco and Iquor	元	yuan	4098	3869	5.9
（二）衣着	Clothing	元	yuan	1020	971	5.1
（三）居住	Residence	元	yuan	3024	2801	8.0
（四）生活用品及服务	Household Facilities, Articles and Services	元	yuan	945	885	6.7
（五）交通通信	Transportation and Communication	元	yuan	2445	2262	8.1
（六）教育文化娱乐	Education, Cultural and Recreation Services	元	yuan	1245	1129	10.3
（七）医疗保健	Health Care and Medical Services	元	yuan	794	717	10.6
（八）其他用品和服务	Other Goods and Services	元	yuan	314	294	6.9

10-20 农村居民家庭基本情况（2019 年）
BASIC CONDITIONS OF RURAL HOUSEHOLDS (2019)

指标名称	Name	单位	Unit	2019 年	2018 年	2019 年比 2018 年增长（±%）2019/2018 (±%)
人均可支配收入	**Per Capita Disposable Income**	**元**	**yuan**	**22573**	**20820**	**8.4**
（一）工资性收入	Income from Wages and Salaries	元	yuan	12580	11684	7.7
（二）经营净收入	Net Income from Household Operations	元	yuan	9270	8487	9.2
（三）财产净收入	Income from Properties	元	yuan	344	310	11.1
（四）转移净收入	Income from Transfers	元	yuan	379	339	12.0
人均消费支出	**Per Capita Consumption Expenditure**	**元**	**yuan**	**14899**	**13885**	**7.3**
（一）食品烟酒	Food, Tobacco and Liquor	元	yuan	4393	4098	7.2
（二）衣着	Clothing	元	yuan	1091	1020	6.9
（三）居住	Residence	元	yuan	3222	3024	6.5
（四）生活用品及服务	Household Facilities, Articles and Services	元	yuan	1004	945	6.3
（五）交通通信	Transportation and Communication	元	yuan	2611	2445	6.8
（六）教育文化娱乐	Education, Cultural and Recreation Services	元	yuan	1389	1245	11.5
（七）医疗保健	Health Care and Medical Services	元	yuan	856	794	7.9
（八）其他用品和服务	Other Goods and Services	元	yuan	333	314	6.0

10-21 农村居民家庭基本情况（2020年）
BASIC CONDITIONS OF RURAL HOUSEHOLDS (2020)

指标名称	Name	单位	Unit	2020年	2019年	2020年比2019年增长（±%） 2020/2019（±%）
人均可支配收入	**Per Capita Disposable Income**	**元**	**yuan**	**23656**	**22573**	**4.8**
（一）工资性收入	Income from Wages and Salaries	元	yuan	13151	12580	4.5
（二）经营净收入	Net Income from Household Operations	元	yuan	9720	9270	4.8
（三）财产净收入	Income from Properties	元	yuan	365	344	6.0
（四）转移净收入	Income from Transfers	元	yuan	421	379	10.9
人均消费支出	**Per Capita Consumption Expenditure**	**元**	**yuan**	**15138**	**14899**	**1.6**
（一）食品烟酒	Food, Tobacco and Liquor	元	yuan	4476	4393	1.9
（二）衣着	Clothing	元	yuan	1096	1091	0.5
（三）居住	Residence	元	yuan	3269	3222	1.4
（四）生活用品及服务	Household Facilities, Articles and Services	元	yuan	1011	1004	0.7
（五）交通通信	Transportation and Communication	元	yuan	2659	2611	1.8
（六）教育文化娱乐	Education, Cultural and Recreation Services	元	yuan	1412	1389	1.7
（七）医疗保健	Health Care and Medical Services	元	yuan	880	856	2.7
（八）其他用品和服务	Other Goods and Services	元	yuan	336	333	1.0

10-22 全体居民家庭消费构成
HOUSEHOLDS CONSUMPTION STRUCTURE

项目	Item	2014年		2015年		2016年	
		年人均支出金额（元）Per Capita Annual Expenditure (yuan)	占消费支出的比重（%）Percentage to Consumption Expenditure (%)	年人均支出金额（元）Per Capita Annual Expenditure (yuan)	占消费支出的比重（%）Percentage to Consumption Expenditure (%)	年人均支出金额（元）Per Capita Annual Expenditure (yuan)	占消费支出的比重（%）Percentage to Consumption Expenditure (%)
消费支出	**Consumption Expenditure**	**19653**	**100**	**21326**	**100**	**23256**	**100**
（一）食品烟酒	Food, Tobacco and Liquor	5970	30.4	6459	30.3	6983	30.0
（二）衣着	Clothing	1944	9.9	2096	9.8	2271	9.8
（三）居住	Residence	4316	21.9	4584	21.5	5018	21.6
（四）生活用品及服务	Household Facilities, Articles and Services	1374	7.0	1485	7.0	1607	6.9
（五）交通通信	Transportation and Communication	2905	14.8	3226	15.1	3479	15.0
（六）教育文化娱乐	Education, Cultural and Recreation Services	1654	8.4	1830	8.6	2075	8.9
（七）医疗保健	Health Care and Medical Services	1002	5.1	1115	5.2	1233	5.3
（八）其他用品和服务	Other Goods and Services	488	2.5	531	2.5	590	2.5

2017年		2018年		2019年		2020年	
年人均支出金额（元）Per Capita Annual Expenditure (yuan)	占消费支出的比重（%）Percentage to Consumption Expenditure (%)	年人均支出金额（元）Per Capita Annual Expenditure (yuan)	占消费支出的比重（%）Percentage to Consumption Expenditure (%)	年人均支出金额（元）Per Capita Annual Expenditure (yuan)	占消费支出的比重（%）Percentage to Consumption Expenditure (%)	年人均支出金额（元）Per Capita Annual Expenditure (yuan)	占消费支出的比重（%）Percentage to Consumption Expenditure (%)
25232	**100**	**27316**	**100**	**29501**	**100**	**30294**	**100**
7489	29.7	7787	28.5	8325	28.2	8520	28.1
2467	9.8	2538	9.3	2657	9.0	2706	8.9
5454	21.6	6365	23.3	6969	23.6	7173	23.7
1747	6.9	1837	6.7	1957	6.6	1998	6.6
3753	14.9	4084	15.0	4369	14.8	4477	14.8
2347	9.3	2571	9.4	2904	9.9	3012	10.0
1350	5.4	1480	5.4	1600	5.4	1679	5.5
625	2.4	654	2.4	720	2.5	729	2.4

10-23 城镇居民家庭消费构成
COMPOSITION OF URBAN HOUSEHOLDS CONSUMPTION

项目	Item	2014 年		2015 年		2016 年	
		年人均支出金额（元）Per Capita Annual Expenditure (yuan)	占消费支出的比重（%）Percentage to Consumption Expenditure (%)	年人均支出金额（元）Per Capita Annual Expenditure (yuan)	占消费支出的比重（%）Percentage to Consumption Expenditure (%)	年人均支出金额（元）Per Capita Annual Expenditure (yuan)	占消费支出的比重（%）Percentage to Consumption Expenditure (%)
消费支出	**Consumption Expenditure**	**24122**	**100**	**26052**	**100**	**28285**	**100**
（一）食品烟酒	Food, Tobacco and Liquor	7295	30.2	7856	30.2	8473	30.0
（二）衣着	Clothing	2497	10.4	2685	10.3	2882	10.2
（三）居住	Residence	5302	22.0	5607	21.5	6105	21.6
（四）生活用品及服务	Household Facilities, Articles and Services	1686	7.0	1819	7.0	1962	6.9
（五）交通通信	Transportation and Communication	3455	14.3	3810	14.6	4089	14.4
（六）教育文化娱乐	Education, Cultural and Recreation Services	2057	8.5	2264	8.7	2553	9.0
（七）医疗保健	Health Care and Medical Services	1227	5.1	1352	5.2	1490	5.3
（八）其他用品和服务	Other Goods and Services	603	2.5	659	2.5	731	2.6

2017年		2018年		2019年		2020年	
年人均支出金额（元） Per Capita Annual Expenditure (yuan)	占消费支出的比重（%） Percentage to Consumption Expenditure (%)	年人均支出金额（元） Per Capita Annual Expenditure (yuan)	占消费支出的比重（%） Percentage to Consumption Expenditure (%)	年人均支出金额（元） Per Capita Annual Expenditure (yuan)	占消费支出的比重（%） Percentage to Consumption Expenditure (%)	年人均支出金额（元） Per Capita Annual Expenditure (yuan)	占消费支出的比重（%） Percentage to Consumption Expenditure (%)
30569	**100**	**32890**	**100**	**35266**	**100**	**35936**	**100**
9059	29.6	9318	28.3	9877	28.0	10025	27.9
3117	10.2	3168	9.6	3276	9.3	3306	9.2
6605	21.6	7751	23.6	8449	24.0	8626	24.0
2121	6.9	2207	6.7	2333	6.6	2365	6.6
4399	14.4	4765	14.5	5062	14.3	5154	14.4
2875	9.4	3122	9.5	3503	9.9	3608	10.0
1624	5.3	1764	5.4	1893	5.4	1977	5.5
769	2.6	795	2.4	873	2.5	876	2.4

10-24 农村居民家庭消费构成
COMPOSITION OF RURAL HOUSEHOLDS CONSUMPTION

项目	Item	2014年		2015年		2016年	
		年人均支出金额（元）Per Capita Annual Expenditure (yuan)	占消费支出的比重（%）Percentage to Consumption Expenditure (%)	年人均支出金额（元）Per Capita Annual Expenditure (yuan)	占消费支出的比重（%）Percentage to Consumption Expenditure (%)	年人均支出金额（元）Per Capita Annual Expenditure (yuan)	占消费支出的比重（%）Percentage to Consumption Expenditure (%)
消费支出	**Consumption Expenditure**	**10277**	**100**	**11127**	**100**	**12006**	**100**
（一）食品烟酒	Food, Tobacco and Liquor	3188	31.0	3442	30.9	3651	30.4
（二）衣着	Clothing	784	7.6	826	7.4	905	7.5
（三）居住	Residence	2248	21.9	2377	21.4	2586	21.5
（四）生活用品及服务	Household Facilities, Articles and Services	720	7.0	765	6.9	814	6.8
（五）交通通信	Transportation and Communication	1751	17.0	1965	17.7	2113	17.6
（六）教育文化娱乐	Education, Cultural and Recreation Services	809	7.9	895	8.0	1004	8.4
（七）医疗保健	Health Care and Medical Services	532	5.2	604	5.4	658	5.5
（八）其他用品和服务	Other Goods and Services	245	2.4	253	2.3	275	2.3

2017年		2018年		2019年		2020年	
年人均支出金额（元） Per Capita Annual Expenditure (yuan)	占消费支出的比重（%） Percentage to Consumption Expenditure (%)	年人均支出金额（元） Per Capita Annual Expenditure (yuan)	占消费支出的比重（%） Percentage to Consumption Expenditure (%)	年人均支出金额（元） Per Capita Annual Expenditure (yuan)	占消费支出的比重（%） Percentage to Consumption Expenditure (%)	年人均支出金额（元） Per Capita Annual Expenditure (yuan)	占消费支出的比重（%） Percentage to Consumption Expenditure (%)
12928	**100**	**13885**	**100**	**14899**	**100**	**15138**	**100**
3869	29.9	4098	29.5	4393	29.5	4476	29.6
971	7.5	1020	7.3	1091	7.3	1096	7.2
2801	21.7	3024	21.8	3222	21.6	3269	21.6
885	6.8	945	6.8	1004	6.8	1011	6.7
2262	17.5	2445	17.6	2611	17.5	2659	17.6
1129	8.7	1245	9.0	1389	9.3	1412	9.3
717	5.5	794	5.7	856	5.8	880	5.8
294	2.4	314	2.3	333	2.2	336	2.2

10-25 城镇住户每百户家庭主要耐用品拥有量（1980-2020 年）

OWNERSHIP OF MAJOR DURABLE CONSUMER GOODS PER 100 URBAN HOUSEHOLDS (1980-2020)

年份 Year	家用电脑（台）Computer (set)	钢琴（架）Piano (set)	空调器（台）Air Conditioner (set)	淋浴热水器（台）Shower Water Heater (unit)	洗衣机（台）Washing Machine (set)	电冰箱（台）Household Refrigerator (set)	家用汽车（辆）Automobile (unit)	彩色电视机（台）Color TV (set)	移动电话（部）Call Phone (unit)	照相机（架）Camera (set)
1980										2
1981					12			1		2
1982					22			2		4
1983					27	1		6		6
1984					30	2		8		8
1985					36	4		18		14
1986					40	5		25		15
1987					52	18		34		18
1988					61	33		47		21
1989					67	50		59		22
1990					66	62		68		26
1991					70	76		82		33
1992		1	0	13	73	83		81		39
1993		2	1	18	83	86		88		50
1994		4	1	17	81	89		92		51
1995		4	3	34	82	89		100		61
1996		5	7	40	83	92		105		63
1997	1	5	9	47	83	93		111	3	63
1998	8	5	17	53	83	92		111	7	69
1999	11	4	22	61	83	94		117	15	69
2000	19	2	25	66	83	94		120	30	70
2001	20	2	24	66	84	93		128	36	69
2002	32	2	38	75	89	93	1	123	80	73
2003	41	3	48	76	91	93	0	125	106	70
2004	46	3	55	79	93	93	2	124	128	68
2005	55	4	69	84	92	95	4	118	153	72
2006	71	8	89	88	97	99	6	125	187	82
2007	75	7	98	93	100	107	8	122	194	83
2008	75	5	94	90	95	103	13	116	191	67
2009	82	7	98	91	96	105	18	118	199	71
2010	86	8	99	91	97	107	20	119	208	71
2011	95	8	103	92	98	108	22	117	219	77
2012	101	9	104	93	98	108	29	115	231	79
2013	105	10	104	93	98	107	32	118	232	79
2014	105	10	104	98	99	105	34	109	235	79
2015	80	9	91	91	91	94	50	101	215	57
2016	86		98	93	90	96	58	100	212	63
2017	80		101	94	91	95	60	100	205	
2018	81		120	101	100	108	62	107	228	
2019	89		126	99	100	111	64	110	233	
2020	82		127	101	100	111	62	105	235	

10-26 农村住户每百户家庭主要耐用品拥有量（1985-2020 年）
OWNERSHIP OF MAJOR DURABLE CONSUMER GOODS PER 100 RURAL HOUSEHOLDS (1985-2020)

年份 Year	家用电脑（台） Computer (set)	空调器（台） Air Conditioner (set)	热水器（台） Water Heater (unit)	自行车（辆） Bicycle (unit)	洗衣机（台） Washing Machine (set)	电冰箱（台） Household Refrigerator (set)	彩色电视机（台） Color TV (set)	移动电话（部） Call Phone (unit)	照相机（架） Camera (set)	家用汽车（辆） Automobile (unit)
1985				147	0.3		3		1	
1986				165	1.1	0.3	4.5		1	
1987				148	2.4	0.5	7		2	
1988				154	2.4	1	9		2	
1989				170	3	1	12		2	
1990				164	4	2	13		2	
1991				173	5	4	16		2	
1992				178	5	7	20		2	
1993				203	7	14	26		2	
1994				204	9	21	35		7	
1995				203	16	28	43		6	
1996				198	13	33	46		8	
1997				191	15	36	56		13	
1998				184	17	39	63		15	
1999				185	20	42	74		10	
2000				165	28	47	86		13	
2001				153	28	53	92		13	
2002				152	36	58	98		16	
2003	6	5	33	137	39	60	100	45	16	2
2004	8	8	39	142	48	68	105	68	21	2
2005	14	14	53	138	57	77	109	91	21	5
2006	17	15	54	116	63	87	112	114	14	7
2007	19	19	63	118	70	94	113	132	17	8
2008	25	23	68	124	76	97	114	148	19	9
2009	28	25	71	127	79	99	115	160	21	11
2010	34	30	75	128	82	102	117	170	21	12
2011	44	32	76	114	85	100	112	202	18	15
2012	55	37	85	119	91	102	114	216	21	16
2013	61	45	88	111	93	105	116	221	26	23
2014	61	49	85		93	102	106	225	24	26
2015	46	54	86		92	105	110	219	21	41
2016	56	70	89		96	107	113	226	21	45
2017	52	78	90		98	106	110	223		48
2018	45	93	88		97	109	105	232		43
2019	42	98	96		98	108	104	227		40
2020	45	97	94		98	107	108	231		49

主要统计指标解释

常住成员 指住户成员中，经常在家居住，或者调查期内居住时间超过一半的人员，以及本住户供养的学生。

可支配收入 指调查户在调查期内获得的、可用于最终消费支出和储蓄的总和，即调查户可以用来自由支配的收入。可支配收入既包括现金，也包括实物收入。按照收入的来源，可支配收入包含四项，分别为：工资性收入、经营净收入、财产净收入和转移净收入。计算公式为：

可支配收入 = 工资性收入 + 经营净收入 + 财产净收入 + 转移净收入

居民人均可支配收入是按居民家庭常住人口计算的平均每人可支配收入

消费支出 指住户用于满足家庭日常生活消费需要的全部支出。根据用途不同，消费支出可划分为食品烟酒、衣着、居住、生活用品及服务、交通通信、教育文化娱乐、医疗保健、其他用品及服务八大类。根据来源不同，消费支出可划分为现金消费支出、实物消费支出（含自产自用、来自单位、来自政府和其他社会组织）。

Explanatory Notes on Main Statistical Indicators

Permanent member refers to residents that live usually in home or more than half of the survey period and students that are supported by them.

Disposable income refers to sum of all income earned within the survey period that can be used for deposit and expense on final consumption, which means the income that can be disposed freely by residents. The disposable income includes not only cash, but also income in kinds, which shall be categorized into four kinds according to source of incomes: salary income, net operating income, net property income, net transfer income. Computing formula is as follows:

Disposable income = salary income + net operating income + net property income + net transfer income

Disposable income per capita of residents is the average disposable income per person calculated based on the number of permanent residents of the family.

Consumer spending refers to all spending of residents to cover daily life consumption demands. According to different usages, the consumer spending shall be classified into eight categories: food, cigarettes and alcohol, clothing, housing, daily use articles and services, transportation & communication, education, culture & entertainment, medical and health care, other articles and services. According to sources, the consumer spending shall be classified as cash consumer spending, consumer spending in kinds (including self-produced, from the unit, from government and other social organization) .

农　业 11

AGRICULTURE

简要说明

一、本篇资料的主要内容

本篇资料主要反映了全市农业生产和农村经济的基本情况，主要包括农林牧渔业总产值、中间消耗、增加值、农村劳动力、耕地、主要农产品产量、农业机械年末拥有量、农业机械化和电气化以及农田水利建设等方面的资料。

二、本篇资料的来源

1. 本篇资料中耕地面积资料来源于市自然资源和规划局。

2. 水产品产量等相关资料来源于市海洋发展局。

3. 农业机械化等相关资料来源于市农业农村局。

4. 农田水利灌溉等相关资料来源于市水务管理局。

5. 植树造林等相关资料来源于市园林和林业局。

三、说明

本篇按照国家统计局规定，根据2016年第三次全国农业普查结果对2007年至2017年历史数据进行了核定和修正。

本篇资料由市统计局农村统计处、市统计局国民经济核算处、国家统计局青岛调查队农业农村调查处整理提供。

Brief Introduction

I. Main Content

Data in this chapter show the basic conditions of agricultural production and rural economy, mainly including agricultural output, intermediate consumption, value added, rural labor force, cultivated land, output of main agricultural produces, agricultural machinery and electrification in rural areas and basic construction on irrigation and drainage.

II. Source of Data

1. Data on area of cultivated land are provided by Qingdao Natural Resources and Planning Bureau.

2. Data on output of aquatic products are provided by Qingdao Marine Development Bureau.

3. Data on Agricultural machinery are provided by Qingdao Rural Agriculture Bureau.

4. Data on farmland water conservancy are provided by Qingdao Water Administration Bureau.

5. Data on forest planting are provided by Qingdao Landscape and Forestry Bureau.

III. Explain

This chapter is in accordance with the provisions of the State Statistical Bureau. According to the results of the third national agricultural census in 2016, the historical data from 2007 to 2017 were verified and revised.

The information in this article was compiled and provided by the Rural Statistics Division of the Qingdao Municipal Bureau of Statistics, the National Economic Accounting Division of the Qingdao Municipal Bureau of Statistics, and the Agricultural and Rural Investigation Division of the Qingdao Investigation Team of the National Bureau of Statistics.

11-1 农村基本情况（2000-2020 年）
BASIC STATISTICS ON RURAL AREA (2000-2020)

项目	Item	单位	Unit	2000	2005	2009	2010	2011	2012	2013
一、年末实有耕地面积	**Year-end Area of Cultivated Land**	**万公顷**	**10 000 hectares**	**48**	**42**	**42**			**53**	**53**
二、农用机械总动力	**Total Agricultural Machinery Power**	**万千瓦**	**10 000 kW**	**459**	**620**	**719**	**764**	**784**	**798**	**809**
拖拉机	Tractors	台	unit	126981	163032	180171	200208	202022	206290	206300
三、农村用电量	**Electricity Consumed in Rural Areas**	**万千瓦时**	**10 000 kW·h**	**189651**	**372645**	**426306**	**426819**	**431646**	**426815**	**359139**
四、农用化肥施用量（折纯）	**Consumption of Chemical Fertilizer (convert to pure amount)**	**万吨**	**10 000 tons**	**33**	**33**	**30**	**30**	**29**	**29**	**29**
五、农药使用量	**Pesticide Usage**	**吨**	**10 000 tons**							
六、耕地机电灌溉面积	**Cultivated Land Electromechanical Irrigation Area**	**万公顷**	**10 000 hectares**	**30**	**30**	**32**	**33**	**33**	**33**	**30**

11-1 续表
Continued

项目	Item	单位	Unit	2014	2015	2016	2017	2018	2019	2020
一、年末实有耕地面积	Year-end Area of Cultivated Land	万公顷	10 000 hectares	52	52	52	52	52	52	52
二、农用机械总动力	Total Agricultural Machinery Power	万千瓦	10 000 kW	827	854	698	728	738	751	754.8
拖拉机	Tractors	台	unit	205065	207809	211689	214799	215668	216496	214845
三、农村用电量	Electricity Consumed in Rural Areas	万千瓦时	10 000 kW · h	404380	401122	385434	382437	377858	388484	359584
四、农用化肥施用量（折纯）	Consumption of Chemical Fertilizer (convert to pure amount)	万吨	10 000 tons	29	28	28	28	27	27	26
五、农药使用量	Pesticide Usage	吨	10 000 tons		6252	6145	5962	5627	5401	5273
六、耕地机电灌溉面积	Cultivated Land Electromechanical Irrigation Area	万公顷	10 000 hectares	32	32	33	33	33	33	36

注：1. 农机机械总动力 2016 年为新统计口径，扣除农用运输汽车数据。
2. 2020 年起有效灌溉面积改为耕地机电灌溉面积，数据由农业农村局提供。

Note: 1. Data of total power of agricultural machinery of 2016 is based on the new statistic caliber, deducted by the data of agricultural vehicle.
2. Starting from 2020, the effective irrigation area will be changed to the electromechanical irrigation area of arable land. The data is provided by the Agriculture and Rural Bureau.

11-2 分区市农药、化肥使用量
AMOUNT OF PESTICIDES AND FERTILIZERS USED IN DISTRICT CITIES

单位：吨 (ton)

市、区名称	Region	农药使用量 Pesticide Usage		化肥施用量（折纯） Fertilizer Application Amount (Converted Pure)	
		2020 年	2019 年	2020 年	2019 年
全市	**Whole Municipality**	**5273**	**5401**	**262756**	**267105**
崂山区	Laoshan District	19	53	357	423
西海岸新区	West Coast New Area	493	504	32630	31165
黄岛区	Huangdao District	493	504	32630	31165
保税港区	Qingdao Free Trade Port Area of China				
城阳区	Chengyang District	17	17	585	619
城阳区（不含高新区）	Chengyang District (Excluding High tech District)	17	17	585	619
高新区	High tech District				
即墨区	Jimo District	592	592	31980	32445
胶州市	Jiaozhou	1042	1062	33816	34305
平度市	Pingdu	1670	1711	110978	114956
莱西市	Laixi	1440	1461	52409	53192

11-3 主要年份农、林、牧、渔业总产值（按现价计算）
MAJOR YEAR'S GROSS OUTPUT VALUE OF FARMING, FORESTRY, ANIMAL HUSBANDRY AND FISHERY (CURRENT PRICE)

单位：万元 (10 000 yuan)

年份 Year	农、林、牧、渔业总产值 Gross Output Value of Farming, Forestry, Animal Husbandry and Fishery	农业产值 Farming	林业产值 Forestry	畜牧业产值 Animal Husbandry	渔业产值 Fishery
1949	16511	14755	325	1200	231
1952	24428	21353	479	1888	708
1957	26189	22717	644	2218	610
1962	15356	13257	230	1243	626
1965	25123	21488	854	2110	671
1970	44078	36889	1851	3817	1521
1975	93213	79208	2144	7923	3938
1978	121497	94397	3112	17293	6695
1980	149436	117547	2953	22215	6721
1985	299139	215729	8986	53894	20530
1987	378981	263066	5949	73271	36695
1989	463952	303679	19134	91885	49254
1990	579877	381287	13801	119208	65581
1991	664779	417111	12875	144909	89884
1992	703433	400471	15252	150942	136768
1993	989763	509601	20845	232143	227174
1994	1424074	763366	23101	356734	280873
1995	1923771	1021413	26765	503999	371594
1996	2317434	1145399	29100	692362	450573
1997	2047712	939922	24052	578443	505295
1998	2386303	1198043	16760	633735	537765
1999	2382320	1169596	17122	618020	577582
2000	2483256	1116397	19102	692782	654975
2001	2615228	1135816	20433	758313	700666
2002	2688532	1110671	23157	796007	758697
2003	2759692	1062576	36183	859915	801018
2004	2967389	1181009	32831	937494	816055
2005	3205057	1265695	25246	1070831	843285
2006	3396096	1360755	23546	1076254	855131
2007	3665342	1460800	20801	1143644	916648
2008	3995027	1723855	24356	1195857	907793
2009	4070777	1771982	22133	1133732	980995
2010	4802184	2197935	19090	1225222	1181911
2011	5345885	2188072	19049	1500469	1426786
2012	5672486	2270097	20221	1510234	1633469
2013	6105875	2547805	21875	1553621	1711549
2014	6279086	2644851	22266	1559709	1739234
2015	6123485	2469656	21789	1529587	1814625
2016	6690910	2844023	27741	1621935	1777293
2017	6978980	3003367	30891	1663278	1830324
2018	7369968	3290651	36575	1631422	1920519
2019	7781197	3600911	43066	1671765	1936932
2020	8071003	3732576	44453	1800325	1933437

注：2007 年 -2017 年数据为根据第三次农业普查结果核定修正后数据。
Note: The 2007-2017 data are the approved revised data based on the results of the third agricultural census.

11-4 分市、区农、林、牧、渔业总产值(2020年，现价)
GROSS OUTPUT VALUE OF FARMING, FORESTRY, ANIMAL HUSBANDYRY AND FISHERY BY REGION (2020, CURRENT PRICE)

单位：万元 (10 000 yuan)

市、区名称	Region	农、林、牧、渔业总产值 Gross Output Value of Farming, Forestry, Animal Husbandry and Fishery	农业 Farming	林业 Forestry	畜牧业 Animal Husbandry	渔业 Fishery	服务业 Services
全市	**Whole Municipality**	**8071003**	**3732576**	**44453**	**1800325**	**1933437**	**560212**
崂山区	Laoshan District	119252	17554	428		79203	22067
西海岸新区	West Coast New Area	1550355	530931	6091	178929	735515	98890
黄岛区	Huangdao District	1550355	530931	6091	178929	735515	98890
保税港区	Qingdao Free Trade Port Area of China						
城阳区	Chengyang District	317915	37297	1202	23715	249580	6122
城阳区(不含高新区)	Chengyang District (Excluding High tech District)	317915	37297	1202	23715	249580	6122
高新区	High tech District						
即墨区	Jimo District	1489538	484091	6228	258514	603655	137049
胶州市	Jiaozhou	1099441	510038	6071	221329	256637	105366
平度市	Pingdu	2096230	1473087	13573	508278	2140	99151
莱西市	Laixi	1398272	679578	10860	609560	6707	91567

11-5 分市、区农、林、牧、渔业增加值（2020 年，现价）
VALUE-ADDED OF FARMING, FORESTRY, ANIMAL HUSBANDRY AND FISHERY BY REGION (2020, CURRENT PRICE)

单位：亿元 (100 million yuan)

市、区名称	Region	农、林、牧、渔业增加值 Added Value Of Farming, Forestry, Animal Husbandry and Fishery	农、林、牧、渔专业及辅助性活动 Agriculture, forestry, animal husbandry, fishery and supporting activities
全市	**Whole Municipality**	**453.21**	**27.80**
崂山区	Laoshan District	7.02	1.08
西海岸新区	West Coast New Area	87.02	4.77
黄岛区	Huangdao District	87.02	4.77
保税港区	Qingdao Free Trade Port Area of China		
城阳区	Chengyang District	18.24	0.29
城阳区（不含高新区）	Chengyang District (Excluding High tech District)	18.24	0.29
高新区	High tech District		
即墨区	Jimo District	83.80	6.83
胶州市	Jiaozhou	63.09	5.30
平度市	Pingdu	118.51	5.07
莱西市	Laixi	73.34	4.43

11-6 主要年份耕地面积与播种面积
MAJOR YEAR'S CULTIVATED AND SOWN AREA

单位：万公顷 (10 000 hectares)

年份 Year	年末实有耕地面积 Year-end Area of Cultivated Land	农作物播种面积 Sown Area of Farm Crops	#粮食作物 Grain Crops	#经济作物 Economic Crops
1949		93.47	84.00	7.20
1952		97.53	85.07	10.80
1957		97.87	87.07	10.53
1962		81.47	72.53	5.80
1965		82.80	71.80	8.33
1970		80.73	68.27	10.07
1975		79.82	65.84	11.01
1978		77.60	63.60	10.40
1980		75.87	60.33	12.00
1985		78.27	57.33	15.73
1987		76.67	55.87	15.93
1989		74.78	54.28	16.06
1990		76.85	56.99	15.53
1991		76.98	56.89	15.69
1992		76.96	56.37	15.64
1993	56.90	77.75	56.22	15.71
1994		76.61	54.08	16.20
1995		76.54	53.71	15.65
1996	55.01	77.26	54.81	14.90
1997		75.04	52.32	14.40
1998		77.18	53.05	14.54
1999		77.56	50.61	13.24
2000		76.47	45.07	13.98
2001		73.69	41.91	14.54
2002		72.32	40.83	13.95
2003		67.82	36.05	14.50
2004		71.33	41.40	14.11
2005	42.10	75.02	49.93	11.89
2006	41.29	74.86	49.79	11.75
2007	41.31	64.13	39.16	24.98
2008	41.79	65.29	42.56	22.73
2009	41.87	63.72	42.01	21.72
2010		64.10	42.65	21.45
2011		64.53	43.84	20.70
2012	52.81	64.36	43.95	20.40
2013	52.55	66.16	45.69	20.48
2014	52.42	66.70	46.75	19.95
2015	52.22	67.10	47.93	19.17
2016	52	68.19	48.49	19.70
2017	51.86	67.32	47.79	19.54
2018	51.86	68.37	48.11	20.26
2019	51.62	66.73	47.50	19.23
2020	51.62	66.40	46.95	19.45

注：1. 2009 年前本表数据由市统计局提供。
2. 2010 年起，耕地面积由国土部门提供，粮食作物面积由青岛调查队提供，经济作物面积由市统计局提供。
3. 2007 年 -2017 年农作物播种面积为根据第三次农业普查结果核定修正后数据。
4. 耕地面积由市自然资源和规划局错年提供，2019 年起为 2018 年度变更调查数据。

Note: 1. Those of before 2009 were provided by the National Bureau of Statistics.
2. Since 2010, the area of arable land has been provided by the Ministry of Land and Resources, the area of grain crops has been provided by the Qingdao survey team, and the area of cash crops has been provided by the Municipal Statistics Bureau.
3. Sown Area of Farm Crops from 2007 to 2017 is revised according to the results of the third agricultural census.
4. The area of arable land is provided by the Municipal Bureau of Natural Resources and Planning each year from the previous year's data. Starting from 2019, it will be the 2018 survey data.

11-7 分市、区耕地面积（2020年）
AREA OF CULTIVATED LAND BY REGION (2020)

单位：公顷 (hectares)

市、区名称	Region	年末耕地面积 Year-end Area of Cultivated Land	#旱田 Dry Farmland
全市	**Whole Municipality**	**516213**	**272377**
崂山区	Laoshan District	896	864
西海岸新区	West Coast New Area	73685	71360
黄岛区	Huangdao District	73685	71360
保税港区	Qingdao Free Trade Port Area of China		
城阳区	Chengyang District	6450	5058
城阳区（不含高新区）	Chengyang District (Excluding High tech District)	6450	5058
高新区	High tech District		
即墨区	Jimo District	98918	85813
胶州市	Jiaozhou	62720	23477
平度市	Pingdu	184286	12874
莱西市	Laixi	89228	72901

11-8 分市、区农作物播种面积（2020年）
SOWN AREA OF FARM CROPS BY REGION (2020)

单位：万公顷（10 000 hectares）

市、区名称	Region	总播种面积 Total Sown Area	#粮食 Grain	#棉花 Cotton	#花生 Peanut	#烟叶 Tobacco	#蔬菜 Vegetable
全市	**Whole Municipality**	**66.40**	**46.95**	**0.01**	**7.47**	**0.03**	**10.95**
崂山区	Laoshan District	0.04			0.01		0.03
西海岸新区	West Coast New Area	7.65	4.76		1.93	0.03	0.86
黄岛区	Huangdao District	7.65	4.76		1.93	0.03	0.86
保税港区	Qingdao Free Trade Port Area of China						
城阳区	Chengyang District	0.21	0.09		0.00		0.11
城阳区（不含高新区）	Chengyang District (Excluding High tech District)	0.21	0.09		0.00		0.11
高新区	High tech District						
即墨区	Jimo District	9.99	7.62		1.20		1.05
胶州市	Jiaozhou	8.65	5.91	0.00	0.63	0.00	2.07
平度市	Pingdu	27.29	19.94	0.01	2.09	0.00	4.86
莱西市	Laixi	12.57	8.64		1.62		1.96

11-9 分市、区部分农作物产量（2020 年）
OUTPUT OF FARM CROPS BY REGION (2020)

单位：吨 (ton)

市、区名称	Region	粮食 Grain	棉花 Cotton	花生 Peanut	烟叶 Tobacco	蔬菜 Vegetable
全市	**Whole Municipality**	**3045755**	**136**	**360029**	**750**	**6558479**
崂山区	Laoshan District			163		10999
西海岸新区	West Coast New Area	256413		94737	650	600322
黄岛区	Huangdao District	256413		94737	650	600322
保税港区	Qingdao Free Trade Port Area of China					
城阳区	Chengyang District	5107		123		38839
城阳区（不含高新区）	Chengyang District (Excluding High tech District)	5107		123		38839
高新区	High tech District					
即墨区	Jimo District	434063		52512		628011
胶州市	Jiaozhou	361829	3	26663	46	1094062
平度市	Pingdu	1433515	133	104271	54	2933990
莱西市	Laixi	554829		81559		1252257

11-10 分市、区部分农作物单位面积产量（2020年）
OUTPUT OF FARM CROPS PER HECTARE BY REGION (2020)

单位：千克/公顷 (kg/hectares)

市、区名称	Region	粮食 Grain	棉花 Cotton	花生 Peanut	烟叶 Tobacco	蔬菜 Vegetable
全市	**Whole Municipality**	**6487**	**1460**	**4817**	**2348**	**59880**
崂山区	Laoshan District			3185		31868
西海岸新区	West Coast New Area	5389		4904	2379	69887
黄岛区	Huangdao District	5389		4904	2379	69887
保税港区	Qingdao Free Trade Port Area of China					
城阳区	Chengyang District	5845		4847		34877
城阳区（不含高新区）	Chengyang District (Excluding High tech District)	5845		4847		34877
高新区	High tech District					
即墨区	Jimo District	5697		4376		59807
胶州市	Jiaozhou	6119	1362	4224	2850	52796
平度市	Pingdu	7191	1463	4994	1800	60335
莱西市	Laixi	6421		5051		63803

11-11 主要年份农作物总产量
MAJOR YEAR'S OUTPUT OF FARM CROPS

单位：吨 (ton)

年份 Year	粮食 Grain	#小麦 Wheat	#玉米 Corn	棉花 Cotton	花生 Peanut	水果 Fruit	蔬菜 Vegetable
1949	723190	158815	25810	1280	71080	9955	356015
1952	967640	200380	58130	6025	115585	13468	284050
1957	921920	210690	141540	3520	90445	18869	625220
1962	628930	104340	53010	1280	35470	8366	524455
1965	917635	180610	135595	6090	88390	16034	465850
1970	1175985	243945	244530	16490	96280	33907	541145
1975	1899540	430135	420095	15390	98495	59206	693970
1978	1900850	514570	510635	8720	114370	82819	921140
1980	2164415	520045	819930	19630	160670	80840	996565
1985	2331060	961055	739455	19335	475270	200515	1253075
1987	2626029	996165	1030926	13819	394296	249655	1489250
1989	2654334	993406	1084441	14638	391782	288757	1664238
1990	2998246	1265157	1210687	17490	413636	292366	1786041
1991	3180893	1421143	1285043	25965	446880	294349	1837265
1992	2675641	1235755	981490	8160	321145	341415	2030327
1993	3164812	1463759	1248780	15344	419109	383368	2705349
1994	3106562	1392977	1252952	8326	494827	423024	3002318
1995	3291587	1480385	1365167	8177	510662	478685	3221507
1996	3390033	1513479	1466668	4001	486574	505711	3405056
1997	2523064	1584478	743199	2000	308233	438398	3333181
1998	3469821	1627261	1484182	4159	546786	529592	4036992
1999	3331124	1501182	1499775	3668	572941	606800	5459140
2000	2780481	1353445	1169649	2077	534174	651591	6649322
2001	2539257	1143679	1178851	3409	579441	675244	6250361
2002	2383802	1085936	1094731	3755	557714	579703	6847570
2003	2221697	931787	1117704	5324	568798	677361	7305618
2004	2650952	1301791	1202063	7216	580290	748516	6720886
2005	3150203	1535471	1478616	4042	503941	737300	5792110
2006	3039266	1548928	1372166	3954	471853	827755	6051239
2007	2319354	1118044	1106106	3546	495458	1366106	6180515
2008	2602592	1234264	1279002	3163	470424	1276385	6164760
2009	2590287	1276029	1228485	3213	467937	1294706	5743437
2010	2553744	1206593	1272970	2411	439872	1267226	5895190
2011	2678626	1213908	1386365	2375	441237	1262896	5948249
2012	2707295	1242299	1396704	2334	456372	1201836	5826702
2013	2791826	1295227	1432355	2057	440426	1217969	5906625
2014	2780244	1302282	1418469	1392	394461	1188690	6134061
2015	2878062	1332125	1497121	1279	342034	1189312	5988945
2016	2940668	1345273	1551200	408	365207	1207498	5915380
2017	2968896	1264073	1670338	420	383668	1187041	6277779
2018	3100964	1376646	1690817	977	384918	1092176	6443615
2019	3026054	1426280	1544645	434	342424	1185951	6261517
2020	3045755	1334205	1635225	136	360029	1164739	6558479

注：2007 年 -2017 年数据为根据第三次农业普查结果核定修正后数据。
Note: Agricultural data from 2007 to 2017 are revised according to the results of the third agricultural census.

11-11 续表 1 分市、区部分蔬菜产量（2020 年）

Continued OUTPUT OF SOME VEGETABLES BY CITY AND DISTRICT (2020)

单位：吨 (ton)

市、区名称	Region	蔬菜 Vegetable	#大白菜 Cabbage	#芹菜 Celery	#胡萝卜 Carrot	#马铃薯 Potato
全市	**Whole Municipality**	**6558479**	**1309642**	**150707**	**707781**	**1205889**
崂山区	Laoshan District	10999	5284	32	41	2208
西海岸新区	West Coast New Area	600322	271439	27179	1021	117054
黄岛区	Huangdao District	600322	271439	27179	1021	117054
保税港区	Qingdao Free Trade Port Area of China					
城阳区	Chengyang District	38839	4031	1239	580	3908
城阳区（不含高新区）	Chengyang District (Excluding High tech District)	38839	4031	1239	580	3908
高新区	High tech District					
即墨区	Jimo District	628011	126926	11476	82240	94076
胶州市	Jiaozhou	1094062	269854	58195	5849	409506
平度市	Pingdu	2933990	468224	23173	388645	519743
莱西市	Laixi	1252257	163883	29412	229404	59394

11-11 续表 2 分市、区部分蔬菜产量（2020 年）

Continued OUTPUT OF SOME VEGETABLES BY CITY AND DISTRICT (2020)

单位：吨 (ton)

市、区名称	Region	#黄瓜 Cucumber	#西红柿 Tomato	#大葱 Green onion	#蒜头 Garlic	#食用菌 Edible fungi
全市	**Whole Municipality**	**402368**	**439173**	**745090**	**103895**	**39151**
崂山区	Laoshan District	447	134	139	25	
西海岸新区	West Coast New Area	14396	51657	4267	961	17571
黄岛区	Huangdao District	14396	51657	4267	961	17571
保税港区	Qingdao Free Trade Port Area of China					
城阳区	Chengyang District	9023	7497	346	27	739
城阳区（不含高新区）	Chengyang District (Excluding High tech District)	9023	7497	346	27	739
高新区	High tech District					
即墨区	Jimo District	53886	27586	64627	1590	14450
胶州市	Jiaozhou	22942	18731	54490	779	552
平度市	Pingdu	38926	108297	608219	90942	3851
莱西市	Laixi	262748	225271	13003	9572	1988

11-12 分市、区猪、羊及家禽存养量（2020年）
HOGS, SHEEP, GOATS AND POULTRY IN STOCK BY REGION (2020)

单位：万头、万只 (10 000 head)

市、区名称	Region	年末生猪存养量 Hoga in Stock (year-end)	#母猪 Sow	牛 Cattle and Buffaloes	#奶牛 Cows	年末羊存养量 Sheep and Goats in Stock (year-end)	年末家禽存栏 Poultry stock at the eng of the year	#蛋禽 Egg Poultry
全市	**Whole Municipality**	**169.24**	**19.38**	**13.34**	**9.37**	**17.58**	**4531.18**	**1460.81**
崂山区	Laoshan District							
西海岸新区	West Coast New Area	26.09	1.97	0.73	0.02	2.59	407.87	132.02
黄岛区	Huangdao District	26.09	1.97	0.73	0.02	2.59	407.87	132.02
保税港区	Qingdao Free Trade Port Area of China							
城阳区	Chengyang District	1.52	0.22	0.15	0.15	0.11	33.60	29.30
城阳区（不含高新区）	Chengyang District (Excluding High tech District)	1.52	0.22	0.15	0.15	0.11	33.60	29.30
高新区	High tech District							
即墨区	Jimo District	22.54	3.11	2.54	2.01	1.53	1191.22	555.82
胶州市	Jiaozhou	22.05	2.58	0.65	0.13	3.12	361.12	206.10
平度市	Pingdu	57.08	5.37	1.00	0.33	7.02	1262.84	233.82
莱西市	Laixi	39.96	6.13	8.26	6.72	3.21	1274.54	303.75

11-13 分市、区肉、蛋、奶产量（2020年）
OUTPUT OF MEAT, EGGS AND MILK BY REGION (2020)

单位：万吨 (10 000 tons)

市、区名称	Region	肉类产量 Output of Meat	#猪肉 Port	#禽肉 Poultry Meat	禽蛋 Poultry Eggs	牛奶 Milk
全市	**Whole Municipality**	**48.03**	**16.55**	**29.84**	**24.70**	**30.67**
崂山区	Laoshan District					
西海岸新区	West Coast New Area	4.95	2.72	1.95	2.53	0.25
黄岛区	Huangdao District	4.95	2.72	1.95	2.53	0.25
保税港区	Qingdao Free Trade Port Area of China					
城阳区	Chengyang District	0.25	0.19	0.05	0.46	0.82
城阳区（不含高新区）	Chengyang District (Excluding High tech District)	0.25	0.19	0.05	0.46	0.82
高新区	High tech District					
即墨区	Jimo District	5.99	1.93	3.90	8.34	5.81
胶州市	Jiaozhou	3.15	2.38	0.51	3.92	0.68
平度市	Pingdu	15.50	5.21	9.86	4.25	1.38
莱西市	Laixi	18.20	4.13	13.57	5.20	21.72

11-14 分市、区渔业养殖面积
AQUACULTURE AREA BY REGION

单位：公顷 (hectare)

市、区名称	Region	2020年 养殖面积 Aquaculture Area	#海水 Seawater	#淡水 Fresh Water	2019年 养殖面积 Aquaculture Area	#海水 Seawater	#淡水 Fresh Water
全市	**Whole Municipality**	**35214**	**32233**	**2981**	**34460**	**31516**	**2944**
崂山区	Laoshan District	986	986		986	986	
西海岸新区	West Coast New Area	12845	12436	409	11864	11438	426
黄岛区	Huangdao District	12845	12436	409	11864	11438	426
保税港区	Qingdao Free Trade Port Area of China						
城阳区	Chengyang District	6215	6062	153	7005	6741	264
城阳区（不含高新区）	Chengyang District (Excluding High tech District)	6215	6062	153	7005	6741	264
高新区	High tech District						
即墨区	Jimo District	11186	10916	270	10801	10600	201
胶州市	Jiaozhou	2524	1833	691	2442	1751	691
平度市	Pingdu	513		513	430		430
莱西市	Laixi	945		945	932		932

11-15 分市、区水产品总产量（2020年）
OUTPUT OF AQUATIC PRODUCTS BY REGION (2020)

单位：吨 (ton)

市、区名称	Region	水产品总产量 Output of Aquatic Products	#养殖产量 Aquaculture Output	#捕捞产量 Catch	#鱼类 Fish	#甲壳类 Crust	#贝类 Shellfish	#藻类 Algae
全市	**Whole Municipality**	**1010510**	**815740**	**194770**	**149695**	**53934**	**731570**	**840**
崂山区	Laoshan District	35198	11894	23304	15160	2547	12929	
西海岸新区	West Coast New Area	350527	287718	62809	78487	17353	219381	
黄岛区	Huangdao District	350527	287718	62809	78487	17353	219381	
保税港区	Qingdao Free Trade Port Area of China							
城阳区	Chengyang District	236375	201709	34666	13621	5879	199161	
城阳区（不含高新区）	Chengyang District (Excluding High tech District)	236375	201709	34666	13621	5879	199161	
高新区	High tech District							
即墨区	Jimo District	283955	233393	50562	14503	22248	230714	840
胶州市	Jiaozhou	101068	77915	23153	24605	5842	69385	
平度市	Pingdu	1170	1170		1102	65		
莱西市	Laixi	2217	1941	276	2217			

11-16 分市、区植树及造林面积（2020年）

OUTPUT OF AQUATIC PRODUCTS BY REGION (2020)

市、区名称	Region	当年造林面积（公顷）Area of Afforestation in the Year (hectare)	育苗数量（万株）Number of Seedlings (10 000trees)	森林抚育作业面积（公顷）Forest Tending Area (hectare)	零星（四旁）植树（万株）Surrounding Tree Planting (10 000trees)
全市	**Whole Municipality**	**1482**	**9771.6**	**7733**	**245.0**
崂山区	Laoshan District		29.0	182	11.0
西海岸新区	West Coast New Area	83	3898.0	75	
黄岛区	Huangdao District	83	3898.0	75	
保税港区	Qingdao Free Trade Port Area of China				
城阳区	Chengyang District	60	425.0	800	37.5
城阳区（不含高新区）	Chengyang District (Excluding High tech District)	60	425.0	800	37.5
高新区	High tech District				
即墨区	Jimo District		2700.0	267	
胶州市	Jiaozhou	354	690.1	232	18.0
平度市	Pingdu	751	1628.0	6000	130.3
莱西市	Laixi	234	401.5	177	48.2

11-17 分市、区水果产量（2020年）

AREA OF FORESTATION AND OUTPUT OF FRUITS BY REGION (2020)

单位：吨 (ton)

市、区名称	Region	水果总产量 Output of Fruits (ton)	#园林水果 Garden Fruits	#瓜果类水果 Melon Fruits
全市	**Whole Municipality**	**1164739**	**749900**	**414839**
崂山区	Laoshan District	6841	6759	82
西海岸新区	West Coast New Area	125800	101788	24012
黄岛区	Huangdao District	125800	101788	24012
保税港区	Qingdao Free Trade Port Area of China			
城阳区	Chengyang District	18712	16926	1786
城阳区（不含高新区）	Chengyang District (Excluding High tech District)	18712	16926	1786
高新区	High tech District			
即墨区	Jimo District	52915	31340	21575
胶州市	Jiaozhou	58625	42447	16178
平度市	Pingdu	448223	244431	203792
莱西市	Laixi	453624	306209	147415

11-17 续表
Continued

单位：吨 (ton)

市、区名称	Region	#苹果 Apple	#梨 Pear	#桃 Peach	#葡萄 Grape	#杏 Apricot	#山楂 Hawthorn	#西瓜 Watermelon	#甜瓜 Muskmelon
全市	**Whole Municipality**	**253257**	**111323**	**140164**	**154574**	**11389**	**2464**	**232296**	**112367**
崂山区	Laoshan District	88	55	1687	9	1566	2		
西海岸新区	West Coast New Area	40851	4077	24074	3640	300	58	15566	815
黄岛区	Huangdao District	40851	4077	24074	3640	300	58	15566	815
保税港区	Qingdao Free Trade Port Area of China								
城阳区	Chengyang District	1020	207	5500	4331	3843	1	4	2
城阳区（不含高新区）	Chengyang District (Excluding High tech District)	1020	207	5500	4331	3843	1	4	2
高新区	High tech District								
即墨区	Jimo District	8227	2366	13032	3393	216	46	14034	2751
胶州市	Jiaozhou	15914	3582	9675	4292	5444	71	14811	276
平度市	Pingdu	58572	23789	51414	76426	20	438	162645	1873
莱西市	Laixi	128586	77246	34782	62482	0	1847	25237	106649

11-18 分市、区果园、茶园面积和茶叶产量（2020年）
AREA OF ORCHARD AND TEA GARDEN AND PRODUCTION OF TEA BY CITY AND DISTRICT (2020)

单位：公顷 (hectare)，吨 (ton)

市、区名称	Region	果园面积 Area of Orchards	#苹果园 Apple Orchard	#梨园 Pear Orchard	#葡萄园 Vineyard	#桃园 Peach Orchard	茶园面积 Area of Tea Plantations	茶叶产量 Tea Yield
全市	**Whole Municipality**	**31179**	**8271**	**3453**	**4681**	**6390**	**4583**	**4632**
崂山区	Laoshan District	616	3	3	1	65	1121	1294
西海岸新区	West Coast New Area	5517	1062	151	174	1440	3036	2791
黄岛区	Huangdao District	5517	1062	151	174	1440	3036	2791
保税港区	Qingdao Free Trade Port Area of China							
城阳区	Chengyang District	901	37	6	150	216	31	50
城阳区（不含高新区）	Chengyang District (Excluding High tech District)	901	37	6	150	216	31	50
高新区	High tech District							
即墨区	Jimo District	1659	293	182	136	819	304	489
胶州市	Jiaozhou	1564	431	100	114	417	30	5
平度市	Pingdu	11175	2685	943	2062	1683	47	5
莱西市	Laixi	9746	3758	2068	2044	1750	13	

11-19 主要年份主要农业机械拥有量
MAJOR YEAR'S OWNERSHIP OF AGRICULTURAL MACHINERY

年份 Year	农业机械总动力（万千瓦）Total Agricultural Machinery Power (10 000kW)	农用拖拉机 Agricultural Tractors		大、中型机引农具（万台）Large and Medium Towing Farm Machinery (10 000 sets)	排灌机械 Drainage and Irrigation Machinery	
		混合台 set	千瓦 kW		台 set	万千瓦 10 000kW
1949						
1952						
1957	0.22	59	2.2	0.01		
1962	2.47	254	11.47	0.06		
1965	3.49	296	13.2	0.08		
1970	10.40	602	7 963	0.07		
1975	43.94	6447	103 476	0.48		
1978	75.45	15576	309 287	1.02		
1980	110.44	24278	502 731	1.72		
1985	174.76	33097	506 217	1.71	67794	54.92
1990	253.52	55363	680 903	2.03	105574	74.63
1991	250.58	57404	691 332	2.20	134900	73.77
1992	253.94	57182	684 182	2.28	124800	82.68
1993	261.24	56335	678 161	2.34	144460	78.96
1994	278.41	58698	688 886	2.39	147259	80.81
1995	289.23	56391	657 025	2.28	138625	73.98
1996	303.57	59698	680 447	2.32	148313	81.53
1997	326.72	66841	744 424	2.42	155629	88.09
1998	364.21	87226	894 985	2	156565	86.68
1999	411.44	105743	1 075 907	3	170875	96.20
2000	459.21	126981	1 253 210	3	182646	108.26
2001	496.27	141409	1 394 114	4	178437	104.18
2002	534.92	152920	1 537 544	5	182799	107.35
2003	560.94	160676	1 666 185	5	192930	109.44
2004	599	168061	1 818 276	5	192144	110
2005	620	163032	1757177	6	188689	112
2006	651	171155	1890402	6	192010	116
2007	680	173326	1958047	7	195050	118
2008	697	176156	2034453	8	208711	134
2009	719	180171	2266697	9	207648	134
2010	764	200208	2331867	10	190770	123
2011	784	202022	2649283	10	189834	127
2012	798	206290	2759004	10	190134	127
2013	809	206309	2968332	10	190433	127
2014	827	205065	2960438	10	190584	128
2015	854	207809	3176870	10	191152	128
2016	698	211689	3372681	10	191283	128
2017	728	214799	3550005	11	191417	128
2018	738	215668	3668505	0.8	232943	
2019	752	216496	3769281	1.7	232952	
2020	755	214845	3789730			

注：1. 大、中型机引农具 2018 年为新统计口径，只统计功率 58.8 千瓦以上机引农具。
2. 2020 年起，农业农村局不再提供大、中型机引农具及排灌机械数据。

Note: 1.Large and medium type agricultural tools are the new statistical caliber in 2018, and only the statistical power is 58.8 kilowatts or more.
2.Starting in 2020, the Bureau of Agriculture and Rural Affairs will no longer provide data on large and medium-sized mechanically-introduced agricultural tools and irrigation and drainage machinery.

11-20 主要年份农业机械化用电量、化肥施用量

MAJOR YEAR'S MECHANIZATION, ELECTRICITY AND CHEMICAL FERTILIZER CONSUMPTION

年份 Year	耕地机电灌溉面积（公顷） Cultivated Land Electromechanical Irrigation Area (hectare)	配套机电井（眼） Number of Electromechanical Well (unit)	机耕面积（公顷） Area of Motorized Cultivation (hectare)	机播面积（公顷） Area of Motorized Planting (hectare)	机收面积（公顷） Area of Motorized Harvesting (hectare)	农村用电量（万千瓦时） Electricity Consumption in Rural Area (10 000kW・h)	化肥施用量（折纯万吨） Chemical Fertilizer Consumption (convert to 10 000tons)
1949	8340						
1952	14980						
1957	59353		12800	13			0.19
1962	55213	191	65680	927	927	55	0.10
1965	80000	125	11433	573	247	128	0.55
1970	147613	3947	143700	2527	133	1208	1.76
1975	233980	12820	248867	54507	953	2522	2.77
1978	276660	21017	329213	178533	15060	13975	3.64
1980	296606	22472	444800	187980	55333	20492	12.06
1985	302647	42925	366786	148433	56447	41524	11.66
1990	274680	56821	426680	220593	143133	67616	20.47
1991	281500	58987	431293	254266	192946	81200	22.53
1992	281610	62100	438533	270453	207780	88024	22.60
1993	284080	63954	439300	260287	225807	102501	28.04
1994	286750	64877	436820	262846	238693	121307	28.73
1995	287020	64651	435213	271707	250267	134284	31.45
1996	289320	65237	438947	280480	235933	143740	31.36
1997	292130	66783	442213	308267	266147	150971	28.99
1998	294120	64109	442920	359447	285513	153113	32.0
1999	294790	64734	440967	396180	286367	169337	32.6
2000	295190	65179	439980	346480	292787	189651	32.5
2001	296980	65547	436576	382870	265730	228069	31.7
2002	294310	65588	433660	364680	267690	256453	31.1
2003	292410	65406	415790	404980	256600	299425	31.9
2004	292520	65501	415220	454800	314680	330609	32.5
2005	296450	65303	409610	493240	367740	372644	33.0
2006	303070	65981	403980	493750	398700	413762	32.6
2007	305760	66400	400480	499590	429630	425715	33.9
2008	313920	66828	404080	517540	455120	424292	31.1
2009	322710	67027	404080	538220	481176	426306	30.2
2010	328960	67242	578726	558611	499248	426819	29.9
2011	331690	62104	600451	567947	547108	431646	29.4
2012	333850	62112	610382	627701	566653	426815	29.1
2013	302790	170008	410601	627701	566653	359138	29.1
2014	321670	169491	411355	590798	545360	404380	28.9
2015	323400	155074	417991	640022	600696	401122	28.5
2016	327600	135057	362912	561022	511000	385434	28.37
2017	329620	139342	360085	566264	516763	382437	27.83
2018	331240	136785	359238	578082	531733	377858	27.05
2019	329390	136963	353624	563689	527199	388484	26.71
2020	355077		334148	563410	516895	359584	26.28

注：1.2020 年起有效灌溉面积改为耕地机电灌溉面积，数据由农业农村局提供。
　　2.2020 年起，部门不再提供配套机电井数据。

Note: 1. Starting from 2020, the effective irrigation area will be changed to the electromechanical irrigation area of arable land. The data is provided by the Agriculture and Rural Bureau.
2. Starting from 2020, the department will no longer provide supporting electromechanical well data.

11-21 分市、区农业机械化和电气化（2020 年）
MECHANIZATION AND ELECTRIFICATION IN AGRICULTURE BY REGION (2020)

市、区名称	Region	农村用电量（万千瓦小时）Electricity Consumed in Rural Areas (10 000kW·h)	机耕作业面积 Area of Motorized Cultivation (hectare)	机播地面积 Area of Motorized Planting (hectare)	机收面积 Area of Motorized Harvesting (hectare)
			面积 Area（公顷）(hectare)		
全市	**Whole Municipality**	**359584**	**334148**	**563410**	**516895**
崂山区	Laoshan District	10455			
西海岸新区	West Coast New Area	35681	45475	66249	61043
黄岛区	Huangdao District	35681	45475	66249	61043
保税港区	Qingdao Free Trade Port Area of China				
城阳区	Chengyang District	51289	945	940	932
城阳区（不含高新区）	Chengyang District (Excluding High tech District)	51289	945	940	932
高新区	High tech District				
即墨区	Jimo District	61875	46901	86619	82282
胶州市	Jiaozhou	99744	32261	70073	68438
平度市	Pingdu	64718	145453	233722	211224
莱西市	Laixi	35823	63114	105806	92976

11-22 分市、区农用化肥施用量（2020 年）
CONSUMPTION OF CHEMICAL FERTILIZERS BY REGION (2020)

单位：吨（折纯）(convert to pure amount)

市、区名称	Region	农用化肥施用量 Consumption of Chemical Fertilizers	氮肥 Nitrogenous Fertilizer	磷肥 Phosphate Fertilizer	钾肥 Potash Fertilizer	复合肥 Compound Fertilizer	附：平均每公顷耕地施用化肥量（折纯千克）Annotation: Consumption of Chemical Fertilizer Per Hectare (convert to pure volume)
全市	**Whole Municipality**	**262756**	**35984**	**10851**	**14626**	**201295**	**509**
崂山区	Laoshan District	357	7	2	2	345	398
西海岸新区	West Coast New Area	32630	5788	2501	4311	20031	443
黄岛区	Huangdao District	32630	5788	2501	4311	20031	443
保税港区	Qingdao Free Trade Port Area of China						
城阳区	Chengyang District	585	111	51	52	371	91
城阳区（不含高新区）	Chengyang District (Excluding High tech District)	585	111	51	52	371	91
高新区	High tech District						
即墨区	Jimo District	31980	9654	2107	1398	18821	323
胶州市	Jiaozhou	33816	5399	823	3687	23908	539
平度市	Pingdu	110978	5903	2073	3026	99975	602
莱西市	Laixi	52409	9122	3294	2150	37844	587

11-23　分市、区农田水利情况（2020 年）
FARMLAND WATER CONSERVANCY BY REGION（2020）

市、区名称	Region	耕地机电灌溉面积（公顷）Cultivated Land Electromechanical Irrigation Area (hectare)	机电灌溉面积占耕地面积比重（%）Proportion of Electromechanical Irrigation Area in Cultivated Land Area (%)
全市	**Whole Municipality**	**355077**	**68.8**
崂山区	Laoshan District		
西海岸新区	West Coast New Area	43254	58.7
黄岛区	Huangdao District	43254	58.7
保税港区	Qingdao Free Trade Port Area of China		
城阳区	Chengyang District	935	14.5
城阳区（不含高新区）	Chengyang District (Excluding High tech District)	935	14.5
高新区	High tech District		
即墨区	Jimo District	65520	66.2
胶州市	Jiaozhou	18500	29.5
平度市	Pingdu	172958	93.9
莱西市	Laixi	53910	60.4

11-24 分市、区主要农业机械拥有量（2020年）
OWNERSHIP OF MAJOR AGRICULTURAL MACHINERY BY REGION (2020)

市、区名称	Region	农业机械总动力（万千瓦） Agricultural Machinery Power (10 000kW)	平均每公顷耕地拥有量（千瓦） Power Per Hectare of Cultivated Land (kW)	大中型拖拉机 Large and Medium Tractors		小型拖拉机 Small Tractors	
				台 set	千瓦 kW	台 set	千瓦 kW
全市	**Whole Municipality**	**754.8**	**14.6**	**45751**	**2329335**	**169094**	**1460395**
崂山区	Laoshan District						
西海岸新区	West Coast New Area	83.2	11.3	2762	135832	44627	282247
黄岛区	Huangdao District	83.2	11.3	2762	135832	44627	282247
保税港区	Qingdao Free Trade Port Area of China						
城阳区	Chengyang District	26.2	40.6	54	3102	189	1133
城阳区（不含高新区）	Chengyang District (Excluding High tech District)	26.2	40.6	54	3102	189	1133
高新区	High tech District						
即墨区	Jimo District	112.9	11.4	4466	251510	34600	318582
胶州市	Jiaozhou	111.5	17.8	5130	342780	19836	283994
平度市	Pingdu	283.0	15.4	25422	1217109	33723	320365
莱西市	Laixi	138.0	15.5	7917	379002	36119	254074

11-24 续表
Continued

市、区名称	Region	机引犁（部） Towing Ploughs (unit)	机引耙（部） Towing Rakes (unit)	粮食加工机械（台） Grain Processing Machinery (unit)	油料加工机械（部） Oil Processing Machinery (unit)	棉花加工机械（部） Cotton Processing Machinery (unit)	饲草料加工机械（台套） Forage Processing Machinery (unit)
全市	**Whole Municipality**	**160472**	**32230**	**25700**	**9139**	**132**	**22652**
崂山区	Laoshan District						
西海岸新区	West Coast New Area	32937	109	1117	256		2999
黄岛区	Huangdao District	32937	109	1117	256		2999
保税港区	Qingdao Free Trade Port Area of China						
城阳区	Chengyang District	1196	197	1602	515	17	338
城阳区（不含高新区）	Chengyang District (Excluding High tech District)	1196	197	1602	515	17	338
高新区	High tech District						
即墨区	Jimo District	19959	1680	3259	1472		1481
胶州市	Jiaozhou	15145	5242	3070	2125		3589
平度市	Pingdu	21850	16500	4372	1421	6	7538
莱西市	Laixi	69385	8502	12280	3350	109	6707

主要统计指标解释

农业总产值 是以货币表现的农、林、牧、渔业全部产品的总量，它反映一定时期内农业生产的总规模和总成果。

农、林、牧、渔业的统计范围是：

（1）农业包括农作物种植业和其他农业。

农作物种植业包括谷物、豆类、薯类、棉、油料、糖料、麻类、烟叶、蔬菜、药材、瓜类和其他农作物的种植，以及茶园、桑园、果园的生产经营。其他农业包括采集野生植物的果实、纤维、树胶、树脂、油料以及柴草、野生药材、菌类等及农民家庭兼营的商品性工业。

（2）林业包括林木的栽培（不包括茶园、桑园和果园的栽培、管理和收获等活动）、林产品的采集和村及村以下合作经济组织和农户的竹木采伐。

（3）畜牧业包括除渔业养殖以外的一切动物饲养和放牧，以及野生动物的捕猎和饲养。

（4）渔业包括水生动物和海藻类植物的养殖和捕捞。

（5）农、林、牧、渔专业及辅助性活动指对农业提供的各种专业及辅助性生产活动，不包括各种科学技术和专业技术服务。

粮食产量 指稻谷、小麦、玉米、高粱等谷物及薯类和豆类的全社会产量。包括国有经济经营的、集体统一经营的和农民家庭经营的粮食产量，还包括工矿企业办的农场和其他生产单位的产量。其产量计算方法，豆类按去豆荚后的干豆计算；薯类（不包括芋头、木薯和马铃薯）按5公斤鲜薯折1公斤粮食计算；马铃薯作为蔬菜统计；其他粮食一律按脱粒后的原粮计算。

水产品产量 指人工养殖的水产品和天然生长的水产品的捕捞量．包括海水的鱼类、虾蟹类、贝类和藻类以及内陆水域的鱼类、虾蟹类和贝类，不包括淡水生植物。

猪、牛、羊肉产量 指当年出栏并已屠宰、除去头蹄下水后带骨头肉（即胴体重）的重量。其统计范围为全社会。

农用化肥施用量 指本年内实际用于农业生产的化肥数量，包括氮肥、磷肥、钾肥和复合肥。化肥施用量要求按折纯量计算数量。折纯量是指把氮肥、磷肥、钾肥分别按含氮、含五氧化二磷、含氧化钾的百分之百成分进行折算后的数量。复合肥按其所含主要成分折算。

公式：折纯量 = 实物量 × 某种化肥有效成分含量的百分比

农业机械总动力 指用于农、林、牧、渔业生产的各种动力机械的动力总和。动力机械包括耕作、排灌、种植、植物保护、收获、农产品加工、运输、畜牧、渔业、农田水利等各种机械。不包括专门用于乡办工业、基本建设、非农业运输、科学试验和教学等非农业生产方面用的动力机械与作业机械的数量。

Explanatory Notes on Main Statistical Indicators

Gross Output Value of Agriculture refers to the total volume of products of farming, forestry, animal husbandry, and fishery expressed in the monetary terms. It reflects the overall scale and achievements of agricultural production during a given period of time.

The scope of statistics on farming, forestry, animal husbandry, and fishery are as follows:

Farming includes cultivation of farm crops and other agricultural activities.

Cultivation of farm crops include cultivation of grain crops, legume crops, tuber-crops, cotton, oil-bearing crops, sugar crops, and cultivation and management of tea plantations, mulberry fields and orchards. Other agricultural activities include harvesting wild fruits, fiber, tree gum, resin, oil-bearing plants, firewood, wild medicinal herbs, fungus, and rural-household commodity industries.

Forestry refers to planting trees of various kinds (excluding tea plantations, mulberry fields and orchards), collection of forestry products and cutting and felling of bamboo and trees by villages and other cooperative organizations under village level.

Animal husbandry refers to raising and grazing of all kinds of farm animals except fishing and aquatic cultivating, and hunting and rising of wild animals.

Fishery refers to cultivation and catching of fish and other aquatic products and cultivation and collection of seaweed and other aquatic plants.

Agriculture, forestry, animal husbandry, and fishery professions and auxiliary activities refer to various professional and auxiliary production activities provided to agriculture, excluding various scientific and technical and professional technical services.

Grain Output refers to the total output of rice, wheat, corn, sorghum, millet and other miscellaneous grains as well as tubers and bean in the whole country including grains produced by states farms, collective unit, industrial enterprises and mines, output of beans refers to dry beans without pods, the output of tubers (excluding taros,cassava and potatoes) was converted into that of grain at the ratio 5 ∶ 1, i. e. 5 kilograms of fresh tubers was equivalent to 1 kilogram of grain. Statistics of potatoes as vegetables. Output of all other grains refers to husked grain.

Output of Aquatic Products refers to catches of both artificially cultured and naturally grown aquatic products, including fish, shrimps, crabs and shellfish in sea and inland water as well as seaweed. Freshwater plants are not included.

Output of Pork, Beef, and Mutton refers to the meat of slaughtered hogs, cattle, sheep and goats with head, feet, and offal taken away. Data refers to the production of the whole country.

Consumption of Chemical Fertilizers in Agriculture refers to the quantity of chemical fertilizers applied in agriculture in the year, including nitrogenous fertilizer, phosphate fertilizer, potash fertilizer, and compound fertilizer. The consumption of chemical fertilizers is required in calculation to convert the gross weight into weight containing 100% effective component (e.g. 100% nitrogen content in nitrogenous fertilizer, 100% phosphorous pent oxide contents in phosphate fertilizer, 100% potassium oxide contents in potash fertilizer) . Compound fertilizer is converted with its major component. The formula is:

Volume of effective component= physical quantity x effective component of certain chemical fertilizer (%)

Total Power of Agriculture Machinery Refers to the total mechanical power of machinery used in farming forestry animal husbandry and fishery, including machines used for ploughing, irrigation and drainage, crop growing, plant protection, harvesting, farm product processing, transport, stock breeding, fishery and water conservancy, machinery employed for non agricultural purposes such as township industry, capital construction, non–agricultural transport, scientific experiments and for teaching is excluded.

12 工　业

INDUSTRY

简 要 说 明

一、本篇资料的主要内容

本篇资料主要反映了全市工业生产和基本效益情况，主要包括工业企业单位数、历年工业总产值、规模以上工业、国有控股工业、国有工业、集体工业、外商投资和港澳台投资工业、大中型工业企业的主要经济指标、相关的财务分析指标和主要工业产品产量等方面的内容。

二、本篇资料的来源

本篇中规模以上工业资料来源于工业统计年报，由市统计局工业统计处整理提供。

Brief Introduction

I. Main Content

Data in this chapter show the basic condition of industrial production and benefit in Qingdao, mainly including the number of industrial enterprises, gross industrial output value and indices, the output of major industrial products and major economic and relevant financial indicators of industrial enterprises. Industrial enterprises include enterprises above designated size, state share-holding enterprises, state owned enterprises, collective owned enterprises, foreign funded enterprises, enterprises with funds from Hong Kong, Macao and Taiwan, large and medium sized enterprises.

II. Source of Data

Data on industry above designated size are based on the annual report of industrial statistics, and prepared by the Division of Industry Statistics of Qingdao Municipal Bureau of Statistics.

12-1 规模以上工业企业单位数
NUMBER OF INDUSTRIAL ENTERPRISES ABOVE DESIGNATED SIZE

单位：个 (unit)

项 目	Item	1985 年	1990 年	1995 年	2000 年	2005 年	2006 年
总 计	**Total**	**2411**	**2997**	**4987**	**1504**	**3697**	**4567**
一、按经济类型分	**Grouped by Economic Types**						
国有企业	State-owned	502	568	1084	179	76	74
集体企业	Collective-owned	1907	2386	2731	226	87	72
其他经济类型企业	Other Economic Types	2	43	1172	1099	3534	4421
# 外商及港澳台商投资企业	Foreign Funded Enterprises and Enterprises with Funds from Hong Kong, Macao and Taiwan		35	1027	593	1658	1952
二、按轻重工业分	**Grouped by Light and Heavy Industries**						
轻工业	Light Industry	1398	1730	2858	891	1942	2313
重工业	Heavy Industry	1013	1267	2129	613	1755	2254
三、按企业规模分	**Grouped by Size of Enterprises**						
大型企业	Large	26	42	89	202	51	51
中型企业	Medium	80	168	216	229	441	469
小型企业	Small	2305	2787	4480	1073	3205	4047
四、按行业分	**Grouped by sectors**						
黑色金属矿采选业	Mining of Non-ferrous Metal Ores		4	6	1	2	5
有色金属矿采选业	Mining of Non-ferrous Metal Ores	2	7	9	7	5	5
非金属矿采选业	Mining and Processing of Nometal Ores	43	70	87	29	34	31
食品制造业	Manufacture of Foods	244	324	437	170	121	137
# 粮食及饲料加工	Processing of Gren and Feed	62	57	60	27		
饮料制造业	Manufacture of Beverage	31	44	74	23	29	28
# 饮料酒	Beverage Liquor	20	28	27	19	20	25

12-1 续表 1
Continued

单位：个 (unit)

项 目	Item	2007 年	2008 年	2009 年	2010 年	2011 年
总 计	**Total**	**5032**	**5628**	**5895**	**5674**	**4727**
一、按经济类型分	**Grouped by Economic Types**					
国有企业	State-owned	63	65	163	61	147
集体企业	Collective-owned	72	61	59	53	31
其他经济类型企业	Other Economic Types	4897	5502	5673	5560	4549
#外商及港澳台商投资企业	Foreign Funded Enterprises and Enterprises with Funds from Hong Kong, Macao and Taiwan	2091	2217	2244	2037	1618
二、按轻重工业分	**Grouped by Light and Heavy Industries**					
轻工业	Light Industry	2489	2704	2805	2635	2131
重工业	Heavy Industry	2543	2924	3090	3039	2596
三、按企业规模分	**Grouped by Size of Enterprises**					
大型企业	Large	53	48	50	52	50
中型企业	Medium	489	519	502	525	516
小型企业	Small	4490	5061	5343	5097	4161
四、按行业分	**Grouped by sectors**					
黑色金属矿采选业	Mining of Non-ferrous Metal Ores	7	23	22	12	12
有色金属矿采选业	Mining of Non-ferrous Metal Ores	5	6	6	4	
非金属矿采选业	Mining and Processing of Nometal Ores	33	30	26	26	23
食品制造业	Manufacture of Foods	156	158	174	167	127
#粮食及饲料加工	Processing of Gren and Feed					
饮料制造业	Manufacture of Beverage	33	40	42	42	36
#饮料酒	Beverage Liquor					

12-1 续表 2
Continued

单位：个 (unit)

项　目	Item	1985年	1990年	1995年	2000年	2005年	2006年
烟草制品业	Manufacture of Tobacco	2	2	5	3	2	2
纺织业	Manufacture of Textile	169	225	330	132	300	327
纺织服装、鞋、帽制造业	Manufacture of Textile Wearing Apparel. Footware and Caps	171	194	322	95	272	339
皮革、毛皮、羽毛(绒)及其制品业	Manufacture of Leather, Fur, Feather and Related Products	56	64	161	64	167	194
木材加工制品业	Processing of Wood and Wood Products	71	89	116	19	40	53
家具制造业	Manufacture of Furniture	61	72	88	10	72	103
造纸及纸制品业	Manufacture of Paper and Paper Products	66	74	110	56	102	128
印刷业和记录媒介的复制	Printing, Reproduction of Recording Media	61	81	215	23	44	59
文教体育用品制造业	Manufacture of Articles For Culture, Education and Sport Activities	31	27	93	48	89	91
石油、煤炭及其他燃料加工业	Oil, coal and other fuel processing industries	2	3	13	5	10	6
化学原料及制品	Manufacture of Raw Chemical Materials and Chemical Products	106	156	278	81	178	233
医药制造业	Manufacture of Medicines	16	14	39	20	30	46
化学纤维制造业	Manufacure of Chemical Fibers	2	4	26	15	14	13
橡胶制品业	Manufacture of Rubber	53	57	143	48	116	170
塑料制品业	Manufacture of Plastics	103	131	237	64	153	179
非金属矿物制品业	Manufacture of Non-metallic Mineral Products	230	245	275	62	161	218
黑色金属压延加工业	Smelting and Pressing of Ferrous Metals	11	13	31	15	41	45
有色金属压延加工业	Smelting and Pressing of Non-ferrous Metals	6	8	19	9	28	40
金属制品业	Manufacture of Metal Products	161	186	372	88	186	250
通用设备制造业	Manufacture of General Purpose Machinery	320	398	320	94	299	397
交通运输制造业	Manufacture of Electrical Machinery and Equipment	104	114	358	52	151	194
电气机械及器材制造业	Manufacture of Electrication Machinery and Equipment	86	96	211	79	214	249
通信设备、计算机及其他电子设备制造业	Manufacture of Communication Equipment, Computers and Other Electronic Equipment	32	31	79	34	123	140
仪器仪表及文化、办公用机械制造业	Manufacture of Measuring Instruments and Machinery for Cultural Activity and Office Work	28	33	70	20	40	44
水的生产和供应业	Production and Supply of Water	8	12	12	8	10	10
电力、热力的生产和供应业	Production and Supply of Electric Power and Heat Power	10	16	20	17	27	32
燃气生产和供应业	Production and Supply of Gas	1	4	3	2	5	6
其他工业	Other Industrial Sectors	46	48	209	63	166	534

12-1 续表 3
Continued

单位：个 (unit)

项　目	Item	2007 年	2008 年	2009 年	2010 年	2011 年
烟草制品业	Manufacture of Tobacco	2	2	2	1	1
纺织业	Manufacture of Textile	340	330	322	287	229
纺织服装、鞋、帽制造业	Manfacture of Textile Wearing Apparel. Footware and Caps	362	418	434	392	295
皮革、毛皮、羽毛(绒)及其制品业	Manufacture of Leather, Fur, Feather and Related Products	197	209	210	211	160
木材加工制品业	Processing of Wood and Wood Products	64	66	68	68	49
家具制造业	Manufacture of Furniture	119	130	133	117	97
造纸及纸制品业	Manufacture of Paper and Paper Products	126	133	133	138	101
印刷业和记录媒介的复制	Printing, Reproduction of Recording Media	63	74	79	92	58
文教体育用品制造业	Manufacture of Articles For Culture, Education and Sport Activities	97	96	99	90	75
石油、煤炭及其他燃料加工业	Oil, coal and other fuel processing industries	7	7	9	8	7
化学原料及制品	Manufacture of Raw Chemical Materials and Chemical Products	261	276	275	262	231
医药制造业	Manufacture of Medicines	48	49	56	52	44
化学纤维制造业	Manufacure of Chemical Fibers	12	13	14	12	10
橡胶制品业	Manufacture of Rubber	183	211	214	196	187
塑料制品业	Manufacture of Plastics	199	227	234	233	169
非金属矿物制品业	Manufacture of Non-metallic Mineral Products	259	311	320	327	303
黑色金属压延加工业	Smelting and Pressing of Ferrous Metals	39	24	27	31	29
有色金属压延加工业	Smelting and Pressing of Non-ferrous Metals	40	41	40	35	34
金属制品业	Manufacture of Metal Products	271	347	376	361	294
通用设备制造业	Manufacture of General Purpose Machinery	473	535	592	597	521
交通运输制造业	Manufacture of Electrical Machinery and Equipment	217	264	290	296	263
电气机械及器材制造业	Manufacture of Electrication Machinery and Equipment	274	303	300	281	230
通信设备、计算机及其他电子设备制造业	Manufacture of Communication Equipment, Computers and Other Electronic Equipment	152	163	168	167	124
仪器仪表及文化、办公用机械制造业	Manufacture of Measuring Instruments and Machinery for Cultural Activity and Office Work	47	47	55	54	39
水的生产和供应业	Production and Supply of Water	10	13	14	14	11
电力、热力的生产和供应业	Production and Supply of Electric Power and Heat Power	34	36	39	38	36
燃气生产和供应业	Production and Supply of Gas	7	13	13	14	11
其他工业	Other Industrial Sectors	895	1033	1109	1049	921

12-1 续表 4
Continued

单位：个 (unit)

项 目	Item	2012 年	2013 年	2014 年	2015 年
总计	**Total**	**4817**	**4917**	**4790**	**4876**
一、按经济类型分	**Grouped by Economic Types**				
国有企业	State-owned	144	140	132	141
集体企业	Collective-owned	28	24	19	15
其他经济类型企业	Other Economic Types	4645	4753	4639	4720
#外商及港澳台商投资企业	Foreign Funded Enterprises and Enterprises with Funds from Hong Kong, Macao and Taiwan	1599	1551	1445	1361
二、按轻重工业分	**Grouped by Light and Heavy Industries**				
轻工业	Light Industry	2153	2190	2080	2095
重工业	Heavy Industry	2664	2727	2710	2781
三、按企业规模分	**Grouped by Size of Enterprises**				
大型企业	Large	98	97	91	89
中型企业	Medium	596	599	568	566
小微型企业	Small& Micro-Enterprises	4123	4221	4131	4221
四、按行业分	**Grouped by sectors**				
黑色金属矿采选业	Mining of Ferrous Metal Ores	10	11	8	7
有色金属矿采选业	Mining of Non-ferrous Metal Ores				
非金属矿采选业	Mining and processing of Nometal Ores	14	13	7	6
农副食品加工业	Processing of Food from Agricultural Products	454	468	444	458
食品制造业	Manufacture of Foods	129	123	109	116
酒、饮料和精制茶制造业	Manufacture of Liquor, Beverage and Refind Tea	34	35	34	38
烟草制品业	Manufacture of Tobacco	1	1	1	1
纺织业	Manufacture of Textile	181	175	146	133
纺织服装、服饰业	Manufacture of Texitile Wearing Apparel	312	283	249	244

注：国家统计局根据《国民经济行业分类》(GB/T 4754-2017)，对《三次产业划分规定 (2012)》中行业类别进行了对应调整，其中“石油加工、炼焦和核燃料加工业”更名为“石油、煤炭及其他燃料加工业”，并将 2011 版《国民经济行业分类》4500 中部分内容和 4120 全部内容调到此类。

Note: According to the national economic industry classification (GB/ T 4754-2017), the National Bureau of Statistics carries out a corresponding adjustment to the three industries according to the classification of the national economy (GB/ T 4754-2017), in which the petroleum processing, coking and nuclear fuel processing industry is changed to petroleum, coal and other fuel processing industries, and the content of part of the content and 4,120 of the 2011 edition of the national economy industry category 4,500 are transferred to this category.

12-1 续表 5
Continued

单位：个 (unit)

项 目	Item	2016 年	2017 年	2018 年	2019 年	2020 年
总计	**Total**	**4431**	**3569**	**3508**	**3536**	**3856**
一、按经济类型分	**Grouped by Economic Types**					
国有企业	State-owned	128	131	145	175	189
集体企业	Collective-owned	11	5	4	5	5
其他经济类型企业	Other Economic Types	4292	3433	3359	3356	3662
#外商及港澳台商投资企业	Foreign Funded Enterprises and Enterprises with Funds from Hong Kong, Macao and Taiwan	1205	1037	938	868	825
二、按轻重工业分	**Grouped by Light and Heavy Industries**					
轻工业	Light Industry	1875	1522	1448	1400	1469
重工业	Heavy Industry	2556	2047	2060	2136	2387
三、按企业规模分	**Grouped by Size of Enterprises**					
大型企业	Large	85	78	76	86	77
中型企业	Medium	516	459	383	386	396
小微型企业	Small& Micro-Enterprises	3830	3032	3049	3064	3383
四、按行业分	**Grouped by sectors**					
黑色金属采选业	Mining of ferrous metal Ores	1				
有色金属采选业	Mining of non-ferrous Metal Ores			1	1	2
非金属矿采选业	Mining and processing of Nometal Ores	5	2	1	2	2
农副食品加工业	Processing of Food from Agricultural Products	419	338	331	304	295
食品制造业	Manufacture of Foods	115	111	115	123	142
酒、饮料和精制茶制造业	Manufacture of Liquor, Beverage and Refind Tea	33	18	17	13	13
烟草制品业	Manufacture of Tobacco	0	0	0	0	
纺织业	Manufacture of Textile	111	91	93	103	134
纺织服装、服饰业	Manufacture of Texitile Wearing Apparel	206	152	144	132	121

12-1 续表 6
Continued

单位：个 (unit)

项　目	Item	2012 年	2013 年	2014 年	2015 年
皮革、毛皮、羽毛及其制品和制鞋业	Manufacture of Leather, Fur, Feather & Its Products Footwear	177	148	124	116
木材加工和木、竹、藤、棕、草制品业	Processing of Timbers, Manufacture of Wood, Bamboo, Rattan, Palm and Straw Products	34	40	32	34
家具制造业	Manufacture of Furniture	103	107	96	98
造纸和纸制品业	Manufacture of Paper and Paper Producls	100	71	54	52
印刷和记录媒介复制业	Printing, Reproduction of Recording Media	80	121	150	156
文教、工美、体育和娱乐用品制造业	Manufacture of Articles for Culture, Arts & Crafts, Sports and Entertainment	263	335	348	345
石油、煤炭及其他燃料加工业	Oil, coal and other fuel processing industries	8	8	9	9
化学原料和化学制品制造业	Manufacture of Chemical Raw Material and Chemical Products	224	240	246	249
医药制造业	Manufacture of Medicines	45	49	50	54
化学纤维制造业	Manufacure of Chemical Fibers	9	8	8	8
橡胶和塑料制品业	Manufacture of Rubber and Plastic	350	345	331	310
非金属矿物制品业	Manufacture of Non-metallic Mineral Products	325	333	330	338
黑色金属冶炼和压延加工业	Smelting and Pressing of Ferrous Metals	105	93	87	83
有色金属冶炼和压延加工业	Smelting and Pressing of Non-ferrous Metals	37	36	38	39
金属制品业	Manufacture of Metal Products	399	389	380	388
通用设备制造业	Manufacture of General Purpose Machinery	362	382	395	402
专用设备制造业	Manufacture of Special Purpose Machinery	312	322	314	336
汽车制造业	Manufacture of Vehicle	136	141	145	158
铁路、船舶、航空航天和其他运输设备制造业	Manufacture of Transport Equipment for Railway, Shipping, Aerospace and other uses	145	146	152	168
电气机械和器材制造业	Manufacture of Electrical Machinery & Equipment	202	212	217	226
计算机、通信和其他电子设备制造业	Manufactuter of Computer, Communication Equipment and Other Electronic Equipment	137	136	141	147
仪器仪表制造业	Manufacture of Measuring Instrument	41	49	52	58
其他制造业	Manufacture of Other Products	18	17	13	15
废弃资源综合利用业	Recycling and Disposal of Waste Resources	4	6	6	5
金属制品、机械和设备修理业	Maintenance of Metal Products, Machinery and Equipment	7	7	7	6
电力、热力生产和供应业	Production and Supply of Electric Power and Heat Power	36	39	40	43
燃气生产和供应业	Production and Supply of Gas	12	13	12	14
水的生产和供应业	Production and Supply of water	11	15	15	16

12-1 续表 7
Continued

单位：个 (unit)

项 目	Item	2016年	2017年	2018年	2019年	2020年
皮革、毛皮、羽毛及其制品和制鞋业	Manufacture of Leather, Fur, Feather & Its Products Footwear	89	58	47	39	36
木材加工和木、竹、藤、棕、草制品业	Processing of Timbers, Manufacture of Wood, Bamboo, Rattan, Palm and Straw Producls	31	27	22	28	43
家具制造业	Manufacture of Furniture	88	65	64	59	61
造纸和纸制品业	Manufacture of Paper and Paper Producls	50	40	40	43	64
印刷和记录媒介复制业	Printing, Reproduction of Recording Media	137	110	101	88	66
文教、工美、体育和娱乐用品制造业	Manufacture of Ariticles for Culture, Arts & CraftsSports and Entertainment	310	222	179	131	103
石油、煤炭及其他燃料加工业	Oil, coal and other fuel processing industries	9	9	8	10	10
化学原料和化学制品制造业	Manufacture of Chemical Raw Material and Chemical Products	223	176	171	165	164
医药制造业	Manufacture of Medicines	47	35	34	40	43
化学纤维制造业	Manufacure of Chemical Fibers	6	7	8	7	8
橡胶和塑料制品业	Manufacture of Rubber and Plastic	281	250	252	268	331
非金属矿物制品业	Manufacture of Non-metallic Mineral Products	315	228	218	234	296
黑色金属冶炼和压延加工业	Smelting and Pressing of Ferrous Metals	73	27	30	25	31
有色金属冶炼和压延加工业	Smelting and Pressing of Non-ferrous Metals	30	23	24	29	31
金属制品业	Manufacture of Metal Products	348	289	278	295	343
通用设备制造业	Manufacture of General Purpose Machinery	383	301	316	318	325
专用设备制造业	Manufacture of Special Purpose Machinery	311	233	245	243	275
汽车制造业	Manufacture of Vehicle	154	156	168	200	236
铁路、船舶、航空航天和其他运输设备制造业	Manufacture of Transport Equipment for Railway, Shipping, Aerospace and other uses	156	150	155	164	168
电气机械和器材制造业	Manufacture of Electrical Machinery & Equipment	211	184	186	184	197
计算机、通信和其他电子设备制造业	Manufactuter of Computer, Communication Equipment and Other Electronic Equipment	140	128	114	117	114
仪器仪表制造业	Manufacture of Measuring Insturment	50	46	49	59	67
其他制造业	Manufacture of Other Products	16	10	11	11	16
废弃资源综合利用业	Recycling and Disposal of Waste Resources	6	3	3	3	2
金属制品、机械和设备修理业	Maintenance of Metal Products, Machinery and Equipment	5	6	6	3	7
电力、热力生产和供应业	Production and Supply of Electric Power and Heat Power	42	43	44	58	64
燃气生产和供应业	Production and Supply of Gas	14	14	15	14	17
水的生产和供应业	Production and Supply of water	16	17	18	23	29

12-2　分市、区规模以上工业企业数（2020 年）
NUMBER OF ALL INDUSTRIAL ENTERPRISES BY REGION (2020)

单位：个 (unit)

市、区名称	Region	规模以上 Above Designated	按轻重工业分 Grouped by Light and Heavy Ind		按企业规模分 Grouped by Size of Enterprises		
			轻工业 Light Industry	重工业 Heavy Industry	大型企业 Large	中型企业 Medium	小微型企业 Small& Micro-Enterprises
全　市	**Whole Municipality**	**3856**	**1469**	**2387**	**77**	**396**	**3383**
市南区	Shinan District	8	3	5	1	3	4
市北区	Shibei District	60	13	47	2	11	47
李沧区	Licang District	114	25	89	0	8	106
崂山区	Laoshan District	99	44	55	5	14	80
西海岸新区	West Coast New Area	861	243	618	32	96	733
黄岛区	Huangdao District	833	231	602	30	92	711
保税港区	Qingdao Free Trade Port Area of China	28	12	16	2	4	22
城阳区	Chengyang District	769	294	475	13	76	680
城阳区（不含高新区）	Chengyang District (Excluding High tech District)	642	269	373	12	59	571
高新区	High tech District	127	25	102	1	17	109
即墨区	Jimo District	532	234	298	10	69	453
胶州市	Jiaozhou	690	282	408	4	59	627
平度市	Pingdu	425	185	240	5	33	387
莱西市	Laixi	297	145	152	4	27	266

12-2　续表
Contiued

单位：个 (unit)

市、区名称	Region	按经济类型分 Grouped by Economic Types			
		国有企业 State-owned	集体企业 Collective-owned	其他经济 Others	#外资及港澳台商企业 Foreign Funded Enterprises and Enterprises with Funds from Hong Kong, Macao and Taiwan
全　市	**Whole Municipality**	**189**	**5**	**3662**	**825**
市南区	Shinan District	3		5	1
市北区	Shibei District	13	1	46	13
李沧区	Licang District	13		101	12
崂山区	Laoshan District	8		91	26
西海岸新区	West Coast New Area	65		796	197
黄岛区	Huangdao District	65		768	186
保税港区	Qingdao Free Trade Port Area of China			28	11
城阳区	Chengyang District	32	1	736	219
城阳区（不含高新区）	Chengyang District (Excluding High tech District)	19	1	622	181
高新区	High tech District	13		114	38
即墨区	Jimo District	13		519	110
胶州市	Jiaozhou	10	1	679	110
平度市	Pingdu	20	2	403	82
莱西市	Laixi	11		286	55

12-3 历年全部工业总产值
GROSS INDUSTRIAL OUTPUT VALUE OVER THE YEARS

单位：万元 (10 000 yuan)

年 份 Year	工业总产值 Gross Industrial Output Value	轻工业产值 Light Industry	重工业产值 Heavy Industry
1949	21605	18494	3111
1950	34010	28720	5290
1951	53538	44600	8938
1952	84295	69258	15037
1953	115222	74716	40506
1954	126064	80604	45460
1955	118935	86956	31979
1956	144833	93809	51024
1957	142920	101202	41718
1958	217648	92407	125241
1959	282610	84376	198234
1960	291451	77043	214408
1962	120738	64233	56505
1963	139542	83630	55912
1964	177273	108884	68389
1965	215536	141765	73771
1966	252896	152304	100592
1967	287739	163627	124112
1968	299814	175791	123489
1969	296814	188860	107954
1970	345212	202903	142309

注：本表按当年价格计算，1995 年开始工业总产值按新规定计算。
Note: The data in this form are calculated at current price. Since 1995, new regulations have been adopted in calculating gross industrial output value.

12-3 续表 1
Continued

单位：万元 (10 000 yuan)

年 份 Year	工业总产值 Gross Industrial Output Value	轻工业产值 Light Industry	重工业产值 Heavy Industry
1971	365770	216172	149598
1972	378266	230309	147957
1973	377943	245371	132572
1974	237219	154054	83165
1975	402541	261418	141123
1976	439793	278514	161279
1977	490669	296728	193941
1978	565503	336817	228686
1979	625227	379276	245951
1980	677690	442078	235612
1981	707434	479954	227480
1982	732705	474767	257938
1983	816793	513759	303034
1984	918364	569080	349284
1985	1113891	699524	414367
1986	1316230	833864	482366
1987	1703830	1065873	637957
1988	2481594	1451215	1030379
1989	3191643	1857019	1334624
1990	3571845	2057968	1513878

12-3 续表 2
Continued

单位：万元 (10 000 yuan)

年 份	Year	工业总产值 Gross Industrial Output Value	轻工业产值 Light Industry	重工业产值 Heavy Industry
1991	1991	3986427	2318257	1668170
1992	1992	4826834	2835728	1991106
1993	1993	5929236	3422107	2507129
1994	1994	8456974	4931262	3525712
1995	1995	9412635	5579637	3832998
1996	1996	11173672	6793007	4380665
1997	1997	13704735	8620710	5084025
1998	1998	15794106	10153634	5640472
1999	1999	16822436	10918827	5903609
2000	2000	19408338	12433214	6975124
2001	2001	22398464	14368582	8029882
2002	2002	25794324	14811106	10983218
2003	2003	31195595	17306539	13889056
2004	2004	39590783	21473202	18117581
2005	2005	50017829	24697792	25320037
2006	2006	59188120	28686826	30501294
2007	2007	74306364	33463071	40843293
2008	2008	89467300	37871227	51596073
2009	2009	102556155	42715781	59840374
2010	2010	116148345	44954630	71193715
2011	2011	132779629	50854938	81924691

12-3 续表 3
Continued

单位：万元 (10 000 yuan)

年 份	Year	工业总产值 Gross Industrial Output Value	轻工业产值 Light Industry	重工业产值 Heavy Industry
2012	2012	153102565	60516341	92546833
2013	2013	168971805	66799317	102172488
2014	2014	174442125	67683545	106758580
2015	2015	180194299	71176748	109017551
2016	2016	174157133	68552071	105605062
2017	2017	130197343	48954201	81243142
2018	2018	113897787	39054621	74843166
"一五"时期合计	"First Five-Year Plan" Period	647974	437287	210687
"二五"时期合计	"Second Five-Year Plan" Period	1077075	388406	688669
1963-1965 年合计	1963-1965	532351	334279	198072
"三五"时期合计	"Third Five-Year Plan" Period	1481941	883485	598456
"四五"时期合计	"Fourth Five-Year Plan" Period	1761739	1107324	654415
"五五"时期合计	"Fifth Five-Year Plan" Period	2798882	1733413	1065469
"六五"时期合计	"Sixth Five-Year Plan" Period	4289187	2737084	1552103
"七五"时期合计	"Seventh Five-Year Plan" Period	12265142	7265939	4999204
"八五"时期合计	"Eighth Five-Year Plan" Period	32612106	19087323	13524783
"九五"时期合计	"Ninth Five-Year Plan" Period	76903287	48919392	27983895
"十五"时期合计	"Tenth Five-Year Plan" Period	168996995	92657221	76339774
"十一五"时期合计	"Eleventh Five-Year Plan" Period	175336465	73641456	101695009
"十二五"时期合计	"Twelveth Five-Year Plan" Period	809490422	317030889	492420143

12-4　规模以上工业企业主要指标（2020 年）

MAIN INDICATORS OF INDUSTRIAL ENTERPRISES ABOVE DESIGNATED SIZE (2020)

项目	Indicator	企业单位数（个）Number of Enterprises (unit)
总　计	**Total**	**3856**
按注册登记类型分	**Grouped by Status of Registration**	
国有及国有控股企业	State-owned and State-holding Enterprises	212
集体企业	Collective-owned Enterprises	5
股份有限公司	Share-holding Corporations Ltd	102
外商投资企业	Foreign Funded Enterprises	639
港澳台商投资企业	Invested by HongKong, Macao and Taiwan	186
按轻重工业分	**Grouped by Light and Heavy Industries**	
轻工业	Light Industry	1469
重工业	Heavy Industry	2387
按企业规模分	**Grouped by Size of Enterprises**	
大型企业	Large	77
中型企业	Medium	396
小微型企业	Small & Micro-Enterprises	3383
按所在地分	**Grouped by Location**	
市南区	Shinan District	8
市北区	Shibei District	60
李沧区	Licang District	114
崂山区	Laoshan District	99
西海岸新区	West Coast New Area	861
黄岛区	Huangdao District	833
保税港区	Qingdao Free Trade Port Area of China	28
城阳区	Chengyang District	769
城阳区（不含高新区）	Chengyang District (Excluding High tech District)	642
高新区	High tech District	127
即墨区	Jimo District	532
胶州市	Jiaozhou	690
平度市	Pingdu	425
莱西市	Laixi	297
按行业分	**Grouped by sector**	
煤炭开采和洗选业	Mining and Washing of Coal	
石油和天然气开采业	Extraction of Petroleum and Natural Gas	
黑色金属矿采选业	Mining of Ferrous Metal Ores	
有色金属矿采选业	Mining of Non-ferrous Metal Ores	2
非金属矿采选业	Mining and Processing of Nometal Ores	2
开采辅助活动	Auxiliary Activities of Mining	
其他采矿业	Mining of Other Ores	

单位：万元 (10 000 yuan)

资产合计 Total Assets	流动资产年合计 Total Current Assets	固定资产净值 Net Value of Fixed Assets
110664063	**68299980**	**19748716**
38329390	21875445	8859800
57790	42939	6716
30638681	17536567	2078881
19111327	13162993	3707967
6403834	4359804	1379946
31750280	18644315	4200887
78913784	49655666	15547829
43808017	26004933	5884944
30179487	19339296	6326794
36676560	22955752	7536978
983019	360371	449415
3773973	2039266	924131
2889319	1700029	540286
5011090	3328038	546578
41140346	23728348	7492720
40633830	23378310	7383123
506516	350039	109597
22065969	15283233	3279505
17440338	12253902	2532576
4625632	3029330	746929
11767884	7543186	1894572
10147785	6824409	1648393
7229257	3747650	1702953
5655421	3745452	1270165

12-4 续表 1
Continued

项目	Indicator	营业收入 Revenue from Principal Business
总 计	**Total**	**98281712**
按注册登记类型分	**Grouped by Status of Registration**	
国有及国有控股企业	State-owned and State-holdinig Enterprises	33961229
集体企业	Collective-owned Enterprises	39702
股份有限公司	Share-holding Corporations Ltd	16178029
外商投资企业	Foreign Funded Enterprises	21755581
港澳台商投资企业	Invested by HongKong, Macao and Taiwan	5642688
按轻重工业分	**Grouped by Light and Heavy Industries**	
轻工业	Light Industry	30350888
重工业	Heavy Industry	67930824
按企业规模分	**Grouped by Size of Enterprises**	
大型企业	Large	37056346
中型企业	Medium	27332882
小微型企业	Small & Micro-Enterprises	33892485
按所在地分	**Grouped by Location**	
市南区	Shinan District	287565
市北区	Shibei District	3853426
李沧区	Licang District	3156469
崂山区	Laoshan District	3371365
西海岸新区	West Coast New Area	34552251
黄岛区	Huangdao District	33995583
保税港区	Qingdao Free Trade Port Area of China	556668
城阳区	Chengyang District	17662404
城阳区（不含高新区）	Chengyang District (Excluding High tech District)	14755020
高新区	High tech District	2907384
即墨区	Jimo District	13698909
胶州市	Jiaozhou	9082990
平度市	Pingdu	7670070
莱西市	Laixi	4946263
按行业分	**Grouped by sector**	
煤炭开采和洗选业	Mining and Washing of Coal	
石油和天然气开采业	Extraction of Petroleum and Natural Gas	
黑色金属矿采选业	Mining of Ferrous Metal Ores	
有色金属矿采选业	Mining of Non-ferrous Metal Ores	
非金属矿采选业	Mining and Processing of Nometal Ores	
开采辅助活动	Auxiliary Activities of Mining	
其他采矿业	Mining of Other Ores	

单位：万元 (10 000 yuan)

营业成本 Cost of Principal Business	营业税金及附加 Taxes and Extra Charges on Principal Business	利润总额 Total Profits	全部从业人员年平均人数（人） Annual Average Employed Persons (person)
82923598	**1585926**	**5717894**	**674085**
28795053	1290795	1627320	118552
35777	541	1230	722
13330788	122080	1549356	87190
18030770	119609	1578640	172201
4740688	27563	270355	42856
25512246	181564	2062899	270154
57411353	1404363	3654996	403931
31597126	214012	2864504	173519
22304175	1210557	1260300	213374
29022297	161358	1593091	287192
277564	9409	-6105	2815
3427637	20780	298882	15357
2495962	307219	67606	19230
2520719	23084	339867	24147
29011068	971066	2337263	178875
28556010	968255	2294276	170556
455058	2810	42987	8319
14262520	92855	1391407	140567
12057091	75209	1091314	116739
2205429	17646	300093	23828
12188328	48345	530314	94865
7842972	41116	316460	88031
6618366	51899	244786	67720
4278463	20155	197415	42478

12-4 续表 2
Continued

项目	Indicator	企业单位数(个) Number of Enterprises (unit)
农副食品加工业	Processing of Food from Agricultural Products	295
食品制造业	Manufacture of Foods	142
酒、饮料和精制茶制造业	Manufacture of Liquor, Beverage and Refind Tea	13
烟草制品业	Manufacture of Tobacco	
纺织业	Manufacture of Textile	134
纺织服装、服饰业	Manufacture of Textile Wearing Apparel	121
皮革、毛皮、羽毛及其制品和制鞋业	Processing of Leather, Fur, Feather & Its Products Footwear	36
木材加工和木、竹、藤、棕、草制品业	Processing of Timbers, Manufacture of Wood, Bamboo, Rattan, Palm and Straw Products	43
家具制造业	Manufacture of Furniture	61
造纸和纸制品业	Manufacture of Paper and Paper Products	64
印刷和记录媒介复制业	Printing, Reproduction of Recording Media	66
文教、工美、体育和娱乐用品制造业	Manufacture of Articles for Culture, Arts & Crafts, Sports and Entertainment	103
石油、煤炭及其他燃料加工业	Oil, coal and other fuel processing industries	10
化学原料和化学制品制造业	Manufacture of Chemical Raw Material and Chemical Products	164
医药制造业	Manufacture of Medicines	43
化学纤维制造业	Manufacture of Chemical Fibers	8
橡胶和塑料制品业	Manufacture of Rubber and Plastic	331
非金属矿物制品业	Manufacture of Non-metallic Mineral Products	296
黑色金属冶炼和压延加工业	Smelting and Pressing of Ferrous Metals	31
有色金属冶炼和压延加工业	Smelting and Pressing of Nonferrous Metals	31
金属制品业	Manufacture of Metal Products	343
通用设备制造业	Manufacture of General Purpose Machinery	325
专用设备制造业	Manufacture of Special Purpose Machinery	275
汽车制造业	Manufacture of Vehicle	236
铁路、船舶、航空航天和其他运输设备制造业	Manufacture of Transport Equipment for Railway, Shipping, Aerospace and other uses	168
电气机械和器材制造业	Manufacture of Electrical Machinery & Equipment	197
计算机、通信和其他电子设备制造业	Manufacture of Compute, Communication Equipment and Other Electronic Equipment	114
仪器仪表制造业	Manufacture of Measuring Instrument	67
其他制造业	Manufacture of Other Products	16
废弃资源综合利用业	Recycling and Disposal of Waste Resources	2
金属制品、机械和设备修理业	Manufacture of Metal Products, Machinery and Equipment	7
电力、热力生产和供应业	Production and Supply of Electric Power and Heat Power	64
燃气生产和供应业	Production and Supply of Gas	17
水的生产和供应业	Production and Supply of Water	29

单位：万元 (10 000 yuan)

资产合计 Total Assets	流动资产合计 Total Current Assets	固定资产净值 Net Value of Fixed Assets
4150894	3105936	583570
3189986	2137236	627289
3347503	1665929	351845
1003437	760345	185450
1704820	991495	186800
323320	224467	66642
208357	149007	44005
479228	381861	57362
484027	334077	102632
534390	334525	144553
776689	540225	135599
2188386	1429537	607267
5973031	2896617	1604717
1649427	948157	340074
106183	39137	18040
5168847	2798010	1487921
4598229	3493453	750915
2686223	1210019	846225
525662	173513	218053
5350481	3199637	816915
6481624	4683343	963567
6858043	4987873	764646
9263824	7204241	1384572
13081646	8888615	1422084
14396027	7648442	1022893
5609661	4007264	670929
1694698	1249041	117587
155169	108999	30703
64007	58592	3407
5230190	1685401	2408735
1506944	358735	870952
1769462	581354	858639

12-4 续表 3
Continued

项目	Indicator	营业收入 Revenue from Principal Business
农副食品加工业	Processing of Food from Agricultural Products	8409817
食品制造业	Manufacture of Foods	2462453
酒、饮料和精制茶制造业	Manufacture of Liquor, Beverage and Refind Tea	2465029
烟草制品业	Manufacture of Tobacco	
纺织业	Manufacture of Textile	1491509
纺织服装、服饰业	Manufacture of Textile Wearing Apparel	1554851
皮革、毛皮、羽毛及其制品和制鞋业	Processing of Leather, Fur, Feather & Its Products Footwear	420557
木材加工和木、竹、藤、棕、草制品业	Processing of Timbers, Manufacture of Wood, Bamboo, Rattan, Palm and Straw Products	223177
家具制造业	Manufacture of Furniture	537802
造纸和纸制品业	Manufacture of Paper and Paper Products	630836
印刷和记录媒介复制业	Printing, Reproduction of Recording Media	573218
文教、工美、体育和娱乐用品制造业	Manufacture of Articles for Culture, Arts & Crafts, Sports and Entertainment	847991
石油、煤炭及其他燃料加工业	Oil, coal and other fuel processing industries	4848217
化学原料和化学制品制造业	Manufacture of Chemical Raw Material and Chemical Products	4835346
医药制造业	Manufacture of Medicines	1010906
化学纤维制造业	Manufacture of Chemical Fibers	54470
橡胶和塑料制品业	Manufacture of Rubber and Plastic	4236610
非金属矿物制品业	Manufacture of Non-metallic Mineral Products	3762093
黑色金属冶炼和压延加工业	Smelting and Pressing of Ferrous Metals	3165912
有色金属冶炼和压延加工业	Smelting and Pressing of Nonferrous Metals	704576
金属制品业	Manufacture of Metal Products	4663121
通用设备制造业	Manufacture of General Purpose Machinery	5625382
专用设备制造业	Manufacture of Special Purpose Machinery	4406590
汽车制造业	Manufacture of Vehicle	13239030
铁路、船舶、航空航天和其他运输设备制造业	Manufacture of Transport Equipment for Railway, Shipping, Aerospace and other uses	7844157
电气机械和器材制造业	Manufacture of Electrical Machinery & Equipment	9682876
计算机、通信和其他电子设备制造业	Manufacture of Computer, Communication Equipment and Other Electronic Equipment	6544203
仪器仪表制造业	Manufacture of Measuring Instrument	1036691
其他制造业	Manufacture of Other Products	148983
废弃资源综合利用业	Recycling and Disposal of Waste Resources	
金属制品、机械和设备修理业	Manufacture of Metal Products, Machinery and Equipment	65019
电力、热力生产和供应业	Production and Supply of Electric Power and Heat Power	1498449
燃气生产和供应业	Production and Supply of Gas	859280
水的生产和供应业	Production and Supply of Water	386045

单位：万元 (10 000 yuan)

营业成本 Cost of Principal Business	营业税金及附加 Taxes and Extra Charges on Principal Business	利润总额 Total Profits	全部从业人员年平均人数（人） Annual Average Employed Persons (person)
7930314	12942	206614	43652
1950310	13144	136857	18973
1901146	62083	131973	17603
1314959	7873	51308	16375
1367880	10633	47552	35446
374568	1933	-3510	14109
207997	1196	-6940	2715
456038	2374	22652	9772
575214	2133	10493	6314
468535	3402	36289	7766
692377	4920	50536	16104
3663906	1097032	-46541	2065
4064800	21110	221122	21313
429375	11345	223528	10201
46674	356	1766	600
3525144	25468	303369	46145
3180887	21627	213375	25062
2831859	9667	164918	8032
639969	4133	6197	2835
4097123	21975	168320	40087
4518852	27958	352360	54436
3428297	25227	335639	38133
11814159	53871	621031	50755
6389892	46599	671830	54004
7943610	39232	1096584	54282
5836129	19725	366214	40693
667817	6220	134991	10938
125298	1163	3628	3917
49675	421	8316	1297
1374453	13745	19900	12504
649184	2905	145282	2704
377333	12181	16388	4774

12-5 按行业分国有控股工业企业主要指标（2020年）
MAIN INDICATORS OF STATE-HOLDING INDUSTRIAL ENTERPRISES BY INDUSTRIAL SECTOR (2020)

项目	Indicator	企业单位数（个） Number of Enterprises (unit)
总计	**Total**	**189**
煤炭开采和洗选业	Mining and Washing of Coal	
石油和天然气开采业	Extraction of Petroleum and Natural Gas	
黑色金属矿采选业	Mining of Ferrous Metal Ores	
有色金属矿采选业	Mining of Non-ferrous Metal Ores	2
非金属矿采选业	Mining and Processing of Nometal Ores	1
开采辅助活动	Auxiliary Activities of Mining	
其他采矿业	Mining of Other Ores	
农副食品加工业	Processing of Food from Agricultural Products	1
食品制造业	Manufacture of Foods	3
酒、饮料和精制茶制造业	Manufacture of Liquor, Beverage and Refind Tea	2
烟草制品业	Manufacture of Tobacco	
纺织业	Manufacture of Textile	
纺织服装、服饰业	Manufacture of Textile Wearing Apparel	1
皮革、毛皮、羽毛及其制品和制鞋业	Manufacture of Leather, Fur, Feather & Its Products Footwear	
木材加工和木、竹、藤、棕、草制品业	Processing of Timbers, Manufacture of Wood, Bamboo, Rattan, Palm and Straw Products	2
家具制造业	Manufacture of Furniture	
造纸和纸制品业	Manufacture of Paper and Paper Products	1
印刷和记录媒介复制业	Printing, Reproduction of Recording Media	1
文教、工美、体育和娱乐用品制造业	Manufacture of Articles for Culture, Arts & Crafts, Sports and Entertainment	
石油、煤炭及其他燃料加工业	Oil, coal and other fuel processing industries	2
化学原料和化学制品制造业	Manufacture of Chemical Raw Material and Chemical Products	9
医药制造业	Manufacture of Medicines	4
化学纤维制造业	Manufacture of Chemical Fibers	
橡胶和塑料制品业	Manufacture of Rubber and Plastic	4
非金属矿物制品业	Manufacture of Non-metallic Mineral Products	12
黑色金属冶炼和压延加工业	Smelting and Pressing of Ferrous Metals	8
有色金属冶炼和压延加工业	Smelting and Pressing of Non-ferrous Metals	4
金属制品业	Manufacture of Metal Products	8
通用设备制造业	Manufacture of General Purpose Machinery	11
专用设备制造业	Manufacture of Special Purpose Machinery	12
汽车制造业	Manufacture of Vehicle	6
铁路、船舶、航空航天和其他运输设备制造业	Manufacture of Transport Equipment for Railway, Shipping, Aerospace and other uses	14
电气机械和器材制造业	Manufacture of Electrical Machinery & Equipment	10
计算机、通信和其他电子设备制造业	Manufacture of Computer, Communication Equipment and Other Electronic Equipment	6
仪器仪表制造业	Manufacture of Measuring Instrument	2
其他制造业	Manufacture of Other Products	
废弃资源综合利用业	Recycling and Disposal of Waste Resources	
金属制品、机械和设备修理业	Manufacture of Metal Products, Machinery and Equipment	2
电力、热力生产和供应业	Production and Supply of Electric Power and Heat Power	36
燃气生产和供应业	Production and Supply of Gas	6
水的生产和供应业	Production and Supply of Water	19

单位：万元 (10 000 yuan)

资产合计 Total Assets	流动资产合计 Total Current Assets	固定资产净值 Net Value of Fixed Assets
36641165	**20886192**	**8420414**
94208	60622	2565
1820500	404853	817203
640117	338858	146111
671439	281864	339573
386133	322583	55476
2268708	877121	805904
341004	38916	186512
229651	150484	62287
271598	208191	38689
851423	596547	202444
3971289	3396587	374541
9830923	6693102	960890
983064	606519	181032
2708603	2050914	95549
3742549	1287543	1864503
963820	184767	581283
1612259	503542	805222

12-5 续表
Continued

项目	Indicator	营业收入 Revenue from Principal Business
总计	**Total**	**32612329**
煤炭开采和洗选业	Mining and Washing of Coal	
石油和天然气开采业	Extraction of Petroleum and Natural Gas	
黑色金属矿采选业	Mining of Ferrous Metal Ores	
有色金属矿采选业	Mining of Non-ferrous Metal Ores	
非金属矿采选业	Mining and Processing of Nonmetal Ores	
开采辅助活动	Auxiliary Activities of Mining	
其他采矿业	Mining of Other Ores	
农副食品加工业	Processing of Food from Agricultural Products	
食品制造业	Manufacture of Foods	59220
酒、饮料和精制茶制造业	Manufacture of Liquor, Beverage and Refined Tea	
烟草制品业	Manufacture of Tobacco	
纺织业	Manufacture of Textile	
纺织服装、服饰业	Manufacture of Textile Wearing Apparel	
皮革、毛皮、羽毛及其制品和制鞋业	Manufacture of Leather, Fur, Feather & Its Products Footwear	
木材加工和木、竹、藤、棕、草制品业	Processing of Timbers, Manufacture of Wood, Bamboo, Rattan, Palm and Straw Products	
家具制造业	Manufacture of Furniture	
造纸和纸制品业	Manufacture of Paper and Paper Products	
印刷和记录媒介复制业	Printing, Reproduction of Recording Media	
文教、工美、体育和娱乐用品制造业	Manufacture of Articles for Culture, Arts & Crafts, Sports and Entertainment	
石油、煤炭及其他燃料加工业	Oil, coal and other fuel processing industries	
化学原料和化学制品制造业	Manufacture of Chemical Raw Material and Chemical Products	921189
医药制造业	Manufacture of Medicines	335418
化学纤维制造业	Manufacture of Chemical Fibers	
橡胶和塑料制品业	Manufacture of Rubber and Plastic	382177
非金属矿物制品业	Manufacture of Non-metallic Mineral Products	329270
黑色金属冶炼和压延加工业	Smelting and Pressing of Ferrous Metals	2321136
有色金属冶炼和压延加工业	Smelting and Pressing of Non-ferrous Metals	146478
金属制品业	Manufacture of Metal Products	139461
通用设备制造业	Manufacture of General Purpose Machinery	261160
专用设备制造业	Manufacture of Special Purpose Machinery	506337
汽车制造业	Manufacture of Vehicle	8403876
铁路、船舶、航空航天和其他运输设备制造业	Manufacture of Transport Equipment for Railway, Shipping, Aerospace and other uses	5953930
电气机械和器材制造业	Manufacture of Electrical Machinery & Equipment	967196
计算机、通信和其他电子设备制造业	Manufacture of Computer, Communication Equipment and Other Electronic Equipment	3026249
仪器仪表制造业	Manufacture of Measuring Instrument	
其他制造业	Manufacture of Other Products	
废弃资源综合利用业	Recycling and Disposal of Waste Resources	
金属制品、机械和设备修理业	Manufacture of Metal Products, Machinery and Equipment	
电力、热力生产和供应业	Production and Supply of Electric Power and Heat Power	1243648
燃气生产和供应业	Production and Supply of Gas	341068
水的生产和供应业	Production and Supply of Water	338413

单位：万元 (10 000 yuan)

营业成本 Cost of Principal Business	营业税金及附加 Taxes and Extra Charges on Principal Business	利润总额 Total Profits	全部从业人员年平均人数（人） Annual Average Employed Persons (person)
27565265	**1283777**	**1649731**	**109742**
45963	454	8254	753
759195	3699	89465	3757
117625	3862	94361	2878
351379	2643	-1271	3792
286809	1466	18156	1089
2021924	8205	159560	6238
108415	3206	3457	1143
130262	1422	-11778	805
230299	1344	4448	2281
362890	3262	53621	3565
7634940	33068	408436	10470
4847389	32324	537355	21895
871761	6008	-20915	7847
2786750	7387	140298	8149
1190876	10754	-13493	10214
220489	2087	105004	1052
346890	11902	2994	4343

12-6　按行业分规模以上外商投资和港澳台商投资工业企业主要指标（2020年）
MAIN INDICATORS OF FOREIGN FUNDED ENTERPRISES AND ENTERPRISES WITH FUNDS FROM HONG KONG, MACAO AND TAIWAN ABOVE DESIGNATED SIZE BY INDUSTRIAL SECTOR (2020)

项目	Indicator	企业单位数（个）Number of Enterprises (unit)
总计	**Total**	**825**
煤炭开采和洗选业	Mining and Washing of Coal	
石油和天然气开采业	Extraction of Petroleum and Natural Gas	
黑色金属矿采选业	Mining of Ferrous Metal Ores	
有色金属矿采选业	Mining of Non-ferrous Metal Ores	
非金属矿采选业	Mining and Processing of Nometal Ores	
开采辅助活动	Auxiliary Activities of Mining	
其他采矿业	Mining of Other Ores	
农副食品加工业	Processing of Food from Agricultural Products	73
食品制造业	Manufacture of Foods	34
酒、饮料和精制茶制造业	Manufacture of Liquor, Beverage and Refind Tea	5
烟草制品业	Manufacture of Tobacco	
纺织业	Manufacture of Textile	43
纺织服装、服饰业	Manufacture of Textile Wearing Apparel	44
皮革、毛皮、羽毛及其制品和制鞋业	Manufacture of Leather, Fur, Feather & Its Products Footwear	14
木材加工和木、竹、藤、棕、草制品业	Processing of Timbers, Manufacture of Wood, Bamboo, Rattan, Palm and Straw Products	7
家具制造业	Manufacture of Furniture	16
造纸和纸制品业	Manufacture of Paper and Paper Products	12
印刷和记录媒介复制业	Printing, Reproduction of Recording Media	14
文教、工美、体育和娱乐用品制造业	Manufacture of Articles for Culture, Arts & Crafts, Sports and Entertainment	36
石油、煤炭及其他燃料加工业	Oil, coal and other fuel processing industries	
化学原料和化学制品制造业	Manufacture of Chemical Raw Material and Chemical Products	45
医药制造业	Manufacture of Medicines	10
化学纤维制造业	Manufacture of Chemical Fibers	2
橡胶和塑料制品业	Manufacture of Rubber and Plastic	55
非金属矿物制品业	Manufacture of Non-metallic Mineral Products	34
黑色金属冶炼和压延加工业	Smelting and Pressing of Ferrous Metals	5
有色金属冶炼和压延加工业	Smelting and Pressing of Non-ferrous Metals	2
金属制品业	Manufacture of Metal Products	60
通用设备制造业	Manufacture of General Purpose Machinery	66
专用设备制造业	Manufacture of Special Purpose Machinery	44
汽车制造业	Manufacture of Vehicle	62
铁路、船舶、航空航天和其他运输设备制造业	Manufacture of Transport Equipment for Railway, Shipping, Aerospace and other uses	24
电气机械和器材制造业	Manufacture of Electrical Machinery & Equipment	33
计算机、通信和其他电子设备制造业	Manufacture of Computer, Communication Equipment and Other Electronic Equipment	47
仪器仪表制造业	Manufacture of Measuring Instrument	11
其他制造业	Manufacture of Other Products	5
废弃资源综合利用业	Recycling and Disposal of Waste Resources	
金属制品、机械和设备修理业	Manufacture of Metal Products, Machinery and Equipment	2
电力、热力生产和供应业	Production and Supply of Electric Power and Heat Power	5
燃气生产和供应业	Production and Supply of Gas	10
水的生产和供应业	Production and Supply of Water	5

单位：万元 (10 000 yuan)

资产合计 Total Assets	流动资产合计 Total Current Assets	固定资产净值 Net Value of Fixed Assets
25515161	**17522797**	**5087913**
1530555	1215629	201537
2134458	1471476	412813
206754	140445	48643
444459	356708	70159
522671	409025	56779
199259	134511	51784
58808	48956	7775
135182	105268	22151
187463	143733	36421
231960	153790	47300
398934	268387	85394
1678337	923212	537499
521237	314439	107056
1054634	572684	414851
637547	399640	184786
183873	137933	14365
1475622	979537	364777
1851023	1324365	404616
1401577	1069129	181435
3288457	2603491	527771
2249051	1706487	265124
2107951	1213631	245521
1473309	1029027	328677
407435	344963	16766
110252	68245	27196
217910	42803	115374
560853	216323	214574
153524	59145	78488

12-6 续表
Continued

项目	Indicator	营业收入 Revenue from Principal Business
总计	**Total**	**27398269**
煤炭开采和洗选业	Mining and Washing of Coal	
石油和天然气开采业	Extraction of Petroleum and Natural Gas	
黑色金属矿采选业	Mining of Ferrous Metal Ores	
有色金属矿采选业	Mining of Non-ferrous Metal Ores	
非金属矿采选业	Mining and Processing of Nometal Ores	
开采辅助活动	Auxiliary Activities of Mining	
其他采矿业	Mining of Other Ores	
农副食品加工业	Processing of Food from Agricultural Products	3216471
食品制造业	Manufacture of Foods	1391044
酒、饮料和精制茶制造业	Manufacture of Liquor, Beverage and Refind Tea	241875
烟草制品业	Manufacture of Tobacco	
纺织业	Manufacture of Textile	590778
纺织服装、服饰业	Manufacture of Textile Wearing Apparel	678579
皮革、毛皮、羽毛及其制品和制鞋业	Manufacture of Leather, Fur, Feather & Its Products Footwear	307712
木材加工和木、竹、藤、棕、草制品业	Processing of Timbers, Manufacture of Wood, Bamboo, Rattan, Palm and Straw Products	33756
家具制造业	Manufacture of Furniture	148801
造纸和纸制品业	Manufacture of Paper and Paper Products	199510
印刷和记录媒介复制业	Printing, Reproduction of Recording Media	254955
文教、工美、体育和娱乐用品制造业	Manufacture of Articles for Culture, Arts & Crafts, Sports and Entertainment	379311
石油、煤炭及其他燃料加工业	Oil, coal and other fuel processing industries	
化学原料和化学制品制造业	Manufacture of Chemical Raw Material and Chemical Products	1817527
医药制造业	Manufacture of Medicines	361978
化学纤维制造业	Manufacture of Chemical Fibers	
橡胶和塑料制品业	Manufacture of Rubber and Plastic	910411
非金属矿物制品业	Manufacture of Non-metallic Mineral Products	496056
黑色金属冶炼和压延加工业	Smelting and Pressing of Ferrous Metals	367272
有色金属冶炼和压延加工业	Smelting and Pressing of Non-ferrous Metals	
金属制品业	Manufacture of Metal Products	1674648
通用设备制造业	Manufacture of General Purpose Machinery	1989130
专用设备制造业	Manufacture of Special Purpose Machinery	1068673
汽车制造业	Manufacture of Vehicle	4002418
铁路、船舶、航空航天和其他运输设备制造业	Manufacture of Transport Equipment for Railway, Shipping, Aerospace and other uses	1200970
电气机械和器材制造业	Manufacture of Electrical Machinery & Equipment	2887001
计算机、通信和其他电子设备制造业	Manufacture of Computer, Communication Equipment and Other Electronic Equipment	2086227
仪器仪表制造业	Manufacture of Measuring Instrument	321428
其他制造业	Manufacture of Other Products	95945
废弃资源综合利用业	Recycling and Disposal of Waste Resources	
金属制品、机械和设备修理业	Manufacture of Metal Products, Machinery and Equipment	
电力、热力生产和供应业	Production and Supply of Electric Power and Heat Power	32679
燃气生产和供应业	Production and Supply of Gas	521859
水的生产和供应业	Production and Supply of Water	44705

单位：万元 (10 000 yuan)

营业成本 Cost of Principal Business	营业税金及附加 Taxes and Extra Charges on Principal Business	利润总额 Total Profits	全部从业人员年平均人数（人） Annual Average Employed Persons (person)
22771458	**147172**	**1848995**	**215057**
3037608	4231	43760	15666
1040150	8837	98821	8611
167347	2130	5666	2520
498824	3464	37680	6723
608323	4515	13457	14831
277585	1321	2118	10407
31089	221	-1221	432
125072	1064	3813	3218
178177	884	5268	1572
198593	1763	22121	3492
310691	2150	26578	8572
1592970	8945	-26732	6710
167136	3768	110682	2281
733339	5552	58995	11587
403150	3435	33315	3880
349160	948	3170	961
1464832	8881	100277	14902
1579099	10756	146084	18332
841676	6673	47233	8642
3340730	31045	362425	20302
881660	9576	171038	9750
2278101	13981	313278	14254
1806076	7794	144636	19459
200188	2080	62013	1918
83653	886	-1561	3245
17538	422	11073	200
463774	836	42453	1532
27759	714	9119	336

12-7　按行业分大中型工业企业主要指标（2020 年）
MAIN INDICATORS OF LARGE AND MEDIUM-SIZED INDUSTRIAL ENTERPRISES BY INDUSTRIAL SECTOR (2020)

项目	Indicator	企业单位数（个）Number of Enterprises (unit)
总计	**Total**	**473**
煤炭开采和洗选业	Mining and Washing of Coal	
石油和天然气开采业	Extraction of Petroleum and Natural Gas	
黑色金属矿采选业	Mining of Ferrous Metal Ores	
有色金属矿采选业	Mining of Non-ferrous Metal Ores	
非金属矿采选业	Mining and Processing of Nometal Ores	
开采辅助活动	Auxiliary Activities of Mining	
其他采矿业	Mining of Other Ores	
农副食品加工业	Processing of Food from Agricultural Products	32
食品制造业	Manufacture of Foods	15
酒、饮料和精制茶制造业	Manufacture of Liquor, Beverage and Refind Tea	5
烟草制品业	Manufacture of Tobacco	
纺织业	Manufacture of Textile	10
纺织服装、服饰业	Manufacture of Textile Wearing Apparel	33
皮革、毛皮、羽毛及其制品和制鞋业	Manufacture of Leather, Fur, Feather & Its Products Footwear	11
木材加工和木、竹、藤、棕、草制品业	Processing of Timbers, Manufacture of Wood, Bamboo, Rattan, Palm and Straw Products	2
家具制造业	Manufacture of Furniture	9
造纸和纸制品业	Manufacture of Paper and Paper Products	3
印刷和记录媒介复制业	Printing, Reproduction of Recording Media	6
文教、工美、体育和娱乐用品制造业	Manufacture of Articles for Culture, Arts & Crafts, Sports and Entertainment	14
石油、煤炭及其他燃料加工业	Oil, coal and other fuel processing industries	2
化学原料和化学制品制造业	Manufacture of Chemical Raw Material and Chemical Products	16
医药制造业	Manufacture of Medicines	9
化学纤维制造业	Manufacture of Chemical Fibers	
橡胶和塑料制品业	Manufacture of Rubber and Plastic	23
非金属矿物制品业	Manufacture of Non-metallic Mineral Products	13
黑色金属冶炼和压延加工业	Smelting and Pressing of Ferrous Metals	5
有色金属冶炼和压延加工业	Smelting and Pressing of Non-ferrous Metals	2
金属制品业	Manufacture of Metal Products	26
通用设备制造业	Manufacture of General Purpose Machinery	42
专用设备制造业	Manufacture of Special Purpose Machinery	26
汽车制造业	Manufacture of Vehicle	41
铁路、船舶、航空航天和其他运输设备制造业	Manufacture of Transport Equipment for Railway, Shipping, Aerospace and other uses	31
电气机械和器材制造业	Manufacture of Electrical Machinery & Equipment	39
计算机、通信和其他电子设备制造业	Manufacture of Computer, Communication Equipment and Other Electronic Equipment	30
仪器仪表制造业	Manufacture of Measuring Instrument	8
其他制造业	Manufacture of Other Products	2
废弃资源综合利用业	Recycling and Disposal of Waste Resources	
金属制品、机械和设备修理业	Manufacture of Metal Products, Machinery and Equipment	1
电力、热力生产和供应业	Production and Supply of Electric Power and Heat Power	12
燃气生产和供应业	Production and Supply of Gas	2
水的生产和供应业	Production and Supply of Water	3

单位：万元 (10 000 yuan)

资产合计 Total Assets	流动资产合计 Total Current Assets	固定资产净值 Net Value of Fixed Assets
73987503	**45344229**	**12211739**
1979086	1495985	241501
2116650	1462083	392170
3193586	1572115	309581
297635	242874	45982
1197153	670653	117412
230784	154531	55668
219298	194258	16687
66951	38722	12368
167029	122917	40405
436770	289272	81650
3746318	1512741	1204461
1185273	706872	217299
3340767	1525603	1104419
761643	578137	132697
2219737	823183	791780
2249772	1330981	343140
4151925	2992857	583800
3086671	2468822	332753
7267659	5827872	951568
11262044	7744437	1220670
13119147	6688782	865175
4356657	3250156	471856
1081326	787452	73741
2355866	948474	1140421
910068	315464	461605

12-7　续表
Continued

项目	Indicator	营业收入 Revenue from Principal Business
总计	**Total**	**64389227**
煤炭开采和洗选业	Mining and Washing of Coal	
石油和天然气开采业	Extraction of Petroleum and Natural Gas	
黑色金属矿采选业	Mining of Ferrous Metal Ores	
有色金属矿采选业	Mining of Non-ferrous Metal Ores	
非金属矿采选业	Mining and Processing of Nometal Ores	
开采辅助活动	Auxiliary Activities of Mining	
其他采矿业	Mining of Other Ores	
农副食品加工业	Processing of Food from Agricultural Products	4371833
食品制造业	Manufacture of Foods	1357431
酒、饮料和精制茶制造业	Manufacture of Liquor, Beverage and Refind Tea	2393700
烟草制品业	Manufacture of Tobacco	
纺织业	Manufacture of Textile	499591
纺织服装、服饰业	Manufacture of Textile Wearing Apparel	1034207
皮革、毛皮、羽毛及其制品和制鞋业	Manufacture of Leather, Fur, Feather & Its Products Footwear	332827
木材加工和木、竹、藤、棕、草制品业	Processing of Timbers, Manufacture of Wood, Bamboo, Rattan, Palm and Straw Products	
家具制造业	Manufacture of Furniture	284532
造纸和纸制品业	Manufacture of Paper and Paper Products	67846
印刷和记录媒介复制业	Printing, Reproduction of Recording Media	194362
文教、工美、体育和娱乐用品制造业	Manufacture of Articles for Culture, Arts & Crafts, Sports and Entertainment	380631
石油、煤炭及其他燃料加工业	Oil, coal and other fuel processing industries	
化学原料和化学制品制造业	Manufacture of Chemical Raw Material and Chemical Products	2730109
医药制造业	Manufacture of Medicines	754922
化学纤维制造业	Manufacture of Chemical Fibers	
橡胶和塑料制品业	Manufacture of Rubber and Plastic	1849158
非金属矿物制品业	Manufacture of Non-metallic Mineral Products	590073
黑色金属冶炼和压延加工业	Smelting and Pressing of Ferrous Metals	2145193
有色金属冶炼和压延加工业	Smelting and Pressing of Non-ferrous Metals	
金属制品业	Manufacture of Metal Products	1951377
通用设备制造业	Manufacture of General Purpose Machinery	3426855
专用设备制造业	Manufacture of Special Purpose Machinery	2193852
汽车制造业	Manufacture of Vehicle	10733226
铁路、船舶、航空航天和其他运输设备制造业	Manufacture of Transport Equipment for Railway, Shipping, Aerospace and other uses	6834217
电气机械和器材制造业	Manufacture of Electrical Machinery & Equipment	8178042
计算机、通信和其他电子设备制造业	Manufacture of Computer, Communication Equipment and Other Electronic Equipment	5332964
仪器仪表制造业	Manufacture of Measuring Instrument	574491
其他制造业	Manufacture of Other Products	
废弃资源综合利用业	Recycling and Disposal of Waste Resources	
金属制品、机械和设备修理业	Manufacture of Metal Products, Machinery and Equipment	
电力、热力生产和供应业	Production and Supply of Electric Power and Heat Power	885452
燃气生产和供应业	Production and Supply of Gas	
水的生产和供应业	Production and Supply of Water	131731

单位：万元 (10 000 yuan)

营业成本 Cost of Principal Business	营业税金及附加 Taxes and Extra Charges on Principal Business	利润总额 Total Profits	全部从业人员年平均人数（人） Annual Average Employed Persons (person)
53901301	**1424569**	**4124804**	**386893**
4141020	5457	60236	24806
1010537	7190	92608	8679
1852834	58943	120316	16657
0	0	0	0
441097	2453	16832	5037
900693	7354	54610	25375
295753	1448	-1963	12058
230129	1342	14154	4605
63815	358	-154	1307
151678	1041	16616	2620
290652	2488	36210	7951
2358355	9796	81924	9571
267666	9551	209285	6738
1494021	12267	197322	20794
489262	3071	43370	5942
1850026	8063	157677	6239
1722637	9576	114683	15369
2731482	15958	242724	28580
1675514	13923	205640	16038
9660655	42816	511500	30091
5585027	40347	588728	42143
6624534	34499	1046250	41390
4789755	15739	282027	31068
345655	3873	93125	4978
851062	7718	-17001	7489
181002	9901	-17566	2650

12-8 按行业分规模以上工业企业主要经济效益指标（2020 年）

MAIN INDICATORS ON ECONOMIC BENEFIT OF INDUSTRIAL ENTERPRISES ABOVE DESIGNATED SIZE BY INDUSTRIAL SECTOR (2019)

项目	Indicator	总资产贡献率(%) Ratio of Total Assets to Industrial Output Value (%)
总计	**Total**	**8.2**
煤炭开采和洗选业	Mining and Washing of Coal	
石油和天然气开采业	Extraction of Petroleum and Natural Gas	
黑色金属矿采选业	Mining of Ferrous Metal Ores	
有色金属矿采选业	Mining of Non-ferrous Metal Ores	
非金属矿采选业	Mining and Processing of Nometal Ores	
开采辅助活动	Auxiliary Activities of Mining	
其他采矿业	Mining of Other Ores	
农副食品加工业	Processing of Food from Agricultural Products	5.96
食品制造业	Manufacture of Foods	6.02
酒、饮料和精制茶制造业	Manufacture of Liquor, Beverage and Refind Tea	7.34
烟草制品业	Manufacture of Tobacco	
纺织业	Manufacture of Textile	8
纺织服装、服饰业	Manufacture of Textile Wearing Apparel	5.18
皮革、毛皮、羽毛及其制品和制鞋业	Manufacture of Leather, Fur, Feather & Its Products Footwear	1.1
木材加工和木、竹、藤、棕、草制品业	Processing of Timbers, Manufacture of Wood, Bamboo, Rattan, Palm and Straw Products	-0.88
家具制造业	Manufacture of Furniture	7.42
造纸和纸制品业	Manufacture of Paper and Paper Products	5.06
印刷和记录媒介复制业	Printing, Reproduction of Recording Media	10.31
文教、工美、体育和娱乐用品制造业	Manufacture of Articles for Culture, Arts & Crafts, Sports and Entertainment	7.96
石油、煤炭及其他燃料加工业	Oil, coal and other fuel processing industries	53.1
化学原料和化学制品制造业	Manufacture of Chemical Raw Material and Chemical Products	5.83
医药制造业	Manufacture of Medicines	18.59
化学纤维制造业	Manufacture of Chemical Fibers	2.89
橡胶和塑料制品业	Manufacture of Rubber and Plastic	8.04
非金属矿物制品业	Manufacture of Non-metallic Mineral Products	7.66
黑色金属冶炼和压延加工业	Smelting and Pressing of Ferrous Metals	7.43
有色金属冶炼和压延加工业	Smelting and Pressing of Non-ferrous Metals	3.03
金属制品业	Manufacture of Metal Products	5.11
通用设备制造业	Manufacture of General Purpose Machinery	7.61
专用设备制造业	Manufacture of Special Purpose Machinery	6.88
汽车制造业	Manufacture of Vehicle	9.25
铁路、船舶、航空航天和其他运输设备制造业	Manufacture of Transport Equipment for Railway, Shipping, Aerospace and other uses	7
电气机械和器材制造业	Manufacture of Electrical Machinery & Equipment	8.99
计算机、通信和其他电子设备制造业	Manufacture of Computer, Communication Equipment and Other Electronic Equipment	6.95
仪器仪表制造业	Manufacture of Measuring Instrument	10.56
其他制造业	Manufacture of Other Products	5.12
废弃资源综合利用业	Recycling and Disposal of Waste Resources	
金属制品、机械和设备修理业	Manufacture of Metal Products, Machinery and Equipment	18.28
电力、热力生产和供应业	Production and Supply of Electric Power and Heat Power	2.24
燃气生产和供应业	Production and Supply of Gas	11.51
水的生产和供应业	Production and Supply of Water	2.89

资产负债率 (%) Assets–Liability Ratio (%)	流动资产周转次数(次/年) Number of Times of Annual of Turnover Current Assets (time/year)	工业成本费用利润率 (%) Ratio of Profits to Industrial Costs (%)
57.78	**1.44**	**6.18**
68.7	2.71	2.48
65.74	1.15	6.02
47.34	1.48	5.59
63.04	1.96	3.57
52.68	1.57	3.12
55.3	1.87	–0.85
78.99	1.5	–3.02
66.36	1.41	4.38
65.82	1.89	1.69
57.03	1.71	6.75
50.96	1.57	6.3
48.5	3.39	–1.24
52.57	1.67	4.8
38.68	1.07	28.51
73.76	1.39	3.36
52.76	1.51	7.46
64.4	1.08	6.02
70.42	2.62	5.51
53.01	4.06	0.9
48.94	1.46	3.73
55.21	1.2	6.68
59.27	0.88	8.19
66.43	1.84	4.94
56.81	0.88	9.22
56.59	1.27	12.07
48.37	1.63	5.78
42.8	0.83	14.84
68.55	1.37	2.53
49.48	1.11	14.24
76.32	0.89	1.31
49.65	2.4	19.81
59.62	0.66	3.77

12-9 按行业分国有控股工业企业主要经济效益指标(2020年)

MAIN INDICATORS ON ECONOMIC BENEFIT OF STATE-OWNED AND STATE-HOLDING INDUSTRIAL ENTERPRISES BY INDUSTRIAL SECTOR (2020)

行业	Indicator	总资产贡献率(%) Ratio of Total Assets to Industrial Output Value (%)
总计	**Total**	**9.53**
煤炭开采和洗选业	Mining and Washing of Coal	
石油和天然气开采业	Extraction of Petroleum and Natural Gas	
黑色金属矿采选业	Mining of Ferrous Metal Ores	
有色金属矿采选业	Mining of Non-ferrous Metal Ores	
非金属矿采选业	Mining and Processing of Nometal Ores	
开采辅助活动	Auxiliary Activities of Mining	
其他采矿业	Mining of Other Ores	
农副食品加工业	Processing of Food from Agricultural Products	
食品制造业	Manufacture of Foods	10.67
酒、饮料和精制茶制造业	Manufacture of Liquor, Beverage and Refind Tea	
烟草制品业	Manufacture of Tobacco	
纺织业	Manufacture of Textile	
纺织服装、服饰业	Manufacture of Textile Wearing Apparel	
皮革、毛皮、羽毛及其制品和制鞋业	Manufacture of Leather, Fur, Feather & Its Products Footwear	
木材加工和木、竹、藤、棕、草制品业	Processing of Timbers, Manufacture of Wood, Bamboo, Rattan, Palm and Straw Products	
家具制造业	Manufacture of Furniture	
造纸和纸制品业	Manufacture of Paper and Paper Products	
印刷和记录媒介复制业	Printing, Reproduction of Recording Media	
文教、工美、体育和娱乐用品制造业	Manufacture of Articles for Culture, Arts & Crafts, Sports and Entertainment	
石油、煤炭及其他燃料加工业	Oil, coal and other fuel processing industries	
化学原料和化学制品制造业	Manufacture of Chemical Raw Material and Chemical Products	5.83
医药制造业	Manufacture of Medicines	18.62
化学纤维制造业	Manufacture of Chemical Fibers	
橡胶和塑料制品业	Manufacture of Rubber and Plastic	2.50
非金属矿物制品业	Manufacture of Non-metallic Mineral Products	7.94
黑色金属冶炼和压延加工业	Smelting and Pressing of Ferrous Metals	8.22
有色金属冶炼和压延加工业	Smelting and Pressing of Non-ferrous Metals	2.70
金属制品业	Manufacture of Metal Products	0.98
通用设备制造业	Manufacture of General Purpose Machinery	4.26
专用设备制造业	Manufacture of Special Purpose Machinery	8.30
汽车制造业	Manufacture of Vehicle	12.93
铁路、船舶、航空航天和其他运输设备制造业	Manufacture of Transport Equipment for Railway, Shipping, Aerospace and other uses	7.10
电气机械和器材制造业	Manufacture of Electrical Machinery & Equipment	0.13
计算机、通信和其他电子设备制造业	Manufacture of Computer, Communication Equipment and Other Electronic Equipment	4.37
仪器仪表制造业	Manufacture of Measuring Instrument	
其他制造业	Manufacture of Other Products	
废弃资源综合利用业	Recycling and Disposal of Waste Resources	
金属制品、机械和设备修理业	Manufacture of Metal Products, Machinery and Equipment	
电力、热力生产和供应业	Production and Supply of Electric Power and Heat Power	1.73
燃气生产和供应业	Production and Supply of Gas	13.01
水的生产和供应业	Production and Supply of Water	2.09

资产负债率（%） Assets–Liability Ratio (%)	流动资产周转次数(次/年) Number of Times of Annual of Turnover Current Assets (time/year)	工业成本费用利润率(%) Ratio of Profits to Industrial Costs (%)
60.19	**1.56**	**5.47**
33.87	0.98	15.84
67.13	2.28	10.39
28.44	0.99	39.87
70.48	1.36	–0.32
69.50	1.02	5.86
71.73	2.65	7.41
45.13	3.76	2.71
101.46	0.93	–7.76
69.96	1.25	1.74
68.57	0.85	11.78
69.97	2.47	5.13
58.22	0.89	9.77
66.56	1.59	–2.11
41.82	1.48	4.69
80.95	0.97	–1.04
42.69	1.85	42.10
60.70	0.67	0.75

12-10 按行业分规模以上外商及港澳台商投资工业企业主要经济效益指标（2020 年）

MAIN INDICATORS ON ECONOMIC BENEFIT OF FOREIGN FUNDED ENTERPRISES AND ENTERPRISES WITH FUNDS FROM HONG KONG, MACAO AND TAIWAN ABOVE DESIGNATED SIZE BY INDUSTRIAL SECTOR (2020)

行业	Indicator	总资产贡献率（%） Ratio of Total Assets to Industrial Output Value (%)
总计	**Total**	**9.67**
煤炭开采和洗选业	Mining and Washing of Coal	
石油和天然气开采业	Extraction of Petroleum and Natural Gas	
黑色金属矿采选业	Mining of Ferrous Metal Ores	
有色金属矿采选业	Mining of Non-ferrous Metal Ores	
非金属矿采选业	Mining and Processing of Nometal Ores	
开采辅助活动	Auxiliary Activities of Mining	
其他采矿业	Mining of Other Ores	
农副食品加工业	Processing of Food from Agricultural Products	2.94
食品制造业	Manufacture of Foods	6.15
酒、饮料和精制茶制造业	Manufacture of Liquor, Beverage and Refind Tea	8.61
烟草制品业	Manufacture of Tobacco	
纺织业	Manufacture of Textile	11.02
纺织服装、服饰业	Manufacture of Textile Wearing Apparel	4.81
皮革、毛皮、羽毛及其制品和制鞋业	Manufacture of Leather, Fur, Feather & Its Products Footwear	3.36
木材加工和木、竹、藤、棕、草制品业	Processing of Timbers, Manufacture of Wood, Bamboo, Rattan, Palm and Straw Products	-1.61
家具制造业	Manufacture of Furniture	6.09
造纸和纸制品业	Manufacture of Paper and Paper Products	6.31
印刷和记录媒介复制业	Printing, Reproduction of Recording Media	13.31
文教、工美、体育和娱乐用品制造业	Manufacture of Articles for Culture, Arts & Crafts, Sports and Entertainment	7.97
石油、煤炭及其他燃料加工业	Oil, coal and other fuel processing industries	0.00
化学原料和化学制品制造业	Manufacture of Chemical Raw Material and Chemical Products	2.20
医药制造业	Manufacture of Medicines	26.22
化学纤维制造业	Manufacture of Chemical Fibers	
橡胶和塑料制品业	Manufacture of Rubber and Plastic	7.63
非金属矿物制品业	Manufacture of Non-metallic Mineral Products	7.66
黑色金属冶炼和压延加工业	Smelting and Pressing of Ferrous Metals	3.92
有色金属冶炼和压延加工业	Smelting and Pressing of Non-ferrous Metals	
金属制品业	Manufacture of Metal Products	7.91
通用设备制造业	Manufacture of General Purpose Machinery	9.91
专用设备制造业	Manufacture of Special Purpose Machinery	6.46
汽车制造业	Manufacture of Vehicle	14.94
铁路、船舶、航空航天和其他运输设备制造业	Manufacture of Transport Equipment for Railway, Shipping, Aerospace and other uses	9.72
电气机械和器材制造业	Manufacture of Electrical Machinery & Equipment	17.48
计算机、通信和其他电子设备制造业	Manufacture of Computer, Communication Equipment and Other Electronic Equipment	11.39
仪器仪表制造业	Manufacture of Measuring Instrument	19.15
其他制造业	Manufacture of Other Products	0.72
废弃资源综合利用业	Recycling and Disposal of Waste Resources	0.00
金属制品、机械和设备修理业	Manufacture of Metal Products, Machinery and Equipment	
电力、热力生产和供应业	Production and Supply of Electric Power and Heat Power	6.65
燃气生产和供应业	Production and Supply of Gas	9.20
水的生产和供应业	Production and Supply of Water	9.11

资产负债率（%） Assets–Liability Ratio (%)	流动资产周转次数(次/年) Number of Times of Annual of Turnover Current Assets (time/year)	工业成本费用利润率(%) Ratio of Profits to Industrial Costs (%)
52.15	**1.56**	**7.26**
71.43	2.65	1.38
67.73	0.95	8.01
56.74	1.72	2.41
46.76	1.66	6.86
53.70	1.66	2.03
45.61	2.29	0.70
80.58	0.69	-3.51
60.37	1.41	2.64
56.05	1.39	2.73
51.15	1.66	9.59
52.32	1.41	7.46
0.00	0.00	0.00
51.41	1.97	-1.47
39.19	1.15	44.29
37.46	1.59	6.97
34.52	1.24	7.24
32.91	2.66	0.87
55.08	1.71	6.32
44.78	1.50	7.94
53.98	1.00	4.65
44.12	1.54	10.02
55.09	0.70	16.68
51.79	2.38	12.05
50.93	2.03	7.37
44.31	0.93	24.24
79.14	1.41	-1.63
0.00	0.00	0.00
34.82	0.93	21.49
55.51	2.41	8.48
53.58	0.76	25.44

12-11 按行业分大中型工业企业主要经济效益指标（2020年）

MAIN INDICATORS ON ECONOMIC BENEFIT OF LARGE AND MEDIUM-SIZED INDUSTRIAL ENTERPRISES BY INDUSTRIAL SECTOR (2020)

行业	Indicator	总资产贡献率（%）Ratio of Total Assets to Industrial Output Value (%)
总计	**Total**	**8.94**
煤炭开采和洗选业	Mining and Washing of Coal	
石油和天然气开采业	Extraction of Petroleum and Natural Gas	
黑色金属矿采选业	Mining of Ferrous Metal Ores	
有色金属矿采选业	Mining of Non-ferrous Metal Ores	
非金属矿采选业	Mining and Processing of Nometal Ores	
开采辅助活动	Auxiliary Activities of Mining	
其他采矿业	Mining of Other Ores	
农副食品加工业	Processing of Food from Agricultural Products	3.40
食品制造业	Manufacture of Foods	5.89
酒、饮料和精制茶制造业	Manufacture of Liquor, Beverage and Refind Tea	7.09
烟草制品业	Manufacture of Tobacco	
纺织业	Manufacture of Textile	8.59
纺织服装、服饰业	Manufacture of Textile Wearing Apparel	7.05
皮革、毛皮、羽毛及其制品和制鞋业	Manufacture of Leather, Fur, Feather & Its Products Footwear	1.41
木材加工和木、竹、藤、棕、草制品业	Processing of Timbers, Manufacture of Wood, Bamboo, Rattan, Palm and Straw Products	
家具制造业	Manufacture of Furniture	10.13
造纸和纸制品业	Manufacture of Paper and Paper Products	1.06
印刷和记录媒介复制业	Printing, Reproduction of Recording Media	12.91
文教、工美、体育和娱乐用品制造业	Manufacture of Articles for Culture, Arts & Crafts, Sports and Entertainment	9.04
石油、煤炭及其他燃料加工业	Oil, coal and other fuel processing industries	
化学原料和化学制品制造业	Manufacture of Chemical Raw Material and Chemical Products	4.24
医药制造业	Manufacture of Medicines	23.66
化学纤维制造业	Manufacture of Chemical Fibers	0.00
橡胶和塑料制品业	Manufacture of Rubber and Plastic	7.60
非金属矿物制品业	Manufacture of Non-metallic Mineral Products	8.52
黑色金属冶炼和压延加工业	Smelting and Pressing of Ferrous Metals	8.20
有色金属冶炼和压延加工业	Smelting and Pressing of Non-ferrous Metals	
金属制品业	Manufacture of Metal Products	6.41
通用设备制造业	Manufacture of General Purpose Machinery	7.86
专用设备制造业	Manufacture of Special Purpose Machinery	8.66
汽车制造业	Manufacture of Vehicle	9.24
铁路、船舶、航空航天和其他运输设备制造业	Manufacture of Transport Equipment for Railway, Shipping, Aerospace and other uses	6.96
电气机械和器材制造业	Manufacture of Electrical Machinery & Equipment	9.27
计算机、通信和其他电子设备制造业	Manufacture of Computer, Communication Equipment and Other Electronic Equipment	6.55
仪器仪表制造业	Manufacture of Measuring Instrument	11.10
其他制造业	Manufacture of Other Products	
废弃资源综合利用业	Recycling and Disposal of Waste Resources	0.00
金属制品、机械和设备修理业	Manufacture of Metal Products, Machinery and Equipment	
电力、热力生产和供应业	Production and Supply of Electric Power and Heat Power	2.14
燃气生产和供应业	Production and Supply of Gas	
水的生产和供应业	Production and Supply of Water	-0.22

资产负债率（%） Assets-Liability Ratio (%)	流动资产周转次数(次/年) Number of Times of Annual of Turnover Current Assets (time/year)	工业成本费用利润率(%) Ratio of Profits to Industrial Costs (%)
56.88	**1.42**	**6.87**
73.35	2.92	1.40
70.49	0.93	7.67
47.32	1.52	5.22
58.92	2.06	3.52
50.87	1.54	5.47
47.70	2.15	-0.60
72.77	1.46	5.36
72.23	1.75	-0.23
51.39	1.58	9.40
36.29	1.32	10.40
56.82	1.80	3.10
30.78	1.07	38.69
0.00	0.00	0.00
49.54	1.21	11.01
56.45	1.02	7.94
69.53	2.61	7.97
41.86	1.47	6.19
54.90	1.15	7.61
63.40	0.89	10.30
67.28	1.84	5.02
58.30	0.88	9.25
56.29	1.22	13.72
45.36	1.64	5.46
41.26	0.73	19.28
0.00	0.00	0.00
75.28	0.93	-1.84
51.24	0.42	-8.73

12-12　主要年份规模以上工业主要产品产量
OUTPUT OF MAIN PRODUCTS OF INDUSTRIES ABOVE DESIGNATED SIZE IN MAJOR YEARS

年份 Year	原盐 （万吨） Salt (10 000 tons)	发电量 （亿千瓦小时） Electricity (100 million kW·h)	饮料酒 （万吨） Beverage Liquour (10 000 tons)	#啤酒 Beer	卷烟 （万箱） Cigarettes (10 000 cases)	罐头 （吨） Canned Food (ton)	化学纤维 （吨） Chemical Fiber (ton)	纱 （吨） Yarn (ton)
1949	15.16	1.21	0.18	0.12	2.36			27447
1952	35.08	2.11	0.37	0.18	12.27			59674
1957	44.34	2.92	0.96	0.58	23.41			50699
1962	38.60	3.86	1.58	0.79	16.59		28	17939
1965	41.34	6.80	2.04	1.34	31.34		205	68082
1970	29.96	10.57	3.39	2.55	42.16		621	85591
1975	34.52	10.98	5.30	2.98	36.00		357	79516
1978	60.68	13.63	6.25	3.75	44.00	4743	1413	85233
1980	41.19	12.50	8.49	4.84	48.79	3521	2116	83389
1985	47.34	26.97	13.76	10.05	51.81	6400	1747	91839
1988	53.28	29.35	26.61	15.58	57.01	27200	3393	107720
1990	35.70	40.22	29.18	19.61	61.94		2900	100381
1991	31.39	54.60	36.75	27.38	56.19	130510	5200	96271
1992	46.24	58.63	44.59	37.01	59.37	3200	6000	99043
1993	48.88	59.39	54.74	45.92	63.46	1900	27100	91351
1994	53.02	59.62	60.00	50.92	69.20	2300	21400	86744
1995	50.84	64.69	60.85	54.16	70.96	4609	20973	79492
1996	41.39	83.02	61.79	54.40	73.04	1719	22945	66832
1997	34.11	95.12	66.64	56.06	88.32	554	26300	70402
1998	19.08	79.65	47.33	42.79	77.10		23858	66504
1999	30.30	82.00	126.21	120.10	149.00	379	29967	56431
2000	41.83	90.84	211.47	206.50	148.10	225	65362	69561
2001	31.40	85.73	279.37	274.28	142.95	99	89989	72933
2002	42.50	89.70	323.20	320.60	138.10	11690	91394	70888
2003	36.85	87.69	353.90	351.80	148.00		101752	65919
2004	34.36	89.01	393.30	390.60	147.10	10889	115187	71931
2005	10.00	98.63	439.70	435.20	150.70	10097	95887	72140
2006	15.30	124.54	101.60（本地）	95.60（本地）	95.16（本地）	1668	72381	56128
2007	19.23	155.30	118.10（本地）	112.50（本地）	100.08（本地）	1850	68746	47850
2008	15.90	164.58	132.07（本地）	124.75（本地）	100.02（本地）	1510	51751	43102
2009	5.90	172.66	137.21（本地）	127.12（本地）	100.08（本地）	4706	59852	38566
2010	11.25	181.93	144.66（本地）	141.65（本地）	102.55（本地）	1092	68654	35278
2011		173.69	164.04（本地）	156.50（本地）	104.51（本地）	41204	38640	18556
2012		174.72	174.03（本地）	163.95（本地）	106.03（本地）	35026	32371	19404
2013	1.28	180.11	194.22（本地）	185.17（本地）	108.36（本地）	30203	23647	33687
2014		178.29	169.85（本地）	164.59（本地）	112.06（本地）	23970	22053	32336
2015		173.53	162.66（本地）	157.83（本地）	111.48（本地）	36179	17419	27721
2016		175.40	168.82（本地）	164.27（本地）		53139	14839	33416
2017		181.80	163.41（本地）	159.97（本地）		85942	11565	26493
2018		192.40	165.81（本地）	162.44（本地）		43893	5545	28948
2019		181.03	177.82（本地）	174.80（本地）		5940	39091	40562
2020		172.47	180.84（本地）	178.17（本地）		2699	11855	30269

注：1998 年以前为乡及乡以上工业。

Note: Before 1998, the data refer to those at and above county level.

12-12 续表 1
Continued

年份 Year	布（万米）Cloth (10 000 m)	印染布（万米）Printed Fabric (10 000 m)	机制纸及纸板（万吨）Machine-made Paper and Paperboards (10 000 tons)	硫酸（万吨）Sulfuric Acid (10 000 tons)	烧碱（万吨）Caustic Soda (10 000 tons)	纯碱（万吨）Soda Ash (10 000 tons)
1949	10608	2947	0.98		0.01	
1952	30069	13658	0.44		0.17	
1957	27806	16053	1.54		0.74	
1962	7444	7375	1.45	0.06	0.89	
1965	29538	13670	2.22		1.66	5.32
1970	33660	21994	3.14	0.04	2.14	12.01
1975	31242	22828	3.10	0.53	2.36	9.15
1978	36877	25797	4.55	1.32	3.61	14.04
1980	34937	22900	5.25	4.11	4.33	18.18
1985	34998	17679	6.20	3.34	5.52	26.03
1988	35890	21213	7.42	4.88	6.62	31.12
1990	34066	21446	6.02	4.86	6.73	30.48
1991	34076	19999	5.99	5.62	5.99	29.50
1992	33682	21534	5.95	6.70	5.62	34.60
1993	35912	16606	8.84	6.96	6.07	40.43
1994	43241	16387	12.36	8.33	6.48	43.36
1995	41170	17864	11.06	9.69	7.90	43.20
1996	39023	16881	11.31	10.12	7.30	46.91
1997	43615	15722	7.78	10.16	8.45	50.55
1998	40440	9864	6.91	10.33	9.25	52.80
1999	39576	4340	7.77	12.56	8.96	53.70
2000	41783	3526	10.96	12.96	10.24	56.20
2001	40640	3402	23.05	13.03	11.44	58.47
2002	47609	5592	29.92	5.00	13.80	60.70
2003	35922	10131	31.76	4.50	13.53	62.50
2004	50111	7718	36.38	14.70	14.86	60.80
2005	51307	16027	31.95	14.80	16.10	62.50
2006	55093	20867	15.50	7.00	15.90	63.95
2007	44251	18708	24.04	9.22	14.91	71.02
2008	48399	58907	22.41	13.02	12.78	72.03
2009	31048	27998	34.59	1.40	12.24	68.21
2010	17457	29631	35.43	4.07	13.87	69.35
2011	49617	28449	32.28	5.06	13.20	70.07
2012	48987	32478	22.27	7.22	13.71	63.35
2013	51646	34381	17.95	4.32	11.06	61.66
2014	44593	33653	18.26			67.85
2015	28040	25458	18.29			68.95
2016	24973	28661	18.17		11.33	
2017	23550	21530	17.39		33.89	
2018	46737	22647	14.58		35.36	
2019	11354	27528	11.52		35.11	
2020	16207	31116	26.21		39.17	

12-12　续表 2
Continued

年份 Year	合成氨 （万吨） Synthetic Ammonia (10 000 tons)	化学肥料 （万吨） Chemical Fertilizer (10 000 tons)	化学农药 （吨） Chemical Pesticide (ton)	油漆 （吨） Paint (ton)	染料 （吨） Dye (ton)
1949				30	599
1952				480	2855
1957			1226	1247	4307
1962		0.45	213	910	3560
1965		1.42	2	4727	8667
1970	0.98	5.89	2313	6380	9347
1975	3.46	12.46	4439	7016	5967
1978	7.17	23.66	9714	8786	5877
1980	7.24	7.82	8333	14556	2159
1985	6.31	5.16	2000	26055	4448
1988	8.72	9.41	2400	28943	5527
1990	7.56	7.55	2500	29075	5119
1991	8.52	8.04	2800	33548	5263
1992	10.45	7.85	3400	35058	4821
1993	10.70	8.02	3600	33054	4550
1994	13.04	12.39	3600	29437	5097
1995	14.98	12.62	4934	37772	7185
1996	18.67	12.62	4976	26762	7668
1997	16.94	12.52	4600	19743	11189
1998	22.36	15.30	6755	17594	8274
1999	26.09	20.19	4480	3730	7866
2000	24.64	20.04	3758	693	9306
2001	35.53	28.07	3915	1349	9757
2002	20.30	9.80	4020	1701	9826
2003	21.55	9.70	2039	2106	10734
2004	30.30	19.60	5061	1955	3961
2005	33.80	22.10	6524	1687	13979
2006	33.30	21.30	12544		26544
2007	28.22	25.70	16433	2957	28269
2008	17.93	21.51	12848	12105	18263
2009	17.71	21.23	49684		24893
2010	16.84	14.10	16450		41383
2011	10.78	9.26	23286		
2012	7.71	6.98	28801		
2013	6.48	5.10	27715		
2014			27160		
2015			36853		
2016		14.33	34993		
2017		7.38	18911		
2018		8.08	8507		
2019		8.50	17524		
2020		8.60	11938		

12-12 续表 3
Continued

年份 Year	化学原料药 (吨) Chemical Medicines (ton)	水泥 (万吨) Cement (10 000 tons)	平板玻璃 (万重量箱) Plate Glass (10 000 weight cases)	耐火材料 (万吨) Refractory Material (10 000 tons)	粗钢 (万吨) Crude Steel (10 000 tons)	钢材 (万吨) Rolled-steel (10 000 tons)
1949						0.06
1952				0.78	0.36	0.41
1957				3.39	1.77	4.30
1962		2.09		2.41	4.59	2.94
1965		6.59		2.91	11.72	8.43
1970		7.35	16.31	3.23	19.38	14.56
1975	55	20.93	19.44	4.88	21.25	20.01
1978	185	35.40	8.86	5.93	31.06	27.61
1980	123	44.66	70.13	5.38	37.14	32.82
1984	7228	70.27	91.25	7.98	37.81	32.43
1985	4222	82.70	77.00	4.35	37.51	32.68
1988	7655	141.00	108.81	4.56	50.17	38.26
1990	6913	139.48	83.13	3.91	54.55	38.04
1991	4754	165.66	96.90	3.71	56.96	39.02
1992	5743	191.50	120.00	3.86	63.75	50.09
1993	6566	221.30	148.71	3.55	61.75	44.88
1994	4238	246.50	145.12	3.06	60.82	46.95
1995	1993	213.82	426.40	3.88	67.27	49.60
1996	5505	181.45	423.60	3.54	72.02	50.60
1997	1693	208.04	570.85	2.45	75.71	51.06
1998	910	131.51	509.38	0.99	84.02	64.93
1999	1691	149.41	576.50	0.59	108.10	86.58
2000	2131	137.52	556.58	0.62	101.17	93.35
2001	2534	148.67	421.51	0.51	124.45	119.77
2002	2712	140.30	405.40	0.45	145.90	142.20
2003	3288	154.90	361.40	0.47	204.80	204.30
2004	4394	181.19	163.30	0.69	225.70	230.97
2005	4430	210.80	297.50	1.04	309.70	330.30
2006	32232	232.72	418.74	1.21	325.82	375.52
2007	14139	425.53	397.79	2.38	327.00	365.55
2008	17910	363.57	599.87	3.65	300.19	350.14
2009	19086	397.66	681.02	18.46	307.89	349.63
2010	26170	442.66	662.04	8.17	300.04	333.46
2011	29337	588.08	510.05	20.02	318.27	325.89
2012	49290	556.57	494.54	33.44	252.78	274.67
2013	49081	575.66	610.21	42.34	235.53	230.39
2014	50713	597.35	612.40	39.37	214.43	212.79
2015	45923	532.36	534.99	41.13	154.56	140.63
2016	2248	600.56	576.16	108.76	188.04	191.37
2017	2775	525.42	557.44	109.84	280.97	291.85
2018	1809	284.47	561.51	27.97	309.70	319.90
2019	2616	442.47	393.64	12.18	319.25	336.19
2020	745	414.03	1003.97	19.54	335.19	389.20

12-12 续表 4
Continued

年份 Year	金属切削机床（台） Metal-cutting Machine Tools (unit)	锻压机械（台） Metal Forming Machinery (unit)	交流电动机（万千瓦） AC Motors (10 000 kW)
1949			0.02
1952	105		0.50
1957	76		3.61
1962	167	77	3.85
1965	526	111	6.48
1970	2353	531	14.53
1975	3213	788	15.56
1978	2558	379	21.72
1980	595	444	20.11
1985	900	607	26.08
1988	1336	737	39.60
1990	1049	440	34.28
1991	869	764	44.17
1992	1018	982	61.08
1993	1532	919	64.13
1994	1505	860	37.71
1995	972	2563	39.18
1996	1084	584	22.65
1997	449	416	20.74
1998	280		6.43
1999	251		11.10
2000	384		38.70
2001	472	2477	42.72
2002	588		68.25
2003	990		95.63
2004	1287		96.13
2005	1347		63.50
2006	3636		702.02
2007	3392	1869	119.23
2008	8381	1230	96.89
2009	668		728.03
2010	1120		101.10
2011	1194		74.08
2012	1014		104.48
2013	2689		126.82
2014	2563		114.46
2015	618		104.30
2016	588		98.70
2017	610		202.79
2018	204		230.86
2019	584		110.03
2020	466		173.94

12-12　续表 5
Continued

年份 Year	钢芯铝绞线（吨）Steel-cored Aluminum Stranded Wire (ton)	家用电冰箱（万台）Home Refrigerators (10 000 sets)	家用洗衣机（万台）Home Washing Machines (10 000 sets)	彩色电视机（万台）Color TV Sets (10 000 sets)
1949				
1952				
1957				
1962				
1965	250			
1970	34			
1975	188			
1978	684			
1980	1232			
1985	2327	1.66	0.48	6.60
1988	1571	15.22	42.38	17.00
1990	1880	27.41	45.86	18.50
1991	2463	31.51	45.70	22.27
1992	2248	54.84	46.31	28.07
1993	1144	50.48	56.59	36.08
1994	287	62.50	71.34	60.15
1995	1659	107.91	64.34	60.53
1996	2265	193.80	100.94	56.68
1997	2616	257.10	171.95	124.86
1998	1725	219.23	183.67	96.83
1999	2805	259.60	256.30	285.20
2000	4202	311.10	318.50	379.40
2001	4498	396.30	367.89	455.40
2002	5825	518.20	408.6	593.20
2003	4940	598.30	471.5	671.70
2004	6608	815.03	575.06	957.90
2005	116592	908.80	614.9	1324.30
2006	46974	1290.00	649.4	1205.60
2007	22564	1421.40	769.4	1243.10
2008	29507	723.19	407.54	836.66
2009		827.21	488.72	1064.70
2010		801.22	580.87	1111.19
2011		718.54	604.55	1154.20
2012		575.01	583.6	1439.98
2013		524.35	606.65	1512.05
2014		610.07	590.95	1714.93
2015		872.09	595.11	1736.20
2016		882.22	606.74	2111.71
2017		818.65	603.4	1703.01
2018		886.58	601.72	1695.18
2019		731.81	513.71	1580.42
2020		822.01	575.41	1774.86

12-13 规模以上工业主要产品产量
OUTPUT OF MAJOR INDUSTRIAL PRODUCTS OF INDUSTRY ABOVE DESIGNATED SIZE

产品名称	Name	计算单位	Unit	2020 年	增长 (± %) Increase (± %)
冶金工业产品	**Products of Metallurgical Industry**				
粗钢	Crude Steel	万吨	10 000 tons	335.19	4.58
钢材	Rolled-steel	万吨	10 000 tons	389.20	7.74
耐火材料制品	Refractory Material	万吨	10 000 tons	19.54	0.98
电力工业产品	**Products of Electricity Industry**				
发电量	Electricity	亿千瓦小时	100 million kW · h	172.47	-4.73
化学工业产品	**Products of Chemical Industry**				
原油加工量	Processing Amount of Crude Oill	万吨	10 000 tons	1340.06	11.69
汽油	Petrol	万吨	10 000 tons	370.78	0.53
柴油	Diesel Oill	万吨	10 000 tons	331.79	11.53
燃料油	Fuel Oil	万吨	10 000 tons	121.86	357.07
化学农药	Chemical Pesticides	万吨	10 000 tons	1.19	-3.46
塑料制品	Plastic	万吨	10 000 tons	38.52	8.22
化学药品（原料）	Chemical Medicines (Raw Materials)	万吨	10 000 tons	0.07	-29.43

12-13　续表 1
Continued

产品名称	Name	计算单位	Unit	2020 年	增长 (± %) Increase (± %)
橡胶轮胎外胎	Rubber Tire Casing	万条	10 000 tires	4563.31	4.26
机械工业产品	**Products of Machinery Industry**				
工业锅炉	Industrial Boiler	蒸发量吨	ton (evaporation amount)	19659.64	-20.04
交流电动机	AC Motors	万千瓦	10 000 kW	173.94	11.23
金属切削机床	Metal-cutting Machine	台	set	466	-21.81
改装汽车	Refitted Motor Vehicles	辆	set	71373	-13.07
民用钢质船舶	Civil Steel Ships	载重吨	syn-ton		
电子产品	**Electronic Products**				
彩色电视机	Color TV sets	万台	10 000 sets	1774.86	15.30
电子元件	Electronice	万只	10 000 Units	2623983.09	11.29
建材工业产品	**Products of Construction Industry**				
水泥	Cement	万吨	10 000 tons	414.03	-1.82
平板玻璃	Plate Glass	万重量箱	10 000 weight cases	1003.97	8.89

12-13 续表 2
Continued

产品名称	Name	计算单位	Unit	2020 年	增长 (±%) Increase (±%)
纺织工业产品	**Products of Textile Industry**				
纱	Yarn	吨	ton	30269.23	-23.71
布	Cloth	万米	10 000 m	16206.50	0.89
印染布	Printed Fabric	万米	10 000 m	31115.98	-28.89
化学纤维	Chemical Fibers	吨	ton	11854.74	-60.72
轻工产品	**Products of Light Industry**				
机制纸及纸板	Machine-made Paper and Paperboards	万吨	10 000 tons	26.21	-10.30
家用洗衣机	Home Washing Machines	万台	10 000 sets	575.41	54.89
糖果	Sugar	吨	ton	11972	95.97
食用植物油	Vegetable Oil	万吨	10 000 tons	100.50	6.40
饮料酒	Beverage Liquor	万千升	10 000 KL	178.69	1.26
# 白酒	White Spirit	万千升	10 000 KL	2.09	2.64
# 啤酒	Beer	万千升	10 000 KL	176.05	1.43
塑料制品	Plastic Products	万吨	10 000 tons	38.52	8.22
家具	Furniture	万件	10 000 articles	729.42	6.49
家用电冰箱	Home Refrigerators	万台	10 000 sets	822.01	23.05
皮革鞋靴	Leather Shoes	万双	10 000 pairs	1056.86	-39.32
服装	Clothing	万件	10 000 articles	48325.19	-4.75

12-14 规模以上工业主要产品生产能力
PRODUCTION CAPACITY OF MAJOR PRODUCTS OF INDUSTRY ABOVE DESIGNATED SIZE

产品名称	Name	计算单位	Unit	2020 年 生产能力 Production Capacity of 2020	2019 年 生产能力 Production Capacity of 2019
发电设备容量总计 / 发电量	Total Capacity of Generation Equipment	万千瓦 / 万千瓦小时	10 000 kW/ 10 000 kW·h	450	429
化学纤维	Chemical Fiber	吨	ton	36990	36900
棉纺锭 / 纺纱量	Knitting Spindle	锭 / 吨	spindle/ton	144532	144164
棉布织机 / 布	Cotton Cloth Loom	台 / 万米	set/10 000 m	2428	3121
焦炭	Coke	吨	ton	1700000	1600000
农用氮、磷、钾化学肥料总计（折纯）	Chemical Fertilizer	吨	ton	110000	110000
水泥	Cement	吨	ton	7310000	7300000
平板玻璃	Plate Glass	重量箱	weight cases	11241440	11241440
生铁	Pig Iron	吨	ton	3220000	3220000
粗钢	Crude Steel	吨	ton	3125000	3125000
钢材	Rolled-steel	吨	ton	5610150	5596550
金属切削机床	Metal-cutting Machine	台	set	2293	2593
家用电冰箱	Home Refrigerators	台	set	10453300	10171130
房间空气调节器	Air Conditioner	台	set	15806755	13254158
移动通信手持机（手机）	Cell Phone	台	set	7000000	8400000
彩色电视机	Color TV Sets	台	set	19953200	17877000

主要统计指标解释

工业总产值　是以货币表现的工业企业在一定时期内生产的已出售或可供出售工业产品总量，它是反映一定时间内工业生产的总规模和总水平。

资产总计　指企业拥有或控制的能以货币计量的经济资源，包括各种财产、债权和其他权利。资产按其流动性（即资产的变现能力和支付能力）划分为：流动资产、长期投资、固定资产、无形资产、递延资产和其他资产。

负债合计　指企业所承担的能以货币计量，将以资产或劳务偿付的债务，偿还形式包括货币、资产或提供劳务。负债一般按偿还期长短分为流动负债和长期负债。

利润总额　指企业生产经营活动的最终成果，是企业在一定时期内实现的盈亏相抵后的利润总额（亏损以"–"号表示），它等于营业利润加上补贴收入加上投资收益加上营业外净收入再加上以前年度损益调整。

Explanatory Notes on Main Statistical Indicators

Gross Industrial Output Value　is the total volume of final industrial products produced and industrial services provided during a given period. It reflects the total achievements and overall scale of industrial production during a given period.

Total Assets　refers to the economic resources that can be measured in currency owned or controlled by an enterprise, including various properties, claims and other rights. Assets are divided into: current assets, long–term investments, fixed assets, intangible assets, deferred assets and other assets according to their liquidity (that is, the ability to realize assets and payment capabilities).

Total Liabilities　refers to the debts that an enterprise bears that can be measured in currency and will be repaid in assets or services. The form of repayment includes currency, assets or the provision of services. Liabilities are generally divided into current liabilities and long–term liabilities according to the length of the repayment period.

Total Profits　refer to the final achievements of production and operation of the enterprises, represented by the total profits after deducting losses (loss is expressed by the negative figure). It is the sum of profits from operation, income from subsidies, investment earnings, net income from activities other than operation, and adjustment of profits and losses of previous years.

13 规模以上服务业

SERVICE ENTERPRISES ABOVE DESIGNATED SIZE

简 要 说 明

一、本篇资料的主要内容

本篇资料主要反映了全市规模以上服务业企业主要财务状况，规模以上服务业企业分行业财务状况，规模以上服务业企业分登记注册类型财务状况，分区市规模以上服务业企业财务状况等方面的内容。

二、本篇资料的来源

本篇中规模以上服务业企业资料来源于规模以上服务业统计年报，由市统计局服务业统计处整理提供。

Brief Introduction

I. Main Content

This document mainly reflects the major financial indicators of service enterprises above designated size in the city, the financial indicators of service enterprises above designated size by industry, the financial indicators of service enterprises above designated size by registration type, and the financial indicators of service enterprises above designated size in regional cities content.

This document mainly reflects the major financial indicators of service enterprises above designated size in the city, the financial indicators of service enterprises above designated size by industry, the financial indicators of service enterprises above designated size by registration type, and the financial indicators of service enterprises above designated size in regional cities content.

II. Source of Data

The data of service enterprises above designated size in this chapter are derived from the annual statistical report of service industries above designated size, which are compiled and provided by the Service Statistics Department of the Municipal Statistics Bureau.

13-1 规模以上服务业企业主要财务状况

MAIN FINANCIAL INDICATORS OF SERVICE ENTERPRISES ABOVE THE DESIGNATED

单位：亿元 (100 million yuan)

项目	Item	2020 年	2019 年	2020 年比 2019 年增长 (%) Growth Rate in 2020 Over 2019 (%)
营业收入	Business Revenue	2579.46	2292.20	12.53
营业成本	Business Costs	2151.74	1854.32	16.04
税金及附加	Tax and Extra Charges on Business	12.98	13.79	-5.87
销售费用	Sales Expenses	72.09	73.39	-1.77
管理费用	Management Expenses	179.03	186.92	-4.22
财务费用	Financial Expenses	65.68	48.83	34.51
营业利润	Business Profits	193.09	207.03	-6.73
利润总额	Total Profits	198.81	222.89	-10.80
所得税费用	Income Taxes Payable	39.61	39.28	0.84
应付职工薪酬	Employee Compensation Payable	367.90	353.04	4.21
应交增值税	Value-added Tax Payable	45.86	39.01	17.56

注：增速按可比口径计算。

Note : The growth rates are calculated on comparable coverage.

13-2 规模以上其他营利性服务业企业主要财务状况

MAIN FINANCIAL INDICATORS OF OTHER FOR-PROFIT SERVICE ENTERPRISES ABOVE THE DESIGNATED

单位：亿元 (100 million yuan)

项目	Item	2020 年	2019 年	2020 年比 2019 年增长 (%) Growth Rate in 2020 Over 2019 (%)
营业收入	Business Revenue	937.02	887.32	5.60
营业成本	Business Costs	708.20	662.14	6.96
税金及附加	Tax and Extra Charges on Business	5.55	5.63	-1.42
销售费用	Sales Expenses	42.13	43.71	-3.61
管理费用	Management Expenses	97.44	104.38	-6.65
财务费用	Financial Expenses	14.47	9.71	49.02
营业利润	Business Profits	54.35	60.76	-10.55
利润总额	Total Profits	60.67	70.16	-13.53
所得税费用	Income Taxes Payable	9.68	11.14	-13.11
应付职工薪酬	Employee Compensation Payable	169.49	161.18	5.16
应交增值税	Value-added Tax Payable	22.37	21.40	4.53

注：增速按可比口径计算。

Note : The growth rates are calculated on comparable coverage.

13-3 规模以上服务业企业分登记注册类型财务状况（2020年）
FINANCIAL INDICATORS OF SERVICE ENTERPRISES ABOVE DESIGNATED SIZE BY REGISTRATION TYPE(2020)

单位：亿元 (100 million yuan)

类别	Category	企业单位数（个）Number of Industial Enterprises(unit)	营业收入 Business Revenue	营业成本 Business Costs	税金及附加 Tax and Extra Charges on Business
总计	**Total**	**2229**	**2579.46**	**2151.74**	**12.98**
按登记注册类型分	**by Status of Registration**				
内资企业	**Domestic Funded Enterprises**	**2102**	**2257.09**	**1910.13**	**11.91**
国有企业	State-owned Enterprises	56	94.94	63.04	0.56
集体企业	Collective-owned Enterprises	11	3.09	1.89	0.04
股份合作企业	Cooperative Enterprises	1			
有限责任公司	Limited Liability Corporations	608	1042.66	902.26	6.63
股份有限公司	Share-holding Corporations Limited	65	214.68	177.49	1.34
私营企业	Private Enterprises	1343	895.37	761.42	3.28
其他企业	Other Enterprises	18	6.16	4.01	0.03
港、澳、台商投资企业	**Enterprises with Funds from Hong Kong, Macao and Taiwan**	**46**	**83.25**	**66.25**	**0.41**
合资经营企业（港或澳、台资）	Joint-ventures Enterprises	25	41.99	30.45	0.14
合作经营企业（港或澳、台资）	Cooperative Enterprises	1			
港澳台商独资经营企业	Enterprises with Sole Investment	18	36.32	32.06	0.26
港澳台商投资股份有限公司	Share-holding Corporations Ltd. With Funds from Hong Kong, Macao and Taiwan	2			
其他企业	Other Enterprises				
外商投资企业	**Foreign Funded Enterprises**	**81**	**239.12**	**175.35**	**0.66**
中外合资经营企业	Joint-venture Enterprises	44	186.12	131.36	0.48
中外合作经营企业	Cooperation Enterprises	3	0.40	0.29	0.03
外资企业	Foreign Investment	33	51.38	42.70	0.14
其他企业	Other Enterprises	1			

13-3 续表 1
Continued

单位：亿元 (100 million yuan)

类别	Category	销售费用 Selling Expenses	管理费用 Management Expenses	财务费用 Financial Expenses	营业利润 Business Profits
总计	**Total**	**72.09**	**179.03**	**65.68**	**193.09**
按登记注册类型分	**by Status of Registration**				
内资企业	**Domestic Funded Enterprises**	**67.97**	**161.86**	**59.91**	**140.25**
国有企业	State-owned Enterprises	4.00	8.37	2.14	17.49
集体企业	Collective-owned Enterprises	0.09	1.21	-0.01	-0.12
股份合作企业	Cooperative Enterprises				
有限责任公司	Limited Liability Corporations	27.88	69.42	49.21	64.23
股份有限公司	Share-holding Corporations Limited	8.62	11.10	3.32	33.13
私营企业	Private Enterprises	27.24	70.12	5.25	25.01
其他企业	Other Enterprises	0.15	1.46	-0.01	0.51
港、澳、台商投资企业	**Enterprises with Funds from Hong Kong, Macao and Taiwan**	**2.03**	**3.95**	**2.04**	**9.83**
合资经营企业(港或澳、台资)	Joint-ventures Enterprises	1.74	1.74	1.53	7.57
合作经营企业(港或澳、台资)	Cooperative Enterprises				
港澳台商独资经营企业	Enterprises with Sole Investment	0.28	2.01	0.40	1.28
港澳台商投资股份有限公司	Share-holding Corporations Ltd. With Funds from Hong Kong, Macao and Taiwan				
其他企业	Other Enterprises				
外商投资企业	**Foreign Funded Enterprises**	**2.09**	**13.22**	**3.75**	**43.01**
中外合资经营企业	Joint-venture Enterprises	0.68	9.00	3.34	40.45
中外合作经营企业	Cooperation Enterprises	0.15	0.13	0.01	-0.22
外资企业	Foreign Investment	1.25	4.02	0.40	2.60
其他企业	Other Enterprises				

13-3 续表 2
Continued

单位：亿元 (100 million yuan)

类别	Category	利润总额 Total Profits	所得税费用 Income Taxes Payable	应付职工薪酬 Total Wages Payable	应交增值税 Value-added Tax Payable
总计	**Total**	**198.81**	**39.61**	**367.90**	**45.86**
按登记注册类型分	**by Status of Registration**				
内资企业	**Domestic Funded Enterprises**	**145.67**	**27.01**	**330.95**	**42.73**
国有企业	State-owned Enterprises	18.41	0.57	17.15	1.40
集体企业	Collective-owned Enterprises	-0.12	0.10	0.82	0.08
股份合作企业	Cooperative Enterprises				
有限责任公司	Limited Liability Corporations	66.71	15.49	172.39	21.49
股份有限公司	Share-holding Corporations Limited	33.96	5.45	33.76	3.96
私营企业	Private Enterprises	26.20	5.35	105.27	15.77
其他企业	Other Enterprises	0.51	0.05	1.55	0.02
港、澳、台商投资企业	**Enterprises with Funds from Hong Kong, Macao and Taiwan**	**10.04**	**2.09**	**5.98**	**0.78**
合资经营企业（港或澳、台资）	Joint-ventures Enterprises	7.79	1.48	4.05	0.48
合作经营企业（港或澳、台资）	Cooperative Enterprises				
港澳台商独资经营企业	Enterprises with Sole Investment	1.28	0.45	1.80	0.23
港澳台商投资股份有限公司	Share-holding Corporations Ltd. With Funds from Hong Kong, Macao and Taiwan				
其他企业	Other Enterprises				
外商投资企业	**Foreign Funded Enterprises**	**43.11**	**10.53**	**30.96**	**2.35**
中外合资经营企业	Joint-venture Enterprises	40.40	9.72	24.60	1.93
中外合作经营企业	Cooperation Enterprises	-0.20	0.00	0.13	0.01
外资企业	Foreign Investment	2.73	0.77	6.09	0.39
其他企业	Other Enterprises				

13-4 规模以上服务业企业分行业财务状况（2020 年）

FINANCIAL INDICATORS OF SERVICE ENTERPRISES ABOVE DESIGNATED SIZE BY SECTOR (2020)

行业	Category	企业单位数（个）Number of Industial Enterprises(unit)	营业收入 Business Revenue	营业成本 Business Costs	税金及附加 Tax and Extra Charges on Business
总计	Total	**2229**	**2579.46**	**2151.74**	**12.98**
按行业分	**Grouped by Sector**				
交通运输、仓储和邮政业	Transport, Storage and Postal Services	730	1337.11	1234.69	4.53
信息传输、软件和信息技术服务业	Information Transmission, Software and Information Technology Services	200	434.73	300.82	1.72
房地产业	Real Estate	171	86.95	60.85	2.16
租赁和商务服务业	Leasing and Business Services	581	386.20	332.35	2.09
科学研究和技术服务业	Scientific Research and Technical Services	281	200.24	126.59	1.24
水利、环境和公共设施管理业	Management of Water Conservancy, Environment and Public Facilities	40	32.78	24.42	0.22
居民服务、修理和其他服务业	Households' service, Repair and Other Services	50	22.67	15.65	0.13
教育	Education	19	10.25	6.48	0.03
卫生和社会工作	Health and Social Work	60	27.79	19.21	0.01
文化、体育和娱乐业	Culture, Sports and Entertainment	97	40.73	30.68	0.85

单位：亿元 (100 million yuan)

销售费用 Selling Expenses	管理费用 Management Expenses	财务费用 Financial Expenses	营业利润 Business Profits	利润总额 Total Profits	所得税费用 Income Taxes Payable	应付职工薪酬 Total Wages Payable	应交增值税 Value-added Tax Payable
72.09	**179.03**	**65.68**	**193.09**	**198.81**	**39.61**	**367.90**	**45.86**
15.20	51.85	37.96	98.68	98.01	24.77	135.01	18.29
24.16	23.52	2.50	61.00	62.61	5.36	53.03	9.02
2.81	14.17	11.29	2.02	1.82	1.57	26.23	3.14
9.62	33.29	11.52	4.31	7.20	3.46	54.07	6.96
9.79	34.51	1.08	22.86	23.30	2.79	60.64	6.00
0.34	3.69	0.44	3.57	3.67	0.57	9.67	0.56
2.90	2.17	-0.16	2.04	2.22	0.58	5.45	0.86
0.80	2.22	0.18	0.49	0.71	0.22	3.36	0.17
2.27	5.86	0.28	0.04	0.04	0.19	9.15	0.04
4.20	7.75	0.59	-1.92	-0.77	0.10	11.29	0.82

13-5 规模以上服务业企业分市、区财务状况（2020 年）

FINANCIAL INDICATORS OF SERVICE ENTERPRISES ABOVE DESIGNATED SIZE BY REGION (2020)

区（市）	Region	企业单位数（个）Number of Industial Enterprises(unit)	营业收入 Business Revenue	营业成本 Business Costs	税金及附加 Tax and Extra Charges on Business
全市	**Total**	**2229**	**2579.46**	**2151.74**	**12.98**
市南区	Shinan District	460	753.14	640.81	1.96
市北区	Shibei District	258	241.90	217.69	1.76
李沧区	Licang District	231	88.88	77.22	1.11
崂山区	Laoshan District	246	463.23	361.14	2.24
西海岸新区	West Coast New Area	495	524.40	399.70	2.40
黄岛区	Huangdao District	436	442.38	341.13	2.18
保税港区	Qingdao Free Trade Port Area of China	59	82.02	58.57	0.22
城阳区	Chengyang District	242	212.78	192.92	1.18
城阳区（不含高新区）	Chengyang District (Excluding High tech District)	175	162.77	152.79	0.87
高新区	High tech District	67	50.01	40.13	0.31
即墨区	Jimo District	83	79.84	68.29	0.42
胶州市	Jiaozhou	133	99.92	85.18	0.80
平度市	Pingdu	51	23.27	18.83	0.13
莱西市	Laixi	30	92.09	89.96	0.98

单位：亿元 (100 million yuan)

销售费用 Selling Expenses	管理费用 Management Expenses	财务费用 Financial Expenses	营业利润 Business Profits	利润总额 Total Profits	所得税费用 Income Taxes Payable	应付职工薪酬 Total Wages Payable	应交增值税 Value-added Tax Payable
72.09	**179.03**	**65.68**	**193.09**	**198.81**	**39.61**	**367.90**	**45.86**
20.61	41.05	5.92	48.06	50.81	7.18	83.59	7.74
7.43	22.71	16.21	14.19	14.53	1.94	58.84	4.44
1.37	9.39	2.44	−0.54	−0.15	0.14	11.52	1.40
17.96	35.60	3.62	42.79	44.05	4.55	73.29	10.54
11.42	32.00	16.73	93.11	94.89	21.00	73.58	6.57
10.66	27.23	14.68	74.90	76.40	17.09	61.49	5.63
0.76	4.77	2.05	18.21	18.49	3.91	12.09	0.94
7.66	19.24	9.35	−11.06	−10.01	1.46	44.53	3.43
4.40	14.64	6.16	−12.62	−12.00	1.45	37.34	2.68
3.26	4.60	3.19	1.56	1.99	0.01	7.19	0.75
2.33	6.25	1.93	0.81	−2.04	1.22	5.84	1.43
1.60	6.63	9.13	4.05	4.70	1.46	12.48	2.67
0.54	2.42	0.31	1.38	1.51	0.25	1.97	0.35
1.16	3.73	0.06	0.30	0.53	0.41	2.25	7.29

13-6 规模以上其他营利性服务业企业分行业财务状况（2020 年）

FINANCIAL INDICATORS OF OTHER FOR-PROFIT SERVICE ENTERPRISES ABOVE DESIGNATED SIZE BY SECTOR (2020)

行业	Category	企业单位数（个）Number of Industial Enterprises(unit)	营业收入 Business Revenue	营业成本 Business Costs	税金及附加 Tax and Extra Charges on Business
总计	**Total**	**1194**	**937.02**	**708.20**	**5.55**
按行业分	**Grouped by Sector**				
互联网和相关服务	Internet and Related Services	20	18.48	11.97	0.07
软件和信息技术服务业	Software and Information Technology Services	165	268.70	190.96	1.17
租赁业	Leasing	27	10.05	8.22	0.03
商务服务业	Business Services	554	376.15	324.13	2.06
研究和试验发展	Research and Experimental Development	30	22.71	15.41	0.07
专业技术服务业	Professional Technical Service Industry	231	171.32	106.87	1.15
科技推广和应用服务业	Technology Promotion and Application Service Industry	20	6.22	4.31	0.02
居民服务业	Services to Households	16	5.06	3.09	0.02
机动车、电子产品和日用产品修理业	Motor Vehicle, Electronic Products and Consumer Products Repair	17	14.09	9.55	0.10
其他服务业	Other Services	17	3.52	3.01	0.01
新闻和出版业	News and Publication	9	14.02	8.04	0.17
广播、电视、电影和影视录音制作业	Production of Radio, Television, Film and Video Recording	34	5.99	5.46	0.03
文化艺术业	Culture and Arts	19	10.10	8.04	0.22
体育	Sports	17	5.22	4.90	0.30
娱乐业	Entertainment	18	5.39	4.24	0.13

注：根据核算最新划定标准，规上其他营利性服务业新增科学研究和技术服务业行业门类。

Note: According to the latest accounting standards, the new scientific research and technical service industry categories of other for-profit service industries are stipulated.

单位：亿元 (100 million yuan)

销售费用 Selling Expenses	管理费用 Management Expenses	财务费用 Financial Expenses	营业利润 Business Profits	利润总额 Total Profits	所得税费用 Income Taxes Payable	应付职工薪酬 Total Wages Payable	应交增值税 Value-added Tax Payable
42.13	**97.44**	**14.47**	**54.35**	**60.67**	**9.68**	**169.49**	**22.37**
1.53	3.04	0.00	1.28	1.56	0.00	2.09	0.51
14.08	16.67	1.43	25.79	27.15	2.73	35.94	7.22
0.16	1.28	0.23	0.16	0.20	0.03	0.87	0.38
9.46	32.01	11.30	4.15	7.00	3.44	53.20	6.59
1.02	2.12	0.02	6.73	6.93	0.30	8.80	0.36
8.26	31.44	0.74	16.07	16.34	2.45	50.83	5.52
0.51	0.95	0.32	0.05	0.03	0.05	1.01	0.11
0.37	0.98	0.04	0.57	0.61	0.19	1.41	0.06
2.49	0.82	−0.20	1.40	1.52	0.37	2.40	0.69
0.05	0.37	0.00	0.07	0.09	0.02	1.64	0.11
1.42	1.92	−0.17	2.84	3.10	0.00	2.92	0.44
0.66	1.46	0.02	−1.55	−1.33	−0.01	0.90	0.04
0.63	1.63	0.13	0.00	0.09	0.11	3.02	0.17
0.59	1.38	0.52	−2.10	−1.92	0.00	3.26	0.13
0.90	1.37	0.09	−1.11	−0.70	0.00	1.20	0.04

13-7 规模以上其他营利性服务业企业分市、区财务状况（2020年）
FINANCIAL INDICATORS OF OTHER FOR-PROFIT SERVICE ENTERPRISES ABOVE DESIGNATED SIZE BY REGION (2020)

区（市）	Region	企业单位数（个）Number of Industial Enterprises(unit)	营业收入 Business Revenue	营业成本 Business Costs	税金及附加 Tax and Extra Charges on Business
全市	**Total**	**1194**	**937.02**	**708.20**	**5.55**
市南区	Shinan District	235	209.98	158.40	0.98
市北区	Shibei District	146	116.95	91.52	0.68
李沧区	Licang District	130	46.08	37.68	0.72
崂山区	Laoshan District	165	253.43	171.98	1.36
西海岸新区	West Coast New Area	233	141.03	115.01	0.75
黄岛区	Huangdao District	217	133.86	110.38	0.72
保税港区	Qingdao Free Trade Port Area of China	16	7.17	4.63	0.03
城阳区	Chengyang District	153	88.35	68.93	0.59
城阳区（不含高新区）	Chengyang District (Excluding High tech District)	99	49.41	39.05	0.31
高新区	High tech District	54	38.95	29.88	0.29
即墨区	Jimo District	34	13.04	9.23	0.10
胶州市	Jiaozhou	56	40.39	33.26	0.22
平度市	Pingdu	21	13.29	11.31	0.07
莱西市	Laixi	21	14.48	10.87	0.06

单位：亿元 (100 million yuan)

销售费用 Selling Expenses	管理费用 Management Expenses	财务费用 Financial Expenses	营业利润 Business Profits	利润总额 Total Profits	所得税费用 Income Taxes Payable	应付职工薪酬 Total Wages Payable	应交增值税 Value-added Tax Payable
42.13	**97.44**	**14.47**	**54.35**	**60.67**	**9.68**	**169.49**	**22.37**
10.78	22.50	3.33	9.24	12.06	2.40	41.34	5.07
3.66	10.80	2.13	7.23	7.52	1.22	22.37	3.02
0.54	4.98	1.36	-0.59	-0.35	-0.06	3.53	0.71
12.13	25.51	1.39	32.43	33.05	3.19	47.97	7.52
8.05	13.31	0.97	0.19	1.38	1.30	25.04	2.15
7.75	12.57	0.96	-1.12	0.06	1.05	22.76	1.94
0.30	0.74	0.01	1.31	1.33	0.25	2.27	0.21
4.56	9.90	3.64	3.47	4.14	0.50	17.62	1.89
1.49	5.83	0.52	1.84	2.25	0.53	11.79	1.21
3.07	4.06	3.12	1.62	1.89	-0.03	5.82	0.68
1.05	3.53	1.53	-2.98	-2.88	0.02	3.18	0.13
0.95	2.27	0.12	5.11	5.24	0.99	6.33	1.07
0.30	1.23	-0.01	0.31	0.42	0.10	0.48	0.27
0.11	3.41	0.01	-0.03	0.08	0.01	1.63	0.54

主要统计指标解释

营业收入　指企业经营主要业务和其他业务所确认的收入总额。营业收入合计包括“主营业务收入”和“其他业务收入”。根据会计“利润表”中“营业收入”项目的本年累计数填报。

营业成本　指企业经营主要业务和其他业务所发生的成本总额。包括企业（单位）在报告期内从事销售商品、提供劳务等日常活动发生的各种耗费。包括“主营业务成本”和“其他业务成本”。根据会计“利润表”中“营业成本”项目的本年累计数填报。

税金及附加　指企业因从事生产经营活动按税法规定应缴纳的消费税、城市维护建设税、资源税、教育费附加及房产税、土地使用税、车船使用税、印花税等相关税费。根据会计“利润表”中“税金及附加”项目的本年累计数填报。

销售费用　指企业在销售商品和材料、提供劳务的过程中发生的各种费用，包括保险费、包装费、展览费和广告费、商品维修费、预计产品质量保证损失、运输费、装卸费等以及为销售本企业商品而专设的销售机构（含销售网点、售后服务网点等）的职工薪酬、业务费、折旧费等经营费用。

管理费用　指企业为组织和管理企业生产经营所发生的费用，包括企业在筹建期间内发生的开办费、董事会和行政管理部门在企业经营管理中发生的，或者应当由企业统一负担的公司经费等。根据会计“利润表”中“管理费用”项目的本年累计数填报。

财务费用　指企业为筹集生产经营所需资金等而发生的筹资费用，包括企业生产经营期间发生的利息支出（减利息收入）、汇兑损失（减汇兑收益）以及相关的手续费等。根据会计“利润表”中“财务费用”项目的本年累计数填报。

利润总额　指企业在一定会计期间的经营成果，是生产经营过程中各种收入扣除各种耗费后的盈余，反映企业在报告期内实现的盈亏总额。根据会计“利润表”中“利润总额”项目的本年累计数填报。执行《企业会计准则》或《小企业会计准则》的企业，利润总额为营业利润加上营业外收入，减去营业外支出后的金额；执行其他企业会计制度的企业，利润总额为营业利润加上投资收益、营业外收入，再减去营业外支出后的金额。

应交增值税　指按照税法规定，以销售货物、服务、无形资产、不动产或提供加工、修理修配劳务的增值额和货物进口金额为计税依据而课征的一种流转税。

Explanatory Notes on Main Statistical Indicators

Business Revenue　refers to the total income of the business recognized by business and other business. Total operating revenue includes the main business income and other operating income.Fill in according to the cumulative number of the current year's "Business Revenue " item in the "profit statement" of accounting.

Business Costs　refers to the total amount of costs incurred by an enterprise in operating its main business and other businesses. Including the enterprise (unit) in the reporting period engaged in selling goods, providing labor services and other daily activities of all kinds of consumption. Include "main business cost" and "other business cost". The current year's cumulative counting is reported according to the operating cost item in the accounting "income statement".

Taxes and surcharges　refers to the excise duty, urban maintenance and construction tax, resource tax, education surcharge, property tax, land use tax, vehicle and vessel use tax, stamp tax and other related taxes and fees that the enterprise should pay in accordance with the tax law for its production and business activities.Fill in according to the cumulative number of the current year's "Taxes and surcharges " item in the "profit statement" of accounting.

Sales expense refers to the various expenses incurred by the enterprise in the process of selling goods and materials and providing labor services, including insurance, packaging, exhibition and advertising fees, product maintenance fees, estimated product quality assurance losses, transportation fees, loading and unloading fees, etc. Operating expenses such as employee salaries, business expenses, depreciation expenses and other operating expenses of specialized sales organizations (including sales outlets, after–sales service outlets, etc.) that sell the products of the enterprise.

Management Cost refers to the costs of organizing and managing enterprise operation, including the operational cost of the board of directors and the executive body in management that shall be borne by the enterprise.Fill in according to the cumulative number of the current year's "Management Cost " item in the "profit statement" of accounting.

Financial Cost refers to the cost from raising fund for production and operation, including expenditure of interests, loss of momentary exchange and related charges.Fill in according to the cumulative number of the current year's "Financial Cost " item in the "profit statement" of accounting.

Total Profits refers to the operating results of an enterprise in a certain accounting period. It is the surplus after deducting various expenses from various incomes in the production and operation process, reflecting the total profit and loss realized by the enterprise during the reporting period. Fill in according to the cumulative number of the current year's "Total Profits " item in the "profit statement" of accounting.For companies that implement the "Accounting Standards for Business Enterprises" or "Accounting Standards for Small Businesses," the total profit is the amount of operating profit plus non–operating income, minus non–operating expenses; for companies implementing other corporate accounting systems, the total profit is the operating profit plus Investment income, non–operating income, minus the amount of non–operating expenses.

VAT payable refers to a transfer tax levied on the basis of tax on the value added of goods, services, intangible assets, real estate or the provision of processing, repair and repair services and the amount of import of goods, as stipulated in the tax law.

建筑业 14

CONSTRUCTION

简要说明

一、本篇资料的主要内容

本篇资料主要反映了全市建筑业基本情况，主要包括建筑业总产值、增加值、建筑企业生产指标、财务指标、重点建筑企业名单等方面的内容。

二、本篇资料的来源

本篇资料来源于建筑业统计年报，由市统计局固定资产投资统计处整理提供。

Brief Introduction

I. Main Content

Data in this chapter show the basic conditions of construction of the whole city, mainly including the gross output value of construction, value added, major production and financial indicators and list of key enterprises of construction, etc.

II. Source of Data

Data in this chapter are based on the annual report of construction industry, and complied by the Division of Investment and Construction Statistics of Qingdao Municipal Bureau of Statistics.

14-1 建筑业企业生产情况（2020年）
PRODUCTION SITUATION OF CONSTRUCTION ENTERPRISES (2020)

项目	Item	单位	Unit	合计 Total	#中央 of which: Central Enterprises	国有企业 State-owned Enterprises	集体企业 Collective Enterprises	其他所有制企业 Other Ownership Enterprises
施工企业单位数	Number of Construction Enterprises	个	unit	806	11	19	6	781
建筑业总产值	Gross Output Value of Construction	万元	10 000yuan	30001565	6197858	357470	6001	29638094
#建筑工程	of which: Construction	万元	10 000yuan	26230755	4781918	316428	5991	25908337
安装工程	Installation	万元	10 000yuan	3030363	1233332	13992	10	3016361
建筑业增加值	Value Added of Construction	万元	10 000yuan	11127900				
全年竣工产值	Output Value of Buildings Completed in the Year	万元	10 000yuan	11017287	1440599	175896	3212	10838179
施工房屋面积	Floor Space of Buildings under Construction	万平方米	10 000sp.m	19453	4329		15	19438
#新开工	of which: Newly Operating	万平方米	10 000sp.m	7255	1309			7255
竣工房屋面积	Floor Space of Buildings Completed	万平方米	10 000sp.m	3620	237		1	3619
#住宅	of which: Residential Buildings	万平方米	10 000sp.m	2281	68			2281
计算建筑业劳动生产率平均人数	Average Number of Persons for Calculating the Labor Productivity	人	person	639632	71577	14084	298	625250

14-2 建筑业企业财务状况（2020 年）
FINANCIAL SITUATION OF CONSTRUCTION ENTERPRISES (2020)

项目	Item	单位	Unit	合计 Total
流动资产	Circulating Funds	万元	10000yuan	23940160
#存货	of which：Inventory	万元	10000yuan	3473816
年末固定资产原价	Original Value of Fixed Assets（year–end）	万元	10000yuan	2300467
本年固定资产折旧	Depreciation of Fixed Assets in the Year	万元	10000yuan	146023
年末资产合计	Total Assets（year–end）	万元	10000yuan	29389399
年末负债合计	Total Liabilities（year–end）	万元	10000yuan	23084066
所有者权益合计	Total Owners' Equity	万元	10000yuan	6305333
#实收资本	Paid–in Capitals	万元	10000yuan	3473116
主营业务收入	Revenue from Principal Business	万元	10000yuan	27728172
主营业务成本	Cost of Principal Business	万元	10000yuan	25638095
主营业务税金及附加	Taxes and Extra Charges on Principal Business	万元	10000yuan	110234
管理费用	Management Expenses	万元	10000yuan	713280
利润总额	Total Profits	万元	10000yuan	536808
利税总额	Total Pre–tax Profits	万元	10000yuan	994336
年末应收工程款	Account Receivable（year–end）	万元	10000yuan	8242689

#中央 of which：Central Enterprises	国有企业 State-owned Enterprises	集体企业 Collective Enterprises	其他所有制企业 Other Ownership Enterprises
6948076	510950	7020	23422190
450525	67285	1306	3405225
761771	91943	4429	2204095
53357	3920	67	142036
8225372	638849	13109	28737441
7165542	494702	5433	22583931
1059830	144148	7675	6153510
510665	91061	5042	3377013
7502351	446368	20946	27260858
6955599	402146	19788	25216162
12270	1725	99	108410
113394	15718	862	696700
171691	23560	150	513099
228943	45456	1223	947657
1491942	274281	3789	7964619

14-3 建筑业企业主要经济效益指标（2020 年）
MAIN INDICATOR ON ECONOMIC BENEFIT OF CONSTRUCTION ENTERPRISES (2020)

项目	Item	单位	Unit	合计 Total	#中央 of which: Central Enterprises	国有企业 State-owned Enterprises	集体企业 Collective Enterprises	其他所有制企业 Other Ownership Enterprises
建筑业劳动生产率	**Labor Productivity of Construction**							
按总产值计算	In Terms of Gross Output Value	元／人	yuan/person	469044	865901	253812	201342	474019
竣工率	**Rate of Buildings completed**							
按产值计算	In Terms of Gross output Value	%	%	36.7	23.2	49.2	53.5	36.5
产值工资率	Ratio of Wages to Gross Output Value	%	%	14.2	15.2	16.3	15.1	13.3
资金利润率	Ratio of Profit to Funds	%	%	2.1	2.4	3.7	1.6	1.8
产值利润率	Ratio of Profit to Gross Output Value	%	%	1.8	2.8	6.5	2.5	1.7
流动比率	Current Ratio	%	%	113.3	100.2	107.4	116.5	113.4
资产负债率	Assets-Liability Ratio	%	%	78.5	87.1	77.4	41.4	78.5

14-4 建筑业增加值（2020 年）
VALUE ADDED OF CONSTRUCTION (2020)

单位：亿元 (100 million yuan)

市、区名称	Region	增加值 Value Added
全市总计	**Total**	**1112.79**
市南区	Shinan District	82.14
市北区	Shibei District	113.73
李沧区	Licang District	53.39
崂山区	Laoshan District	121.24
西海岸新区	West Coast New Area	329.22
黄岛区	Huangdao District	324.72
保税港区	Qingdao Free Trade Port Area of China	4.50
城阳区	Chengyang District	75.95
城阳区（不含高新区）	Chengyang District (Excluding High tech District)	65.96
高新区	High tech District	9.99
即墨区	Jimo District	122.55
胶州市	Jiaozhou	115.83
平度市	Pingdu	27.72
莱西市	Laixi	71.07

14-5 重点建筑企业一览表（2020 年）
LIST OF KEY CONSTRUCTION ENTERPRISES (2020)

序号 Precedence	企业单位名称	Name	所在地区 Location	资质等级 Qualification Criteria
1	青建集团股份公司	Qingjian Group Co., Ltd.	市北区 Shibei District	A001
2	中铁建工集团山东有限公司	China Railway Construction Engineering Group Shandong Co., Ltd.	城阳区 Chengyang District	A201
3	中建八局第四建设有限公司	Fourth Construction of China Construction Eight Bureau Co., Ltd.	崂山区 Laoshan District	A001
4	荣华建设集团有限公司	Ronghua Construction Group Co., Ltd.	莱西市 Laixi	A001
5	中青建安建设集团有限公司	Zhongqing Jianan Construction Group Co., Ltd.	市北区 Shibei District	A001
6	中启胶建集团有限公司	Zhongqi Rubber Construction Group Co., Ltd.	胶州市 Jiaozhou	A001
7	中铁二十局集团第四工程有限公司	Fourth Engineering of China Railway twenty Bureau Group Co., Ltd.	崂山区 Laoshan District	A103
8	东亚装饰股份有限公司	East Asia Decoration Limited by Share Ltd.	市北区 Shibei District	B103
9	青岛博海建设集团有限公司	Qingdao Bohai Construction Group Co., Ltd.	市南区 Shinan District	A001
10	中铁十七局集团第一工程有限公司	China Railway No.17 Bureau Group First Engineering Co.,Ltd	黄岛区 Huangdao District	A003
11	山东兴华建设集团有限公司	Shandong Xinghua Construction Group Co., Ltd.	黄岛区 Huangdao District	A001
12	青岛亿联建设集团股份有限公司	Qingdao Elink Construction Group Co., Ltd.	黄岛区 Huangdao District	A001
13	青岛中嘉建设集团有限公司	Qingdao Zhongjia Construction Group Co., Ltd.	市北区 Shibei District	A101
14	中建筑港集团有限公司	Zhongjian Zhu Gang Group Co., Ltd.	市北区 Shibei District	A104
15	山东荣泰建筑工程集团有限公司	Shandong Rongtai Construction Engineering Group Co., Ltd.	黄岛区 Huangdao District	A001
16	青岛海川建设集团有限公司	Qingdao Hai Chuan Construction Group Co., Ltd.	市北区 Shibei District	A001
17	青岛海骊住居科技股份有限公司	Qingdao Hailizhuju Technology Co., Ltd.	胶州市 Jiaozhou	A101
18	中交一航局第二工程有限公司	Second Engineering Company Co., Ltd. of China Communications Central Airlines	市南区 Shinan District	A104
19	青岛一建集团有限公司	Qingdao Yi Jian Group Co., Ltd.	市北区 Shibei District	A001
20	中铁十局集团青岛工程有限公司	China Railway Ten Bureau Group Qingdao Engineering Co., Ltd.	市北区 Shibei District	A110
21	青岛新华友建工集团股份有限公司	Qingdao Xinhuayou Construction Engineering Group Limited by Share Ltd.	崂山区 Laoshan District	A101
22	中铁二十五局集团第五工程有限公司	The 5th Engineering Co., Ltd. of China Railway 25th Bureau Group	崂山区 Laoshan District	A110
23	青岛瑞源工程集团有限公司	Qingdao Ruiyuan Engineering Group Co., Ltd.	黄岛区 Huangdao District	A105
24	青岛恒生源集团建设有限公司	Qingdao Hengshengyuan Group Construction Co., Ltd.	即墨区 Jimo District	A101

14-5 续表 1
Continued

序号 Precedence	企业单位名称	Name	所在地区 Location	资质等级 Qualification Criteria
25	青岛建设集团有限公司	Qingdao Construction Group Co., Ltd.	市南区 Shinan District	B103
26	青岛建祥建设集团有限公司	Qingdao Jian Xiang Construction Group Co., Ltd.	胶州市 Jiaozhou	A101
27	中石化第十建设有限公司	Sinopec tenth Construction Company Limited	黄岛区 Huangdao District	A109
28	德才装饰股份有限公司	Decai Decoration Limited by Share Ltd.	崂山区 Laoshan District	B103
29	山东莱钢建设有限公司	Shandong Laiwu Iron and Steel Construction Co., Ltd.	市南区 Shinan District	A101
30	山东电力建设第三工程有限公司	Third Engineering Co., Ltd. of Shandong Electric Power Construction	崂山区 Laoshan District	A006
31	青建国际集团有限公司	Qingjian International Group Limited	市北区 Shibei District	A101
32	青岛德泰建设工程有限公司	Qingdao De Tai Construction Engineering Co., Ltd.	黄岛区 Huangdao District	A101
33	中国石油天然气第七建设有限公司	China Petroleum and Natural Gas Seventh Construction Co., Ltd.	崂山区 Laoshan District	A109
34	青岛即建建设集团有限公司	Qingdao JiJian Construction Group Co., Ltd.	即墨区 Jimo District	A101
35	青岛市房屋建设集团股份有限公司	Qingdao Housing Construction Group Limited by Share Ltd.	市北区 Shibei District	A101
36	青岛营上建设集团有限公司	Qingdao Yingshang Construction Group Co., Ltd.	即墨区 Jimo District	A101
37	青岛颐金建设装饰集团有限公司	Qingdao Yijin Construction Decoration Group Co., Ltd.	市南区 Shinan District	B103
38	青岛海德工程集团股份有限公司	Qingdao Hyde Road and Bridge Engineering Limited by Share Ltd.	崂山区 Laoshan District	B111
39	青岛平建建筑安装股份有限公司	Qingdao Pingjian Construction and Installation Co., Ltd.	平度市 Pingdu	A101
40	青岛胶城建设集团有限公司	Qingdao Rubber City Construction Group Co., Ltd.	胶州市 Jiaozhou	A101
41	青岛第一市政工程有限公司	Qingdao First Municipal Engineering Co., Ltd.	市北区 Shibei District	A110
42	中诚祥建设工程有限公司	Zhongchengxiang Construction Engineering Co., Ltd.	李沧区 Licang District	A101
43	青岛土木建工集团有限公司	Qingdao Civil Engineering Group Co., Ltd.	黄岛区 Huangdao District	A101
44	青岛城建集团有限公司	Qingdao Urban Construction Group Co., Ltd.	市北区 Shibei District	A110
45	青岛温泉建设集团有限公司	Qingdao Hot Spring Construction Group Co., Ltd.	即墨区 Jimo District	A101
46	青岛滨海建设集团有限公司	Qingdao Binhai Construction Group Co., Ltd.	黄岛区 Huangdao District	A101
47	青岛艺高城市建设工程有限公司	Qingdao Yi Gao City Construction Engineering Co., Ltd.	市北区 Shibei District	A201
48	青岛中建联合集团有限公司	Qingdao Sino United Group Co., Ltd.	崂山区 Laoshan District	A101
49	青岛福瀛建设集团有限公司	Qingdao Fu ying Construction Group Co., Ltd.	黄岛区 Huangdao District	A101
50	中建中新建设工程有限公司	China State Construction Zhongxin Construction Engineering Co.,Ltd	高新区 High tech District	A101

14-5 续表 2
Continued

序号 Precedence	企业单位名称	Name	所在地区 Location	资质等级 Qualification Criteria
51	青岛青房建安集团有限公司	Qingdao Qingfang Jianan Group Co., Ltd.	市南区 Shinan District	A101
52	青岛港务局港务工程公司	Qingdao Port Bureau Port Engineering Company	黄岛区 Huangdao District	A204
53	青城建工集团有限公司	Qingcheng Construction Group Co., Ltd.	高新区 High tech District	A101
54	青岛鑫兴泰建筑工程有限公司	Qingdao Xinxingtai Construction Engineering Co., Ltd.	城阳区 Chengyang District	A201
55	青岛胶州湾建设集团有限公司	Qingdao Jiaozhou Bay Construction Group Co., Ltd.	胶州市 Jiaozhou	A101
56	青岛安装建设股份有限公司	Qingdao Installation and Construction Limited by Share Ltd.	市北区 Shibei District	A112
57	青岛营海建设（集团）有限公司	Qingdao Ying hai Construction Group Co., Ltd.	胶州市 Jiaozhou	A101
58	青岛环城建工集团有限公司	Qingdao Ring City Construction Engineering Group Co., Ltd.	黄岛区 Huangdao District	A101
59	青岛方圆达建设集团有限公司	Qindao Fang Yuan Da Construction Group Co.,Ltd.	李沧区 Licang District	A101
60	山东国建工程集团有限公司	Shandong State Construction Engineering Group Co., Ltd.	崂山区 Laoshan District	A101
61	青岛兰桂建工有限公司	Qingdao Langui Construction Engineering Co., Ltd.	黄岛区 Huangdao District	A301
62	青岛建工建安集团有限公司	Qingdao Construction Engineering Jian'an Group Co., Ltd.	崂山区 Laoshan District	A101
63	青岛建工路桥集团有限公司	Qingdao Construction Engineering Road & Bridge Group Co., Ltd.	崂山区 Laoshan District	A102
64	青岛建设装饰集团有限公司	Qingdao Construction Decoration Group Co.,Ltd.	市南区 Shinan District	B103
65	青岛建设集团建兴工程有限公司	Qingdao construction group LITE-ON Engineering Co., Ltd.	高新区 High tech District	A101
66	青岛康太源建设集团有限公司	Qingdao Kangtine Construction Group.Lnc.	李沧区 Licang District	A101
67	山东莱钢绿建发展有限公司	Shandong Laigang Green Construction Development Co., Ltd.	崂山区 Laoshan District	A101
68	青岛市政空间开发集团有限责任公司	Qingdao Municipal Construction Group Co., Ltd.	市南区 Shinan District	A110
69	青岛华山广泰建设集团有限公司	Qingdao Huashan Guangtai Construction Group Co., Ltd.	即墨区 Jimo District	A201
70	青岛环海工程贸易发展有限公司	Qingdao Huanhai Engineering & Trade Development Co., Ltd.	市北区 Shibei District	A201
71	青岛恒华机房设备工程有限公司	Qingdao Henghua Computer Room Equipment Engineering Co., Ltd.	市南区 Shinan District	B123
72	青岛东捷建设工程有限公司	Qingdao Dong jie Construction Engineering Co., Ltd.	市北区 Shibei District	A101
73	青岛隆昌达建设集团有限公司	Qingdao Longchangda Construction Group Co., Ltd.	胶州市 Jiaozhou	A101
74	青岛元昌盛房建集团有限公司	Qingdao Yuanchangsheng Housing Construction Group Co., Ltd.	胶州市 Jiaozhou	A201
75	青岛嘉恒建设集团有限公司	Qingdao Jiaheng Construction Group Co., Ltd.	市南区 Shinan District	A101

14-5 续表 3
Continued

序号 Precedence	企业单位名称	Name	所在地区 Location	资质等级 Qualification Criteria
76	青岛高新建筑安装工程有限公司	Qingdao High-tech Construction and Installation Engineering Co., Ltd.	崂山区 Laoshan District	A101
77	青岛市崂山区古建建筑工程有限公司	Qingdao Laoshan ancient building engineering Co., Ltd.	崂山区 Laoshan District	A101
78	青岛亿佰建工集团有限公司	Qingdao Yibai Construction Engineering Group Co., Ltd.	黄岛区 Huangdao District	A201
79	青岛地矿岩土工程有限公司	Qingdao Geotechnical Engineering Co., Ltd.	市南区 Shinan District	B101
80	青岛诚通建筑工程有限公司	Qingdao Chengtong Construction Engineering Co., Ltd.	黄岛区 Huangdao District	A201
81	山东世纪阳光建筑科技有限公司	Shandong Century Sunshine Construction Technology Co., Ltd.	市南区 Shinan District	B112
82	青岛前盛业建设工程有限公司	Qingdao Qianshengye Construction Engineering Co., Ltd.	黄岛区 Huangdao District	A101
83	中铁十四局集团青岛工程建设有限公司	Qingdao Engineering Construction Co., Ltd. of China Railway 14th Bureau Group	黄岛区 Huangdao District	A110
84	青岛云川建筑有限公司	Qingdao Yun Chuan Architecture Co., Ltd.	胶州市 Jiaozhou	A210
85	青岛东建建设有限公司	Qingdao Dongjian Construction Co., Ltd.	李沧区 Licang District	A101
86	青岛昆泉建设工程有限公司	Qingdao Kunquan Construction Engineering Co., Ltd.	黄岛区 Huangdao District	A101
87	青岛金沙滩建设集团有限公司	Qingdao Jinsten Construction Group Co., Ltd.	黄岛区 Huangdao District	A101
88	青岛昶德建设集团有限公司	Qingdao Changde Construction Group Co., Ltd.	胶州市 Jiaozhou	A101
89	青岛西海岸市政工程有限公司	Qingdao West Coast municipal Group Municipal Engineering Company	黄岛区 Huangdao District	A110
90	青岛巨源建工集团有限公司	Qingdao Juyuan Construction Engineering Group Co., Ltd.	崂山区 Laoshan District	A110
91	青岛永鑫建筑工程有限公司	Qingdao Yongxin Construction Engineering Co., Ltd.	平度市 Pingdu	A201
92	中铁十四局集团青岛工程有限公司	Qingdao Engineering Co., Ltd. of China Railway 14th Bureau Group Co., Ltd.	城阳区 Chengyang District	A110
93	青岛市宏运公路工程有限责任公司	Qingdao Hongyun Highway Engineering Co., Ltd.	平度市 Pingdu	A202
94	青岛市益水工程股份有限公司	Qingdao Yishui Engineering Co.,Ltd.	市南区 Shinan District	A210
95	青岛福海洋建设集团有限公司	Qingdao Fu Ocean Construction Group Co., Ltd.	胶州市 Jiaozhou	A101
96	青岛望城三宝建设有限公司	Qingdao Wangcheng Sanbao Construction Co., Ltd.	莱西市 Laixi	A101
97	即墨市七级建筑工程有限公司	Jimo Seventh Grade Construction Engineering Co., Ltd.	即墨区 Jimo District	A201
98	青岛盈鑫建设集团有限公司	Qingdao Yingxin Construction Group Co., Ltd.	城阳区 Chengyang District	A201
99	青岛三星工程有限公司	Qingdao Sanxing Engineering Co., Ltd.	城阳区 Chengyang District	A110
100	青岛登科市政工程有限公司	Qingdao Dengke Municipal Engineering Co., Ltd.	城阳区 Chengyang District	A110

主要统计指标解释

建筑业统计单位 指从事房屋、构筑物建造和设备安装活动的法人企业。建筑业法人企业应具有建筑业资质并能够独立核算，同时其应具备以下条件：①依法成立，有自己的名称、组织机构和场所，能够承担民事责任；②独立拥有和使用资产，承担负债，有权与其他单位签订合同；③独立核算盈亏，能够编制资产负债表。

建筑业总产值 是以货币形式表现的建筑业企业在一定时期内生产的建筑业产品和提供的服务的总和。建筑业总产值包括：

（1）建筑工程产值：指列入建筑工程预算内的各种工程价值。

（2）安装工程产值：指设备安装工程价值，不包括被安装设备本身的价值。

（3）其他产值：建筑业总产值中除建筑工程、安装工程以外的产值。包括房屋构筑物修理产值、非标准设备制造产值、总包企业向分包企业收取的管理费以及不能明确划分的施工活动所完成的产值。

建筑业增加值 指建筑业企业在报告期内以货币形式表现的建筑业生产经营活动的最终成果。

建筑业现价增加值 按生产法和分配法（收入法）两种方法计算，以收入法的计算结果为准，即从收入的角度出发，根据生产要素在生产过程中应得的收入份额计算。具体计算方法：经济普查年度建筑业增加值按照《经济普查年度 GDP 核算方案》计算，非经济普查年度建筑业增加值按照《非经济普查年度 GDP 核算方案》计算。

Explanatory Notes on Main Statistical Indicators

Statistical Unit in Construction refers to corporate enterprise engaged in the construction of buildings and structures and in the installation of equipment. A corporate construction enterprise should have qualification certificates with independent accounting system, and should meet the following 3 requirements: 1. being set up in line with relevant legal basis, having its full name, organization and location, and capable of taking civil liabilities; 2. independently possessing and using its assets and assuming its liabilities, and entitled to sign contracts with other institutions; and 3. making independent accounts of its profits and losses, and capable of compiling its own balance sheet.

Gross Output Value of Construction refers to total of construction products and services, expressed in money terms, produced or rendered by construction and installation enterprises during a given period of time. It includes:

1. Output value of construction projects, that is the value of projects covered by the project budgets;

2. Output value of installation projects, that is the value of the installation of equipment, (excluding the value of the equipment to be installed);

3. Output value of others, that is the output value of construction industry excluding that of construction projects and installation projects. It includes: output value of repair of buildings and structures; output value of non-standard equipment manufacturing; overhead expenses received by contracted enterprises to the sub-contracted enterprises and the completed output value of construction activities that have no clear definition.

Added Value Of Construction Industry refers to the final results of construction industry production and operation activities expressed in currency by construction enterprises during the reporting period.

Value Added At Current Price Of Construction Industry Calculate according to the two methods of production method and distribution method (income method). The calculation result of income method shall prevail, that is, from the perspective of income, it is calculated according to the income share of production factors in the production process. Specific calculation method: The annual added value of the construction industry in the economic census is calculated in accordance with the "Annual GDP Accounting Plan for the Economic Census", and the annual added value of the construction industry in the non-economic census is calculated in accordance with the "Non-economic Census Annual GDP Accounting Plan".

运输、邮电 15

TRANSPORT, POSTAL AND
TELECOMMUNICATION SERVICES

简要说明

一、本篇资料的主要内容

本篇资料主要反映了全市交通运输业和邮电业通讯业发展的基本情况，主要包括客货运输及港口吞吐量、民用汽车拥有量、独立核算运输邮电单位主要财务指标、邮电通讯基本情况、邮政行业发展情况、快递企业发展情况、电信行业基本情况、城市轨道交通发展情况等方面的内容。

二、本篇资料的来源

1. 本篇资料中交通运输邮电资料来源于全市交通运输邮电业统计年报。

2. 交通运输资料来源于青岛市交通运输局、青岛港（集团）有限公司、青岛国际机场集团有限公司、青岛地铁集团有限公司。

3. 邮政业资料来源于青岛市邮政管理局、中国邮政集团公司青岛市分公司。

4. 电信业资料来源于青岛市通信管理局、中国电信集团公司山东省青岛市电信分公司、中国电信股份有限公司青岛分公司、中国联合网络通信有限公司青岛市分公司、中国移动通信集团山东有限公司青岛分公司。

5. 民用汽车拥有量资料来源于青岛市公安局交警支队车辆管理所。

本篇资料由市统计局服务业统计处整理提供。

Brief Introduction

I. Main Content

Data in this chapter show the basic conditions of the development of transport, post and telecommunications in Shandong Province, mainly including the freight traffic and passenger traffic, cargo handled at port, possession of civil motor vehicles, major financial indices and basic conditions of transport, postal and telecommunication services, development of the postal services, express company development, development of urban rail transit.

II. Source of Data

1. Data on transport are based on the annual report of transport.

2. Transportation data comes from Qingdao Municipal Transportation Bureau, Qingdao Port (Group) Co., Ltd., Qingdao International Airport Group Co., Ltd., and Qingdao Metro Group Co., Ltd.

3. Data on postal and telecommunication are based on Qingdao Municipal Postal Administration, Qingdao Post Bureau.

4. Data on business of telecommunication services Qingdao Communication Administration, China Telecom Group Corporation Qingdao Branch of Shandong Province, China Telecom Co., Ltd. Qingdao Branch, China United Network Communications Co., Ltd. Qingdao Branch, China Mobile Communications Group Shandong Co., Ltd. Qingdao Branch.

5. Date on possession of civil motor vehicles are provided by Qingdao Municipal Public Security Bureau Traffic Police Detachment Vehicle Management Office.

Data in this chapter are prepared and provide by the Division of Industry Statistics of Qingdao Municipal Bureau of Statistics.

15-1 主要年份客货运输及港口吞吐量
MAJOR YEAR'S PASSENGER & FREIGHT TRAFFIC AND HANDLING CAPACITY OF THE PORTS

年份 Year	客运量（万人）Passenger Traffic (10000 persons)			货运量（万吨）Freight Traffic (10000 tons)			港口货物吞吐量（万吨）Volume of Freight Handled in Ports (10 000 tons)	集装箱吞吐量（万标箱）Containers (10 000 TEU)	航空旅客吞吐量（万人）Air Passenger Throughput (10 000 persons)	航空货邮吞吐量（万吨）Air Cargo and Mail Throughput (10 000 tons)
	铁路 Railways	公路 Highways	海运 Waterways	铁路 Railways	公路 Highways	海运 Waterways				
1949	327	14	9	386	162	22	73			
1952	571	49	13	447	399	44	181			
1957	1054	149	13	747	548	118	269			
1962	3100	141	39	909	524	97	391			
1965	1424	230	19	1257	690	158	524			
1970	1329	373	20	1856	736	232	695			
1975	1803	159	30	2325	817	282	1542			
1978	1986	274	49	2917	1561	528	2081			
1980	1896	713	73	2596	1642	941	1779			
1985	2063	1 894	86	3009	2303	919	2610		2.17	0.06
1988	2083	3 300	234	3418	6486	1160	3153		17.48	0.32
1990	1488	3 639	316	3741	6433	1556	3068		28.12	0.54
1991	1453	4144	366	3774	6896	1789	3194		38.36	0.70
1992	1488	4965	437	3899	6822	1981	3240		54.17	0.57
1993	1499	6436	499	4044	7685	1910	3650		70.77	0.70
1994	1564	6787		4112	8336	1804	4331		92.64	0.88
1995	1480	9785		4205	11788	2185	5165		132.71	1.26
1996	1230	10738		4415	10749	474	6056	81.1	157.61	1.73
1997	1308	11855		4466	11232	544	6944	103.3	178.68	1.96
1998	1549	11754		4028	14311	1792	7044	121.3	184.66	2.15
1999	1674	12103		3919	14550	1926	7282	154.3	203.11	2.89
2000	1780	12145		4256	17234	2998	8661	212.0	243.15	3.44
2001	1678	13686		4778	20906	3432	10423	264.0	281.01	3.62
2002	1530	14516	777	5079	24480	2530	12252	341.0	321.99	4.63
2003	1366	13132	786	4929	27241	2773	14135	424.0	349.10	5.46
2004	1496	16420	862	5119	29937	3503	16303	514.0	480.84	7.55
2005	552	17212	972	2299	31009	4471	18727	630.7	587.96	8.91
2006	810	17752	999	2790	32047	4768	22438	770.0	679.12	10.13
2007	1101	18800	1080	2781	33336	4019	26507	946.6	786.80	11.57
2008	1278	19909	1055	3225	34172	5080	30029	1037.7	820.04	13.05
2009	1425	19612	1145	3772	16297	4332	31668	1027.6	966.01	13.54
2010	1537	20460	1302	5031	17525	4407	35012	1201.0	1110.12	16.37
2011	1693	21560	791	5697	19208	4220	37971	1302.0	1171.64	16.65
2012	1881	22724	414	6126	21312	1791	41465	1450.0	1260.12	17.19
2013	2056	23588	333	6266	23270	1313	45782	1552.0	1451.67	18.62
2014	2301	5588	324	5564	19043	1434	47701	1658.0	1641.18	20.44
2015	2421	5370	288	5486	20073	1456	49749	1743.0	1820.21	20.81
2016	2701	4532	225	5569	20701	1685	51463	1805.0	2050.50	23.69
2017	3179	4534	215	6021	24716	1800	51314	1830.9	2321.06	23.21
2018	3455	4602	161	6280	27453	2502	54250	1931.5	2453.57	22.45
2019	3979	4593	186	6115	29170	2493	57736	2101.2	2555.63	25.63
2020	1240	1844	66	8416	25737	2363	60459	2200.8	1456.16	20.68

注：1. 从 2014 年公路客、货运量统计口径进行调整，与以前年度不可比。
2. 根据市交通运输局提供数据，对航空部分吞吐量历史数据进行了修正。

Note: 1. In 2014, the Ministry of Transportation made an adjustment to the statistical gauge for highway passenger and freight transportation and the data are not comparable directly.
2. According to the data provided by the Municipal Transportation Bureau, some historical data of aviation throughput have been revised.

15-2 民用车辆拥有量（2020 年底）
POSSESSION OF CIVIL MOTOR VEHICLES (END OF 2020)

单位：辆 (unit)

项目	Item	合计 Total 辆数 Number	#个人 of which：Private Vehicles 辆数 Number
一、汽车	**Automobile**	**3141380**	**2731563**
1. 载客汽车	Passenger Vehicles	2826608	2556674
其中：轿车	of which：Sedan	1823235	1675083
2. 载货汽车	Trucks	302652	171020
3. 其他汽车	Other Automobile	16933	8575
二、电车	**Tram**	**103**	**0**
三、摩托车	**Motorcycle**	**118163**	**116240**
四、农用运输车	**Agricultural Transport Vehicle**		
五、挂车	**Trailer Trucks**	**36840**	**372**
六、其他类型车	**Other Vehicles**	**116**	**2**
七、校车	**School Bus**	**2576**	**1**

补充资料：机动车驾驶员（3887637 人）Motor drivers（person）
其中：汽车驾驶员（ 3842415 人）of which：Automobile drivers (person)

15-3 客货运输及港口吞吐量（2020 年）
PASSENGER & FREIGHT TRAFFIC AND HANDLING CAPACITY OF THE PORTS (2020)

项目 Item	货运量（万吨）Freight Traffic (10 000 tons)	货物周转量（亿吨公里）Cargo Turnover (100million tons · km)	客运量（万人）Passenger Traffic (10 000 persons)	旅客周转量（亿人公里）Passenger Turnover (100million persons · km)	项目 Item	旅客吞吐量（万人）Passenger Throughput (10 000 persons)	货物吞吐量（万吨）Cargo Throughput (10 000 tons)	集装箱（万标箱）Containers (10 000 TEU)
总计 Total	**36516**	**1824.29**	**3150**	**56.65**		**1456**	**60479**	**2201**
铁路 Railways	8416	71.93	1240	31.92				
公路 Highways	25737	604.22	1844	24.66				
水运 Waterways	2363	1148.14	66	0.07				
机场 Civil Aviation						1456	21	
港口 Ports							60459	2201

15-4 规模以上运输邮电单位主要财务指标（2020 年）
MAJOR FINANCIAL INDICATORS OF TRANSPORTATION, POST AND TELECOMMUNICATION UNITS ABOVE DESIGNATED SCALE (2020)

单位：亿元 (100 million yuan)

项目	Item	营业收入 Revenue from principal Business	营业成本 Cost of principal Business	营业利润 Operating Profits	营业税金及附加 Business taxes and surtax	利润总额 Total Profits
总计	**Total**	**1484.66**	**1332.57**	**5.02**	**132.63**	**131.90**
铁路运输业	Railway Transport	10.95	12.11	0.02	-8.54	-8.56
道路运输业	Road Transport	325.79	342.79	1.93	7.23	7.93
水上运输业	Water Transport	128.82	83.57	1.12	64.00	64.11
航空运输业	Air Transport	28.85	38.31	0.02	-17.15	-16.52
管道运输业	Pipeline Transport	16.10	6.05	0.05	9.26	9.30
多式联运和运输代理业	Multimodal Transport and Transport Agent	632.06	593.57	0.49	24.44	24.74
装卸搬运和仓储业	Loading And Unloading And Storage	147.48	115.87	0.77	18.71	16.26
邮政业	Post	47.05	42.42	0.14	0.75	0.74
电信、广播电视和卫星传输服务	Telecommunications, Broadcast Television and Satellite Transmission Services	147.56	97.88	0.48	33.93	33.90

注：该表数据来源于规模以上服务业统计年报。
Note: The data in this table comes from the statistical annual report of the service industry above designated size.

15-5 邮政行业基本情况（2020 年）
BASIC SITUATION OF THE POSTAL INDUSTRY(2020)

指标名称	Name	计量单位	Unit	本年实际 Actual this year	去年实际 Actual last year
营业网点	Business Outlets	处	unit	2376	3062
其中：快递营业网点	Of Which: Express Business Outlets	处	unit	1938	2684
邮路总长度	Total Length of Postal Route	公里	km	60587	92795
邮运汽车	Postal Car	辆	unit	605	517
邮筒信箱	Mail Box	个	unit	313	663
平均每一营业网点服务面积	Average Service Area of Each Business Outlet	平方公里	aq.km	4.75	3.69
平均每一营业网点服务人口	Average Service Population of Each Business Outlet	万人	10000 persons	0.42	0.31
平均每人每年发函件数	Average Number of Letters Sent Per Person Per Year	件	articles	0.92	1.51
平均每百人每年订有报刊数	Average Number of Newspapers Per 100 People Per Year	份	copies	8.68	10.77

注：该表数据由青岛市邮政管理局提供。
Note: The data in this table is provided by Qingdao Post Management Bureau.

15-6 邮政行业发展情况
DEVELOPMENT OF THE POSTAL SERVICES

指标名称	Name	计量单位	Unit	2020年	2019年
一、邮政行业业务收入	**Postal Services Business Income**	亿元	**100 million yuan**	**95.02**	**81.68**
1、邮政寄递服务	Postal Delivery Service	亿元	100 million yuan	2.57	2.86
2、快递业务	Express Service	亿元	100 million yuan	78.91	65.53
二、邮政行业业务总量	**Total Business Volume Of Postal Industry**	亿元	100 million yuan	**130.77**	**103.55**
1、邮政寄递服务	Postal Delivery Service	万件	10 000 articles	17590	18153
其中：函件	Number Of Letters	万件	10 000 articles	923	1438
包裹	Package	万件	10 000 articles	30	31
订销报纸累计数	Cumulative number of newspapers ordered and sold	万份	10 000 copies	13576	14309
订销杂志累计数	Cumulative number of magazines ordered and sold	万份	10 000 copies	621	646
汇兑	Exchange	万笔	10 000 sums	6	9
2、快递业务	Express Service	万件	10 000 articles	58711	45325
其中：同城	Same City	万件	10 000 articles	11978	10921
异地	Different Places	万件	10 000 articles	45999	33775
国际 / 港澳台	International/Hong Kong, Macao And Taiwan	万件	10 000 articles	734	629

注：该表数据由青岛市邮政管理局提供。
Note: The data in this table is provided by Qingdao Post Management Bureau.

15-7 快递企业发展情况
EXPRESS COMPANY DEVELOPMENT

指标名称	Name	计量单位	Unit	2020 年	2019 年
快递业务量	**Express Business Volume**	**万件**	**10 000 articles**	**58711**	**45325**
同城	Same City	万件	10 000 articles	11978	10921
异地	Different Places	万件	10 000 articles	45999	33775
国际及港澳台	International/ Hong Kong, Macao And Taiwan	万件	10 000 articles	734	629
快递业务收入	**Express Revenue**	**亿元**	**100 million yuan**	**78.91**	**65.53**
同城	Same City	亿元	100 million yuan	9.54	8.31
异地	Different Places	亿元	100 million yuan	42.25	37.70
国际及港澳台	International/ Hong Kong, Macao And Taiwan	亿元	100 million yuan	14.62	10.10
其他	Others	亿元	100 million yuan	12.51	9.42

注：该表数据由邮政管理局提供。
Note: The data in this table is provided by the postal administration.

15-8 电信行业基本情况
BASIC SITUATION OF TELECOM INDUSTRY

指标名称	Name	计量单位	Unit	2020年	2019年
一、电信业务总量（2015年不变价）	**TOTAL TELECOMMUNICATIONS BUSINESS**	亿元	**100 million yuan**	**983.57**	**812.08**
其中：固定话音业务总量	Total Fixed Voice Service	亿元	100 million yuan	1.47	1.88
固定数据及互联网业务总量	Fixed Data And Total Internet Business	亿元	100 million yuan	23.96	22.44
移动话音业务总量	Total Mobile Voice Service	亿元	100 million yuan	22.70	24.04
移动数据及互联网业务总量	Total Mobile Data And Internet Services	亿元	100 million yuan	902.69	736.89
电信业务收入	Telecommunications Revenue	亿元	100 million yuan	110.95	107.52
二、电信营业网点	**Telecom Business Network**	个	**unit**	**400**	**439**
三、固定电话交换机总容量（含农话）	**Total Capacity Of Fixed Telephone Exchanges(Including Rural Fixed Telephone)**	万门	**10 000 line**	**344**	**334**
固定电话年末用户	Fixed Telephone Year-End User	万户	10 000 households	158	156
其中：新装电话	Newly Installed Telephone	万户	10 000 households	6	9
城市电话用户	Urban Telephone User	万户	10 000 households	137	130
乡村电话用户	Village Phone User	万户	10 000 households	20	25
住宅电话年末用户	Home Phone Year-End User	万户	10 000 households	13	15
城市电话用户	Urban Telephone User	万户	10 000 households	9	10
乡村电话用户	Village Phone User	万户	10 000 households	4	4
四、固定电话本地通话量	**Fixed Telephone Local Call Volume**	万分钟	**10 000 minutes**	**85660**	**165943**
长话电路	Long Distance Circuit	路	line	2592	2592
长途电话通话量	Long Distance Call Volume	万次	10 000 times		
长途电话通话时长	Long-Distance Phone Call Duration	万分钟	10 000 minutes	5693	8084
五、互联网用户数	**Number Of Internet Users**	万户	**10 000 households**	**1526**	**1502**
固定宽带互联网用户数	Number Of Fixed Broadband Internet Users	万户	10 000 households	464	418
移动互联网用户数	Number Of Mobile Internet Users	万户	10 000 households	1062	1084

注：该表数据由青岛市通信管理局、中国电信集团公司山东省青岛市电信分公司、中国电信股份有限公司青岛分公司、中国联合网络通信有限公司青岛市分公司、中国移动通信集团山东有限公司青岛分公司等单位提供。

Note: The data in this table is provided by Qingdao Municipal Communications Administration, China Telecom Group Corporation Qingdao Branch, Shandong Province, China Telecom Co., Ltd. Qingdao Branch, China United Network Communications Co., Ltd. Qingdao Branch, China Mobile Communications Group Shandong Co., Ltd. Provided by Qingdao Branch of the company and other units.

15-8 续表
Continued

指标名称	Name	计量单位	Unit	2020 年	2019 年
六、互联网通信量	**Internet Traffic**				
固定互联网宽带使用时长	Fixed Internet Broadband Usage Time	万分钟	10 000 minutes	82473924	74618437
固定互联网宽带接入流量	Fixed Internet Broadband Access Traffic	万 G	10 000 G	11375	6376
移动互联网接入流量	Mobile Internet Access Traffic	万 G	10 000 G	58463	46119
七、光缆线路长度	**Cable Line Length**				
长途光缆线路长度	Long-Distance Cable Line Length	公里	km	5058	4594
本地网中继光缆线路长度	Line Length of Relay Optical Cable in Local Network	公里	km	21583	10444
接入网光缆线路长度	Optical Cable Line Length In Access Network	公里	km	330443	296568
八、移动通信用户	**Mobile Communication Users**				
移动电话交换机容量	Mobile Phone Switch Capacity	万户	10 000 households	3051	3051
期末移动电话用户数	Number of mobile phone users at the end of the period	万户	10 000 households	1257	1246
其中：3G 移动电话用户	3G Mobile Phone Users	万户	10 000 households	31	79
其中：4G 移动电话用户	4G Mobile Phone Users	万户	10 000 households	1030	1003
九、移动电话通话量	**Mobile Phone Call Volume**				
移动电话通话时长	Mobile Phone Call Duration	万分钟	10 000 minutes	3744372	3919210
十、通信能力	**Communication Ability**				
移动电话交换机容量	Mobile Phone Switch Capacity	万户	10 000 households	3051	3051
移动电话基站数	Number Of Mobile Phone Base Stations	个	unit	68167	63795
其中：3G 移动电话基站数	Number Of 3G Mobile Phone Base Stations	个	unit	9274	9072
其中：4G 移动电话基站数	Number Of 4G Mobile Phone Base Stations	个	unit	37438	37982
其中：5G 移动电话基站数	Number Of 5G Mobile Phone Base Stations	个	unit	10824	4183
十一、互联网通信能力	**Internet Communication Capability**				
互联网宽带接入端口	Internet Broadband Access Port	个	unit	8119129	8547426

注：该表数据由青岛市通信管理局、中国电信集团公司山东省青岛市电信分公司、中国电信股份有限公司青岛分公司、中国联合网络通信有限公司青岛市分公司、中国移动通信集团山东有限公司青岛分公司等单位提供。

Note: The data in this table is provided by Qingdao Municipal Communications Administration, China Telecom Group Corporation Qingdao Branch, Shandong Province, China Telecom Co., Ltd. Qingdao Branch, China United Network Communications Co., Ltd. Qingdao Branch, China Mobile Communications Group Shandong Co., Ltd. Provided by Qingdao Branch of the company.

15-9 城市轨道交通发展情况
DEVELOPMENT OF URBAN RAIL TRANSIT

指标名称	Name	计量单位	Unit	2020 年	2019 年
客运量	**Passenger Traffic**	**万人次**	**10 000 person-times**	**13909**	**18753**
日均客运量	**Average Daily Passenger**	**万人次**	**10 000 person-times**	**38**	**51**
旅客周转量	**Passenger Turnover**	**万人公里**	**10 000 passenger-km**	**119515**	**166857**
运营车数	**Number Of Vehicles Operated**	**辆**	**unit**	**980**	**756**
其中：地铁	Subway	辆	unit	980	756
轻轨	Subway	辆	unit		
运营线路总数	**Total Number Of Operating Lines**	**条**	**line**	**6**	**4**
其中：新增运营线路	New Operating Line	条	line	2	
其中：地铁	Subway	条	line	2	
轻轨	Light Rail	条	line		
运营线路总长度	**Total Length Of Operating Line**	**公里**	**km**	**246**	**176**
其中：新增运营线路长度	New Operating Line Length	公里	km	70	4
其中：地铁	Subway	公里	km	70	4
轻轨	Light Rail	公里	km		
地铁站点总数	**Total Number Of Subway Stations**	**个**	**unit**	**107**	**83**
其中：换乘站点个数	Number Of Transfer Stations	个	unit	4	3
其中：新增站点个数	Number Of New Sites	个	unit	26	3
其中：新增换乘站点个数	Increase The Number Of Transfer Stations	个	unit	1	
总开行次数	**Total Number Of Trips**	**列次**	**train number**	**458491**	**472052**
总运营里程	**Total Operating Mileage**	**公里**	**km**	**15113048**	**15160241**
列车准点率	**Train On Time Rate**	**%**	**%**	**99.98**	**99.99**

注：该表数据由青岛地铁集团有限公司提供。
（2018 年数据由青岛地铁集团有限公司轨道运营公司提供，为了统一数据口径，2019 年起，数据由青岛地铁集团有限公司提供。）
Note：The data in this table is provided by Qingdao Metro Group Co., Ltd.
(The data for 2018 are provided by Qingdao Metro Group Co., Ltd. Rail Operation Company. In order to unify the data, the data will be provided by Qingdao Metro Group Co., Ltd. from 2019 onwards.)

15-10 按行业分企业信息化及电子商务情况（2020年）
INFORMATIZATION AND E-COMMERCE OF ENTERPRISES BY INDUSTRIAL SECTOR (2020)

行业	Industry	企业数（个） Number of Enterprises (unit)	期末使用计算机数（台） Computers Used at the End of Period (unit)	每百人使用计算机数（台） Computers Used Per 100 Persons (unit)
总计	**Total**	**11768**	**589253**	**41**
采矿业	Mining	4	76	17
制造业	Manufacturing	3715	221721	34
电力、热力、燃气及水生产和供应业	Production and Supply of Electricity, Heat, Gas and Water	110	9568	47
建筑业	Construction	814	61076	26
批发和零售业	Wholesale and Retail Trades	3126	77215	62
交通运输、仓储和邮政业	Transport, Storage and Post	725	42441	39
住宿和餐饮业	Hotels and Catering Services	591	12786	30
信息传输、软件和信息技术服务业	Information Transmission, Software and Information Technology Services	199	46774	142
房地产业	Real Estate	1360	39822	58
租赁和商务服务业	Leasing and Business Services	579	25281	42
科学研究和技术服务业	Scientific Research and Technical Services	281	35002	82
水利、环境和公共设施管理业	Management of Water Conservancy, Environment and Public Facilities	39	1953	9
居民服务、修理和其他服务业	Service to Households, Repair and Other Services	49	2028	31
教育	Education	19	3075	71
卫生和社会工作	Health and Social Service	60	5108	57
文化、体育和娱乐业	Culture, Sports and Entertainment	97	5327	62

注：有电子商务交易活动的企业是指通过计算机网络开展电子商务销售或电子商务采购的企业。
Note: Enterprises with E-Commerce Transactions refers to those enterprises which performed sales or purchases through internet.

单位：亿元 (100 million yuan)

企业拥有网站数（个） Websites of Enterprises(unit)	每百家企业拥有网站数（个） Websites Per 100 Enterprises (unit)	有电子商务交易活动 With E-Commerce Transactions		电子商务销售额（万元） Sales of E-Commerce (10 000 yuan)	电子商务采购额（万元） Purchases of E-Commerce (10 000 yuan)
		企业数（个） Enterprises(unit)	比重 (%) Proportion(%)		
6292	**54**	**3560**	**30.3**	**43709538**	**27549889**
2	50	1	25.0	3	
2734	74	1314	35.4	19004897	7915878
44	40	38	34.5	13448	33135
405	50	216	26.5	1520158	1516072
1144	37	824	26.4	20219875	16849986
332	46	163	22.5	1915905	716182
185	31	298	50.4	299601	1900
189	95	96	48.2	411523	329800
594	44	190	14.0	19623	10725
284	49	167	28.8	153171	99228
209	74	125	44.5	55828	63908
13	33	18	46.2	2441	1119
27	55	15	30.6	11579	9004
21	111	10	52.6	20560	575
43	72	30	50.0	2941	1475
66	68	55	56.7	57981	901

15-11 区（市）企业信息化及电子商务情况（2020年）
INFORMATIZATION AND E-COMMERCE OF ENTERPRISES BY REGION (2020)

区（市）	Region	企业数（个）Number of Enterprises (unit)	期末使用计算机数（台）Computers Used at the End of Period (unit)	每百人使用计算机数（台）Computers Used Per 100 Persons (unit)
全市	**Total**	**11768**	**589253**	**41**
市南区	Shinan District	1249	99711	69
市北区	Shibei District	899	61262	53
李沧区	Licang District	827	19393	39
崂山区	Laoshan District	757	76406	58
西海岸新区	West Coast New Area	2660	128386	37
黄岛区	Huangdao District	2416	118068	36
保税港区	Qingdao Free Trade Port Area of China	244	10318	52
城阳区	Chengyang District	1677	93676	43
城阳区（不含高新区）	Chengyang District (Excluding High tech District)	1380	71167	39
高新区	High tech District	297	22509	64
即墨区	Jimo District	995	35343	28
胶州市	Jiaozhou	1369	37576	27
平度市	Pingdu	797	22818	28
莱西市	Laixi	538	14682	16

注：有电子商务交易活动的企业是指通过计算机网络开展电子商务销售或电子商务采购的企业。
Note: Enterprises with E-Commerce Transactions refers to those enterprises which performed sales or purchases through internet.

单位：亿元（100 million yuan）

企业拥有网站数（个）Websites of Enterprises(unit)	每百家企业拥有网站数（个）Websites Per 100 Enterprises (unit)	有电子商务交易活动 With E-Commerce Transactions		电子商务销售额（万元）Sales of E-Commerce (10 000 yuan)	电子商务采购额（万元）Purchases of E-Commerce (10 000 yuan)
		企业数（个）Enterprises(unit)	比重 (%) Proportion(%)		
6292	**54**	**3560**	**30.3**	**43709538**	**27549889**
748	60	393	31.5	11778915	5507459
418	47	233	25.9	1344837	1505665
319	39	305	36.9	2021311	2162276
447	59	369	48.7	12032758	10205387
1372	52	606	22.8	7560577	5701933
1280	53	540	22.4	7187849	5451101
92	38	66	27.0	372728	250832
898	54	583	34.8	1290048	1594792
680	49	480	34.8	1155094	1417509
218	73	103	34.7	134954	177283
598	60	308	31.0	3738751	441040
785	57	471	34.4	2448158	212744
421	53	193	24.2	149712	149454
286	53	99	18.4	1344471	69139

主要统计指标解释

货（客）运量 指在一定时期内，各运输部门实际运送的货物（旅客）数量。是反映运输业为国民经济和人民生活服务的数量指标，也是制定和检查运输生产计划，研究运输发展规模和速度的重要指标。货运按吨计算，客运按人计算。货物不论运输距离长短，货物类别，均按实际重量统计；旅客不论行程远近或票价多少，均按一人一次作为客运量统计。半价票、小孩票也按一人统计。

货物（旅客）周转量 指在一定时期内，由各种运输工具运送的货物（旅客）数量与其相应运输距离的乘积之总和，是反映运输业生产总成果的重要指标，也是编制和检查运输生产计划，计算运输效益、劳动生产率以及核算运输单位成本的主要基础资料。通常以吨公里和人公里为计算单位。计算货物周转量通常按发出站与到达站之间的最短距离，也就是计费距离计算。

港口货物吞吐量 指经水运进出沿海主要港区范围，并经过装卸的货物数量，包括邮件及办理托运手续的行李、包裹以及补给运输船舶的燃、物料和淡水。货物吞吐量按货物流向分为进口、出口吞吐量，按货物交流性质分为外贸货物吞吐量和国内贸易货物吞吐量。货物吞吐量的货类构成及其流向，是衡量港口生产能力大小的重要指标。

邮政行业业务总量 指以货币形式表现的邮政企业为社会提供各类邮政通信服务或其他服务的总数量。计算方法为各类邮政通信服务业务的实物量分别乘以相应的不变单价，求出各类业务的货币量后加总求得。该指标反映了一定时期邮政通信业务发展的总成果，是观察邮政通信业务发展变化总趋势的综合性指标。

快递业务量 指企业收寄的各类快递业务总数量，由受理用户委托的企业负责统计。包括国内同城快递业务量、国内异地快递业务量、港澳台快递业务量、国际快递业务量。

电信业务总量 指以货币形式表示的电信企业为社会提供的各类电信服务的总数量。包括固定话音业务总量、固定数据及互联网业务总量、固定增值及其他业务总量、移动话音业务总量、移动数据及互联网业务总量、移动增值及其他业务总量。

长途光缆线路长度 指长途光缆线路的实际长度。架空的光缆按实际杆路长度统计，埋设地下、水底的光缆按沟长统计。

本地网中继光缆线路长度 指本地网内各业务节点之间，从起点至终点所经由的光缆线路实际长度。架空光缆按实际杆路长度统计，埋设地下、水底的光缆按埋设光缆的沟长统计。

移动电话基站数 指为小区服务的无线收发信设备，处理基站与移动台之间的无线通信，在移动交换机与移动台之间起中继作用，监视无线传输质量的全套设备数。

3G 移动电话基站数 指报告期末本电信企业 3G 移动通信网络上实际使用的 NoFe-B 数量。包括 TF-SCFMA 基站、WCFMA 基站和 CFMA2000 基站。

4G 移动电话基站数 指报告期末本电信企业 4G 移动通信网络上实际使用的 Node-B 数量。包括 TD-LTE 基站和 FDD-LTE 基站。

互联网宽带接入端口 指用于接入互联网用户的各类实际安装运行的宽带接入端口的数量。

网站数 指报告期末企业拥有和维护的，在互联网上可浏览的网站数，不包括企业内网。网站是指在公共互联网上，面向公众使用的，基于 TCP/IP 协议的计算机系统，以域名本身或者“WWW.＋域名”为网址的 web 站点，由地址、软件、硬件和内容组成。

电子商务销售金额 指报告期内企业（单位）借助网络订单而销售的商品和服务总额。借助网络订单指通过网络接受订单，付款和配送可以不借助于网络。

电子商务采购金额 指报告期内企业（单位）借助网络订单而采购的商品和服务总额。借助网络订单指通过网络发送订单，付款和配送可以不借助于网络。

电子商务交易平台 指在电子商务活动中为交易双方或多方提供交易撮合及相关服务的信息网络系统的总和。

Explanatory Notes on Main Statistical Indicators

Freight (Passenger)Traffic refers to the volume of freight (passenger)transported with various means. Freight transport is calculated in tons and passenger traffic is calculated in the number of persons. Despite the type of freight and traveling distance, the freight transport is calculated in the actual weight of the goods; and despite the traveling distance and ticket price, the passenger traffic is calculated by the principle that one person can be counted only once in one travel. The passengers who travel with a half price ticket or a child ticket is also calculated as one person. The freight (passenger) traffic provides a quantitative measure to show how the transport industry serves the national economy and people, and is also an important indicator for planning the transport industry and for studying the development scale and speed of the transport industry.

Freight Ton-kilometers (Passenger-kilometers) refer to the sum of the products of the volume of transported cargo (passengers) multiplying by the transport distance. It is an important indicator to reflect the achievement of transportation industry. Normally, the shortest distance between the departure station and the destination station (i.e., the payable distance) is the basis to calculate the freight ton-kilometers. This is an important indicator to show the total results of the transport industry, to prepare and examine the transport plan and to measure the efficiency, the labour productivity and the unit cost of transport.

Volume of Freight Handled in Ports refers to the volume of cargo passing in and out the harbor area of the major coastal ports and having been loaded and unloaded. The volume includes that of the postal matters, registered luggage and fuels, materials and fresh water as supplies of the ships. The volume of freight handled may be classified by direction of flow as freight for import and freight for export, or by nature of cargo as freight for domestic trade and freight for foreign trade. As an important indicator, the volume of freight handled by type of cargo and by main flow direction reflects the production capacity of ports.

Business Volume of Post Services refers to the total amount of post services or other services provided by the post departments for society. The calculation method is that the physical quantity of each type of postal communication service business is multiplied by the corresponding constant unit price, and the monetary quantity of each type of service is obtained and summed up. This indicator reflects the total results of the development of postal communication services in a certain period of time, and is a comprehensive indicator for observing the general trend of development and change of postal communication services.

Business Volume of Express Services refers to the total number of various types of express delivery services received and received by the enterprise, and the enterprises entrusted by the user are responsible for statistics. Including domestic city express business volume, domestic off-site express business volume, Hong Kong, Macao and Taiwan express business volume, international express business volume.

Business Volume of Telecommunication Services refers to the total number of telecommunication services provided by telecommunication enterprises in the form of money for the society. Including the total volume of fixed voice services, fixed data and total

Internet services, fixed value–added and other services, total mobile voice services, total mobile data and Internet services, mobile value–added and other business.

Long–Distance Cable Line Length refers to the actual length of the long–distance cable line. The overhead optical cable is counted according to the actual length of the pole. The underground and underwater cables are counted according to the length of the trench.

Local Network Trunk Cable Length Refers to the actual length of the cable line between the service nodes in the local network and from the starting point to the destination. The overhead optical cable is counted according to the actual length of the pole. The underground and underwater optical cables are counted according to the length of the buried optical cable.

Number of Mobile Phone Base Stations refers to the wireless transceiver device serving the cell, handles the wireless communication between the base station and the mobile station, and acts as a relay between the mobile switch and the mobile station to monitor the total number of devices for wireless transmission quality.

Number of 3G Mobile Phone Base Stations refers to the number of NoFe–B actually used on the 3G mobile communication network of the telecommunications enterprise at the end of the reporting period. It includes TF–SCFMA base station, WCFMA base station, and CFMA2000 base station.

Number of 4G Mobile Phone Base Stations refers to the number of Node–B actually used on the 4G mobile communication network of the telecommunications enterprise at the end of the reporting period. It includes TD–LTE base station and FDD–LTE base station.

Internet Broadband Access Port refers to the number of broadband access ports that are actually installed and operated for accessing Internet users.

Websites refers to the number of websites owned and maintained by enterprises at the end of the reporting period, excluding the intranet. A website is a web site on the public Internet, accessible to the public, based on the TCP/IP protocol, with the domain name itself or the "WWW.+ domain name" as its URL, consisting of address, software, hardware and content.

E–commerce sales amount refers to the total amount of goods and services sold by an enterprise (unit) through online orders during the reporting period. With the help of a network order refers to the acceptance of orders over the network, payment and distribution can be made without the help of the network.

E–commerce purchase amount refers to the total amount of goods and services purchased by an enterprise (unit) through the help of a network order during the reporting period. With the help of a network order, an order is sent over the network, and payment and distribution can be made without the help of the network.

E–commerce trading platform refers to the sum of information network systems that provide transaction matching and related services for both parties or parties in e–commerce activities.

16 批发和零售业
WHOLESALE AND RETAIL TRADES

简 要 说 明

一、本篇资料的主要内容

本篇资料主要反映了全市批发和零售业经营情况和效益情况，主要包括批发和零售业商品流转及财务情况、亿元以上商品交易市场、社会消费品零售总额等内容。

二、本篇资料的来源

本篇资料来源于批发和零售业统计年报和定期报表统计资料。由市统计局外经贸易统计处整理提供。

Brief Introduction

I. Main Content

Data in this chapter show the development of wholesale and retail trade of the whole city, mainly including the circulation and financial indices of commodities in the wholesale and retail trade, commodity exchange markets over 100 million yuan, total retail sales of consumer goods, etc.

II. Source of Data

Data in this chapter are based on annual report and regular reports of wholesale and retail trade. Data in this chapter are prepared and compiled by the Division of Trade and External Economic Relations Statistics of Qingdao Municipal Bureau of Statistics.

16-1 社会消费品零售总额（1985-2020年）

TOTAL RETAIL SALES OF CONSUMER GOODS (1985-2020)

单位：万元 (10 000 yuan)

年份 Year	消费品零售总额 Total Retail Sales of Consumer Goods	批发零售业 Wholesale and Retail Trades	住宿餐饮业 Hotels and Catering Services	其他行业 Others
1985	307222	231477	16996	18753
1986	364091	269418	21384	27118
1987	432569	310658	23319	32617
1988	590538	434572	32304	45449
1989	619941	450812	34083	56303
1990	658264	484770	35568	67863
1991	760562	566767	43320	56812
1992	888411	666911	53045	67392
1993	1381791	1029750	79918	96567
1994	1873212	1346723	126809	202134
1995	2362682	1627640	184925	304133
1996	2687133	1858214	218582	318787
1997	2979302	2084958	239542	357685
1998	3328902	2294750	274412	406348
1999	3710897	2678209	310962	385994
2000	4215480	3067944	381840	397499
2001	4824874	3498744	498046	426179
2002	5464940	4080963	625827	394750
2003	6315866	5169609	830717	315540
2004	7299288	6119422	993279	186587
2005	8479672	7118804	1146604	214264
2006	9885247	8226694	1403617	254936
2007	11805893	9702897	1783908	319089
2008	14456246	12590079	1505564	360603
2009	16728814	13761257	2464719	502838
2010	18923835	16550240	2373595	
2011	22172581	19408076	2764505	
2012	25331596	22147219	3184377	
2013	28650167	25076367	3573800	
2014	32182505	28179596	4002909	
2015	35481601	31012690	4468911	
2016	39141939	34175128	4966811	
2017	43214295	37751718	5462577	
2018	47427204	41340208	6086996	
2019	51265971	44158221	7107750	
2020	52034957	46836540	5198417	

注：1. 自2003年开始消费品零售总额不再包括制造业零售额和农民对非农居民的销售额分组。
2. 自2005年起，住宿业从其它行业调整到住宿餐饮业中。
3. 根据第四次经济普查结果，对1993年以来的历史数据进行了调整。

Note: 1. Since 2003, retail sales of manufacturing and retail sales of rural residents to urban residents are excluded in total retail sales of consumer goods.
2. Since 2005, hotels is adjusted to hotels and catering services from the others.
3. Historical data since1993 have been adjusted according to results of the Four China Economic Census.

16-2 分市、区社会消费品零售总额（2020 年）
TOTAL RETAIL SALES OF CONSUMER GOODS BY REGION (2020)

单位：万元 (10 000 yuan)

市、区名称	Region	消费品零售总额 Total Retail Sales of Consumer Goods	按行业分	
			批发零售业 Wholesale and Retail Trades	住宿餐饮业 Hotels and Catering Services
全　市	**Whole Municipality**	**52034957**	**46836540**	**5198417**
市南区	Shinan District	6435227	5584127	851100
市北区	Shibei District	6429180	5752014	677166
李沧区	Licang District	4012192	3754271	257921
崂山区	Laoshan District	3753745	3436255	317490
西海岸新区	West Coast New Area	11263599	10049737	1213862
黄岛区	Huangdao District	11128668	9916766	1211902
保税港区	Qingdao Free Trade Port Area of China	134931	132971	1960
城阳区	Chengyang District	3828946	3392185	436760
城阳区（不含高新区）	Chengyang District (Excluding High tech District)	3677058	3257457	419601
高新区	High tech District	151888	134728	17160
即墨区	Jimo District	4720192	4400203	319990
胶州市	Jiaozhou	5674755	5221451	453304
平度市	Pingdu	3127811	2822958	304853
莱西市	Laixi	2789310	2423338	365971

16-3 限额以上批发和零售业商品销售、库存情况(2020年)
SALES AND INVENTORIES OF WHOLESALE AND RETAIL COMMODITIES ABOVE DESIGNATED SIZE (2020)

单位：万元(10 000 yuan)

项目	Item	商品销售额 Commodity Sales	#批发额 Wholesale Amount	零售额 Retail Sales	库存额 Inventory
总　计	**Total**	**112809415.2**	**97116245.4**	**15693169.8**	**5722830.3**
国有企业	State-owned Enterprises	2348050.6	2314943.0	33107.6	97958.1
集体企业	Collective-owned Enterprises	101884.9	101884.9	0.0	5.8
其它企业	Other Enterprises	110359479.7	94699417.5	15660062.2	5624866.4
农、林、牧产品批发	Products Wholesale of Agriculture, Forestry and Animal Husbandry Products Wholesale	3424750.3	3403242.5	21507.8	241975.8
食品、饮料及烟草制品批发	Wholesale of Food, Beverages and Tobaccos	9125122.6	8856890.3	268232.3	696456.6
纺织、服装及家庭用品批发	Retail of Textiles, Garments and Daily Consumer Articles	13643978.6	13294883.5	349095.1	342297.4
文化、体育用品及器材批发	Wholesale of Culture, Sports Appliances and Equipment	1352292.4	1339040.1	13252.3	91909.1
医药及医疗器材批发	Wholesale of Medicines and Medical Appliances	3629360.5	3621112.5	8248.0	350789.9
矿产品、建材及化工产品批发	Wholesale of Mineral Products, Building Materials and Chemical Products	57119179.8	56964396.9	154782.9	1835654.0
机械设备、五金产品及电子产品批发	Wholesale of Machinery, Hardware and Electronic Equipment	7633200.9	7480040.6	153160.3	410124.8
贸易经纪与代理	Trade Broker and Agency	550153.2	473801.9	76351.3	19715.7
其它批发业	Other Wholesale not Classified Elsewhere	684899.9	682541.6	2358.3	11903.9
综合零售	Integrated Retail Trade	2473192.1	50508.3	2422683.8	449239.1
食品、饮料及烟草制品专门零售	Retail of Food, Beverages and Tobaccos	316467.7	72534.9	243932.8	46903.4
纺织、服装及日用品专门零售	Retail of Textiles, Garments and Daily Consumer Articles	1160259.7	201617.1	958642.6	286920.1
文化、体育用品及器材专门零售	Retail of Culture, Sports Appliances and Equipment	252903.0	57559.9	195343.1	86216.6
医药及医疗器材专门零售	Retail of Medicines and Medical Appliances	859001.7	104825.5	754176.2	93244.7
汽车、摩托车、燃料及零配件专门零售	Retail of Motor Vehicles, Motorcycles, Fuel and Parts	5951565.7	202814.3	5748751.4	485726.5
家用电器及电子产品专门零售	Retail of Household Electric Appliances and Electronic Products	691411.3	69186.1	622225.2	50628.0
五金、家具及室内装饰材料专门零售	Retail of Hardware, Furniture and Decoration Materials	79606.1	87.3	79518.8	16805.3
货摊、无店铺及其他零售业	Non-shop and Other Retails	3862069.7	241162.1	3620907.6	206319.4

16-4 限额以上批发和零售业商品分类销售额（2019年）

CLASSIFIED SALES OF WHOLESALE AND RETAIL AND RETAIL COMMODITIES ABOVE DESIGNATED SIZE (2019)

单位：万元 (10 000 yuan)

项目	Item	销售总额 Total Sales Value	#批发总额 Wholesale Value	零售总额 Retail Value
销售总额	**Total Sales Value**	**103720056.9**	**88370055.2**	**15350001.7**
1. 粮油、食品类	Grain & Oil and Food	7306737.8	5755802.7	1550935.1
其中：粮油类	Which of: Grain and Oil	1783476.4	1562788.4	220688.0
肉禽蛋类	Meat, Poultry and Eggs	2581454.4	2322464.5	258989.9
水产品类	Aquatic Products	590513.3	550696.1	39817.2
蔬菜类	Vegetable and Fruit	239734.2	150340.3	89393.9
干鲜果品类	Dried and Fresh Fruit	758525.0	519010.3	239514.7
2. 饮料类	Beverages	443135.5	125341.7	317793.8
3. 烟酒类	Tobacco and Liquor	2066357.6	1713897.2	352460.4
4. 服装、鞋帽、针纺织品类	Clothing, Shoes, Hats and Textiles	3381646.8	2073212.8	1308434.0
（1）服装类	Clothing	1553848.7	779339.9	774508.8
（2）鞋帽类	Shoes and Hats	692052.2	225412.1	466640.1
（3）针纺织品类	Knitwear and Textiles	1079104.8	1023188.6	55916.2
5. 化妆品类	Cosmetics	273217.6	68485.8	204731.8
6. 金银珠宝类	Gold, Silver and Jewellery	292655.9	72109.5	220546.4
7. 日用品类	Articles for Daily Use	1172620.7	613980.8	558639.9
其中：可穿戴智能设备	Which of: Wearable smart devices	35240.4	25205.8	10034.6
8. 五金、电料类	Hardware and Electrical Materials	414237.0	397103.8	17133.2
9. 体育、娱乐用品类	Sports and Recreation Articles	134713.2	46915.8	87797.4
其中：照相器材类	Which of: Photographic Apparatus	26563.9	2298.2	24265.7
10. 书报杂志类	Newspapers and Magazines	181599.4	55031.8	126567.6
11. 电子出版物及音像制品类	E-journals and Video Products	4191.8	844.5	3347.3
12. 家用电器和音像器材类	Household Appliances and Video Appliances	12713310.2	9922355.7	2790954.5
其中：能效等级为1级和2级的商品	Which of: Products with energy efficiency grades 1 and 2	2667160.2	956356.5	1710803.7
其中：智能家用电器和音像器材	Which of: Smart household appliances and audio-visual equipment	1068162.3	664775.7	403386.6
13. 中西药品类	Traditional Chinese and Western Medicines	2801575.2	2069568.0	732007.2
其中：西药类	Which of: Western Medicines	2221999.2	1681477.8	540521.4
中草药及中成药类	Traditional Chinese Medicines	140438.8	60382.1	80056.7
14. 文化办公用品类	Cultural and Offices Appliances	1662771.7	1021486.4	641285.3
其中：计算机及其配套产品	Which of: Computer and Related Products	1164750.2	832088.3	332661.9
15. 家具类	Furniture	209568.2	160223.4	49344.8
16. 通讯器材类	Communication Appliances	627808.9	320756.7	307052.2
其中：智能手机	Which of: Smart phones	566317.1	278998.7	287318.4
17. 煤炭及制品类	Coal and Related Products	4076822.4	4058639.1	18183.3
18. 木材及制品类	Wood and Wooden Products	1139725.0	1139725.0	
19. 石油及制品类	Petroleum and Related Products	14236362.1	12404366.2	1831995.9
20. 化工材料及制品类	Chemical Materials and Related Products	7821864.6	7821864.6	
其中：化肥类	Which of: Fertilizers	267396.1	267396.1	
21. 金属材料类	Metal Materials	24845887.9	24845887.9	
22. 建筑及装潢材料类	Building and Decoration Materials	1323105.7	1260783.2	62322.5
23. 机电产品及设备类	Mechanical and Electrical Products	2441519.2	2397346.4	44172.8
其中：农机类	Which of: Agricultural Machineries	10798.5	10798.5	
24. 汽车类	Automobiles	6062417.6	2084438.4	3977979.2
其中：新能源汽车	Which of: New energy vehicles	308173.8	169917.0	138256.8
25. 种子饲料类	Seeds and Feedstuff	1786448.1	1786448.1	
26. 棉麻类	Cotton, Flax	411941.6	407516.1	4425.5
27. 其他类	Others	5887815.2	5745923.6	141891.6

注：此表为定期报表数据。
Note: The data are from regular reports.

16-5 限额以上批发业财务状况（2020年）
FINANCIAL POSITION OF ENTERPRISES ABOVE DESIGNATED SIZE OF WHOLESALE TRADE (2020)

单位：万元 (10 000 yuan)

指标	Indicator	合计 Total	国有经济 State-owned Enterprises	集体经济 Collective-owned Enterprises	外商及港澳台经济 Foreign Funded Enterprises and Enterprises with Funds from Hong Kong, Macao and Taiwan	其它 Other Enterprises
单位数	**Number of Enterprises**	**2431**	**25**	**2**	**77**	**2327**
年末资产负债	**Year-end Assets-Liability**					
资产总计	Total Assets	42658363	1052769		2637419	38904667
流动资产合计	Sub-total of Current Assets	37219773	894978		1973016	34290506
负债合计	Total Liabilities	34439768	851343		1592313	31942376
所有者权益合计	Total Owners' Equity	8188053	198383		1045106	6934793
损益及分配	**Loss, Profits and Distribution**					
营业收入	Revenue from Principal Business	88228855	2097830		2834235	83214208
营业成本	Cost of Principal Business	84940334	2060936		2697342	80107755
营业税金及附加	Taxes and Extra Charges on Principal Business	228397	1149		3287	223791
营业利润	Profits from Principal Business	666310	10812		47537	607024
其他业务利润	Profits from other Business	606300	16		6546	599738
销售费用	Operating Costs	1595313	15425		62715	1515881
管理费用	Management Expenses	740783	7707		46120	678230
财务费用	Financial Expenses	270940	7886		7767	255316
利润总额	Total Profits	723231	13427		48143	660719
经济效益	**Economic Benefit**					
商品经营费用率 %	Ratio of Operating Costs to Revenue from Principal Business	1.81	0.74		2.21	1.82
商品销售利润率 %	Ratio of Profit to Sales Revenue	0.82	0.64		1.70	0.79

注：限额以上批发业企业中，由于包含了部分视同法人单位，因此财务指标数据资产≠负债+所有者权益。
Note: In wholesale enterprises above designated size, as some deemed legal entities are included, the financial index data asset ≠ liability + owner's equity.

16-6 限额以上零售业财务状况（2020年）
FINANCIAL POSITION OF ENTERPRISES ABOVE DESIGNATED SIZE OF RETAIL TRADE (2020)

单位：万元 (10 000 yuan)

指标	Indicator	合计 Total	国有经济 State-owned Enterprises	集体经济 Collective-owned Enterprises	外商及港澳台经济 Foreign Funded Enterprises and Enterprises with Funds from Hong Kong, Macao and Taiwan	其它 Other Enterprises
单位数	**Number of Enterprises**	**764**	**6**		**41**	**717**
年末资产负债	**Year-end Assets-Liability**					
资产总计	Total Assets	7484818	27142		1158703	6298973
流动资产合计	Sub-total of Current Assets	5438446	16042		884980	4537424
负债合计	Total Liabilities	6405678	10648		820804	5574227
所有者权益合计	Total Owners' Equity	1509101	16390		337899	1154812
损益及分配	**Loss, Profits and Distribution**					
营业收入	Revenue from Principal Business	14174408	29363		2065747	12079299
营业成本	Cost of Principal Business	12423224	19892		1719625	10683707
营业税金及附加	Taxes and Extra Charges on Principal Business	37428	111		9740	27577
营业利润	Profits from Principal Business	140836	4405		51475	84957
其他业务利润	Profits from other Business	147681	18		22811	124853
销售费用	Operating Costs	1135025	2387		185157	947480
管理费用	Management Expenses	382814	2607		109638	270569
财务费用	Financial Expenses	69799	35		2800	66963
利润总额	Total Profits	154633	4679		52614	97340
经济效益	**Economic Benefit**					
商品经营费用率 %	Ratio of Operating Costs to Revenue from Principal Business	8.01	8.13		8.96	7.84
商品销售利润率 %	Ratio of Profit to Sales Revenue	1.09	15.94		2.55	0.81

注：限额以上零售业企业中，由于包含了部分视同法人单位，因此财务指标数据资产≠负债+所有者权益。
Note: In retail enterprises above designated size, as some deemed legal entities are included, the financial index data asset ≠ liability + owner's equity.

16-7 分市、区城乡亿元商品交易市场分布情况（2020年）
BASIC STATISTICS ON COMMODITY EXCHANGE MARKETS OF TRANSACTION VALUE OVER 100 MILLION YUAN BY REGION (2020)

市、区名称	Region	亿元商品交易市场数量（个）Number of Commodity Exchange Markets of Transaction Value over 100 Million Yuan (unit)			亿元商品交易市场成交额（亿元）Turnover of Commodity Exchange Markets of Transaction Value over 100 Million yuan (100 million yuan)		
		合计 Total	#综合市场 Integrated Markets	#专业市场 Special Markets	合计 Total	#综合市场 Integrated Markets	#专业市场 Special Markets
全　市	**Whole Municipality**	**59**	**17**	**42**	**1259**	**519**	**740**
市南区	Shinan District						
市北区	Shibei District	7	1	6	70	43	27
李沧区	Licang District	4	1	3	36	10	26
崂山区	Laoshan District	2		2	4		4
西海岸新区	West Coast New Area	8	2	6	59	23	36
黄岛区	Huangdao District	7	2	5	53	23	30
保税港区	Qingdao Free Trade Port Area of China	1		1	6		6
城阳区	Chengyang District	1	1		243	243	
城阳区（不含高新区）	Chengyang District (Excluding High tech District)	1	1		243	243	
高新区	High tech District						
即墨区	Jimo District	9	1	8	610	138	472
胶州市	Jiaozhou	19	9	10	167	45	122
平度市	Pingdu	9	2	7	70	18	52
莱西市	Laixi						

主要统计指标解释

社会消费品零售总额　指各种经济类型的批发和零售业、住宿和餐饮业以及其他行业对城乡居民和社会集团的消费品零售额总和。该指标从2003年开始不再包括制造业零售额和农民对非农居民的零售额。

商品购进总额　指从本企业（单位）以外的单位和个人购进（包括从国外直接进口）作为转卖或加工后转卖的商品。这个指标反映批发零售贸易业从国内、国外市场上购进商品的总量。商品购进总额包括：(1)从工农业生产者购进的商品；(2)从出版社、报社的出版发行部门购进的图书、杂志和报纸；(3)从各种类型的批发零售贸易企业（单位）购进的商品；(4)从其他单位购进的商品，如从机关、团体、企业、单位购进的剩余物资，从餐饮业、服务业购进的商品，从海关、市场管理部门购进的缉私和没收的商品，向居民收购的废旧商品等；(5)从国（境）外直接进口的商品，但不包括企业（单位）为自身经营用和未通过买卖行为而收入的商品以及销售退回、商品损益等。

商品销售总额　指对本企业（单位）以外的单位和个人出售（包括对国（境）外直接出口）的商品。这个指标反映批发零售贸易业在国内市场上销售商品以及出口商品的总量。商品销售总额包括：(1)售给城乡居民和社会集团消费用的商品；(2)售给工业、农业、建筑业、运输邮电业、批发零售贸易业、餐饮业、服务业等作为生产、经营使用的商品；(3)售给批发零售贸易业作为转卖或加工后转卖的商品；(4)对国（境）外直接出口的商品。不包括：出售本企业（单位）自用的废旧包装用品，未通过买卖行为付出的商品，经本单位介绍，由买卖双方直接结算，本单位只收取手续费的业务，购货退出的商品以及商品损耗和损失等。

Explanatory Notes on Main Statistical Indicators

Total Retail Sales of Consumer Goods　refers to the sum of retail sales of consumer goods sold by all sectors of the national economy to urban and rural residents and social groups. Sectors of the national economy include wholesale and retail trade, accommodation and catering trade and others.Since 2003, retail sales of manufacture and retail sales of rural residents to urban residents are excluded in total retail sales.

Total Purchases of Commodities　refers to the total value of purchases of commodities by the enterprises (establishments) from other establishments or individuals (including direct import from abroad) for the purpose of re-selling, either with or without further processing of the commodities purchased. This indicator is used to show the total value of purchases of commodities by wholesale and retail establishments from domestic and overseas markets. The total purchases include：1. agricultural and industrial products purchased from producers；2. books, magazines and newspapers purchased from distribution departments of the publishers；3. commodities purchased from wholesale and retail establishments of different status of registration；4. commodities purchased from other units, such as surplus materials purchased from government agencies, enterprises or institutions, commodities purchased from catering and service establishments, confiscated goods purchased from customs authorities or market management agencies, second-hand goods and wastes purchased from residents；and 5.commodities directly imported from abroad. Excluded are commodities purchased by enterprises (establishments) for use in their own business operation, commodities obtained without buying or selling procedures, rejected commodities, etc.

Total Sales of Commodities　refers to value of commodities sold by the establishments to other establishments and individuals (including direct export). This indicator is used to show the total value of sales of commodities at domestic markets and export. The total sales include：1. commodities sold to urban and rural residents and social groups for their consumption；2. commodities sold to establishments in industry, agriculture, construction, transportation, post and telecommunications, wholesale and retail trades, hotels and catering services, and public utility for their production and operation；3. commodities sold to wholesale and retail establishments for re-selling, with or without further processing；and 4. commodities for direct export to other countries. Excluded are selling of waste packaging materials used by the establishments (units) themselves, commodities transferred without buying or selling procedures, commission income from brokerage in transactions for which settlement is directly handled by buyers and sellers, rejected commodities in the purchase, loss in commodities, etc.

住宿、餐饮业和旅游 17

HOTELS, CATERING SERVICES AND TOURISM

简 要 说 明

一、本篇资料的主要内容

本篇资料主要反映了全市住宿和餐饮业的经营情况和效益情况以及旅游的基本情况，主要包括住宿和餐饮业经营情况和财务情况、涉外以及国内旅游基本情况等方面的内容。

二、本篇资料的来源

本篇资料中住宿和餐饮业经营情况和财务情况资料来源于住宿和餐饮业统计年报和定期报表统计资料；旅游资料来源于市文化和旅游局。由市统计局外经贸易统计处整理提供。

Brief Introduction

I. Main Content

The information in this chapter mainly reflects the operating conditions and benefits of the accommodation and catering industry in the city, as well as the basic conditions of tourism, mainly including the operating conditions and financial conditions of the accommodation and catering industry, foreign-related and domestic tourism, and other aspects.

II. Source of Data

The information on the operating and financial status of the accommodation and catering industry in this article comes from the accommodation and catering industry statistical annual reports and periodic statement statistics; the tourism information comes from the Qingdao Municipal Bureau of Culture and Tourism. Provided by the Foreign Economic and Trade Statistics Department of Qingdao Municipal Bureau of Statistics.

17-1 限额以上住宿和餐饮业经营情况（2020 年）
OPERATION OF ACCOMMODATION AND CATERING SERVICES ABOVE DESIGNATED SIZE (2020)

单位：万元 (10 000 yuan)

项目	Item	营业额 Turnover	客房收入 Income from Guest Rooms	餐费收入 Catering Income	商品销售收入 Income from Commodity Sales	其他收入 Other Income
总　计	**Total**	**1034766.8**	**196862.7**	**763268.6**	**17082.4**	**57553.1**
一、住宿业	**Hotels**	**357220.3**	**184588.4**	**126384.3**	**5146.4**	**41101.2**
国有企业	State-owned Enterprises	48969.1	18015.7	21811.4	979.3	8162.7
集体企业	Collective-owned Enterprises	403.3	214.2	189.1	0.0	0.0
其他企业	Other Enterprises	307847.9	166358.5	104383.8	4167.1	32938.5
独立门店	Freestanding Stores	313798.3	152116.8	117731.0	4745.2	39205.3
连锁总店（总部）	General Chain Stores (Headquarters)	3001.6	1451.8	1250.5	248.4	50.9
连锁直营店	Chain Store	2515.1	1893.2	1.5	5.6	614.8
连锁加盟店	Franchise Store	18143.9	17216.4	337.7	39.2	550.6
其他	Others	19761.4	11910.2	7063.6	108.0	679.6
五星	Five Star Class	52410.1	18075.0	25384.8	1316.6	7633.7
四星	Four Star class	59838.8	23900.1	29190.6	992.9	5755.2
三星	Three Star class	32334.9	16398.6	11364.9	657.8	3913.6
二星	Two Star class	101.1	101.1	0.0	0.0	0.0
一星	One Star class	2203.2	1706.5	492.5	0.0	4.2
其他	Others	210332.2	124407.1	59951.5	2179.1	23794.5
二、餐饮业	**Catering Services**	**677546.5**	**12274.3**	**636884.3**	**11936.0**	**16451.9**
国有企业	State-owned Enterprises	8365.3	2114.2	6089.7	37.3	124.1
集体企业	Collective-owned Enterprises	1898.8	249.5	789.6	666.2	193.5
其他企业	Other Enterprises	667282.4	9910.6	630005.0	11232.5	16134.3
独立门店	Freestanding Stores	286998.1	10777.2	253243.8	7298.5	15678.6
连锁总店	General Chain Stores	260588.4	0.0	257461.9	2886.5	240.0
连锁直营店	Chain Store	12453.1	0.0	12333.9	87.7	31.5
连锁加盟店	Franchise Store	45254.2	0.0	45180.4	73.8	0.0
其他	Others	72252.7	1497.1	68664.3	1589.5	501.8

17-2 限额以上住宿业财务状况（2020 年）
FINANCIAL SITUATION OF HOTELS ABOVE DESIGNATED SIZE (2020)

单位：万元 (10 000 yuan)

指标	Indicator	合计 Total	国有经济 State-owned Enterprises	集体经济 Collective-owned Enterprises	外商及港澳台经济 Foreign Funded Enterprises and Enterprises with Funds from Hong Kong, Macao and Taiwan	其它 Other Enterprises
单位数	**Number of Enterprises**	**273**	**21**	**1**	**8**	**243**
年末资产负债	**Year-end Assets-Liability**					
资产总计	Total Assets	1336137	124348		175007	1035609
流动资产合计	Sub-total of Current Assets	710708	64234		71295	574913
负债合计	Total Liabilities	1062007	78313		136542	846784
所有者权益合计	Total Owners' Equity	280275	45260		38465	195745
损益及分配	**Loss,Profits and Distribution**					
营业收入	Revenue from Principal Business	343335	47574		36640	258725
营业成本	Cost of Principal Business	127913	14657		11900	101224
营业税金及附加	Taxes and Extra Charges on Principal Business	1470	194		59	1217
营业利润	Profits from Principal Business	-67922	-9211		-4024	-54656
其他业务利润	Profits from other Business	6597	999		3007	2591
销售费用	Operating Costs	126157	25024		7025	93846
管理费用	Management Expenses	138061	17858		18979	101192
财务费用	Financial Expenses	19521	-113		2811	16823
利润总额	Total Profits	-61335	-6160		-3462	-51684
其他	**Others**					
应付职工薪酬	Employee Compensation Payable	113494	23962		12329	77039
营业利润率	Operating Profit Margin	-19.78	-19.36		-10.98	-21.13

17-3 限额以上餐饮业财务状况（2020年）
FINANCIAL SITUATION OF CATERING SERVICES ABOVE DESIGNATED SIZE (2020)

单位：万元 (10 000 yuan)

指标	Indicator	合计 Total	国有经济 State-owned Enterprises	集体经济 Collective-owned Enterprises	外商及港澳台经济 Foreign Funded Enterprises and Enterprises with Funds from Hong Kong, Macao and Taiwan	其它 Other Enterprises
单位数	**Number of Enterprises**	**339**	**8**	**1**	**16**	**314**
年末资产负债	**Year-end Assets-Liability**					
资产总计	Total Assets	515875	15330		166048	333981
流动资产合计	Sub-total of Current Assets	282641	11583		60585	209986
负债合计	Total Liabilities	430069	4471		148072	276757
所有者权益合计	Total Owners' Equity	86724	10859		19055	57062
损益及分配	**Loss, Profits and Distribution**					
营业收入	Revenue from Principal Business	662238	8084		255234	397158
营业成本	Cost of Principal Business	393683	6300		132495	252997
营业税金及附加	Taxes and Extra Charges on Principal Business	409	16		161	231
营业利润	Profits from Principal Business	6576	-110		17958	-11026
其他业务利润	Profits from other Business	3558	0		1540	2018
销售费用	Operating Costs	173104	596		77522	94986
管理费用	Management Expenses	81414	2270		25109	53911
财务费用	Financial Expenses	6127	6		2506	3616
利润总额	Total Profits	13859	7		19889	-5792
其他	**Others**					
应付职工薪酬	Employee Compensation Payable	129783	2079		44024	83295
营业利润率	Operating Profit Margin	0.99	-1.36		7.04	-2.78

17-4 入境旅游人数（2000-2020 年）
NUMBER OF OVERSEA VISITOR ARRIVALS (2000-2020)

项目	Item	2000 年	2005 年	2009 年	2010 年	2011 年
总计	**Total**	**260592**	**684407**	**1000670**	**1080511**	**1156391**
一、外国人	**Foreigner**	**177098**	**596177**	**801424**	**826628**	**809043**
# 韩国	Korea	69878	295111	363181	382225	298096
日本	Japan	67215	177121	261553	242082	216755
美国	USA	10384	23284	28745	35539	45842
俄罗斯	Russia	4820	12062	9525	15793	15750
德国	Germany	3820	10646	14735	21626	26178
新加坡	Singapore	6321	6060	17453	13444	16626
英国	UK	2798	5744	9103	17639	23955
加拿大	Canada	1865	4397	7741	9279	12007
法国	France	2491	5166	7030	11766	12019
意大利	Italy	1555	3963	3747	3867	7028
澳大利亚	Australia	1817	4257	6641	8223	15465
菲律宾	Philippines	7947	3459	7800	14140	14259
泰国	Thailand	780	3261	3685	2572	3271
印尼	Indonesia	1 241	2349	4221	7863	8128
新西兰	New Zealand	442	710	2029	1597	6265
二、港澳和台湾同胞	**Chinese Compatriots from Hong Kong, Macao and Taiwan**	**60367**	**88230**	**199246**	**253883**	**347348**

17-5 入境旅游收入（2000-2019 年）
EARNINGS FROM INTERNATIONAL TOURISM (2000-2019)

项目	Item	2000 年	2005 年	2008 年	2009 年	2010 年
总计	**Total**	**118164**	**340899**	**347645**	**377000**	**399688**
旅游购物	Shopping	20742	67047	66053	70763	74104
住宿费	Accommodation	17443	37277	37198	41093	43933
餐饮费	Dining	11223	33557	33374	36569	38747
交通费	Transportation	35252	128112	9039	9877	145551
邮电费	Postal and Telecommunication	5502	18394	17382	18812	19081
文化娱乐费	Culture and Entertainment	6894	20240	20163	22394	24032
游览	Sightseeing			18773	21037	22978
其他	Other Services		36272	145663	29745	31262

注：因新冠疫情影响，2020 年未开展此项统计。
Note: Due to the impact of the new crown epidemic, this statistics will not be carried out in 2020.

单位：人次 (person-time)

2012 年	2013 年	2014 年	2015 年	2016 年	2017 年	2018 年	2019 年	2020 年
1270113	**1282814**	**1280526**	**1338098**	**1410494**	**1443715**	**1535733**	**1702568**	**188361**
877593	**905415**	**951732**	**996191**	**1042213**	**1056800**	**1118860**	**1258240**	**155124**
338383	338191	366584	389832	68010	432430	451046	507854	73266
185613	146080	135179	140762	151832	164095	174147	192257	41274
48431	54178	57907	62771	68010	73905	79392	87014	9079
26432	26519	25356	28529	30534	32540	37053	44720	4896
26311	19014	21723	23425	25456	26636	28646	33256	5874
16316	16305	19975	21310	23713	25257	26060	29001	3942
28385	19496	22817	23812	26133	28006	28942	31577	3582
11678	9727	9483	10659	11592	12544	15473	16849	2245
15595	21422	17828	19388	21836	23507	25035	27218	2708
5622	5679	7705	8747	9234	10627	11559	12904	1563
16644	11149	15339	16798	18839	20304	21491	23344	1679
7546	18630	6668	7300	7891	8489	9837	11300	1327
2369	3692	4803	5331	5784	6628	7367	8331	2075
4571	10011	6568	5692	6220	7388	9816	11161	515
6448	1452	2549	2872	3352	4230	7367	7965	429
392520	**377399**	**328794**	**342511**	**368281**	**386915**	**416873**	**444328**	**33237**

单位：万元 (10 000 yuan)

2011 年	2012 年	2013 年	2014 年	2015 年	2016 年	2017 年	2018 年	2019 年
441171	**519495**	**511158**	**503900**	**566742**	**656966**	**694103**	**798374**	**1084000**
80823	93872	94055	109246	122473	141970	129381	102192	264604
59823	59378	58577	62232	69879	81004	77184	150893	134308
40191	51378	51065	44041	49589	57483	68091	122950	95717
134425	170238	180945	160492	180791	209573	249113	273842	351975
16720	23014	22950	19400	21593	25031	33248	16766	42059
36132	32832	32103	33409	36271	42045	42201	62273	70243
51705	32832	32152	44192	49930	57879	40674	33532	90839
21353	55951	39311	30888	36216	41982	54211	35927	34254

17-6 国内旅游人数及收入（2020 年）
NUMBER OF DOMESTIC TOURISTS AND INCOME (2020)

指标	Indicator	单位	Unit	2020 年
国内旅游人数	Number of Domestic Tourists	万人次	10000 person-times	6293.5
1. 过夜旅游者人数	Number of Overnight Tourists	万人次	10000 person-times	2294
2. 不过夜旅游者（一日游人数）	Number of Non-overnight (One-day Sightseeing) Tourists	万人次	10000 person-times	3999.5
国内旅游人均花费	Per Capita Expenditure of Domestic Tourist	元	yuan	1605.9
国内旅游收入	Earnings from Domestic Tourism	亿元	100 million yuan	1010.7
1. 接待过夜旅游者收入	Earnings from Overnight Tourists	万元	10000 yuan	6133000
2. 接待不过夜旅游者（一日游）收入	Earnings form Non-overnight (One-day Sightseeing) Tourists	万元	10000 yuan	3974000

主要统计指标解释

住宿餐饮业营业额　指住宿和餐饮业法人企业、产业活动单位在经营活动中因提供服务或销售商品等取得的收入，包括客房收入、餐费收入、商品销售收入和其他收入。客房收入指住宿和餐饮业法人企业、产业活动单位在经营活动中因提供住宿服务取得的客房收入。餐费收入指住宿和餐饮业法人企业、产业活动单位因为顾客提供就餐服务取得的收入，包括经烹饪、调制加工后出售的各种食品，如主食、炒菜、凉拌菜等的收入。商品销售收入指住宿和餐饮业法人企业、产业活动单位伴随服务而出售商品所取得的收入。其他收入指营业收入中除客房收入、餐费收入、商品销售收入以外的其他收入，包括娱乐、健身和商务服务等。

国内旅游者　是指不以谋求职业、获取报酬为目的，离开惯常居住环境，到国内其它地方从事参观、游览、度假等旅游活动（包括外出探亲、疗养、考察、参加会议和从事商务、科技、文化、教育、宗教活动过程中的旅游活动），出行距离超过 10 公里，出游时间超过 6 小时，但不超过 12 个月的我国大陆居民。

入境旅游者　指来我国参观、访问、旅行、探亲、访友、休养、考察、参加会议和从事经济、科技、文化、教育、体育、宗教等活动的外国人、华侨、港澳和台湾同胞的人数。不包括外国在我国的常驻机构，如领事馆、通讯社、企业办事处的工作人员；来我国常住的外国专家、留学生以及在岸逗留不过夜人员。

Explanatory Notes on Main Statistical Indicators

Business Revenue of Hotels and Catering Services refers to revenue received from providing services or selling commodities by corporate enterprises and establishments engaged in hotel and catering services, including income from hotel rooms, from catering services, from selling of commodities and from other services. Income from hotel rooms refers to income of corporate enterprises and establishments by providing lodging services. Income from catering services refers to income of corporate enterprises and establishments by providing catering services, including selling of cooked or prepared foods such as stable food, cooked dishes or cold dishes. Income from selling of commodities refers to income of corporate enterprises and establishments by selling commodities that accompany the services they provide. Income from other activities refers to income received other than income from hotel rooms, catering services or selling of commodities, such as income from providing recreation, fitness or business services.

Domestic Tourists refers to residents in mainland China who are not for the purpose of seeking employment, remuneration, and leaving the usual living environment, elsewhere to engage in domestic visitors, sightseeing, vacation travel (including to go out to visit relatives, infirmary, observing, participate in the meeting and engage in business, science and technology, culture, education, religious activities in the course of tourism activities), trip distance of more than 10 km, trips longer than six hours, but not more than 12 months.

Entrance Tourists refers to foreigners, overseas Chinese, Chinese compatriots from Hong Kong, Macao and Taiwan coming to China for sight-seeing, visits, tours, family reunions, vacations, study tours, conferences and other activities of a business, scientific and technological, cultural, educational and religious nature. It does not include representatives and employees of resident institutions of foreign countries in China such as embassies, consulates, news agencies and offices of foreign companies and organizations, nor does it include long-term foreign experts or students residing in China, or persons in transition without spending a night in China.

教育、科技和文化 18

EDUCATION SCIENCE & TECHNOLOGY AND CULTURE

简要说明

一、本篇资料的主要内容

本篇资料主要反映了全市教育、科技和文化事业基本情况。教育部分主要包括高等教育、中等教育、初等教育、成人教育、职业教育、幼儿园等方面的基本情况。科技部分主要包括科研机构、科学技术奖励、大中型工业企业技术开发情况。文化部分主要包括文化、文物、广播、电视、报纸杂志出版、图书出版等方面的发展状况。

二、本篇资料的来源

1. 教育部分，技工学校的资料来源于市人力资源和社会保障局，其他资料来源于市教育局。

2. 科技部分，科研机构及科技奖励资料来源于市科技局，大中型工业企业科技活动资料来源于市统计局统计调查年报。

3. 文化部分，图书、杂志、报纸出版有关资料来源于青岛出版集团、海大出版社其他资料来源于市文化和旅游局。

本篇资料由市统计局人口就业和社会科技文化统计处整理提供。

Brief Introduction

I. Main Content

Data in this chapter show the basic conditions of education, science & technology and culture. Data on education show the development of higher education, secondary education, primary education, adult education, vocational education and kindergartens. Data on science & technology show the basic conditions of science research institutions, scientific and technological achievements and prizes, scientific & technological activities of large and medium-size industrial enterprises. Data on culture show the basic conditions of arts, cultural relics, broadcasting, television and publication of newspapers, magazines and books.

II. Source of Data

1.In education component, data on the basic conditions of technical schools are provided by Qingdao Municipal Bureau of Human Resources and Social Security, and the other data on education are provided by Qingdao Municipal Bureau of Education.

2. In science & technology component, data on science research institutions and scientific & technological achievements and prizes are provided by Qingdao Municipal Bureau of Science and Technology. Data on scientific and technological activities are from the annual report of scientific and technological activities, which is provided by Qingdao Municipal Bureau of Statistics.

3. In the cultural part, the related materials for books, magazines, and newspapers are from Qingdao Publishing Group and Haida Publishing House. Other materials are from the Municipal Bureau of Culture and Tourism.

The information in this article was compiled and provided by the Population, Employment and Social Science, Technology and Culture Statistics Department of Qingdao Bureau of Statistics.

18-1 各级各类学校基本情况（2020 年）
BASIC STATISTICS ON SCHOOLS BY LEVEL AND TYPE OF SCHOOL (2020)

项目	Item	学校数（所）Schools (unit)	毕业生数（人）Graduates (person)	招生数（人）New Students Enrollment(person)	在校学生数（人）Students Enrollment(person)	教职工数（人）Teachers and Staff (person)	#专任教师 of which : Full-time Teachers
研究生	Postgraduates	8	12930	19504	53188		
普通高等学校	Regular Institutions of Higher Education	27	107147	133158	430671	35540	24321
中等专业学校	Specialized Secondary Schools	6	9964	12925	33122	735	594
技工学校	Technical Schools	23	7457	10180	33432	2318	1924
职业学校	Vocational Schools	44	17144	15808	49767	7499	6325
普通中学	Regular Secondary Schools	340	132668	157824	430426	44894	41460
初中	Junior Secondary Schools	259	93575	97496	286078	27700	26168
高中	Senior Secondary Schools	81	39093	60328	144348	17194	15292
小学	Primary Schools	706	97886	115758	603763	36448	35288
特殊教育学校	Special Education Schools	14	275	437	2292	743	623
幼儿园	Kindergartens	2527	99183	127609	344579	43070	26058
成人高等学校	Adult Institutions of Higher Education	1	48870	82597	172423		
成人中等学校	Adult Institutions of Secondary Education	2	136	964	976	15	7
成人初等学校	Adult Primary Education Schools						

18-2 主要年份各级各类学校在校学生数

MAJOR YEAR'S STUDENTS ENROLLMENT OF SCHOOLS BY LEVEL AND TYPE OF SCHOOL

单位：人 (person)

年份 Year	普通高等学校 Regular Institutions of Higher Education	中等学校 Secondary Schools	中等专业学校 Specialized Secondary Schools	普通中学 Regular Secondary Schools	职业中学 Vocational Schools	技工学校 Technical Schools	小学 Primary Schools
1949	1007	13804	1600	12204			213470
1952	2761	27951	3770	24181			413286
1957	3133	56689	4985	51604	100		482397
1962	4381	62646	2791	58639	243	973	522921
1965	2987	99605	9405	88187	1490	523	788485
1970	320	222521	105	220262	2154		728433
1975	1151	350309	3144	346403		762	928153
1978	3465	464584	4269	457460	2000	865	634905
1980	6783	325935	5195	318193	1344	1203	816970
1985	10631	327446	11475	279915	33945	2111	691341
1988	14408	352576	11819	306943	28933	4881	629212
1990	15433	351365	15118	296163	34568	5516	632314
1991	15491	353410	14618	298568	34421	5803	612772
1992	16470	367480	14763	307903	38242	6572	585381
1993	23858	383043	16877	318179	40743	7244	583585
1994	25018	420077	20582	347667	43734	8094	593419
1995	24908	450212	23744	372335	46044	8089	595891
1996	26076	468561	26951	382760	50131	8719	607284
1997	27434	463619	28543	362305	61640	11131	626749
1998	29507	442525	28757	336918	65989	10861	625308
1999	33681	459520	26955	352238	70236	10091	583594
2000	46131	497391	25192	398458	63894	9847	534922
2001	60728	542400	25358	443693	62003	11346	499147
2002	82539	575599	27421	467628	67085	13465	478634
2003	168439	586704	28948	461435	75221	21100	467560
2004	201739	598804	30881	436117	101553	30253	476897
2005	239761	569230	33522	391148	106400	38160	479781
2006	260339	554308	32051	365192	116487	40578	483892
2007	264917	558527	28011	360410	130156	39950	484775
2008	269314	582932	25330	373884	143126	40592	477230
2009	275157	564476	22739	377427	127792	36518	465031
2010	284788	535079	24014	380025	98560	32480	462722
2011	291453	505051	25905	373226	74892	31028	479513
2012	296645	489103	27005	369580	65419	27099	484985
2013	300246	484025	28389	365110	61594	28932	496343
2014	313486	479260	28751	362599	58170	29740	516529
2015	322260	467231	33038	355401	48590	30202	536492
2016	340875	470333	32710	356107	50927	30589	547231
2017	346328	490796	32882	372196	52539	33179	550540
2018	397982	500872	31879	385443	51440	32110	569923
2019	415824	521758	30555	408953	49517	32733	583784
2020	430671	546747	33122	430426	49767	33432	603763

18-3 主要年份普通高等学校基本情况
MAJOR YEAR´S BASIC STATISTICS ON REGULAR INSTITUTIONS OF HIGHER EDUCATION

单位：人 (person)

年份 Year	学校数（所）Schools (unit)	毕业生数 Graduates	招生数 New Students Enrollment	在校学生数 Students Enrollment	教职工数 Teachers and Staff	#专任教师 of which：Full-time Teachers
1949	1		250	1007	779	226
1952	2	262	565	2761	12530	308
1957	2	356	755	3133	1308	622
1962	5	647	653	4381	1866	749
1965	3	741	529	2987	1539	623
1970	2	684		320	1178	486
1975	2	460	473	1151	1353	582
1978	4	739	1782	3465	2829	1176
1980	6	431	1717	6783	4182	1606
1985	7	1828	3823	10631	5561	2181
1988	7	3496	4687	14408	6875	2499
1990	7	4495	4745	15433	7305	2624
1991	7	4880	4954	15491	7282	2489
1992	7	4458	5428	16470	7344	2523
1993	7	3140	9449	23858	7366	2520
1994	4	7059	8042	25018	7466	2650
1995	4	7828	7978	24908	7545	2682
1996	4	6691	7956	26076	7606	2745
1997	4	7091	8503	27434	7790	2813
1998	4	6912	8849	29507	7662	2907
1999	4	7202	11584	33681	7662	2928
2000	6	7128	18427	46131	8030	3278
2001	6	8991	22787	60728	8706	4058
2002	7	13053	29731	82539	9517	4723
2003	25	25747	61975	168439	18911	10293
2004	25	34860	70022	201739	21437	12347
2005	25	46114	79725	239761	23078	13894
2006	25	55931	79094	260339	24881	15195
2007	25	68354	78728	264917	25956	16005
2008	25	75198	86878	269314	26654	16805
2009	25	69475	81025	275157	26983	16870
2010	25	70450	82220	284788	28145	16996
2011	22	79466	84434	291453	28151	17120
2012	22	79791	87981	296645	29445	18183
2013	22	78974	85707	300246	28958	18396
2014	22	77503	90127	313486	28944	18587
2015	24	79784	92251	322260	29620	19213
2016	26	86270	100525	340875	30390	20151
2017	25	95006	98983	346238	32013	21231
2018	25	105580	118247	397982	32628	21576
2019	24	103684	126423	415824	34259	22849
2020	27	107147	133158	430671	35540	24321

18-4 各类成人教育基本情况（2020 年）
BASIC STATISTICS ON ADULT EDUCATION (2020)

单位：人 (person)

各类学校	Schools by Type of School	学校数（所） Schools (unit)	毕业生数 Graduates	招生数 New Students Enrollment	在校学生数 Students Enrollment	教职工数 Teachers and Staff	#专任教师 of which : Full-time Teachers
总 计	**Total**	**3**	**49006**	**83561**	**173399**	**15**	**7**
成人高等教育	Adult Higher Education	1	48870	82597	172423		
成人中等教育	Adult Secondary Education	2	136	964	976	15	7
成人中等专业学校	Adult Specialized Secondary Schools	2	136	964	976	15	7

18-5 分市、区普通中学情况（2020 年）
BASIC STATISTICS ON REGULAR SECONDARY SCHOOLS BY REGION (2020)

单位：人 (person)

市、区名称	Region	普通高中 Regular Senior Secondary Schools				普通初中 Regular Junior Secondary Schools			
		学校数 Schools (unit)	毕业生数 Graduates	招生数 New Students Enrollment	在校生数 Students Enrollment	学校数 Schools (unit)	毕业生数 Graduates	招生数 New Students Enrollment	在校生数 Students Enrollment
合　计	**Whole Municipality**	**81**	**39093**	**60328**	**144348**	**259**	**93575**	**97496**	**286078**
市直属	Municipal Level	22	9937	13691	34692	3	2580	2912	8445
市南区	Shinan District					11	2832	3474	9554
市北区	Shibei District	1	149	222	610	24	7360	8996	24298
李沧区	Licang District	2	20	12	32	14	4162	4998	13580
崂山区	Laoshan District	2				12	2518	3438	8656
西海岸新区	West Coast New Area	14	6113	10207	22970	41	16326	17071	48623
城阳区	Chengyang District	8	2749	4486	10563	19	8115	9980	26929
即墨区	Jimo District	12	6206	8987	21684	32	15138	15689	45642
胶州市	Jiaozhou	7	4430	7407	17565	24	12000	11561	33527
平度市	Pingdu	8	6048	9956	23205	47	14506	12216	36772
莱西市	Laixi	4	3441	5330	12849	30	8038	6805	28884
高新区	High tech District	1		30	178	2		356	1168

18-6 分市、区职业中学、小学情况（2020年）
BASIC STATISTICS ON VOCATIONAL SECONDARY SCHOOLS AND PRIMARY SCHOOLS BY REGION (2020)

单位：人 (person)

市、区名称	Region	职业中学（职业高中） Vocational Secondary Schools(Vocational High Schools)				小学 Primary School			
		学校数 Schools (unit)	毕业生数 Graduates	招生数 New Students Enrollment	在校生数 Students Enrollment	学校数 Schools (unit)	毕业生数 Graduates	招生数 New Students Enrollment	在校生数 Students Enrollment
全　市	**Whole Municipality**	**44**	**17144**	**15808**	**49767**	**706**	**97886**	**115758**	**603763**
市直属	Municipal Level	22	2854	2034	6884		43	82	408
市南区	Shinan District					27	5464	6595	34816
市北区	Shibei District					64	9711	11628	62949
李沧区	Licang District					38	5514	8840	43129
崂山区	Laoshan District					29	4101	4973	25810
西海岸新区	West Coast New Area	10	5511	5392	16531	99	16925	21737	111619
城阳区	Chengyang District	3	1092	966	2974	51	10248	14847	74311
即墨区	Jimo District	3	1876	1633	4660	158	15324	15489	84935
胶州市	Jiaozhou	1	2281	2243	6996	75	11333	12107	64120
平度市	Pingdu	2	1531	1884	5067	102	12229	11541	67208
莱西市	Laixi	3	1999	1656	6655	62	6750	7110	31456
高新区	High tech District					1	244	809	3002

注：市直属中有一所十二年一贯制学校，校数在高中中统计。
Note: There is a twelve-year consistent school in the municipality, and the number of schools is counted in high schools.

18-7 分市、区中小学教职工情况（2020年）

BASIC STATSTICS ON TEACHERS AND STAFF IN SECONDARY AND PRIMARY SCHOOLS BY REGION (2020)

单位：人 (person)

市、区名称	Region	普通中学 Regular Secondary Schools		职业中学 Vocational Secondary Schools		小学 Primary School	
		教职工数 Teachers and Staff	#专任教师 of which：Full-time Teachers	教职工数 Teachers and Staff	#专任教师 of which：Full-time Teachers	教职工数 Teachers and Staff	#专任教师 of which：Full-time Teachers
全　市	**Whole Municipality**	**44894**	**41460**	**7499**	**6325**	**36448**	**35228**
市直属	Municipal Level	4269	3493	2452	1961		
市南区	Shinan District	1328	1154			2134	2024
市北区	Shibei District	2762	2587			3544	3392
李沧区	Licang District	1601	1452			2177	2105
崂山区	Laoshan District	1076	1028			1711	1651
西海岸新区	West Coast New Area	7263	6775	1610	1436	6254	6094
城阳区	Chengyang District	3897	3565	634	560	3713	3579
即墨区	Jimo District	6943	6617	768	657	5460	5273
胶州市	Jiaozhou	4451	4179	649	530	4288	4195
平度市	Pingdu	6498	6107	708	632	4687	4535
莱西市	Laixi	4313	4073	678	549	2434	2337
高新区	High tech District	493	430			46	43

18-8 分市、区幼儿园基本情况（2020年）
BASIC STATISTICS ON KINDERGARTENS BY REGION (2020)

单位：人 (person)

市、区名称	Region	幼儿园（所） Kindergartens (unit)	幼儿数 Children	教职工数 Teachers and Staff	#专任教师 of which: Full-time Teachers
全　市	**Whole Municipality**	**2527**	**344579**	**43070**	**26058**
市直属	Municipal Level				
市南区	Shinan District	68	14795	2433	1231
市北区	Shibei District	217	38255	4515	2471
李沧区	Licang District	113	31074	3998	1898
崂山区	Laoshan District	116	16116	2587	1490
西海岸新区	West Coast New Area	500	71325	8874	5359
城阳区	Chengyang District	193	38321	5067	3290
即墨区	Jimo District	464	43080	5708	3240
胶州市	Jiaozhou	323	40904	5029	3100
平度市	Pingdu	388	34166	3096	2560
莱西市	Laixi	145	16543	1763	1419
高新区	High tech District				

18-9 科研机构基本情况（1978-2020 年）
BASIC STATISTICS ON SCIENTIFIC RESEARCH INSTITUTIONS (1978-2020)

年份 Year	独立自然科研机构（个） Independent Institutions of Natural Scientific Research (unit)	独立自然科研机构中科技人员（个） Personnel of Independent Institutions of Natural Scientific Research (person)	完成科研项目（项） Number of Scientific Research Projects Completed (item)	取得科技成果（项） Number of Achievements in S&T (item)
1978	31	2701	306	306
1980			481	297
1982	41	2345	451	451
1983	48	3182	530	530
1984	53	3312	507	507
1985	52	3673	552	552
1986	63	3998	577	577
1988	101	5199	544	510
1990	141	6046	414	931
1991	72	5665	753	753
1992	71	5726	659	659
1993	69	5545	546	546
1994	69	5540	467	467
1995	59	5286	441	441
1996	58	4738	613	613
1997	54	4577	418	418
1998	52	4142	517	517
1999	58	3771	606	606
2000	54	3637	621	621
2001	50	3191	457	457
2002	52	3248	406	406
2003	53	3246	589	589
2004	50	3226	506	506
2005	50	3234	438	438
2006	50	3291	548	548
2007	50	3432	506	506
2008	42	3709	416	416
2009	43	3727	572	572
2010	44	4088	472	472
2011	47	4548	345	345
2012	48	4967	304	304
2013	48	6057	433	433
2014	50	5438	415	415
2015	54	6037	639	639
2016	57	5722	606	606
2017	57	6017	588	588
2018	58	6017	406	406
2019	58	6417	400	400
2020	49	7379	1309	984

注：1991 年以后不包括民办科研机构。
Note: Since 1991, private institutions of scientific research are not included.

18-10 独立科学研究机构情况（2020年）
BASIC STATISTICS ON INDEPENDENT INSTITUTIONS OF SCIENTIFIC RESEARCH (2020)

项目	Item	计量单位	Unit	总计 Total	中央属 Central	地方属 Local
机构数	Number of Institutions	个	unit	49	16	33
职工人数	Staff and Workers	人	person	9162	6377	2785
科技人员	Personnel Engaged in S&T	人	person	7379	5117	2262
经费收入	Funding for S&T	万元	10 000 yuan	520620	372115	148505
经费支出	Expenditures for S&T	万元	10 000 yuan	558290	382449	175841

18-11 科学技术奖励情况（2020年）
AWARD STATISTICS ON SCIENCE AND TECHNOLOGY (2020)

项目	Item	单位	Unit	自然科学奖 Natural Science Prizes Awarded	技术发明奖 Invention Prizes Awarded	科技进步奖 Scientific and Technological Progress Prizes Awarded	国际科技合作奖 International S&T Cooperation Prizes Award	最高奖 Highest Prizes Award
国家级	National Level	项	Item	0	2	11	0	0
特等	Special Grade	项	Item	0	0	1		
#一等	First Prize	项	Item	0	0	1		
二等	Second Prize	项	Item	0	2	9		
省级	Provincial Level	项	Item	11	5	74	1	1
#一等	First Prize	项	Item	0	0	11		
二等	Second Prize	项	Item	11	3	27		
三等	Third Prize	项	Item	0	2	36		
市级	Municipal Level	项	Item	10	9	131	4	2
#一等	First Prize	项	Item	1	0	17		
二等	Second Prize	项	Item	6	4	72		
三等	Third Prize	项	Item	3	5	42		

注：1. 国际科技合作奖、最高奖不分等级。
　　2. 国家级科学技术奖励为初评公示结果，最终结果暂未公布。

Note: 1.There is no grade in international scientific and technological cooperation prizes award and highest prizes award.
　　2.The national science and technology awards are the results of the preliminary evaluation and the final results have not yet been announced.

18-12　文化、文物事业机构、人员数（2020 年）
NUMBER OF CULTURAL AND CULTURAL RELIC INSTITUTIONS AND PERSONNEL (2020)

项目	Item	文化机构数（个） Number of Cultural Institutions (unit)		文化人员数（人） Number of Cultural Personnel (Person)	
		2020 年	2019 年	2020 年	2019 年
一、艺术事业	**Art**				
1.艺术表演团体	Art Performance Troupes	9	9	908	852
2.艺术表演场所	Art Centers	7	9	156	194
3.艺术展览创作机构	Art Creation Institutions	3	4	30	26
4.艺术研究机构	Art Research Institutions				
5.艺术展览机构	Art Exhibition Institutions				
6.其他	Others				
二、图书馆事业	**Libraries**				
公共图书馆	Public Libraries	12	12	272	278
#县（区）级图书馆	County Libraries	11	11	177	180
三、群众文化事业	**Mass Culture**				
1.群众艺术馆	Mass Art Centers				
2.文化馆	Cultural Palaces	12	12	211	221
3.文化站	Cultural Centers	138	134	619	553
4.其他	Others				

18-13 文化部门艺术剧团情况（2020 年）
STATISTICS ON ART TROUPES OF CULTURAL DEPARTMENT (2020)

项目	Item	剧团数（个）Number of Troupes (unit)	职工人数（人）Staff and Workers (person)	演出场次（场）Number of Performances (show)	观众人数（万人次）Number of Spectators (10000 person-times)	演出收入（万元）Income from Ticket Sales (10000 yuan)	#财政补贴（万元）Appropriation Funds (10000 yuan)
总　计	**Total**	**9**	**908**	**1400**	**57.62**	**1933.9**	**13471.5**
一、按单位性质分	**Divided by unit nature**						
事业	Career	6	405	900	41.23	1102.9	7072.9
企业	Enterprise	3	503	500	16.42	831	6398.6
二、按剧种分	**Grouped by Type of Drama**						
1. 话剧团	Drama Troupes	1	103	200	8.4	198.6	1757.6
2. 歌舞团	Song and Dance Troupes	1	313	129	2.8	78.2	3646.4
3. 戏曲剧团	Local Opera Troupes	4	195	600	29.2	596.6	2316.9
#京剧	of which：Beijing Opera	1	87	100	3.0	136.9	994.6
4. 曲艺团	Recitation and Ballad Troupes						
5. 文工团（艺术团）	Cultural and Performance Troupes						

18-14 图书馆、文化馆情况
STATISTICS ON LIBRARIES AND CULTURAL CENTERS

项目	Item	单位	Unit	2020 年		2019 年	
				全市合计 Total	#市区 Urban Area	全市合计 Total	#市区 Urban Area
公共图书馆	**Pubilc Libraries**	个	unit	**12**	**9**	**12**	**9**
工作人员	Staff and Workers	人	person	272	216	278	229
藏书册数	Collection Books	千册	1000 copies	8402	7365	8121	7127
阅览席位	Seating Capacity of Reading Rooms	张	piece	5984	4663	6400	5143
读者人数	Readers	万人次	10000 person/times	233.55	201.74	520	454.5
文化馆	**Cultural Centers**	个	unit	**12**	**9**	**12**	**9**

主要统计指标解释

普通高等学校 指通过国家普通高等教育招生考试，招收高中毕业生为主要培养对象，实施高等学历教育的全日制大学、独立设置的学院、独立学院和高等专科学校、高等职业学校及其他普通高教机构。

大学、独立设置的学院主要实施本科及本科层次以上的教育。独立学院主要实施本科层次的教育。高等专科学校、高等职业学校实施专科层次的教育。其他普通高教机构是指承担国家普通招生计划任务不计校数的机构，包括普通高等学校分校、大专班等。

成人高等学校 指通过国家成人高等教育招生考试，招收具有高中毕业或同等学力的人员为主要培养对象，利用函授、业余、脱产等多种形式，对其实施高等学历教育的学校。包括：开放大学、管理干部学院、教育学院、独立函授学院、其他成人高教机构等。其他成人高教机构是指承担国家成人招生计划任务不计校数的机构。

科技活动人员 指直接从事科技活动、专门从事科技活动管理和为科技活动提供直接服务，累计的实际工作时间占全年制度工作时间 10% 及以上的人员。

文化事业机构 指从事专业文化工作和为专业文化工作服务的独立建制的单独核算的单位。不包括这些单位另外举办独立核算的其他机构和各部门的业余文化组织。

Explanatory Notes on Main Statistical Indicators

Colleges and Universities refers to full-time universities, independently established colleges, independent colleges and technical colleges, higher vocational schools and other general higher education institutions that have passed the national general higher education enrollment examination and recruited high school graduates as the main training objects.

Universities and independent colleges mainly implement education at the undergraduate level and above. Independent colleges mainly implement education at the undergraduate level. Higher technical colleges and higher vocational schools implement college-level education. Other general higher education institutions refer to institutions that undertake the tasks of the national general enrollment plan without counting the number of schools, including general higher education branch schools, college classes, etc.

Adult Higher School refers to a school that has passed the national adult higher education enrollment examination, recruited people with high school graduation or equivalent academic ability as the main training object, and implemented higher education for them through various forms such as correspondence, part-time, and full-time education. Including: Open University, Management College, Education College, Independent Correspondence College, other adult higher education institutions, etc. Other adult higher education institutions refer to institutions that undertake the tasks of the national adult enrollment plan without counting the number of schools.

Personnel Engaged in S&T Activities refer to personnel directly engaged in S&T activities, in the management of S&T activities, and in providing direct service to S&T activities, who spend over 10% of the total working hours in a year in S&T activities.

Cultural Institutions refer to units, which have their own organizational system and independent accounting system and specialize in or serve cultural development. They exclude other establishments run by these cultural institutions and amateur cultural groups established by various departments.

体育、卫生和民政、司法 19

SPORTS, PUBLIC HEALTH AND CIVIL AFFAIRS, JUDICIAL AFFAIRS

简要说明

一、本篇资料的主要内容

本篇资料反映了全市体育、卫生、民政、司法等社会事业的基本情况。体育部分主要包括主要年份运动员、教练员、裁判员发展人数、体育运动破纪录、获奖情况。卫生部分主要包括各类卫生机构及其人员、床位数。民政部分主要包括婚姻登记、社会救济、社会福利事业基本情况、殡葬服务情况。司法部分主要包括律师、公证、调解、社会治安基本情况。

二、本篇资料的来源

1. 体育部分来源于市体育局。

2. 卫生部分来源于市卫健委。

3. 民政部分来源于市民政局。

4. 司法部分，社会治安资料来源于市公安局，其他资料来源于市司法局。

本篇资料由市统计局人口就业和社会科技文化统计处整理提供。

Brief Introduction

I. Main Content

Data in this chapter show the basic conditions of sports, public health, civil affairs and judicial affairs. Data on sports are mainly including the number of athletes, coaches and referees, conditions of record and awards. Data on public health are mainly including the number of health institutions, personnel and beds. Data on civil affairs are mainly including the conditions of marriage registration, social relief, social welfare and funeral services. Data on judicial affairs are mainly including the conditions of lawyers, notarization, mediation and social order.

II. Source of Data

1. Data on sports are provided by Qingdao Municipal Bureau of Physical.

2. The health part comes from the Qingdao Municipal Health Commission.

3. Data on civil affairs are provided by Qingdao Municipal Bureau of Civil Affairs.

4. In judicial affairs component, data on social order are provided by Qingdao Municipal Bureau of Public Security and the other data are provided by Qingdao Municipal Bureau of Justice.

The information in this article was compiled and provided by the Population, Employment and Social Science, Technology and Culture Statistics Department of Qingdao Bureau of Statistics.

19-1　体育事业情况（2000-2020 年）

STATISTICS ON SPORTS (2000-2020)

单位：人 (person)

项　目	Item	2000	2005	2007	2009	2010	2011	2012	2013	2014	2015	2016	2017	2018	2019	2020
体育部门职工人数	**Staff and Workers in Sports Commissions**	**849**	**834**	**772**	**910**	**1015**				**847**	**795**	**857**	**654**	**682**	**784**	**780**
# 运动员	Athletes	90	87	55	512	287				287	259		284	1123	2259	2787
教练员	Coaches	174	235	211	106	170	136					120	133	134	131	133
重点体校	Key Sports School	126	117	249	97	115	129						1061	1370	881	980
业余体校	Spare Time Sports Schools	142	223	145	160								1537	1846	1702	1807
体育专业队	Professional Sports Teams	135	132	121	144	192	87	84	42	38	17	17	5	5		
优秀运动员	Excellent Athletes	90	87	55	72	146	57									
优秀运动队专职教练员	Full-time Coaches of Excellent Sports Teams	18	23	47	92	97	54				89	120				
等级裁判员发展人数	**Certified Referees**	**1114**	**275**	**781**	**292**	**212**	**510**	**558**	**512**	**514**	**490**	**167**		**511**	**347**	**519**
# 二级	Second Grades	451	275	781	252	169	510	484	463	514	490	116		319	122	236
三级	Third Grades	616													90	283
等级运动员发展人数	**Certified Athletes**	**343**	**260**	**108**	**512**	**229**	**436**	**362**	**362**	**283**	**259**		**176**	**327**	**829**	**328**
# 二级	Second Grades	209	260	108	448	229	436	256	362	283	259		176	290	730	328
三级	Third Grades	46														
少年级	Junior Grades	88														

19-1 续表
Continued

项 目	Item	单位	Unit	2000	2005	2007	2009	2010	2011	2012	2013	2014	2015	2016	2017	2018	2019	2020
全年获得奖牌数	**Number of Medals Won in the Year**	枚	**piece**	**347.5**	**669**	**481**	**602**	**754**	**829**	**746**	**659**	**576.5**	**596**	**729.5**	**3032**	**849**	**1507.5**	**666.5**
#国家级金牌	Golden Medals at National Level	枚	piece	45	62	61	30	14	105	88	90	48	51	101	104	76	142	40
国家级银牌	Silver Medals at National Level	枚	piece	28	48	38	23	7	49	100	44	21	44	56	91	81	127	32
省级金牌	Golden Medals at Provincial Level	枚	piece	116.5	187	116	207	459	225	193	174.5	202.5	149	219.5	214.5	264	428.5	372.5
省级银牌	Silver Medals at Provincial Level	枚	piece	62	174	93	149	116	155	110	111.5	121.5	126	135	140	161	289	222
体育运动破全国记录	**Records Broken the National Records**																	
项目	Number of Events	项	item		2	1	1	1	2	1						1		
人数	Number of Persons	人	person		2	1	1	1	2	1						1		
次数	Number of Times	人次	person-times		4	1	1	1	2	1						1		
体育运动破全省记录	**Records Broken the Provincial Records**																	
项目	Number of Events	项	item	7	3			1										
人数	Number of Persons	人	person	7	1			1										
次数	Number of Times	人次	person-times	7	3			1								15		

19-2 主要年份卫生事业基本情况

MAJOR YEAR'S BASIC STATISTICS ON PUBLIC HEALTH

年份 Year	卫生机构数（个）Health Institutions (unit)	#医院 of which: Hospitals	医疗床位数（张）Beds in Health Institutions (bed)	#医院 of which: Hospitals	卫生技术人员（个）Medical and Technical Personnel (person)	#医生 of which: Hospitals	每千人口拥有医生数（人）Number of Doctors per 1000 Population (person)	每千人口拥有床位数（张）Number of Hospital Beds per 1000 Population (bed)
1949	80	26	1079	970	2637	1292	0.32	0.27
1952	260	34	2943	1691	3748	1559	0.37	0.70
1957	624	45	5163	2656	6941	2578	0.53	1.07
1962	849	149	7167	4526	8279	2972	0.64	1.55
1965	912	162	8428	5003	9051	3586	0.73	1.72
1970	712	170	8613	6603	9591	3761	0.70	1.60
1975	959	181	10902	9078	13558	4566	0.80	1.90
1978	1192	212	13084	10709	16921	5893	1.01	2.24
1980	1253	212	14170	11345	19265	6781	1.14	2.38
1985	1517	219	18469	13214	23413	9694	1.55	2.95
1990	1563	235	23541	16586	27932	13761	2.08	3.56
1991	1579	235	23727	16796	27772	13227	1.98	3.54
1992	1562	236	24765	17269	28305	13157	1.95	3.67
1993	1540	237	24885	17469	28705	13312	1.97	3.68
1994	1335	242	24732	17882	28938	13535	1.99	3.64
1995	1347	228	25282	18126	29816	13840	2.02	3.69
1996	2216	228	24334	18344	30048	13790	2.00	3.53
1997	2193	239	25201	19046	31121	14400	2.07	3.62
1998	2190	237	24887	19083	31623	14327	2.05	3.56
1999	2185	235	25481	19798	31965	14453	2.06	3.62
2000	2911	231	24392	20057	32160	14860	2.10	3.45
2001	3199	217	24755	20313	32765	15772	2.22	3.48
2002	3050	213	21370	20662	31469	13371	1.87	2.99
2003	3111	213	23980	21605	32337	13452	1.87	3.33
2004	2923	219	25432	23465	32937	13953	1.91	3.48
2005	2609	235	30627	28564	33942	15008	2.03	4.13
2006	2834	232	28724	26653	34360	15451	2.06	3.83
2007	2006	251	30062	28107	33807	15018	1.98	3.97
2008	1985	249	32350	29874	36574	16260	2.14	4.25
2009	2017	252	32803	30527	40217	16734	2.19	4.30
2010	2147	254	36066	33383	43285	17696	2.32	4.72
2011	2549	280	39980	35600	47347	18310	2.39	5.22
2012	2607	288	47254	41186	54488	21593	2.81	6.14
2013	2936	285	44876	39725	59961	24113	3.12	5.80
2014	3126	297	47081	42961	62738	24946	3.20	6.03
2015	3146	308	48601	45066	65264	26270	3.35	6.20
2016	7564	322	50649	47309	87733	27675	3.49	6.39
2017	7927	410	55798	46282	76146	30867	3.84	6.94
2018	8027	421	53154	50842	83975	34578	4.23	6.82
2019	8317	427	60519	58492	90361	37813	4.55	7.28
2020	8531	460	64423	62450	94854	39708	4.74	7.70

注：自 2016 年起，卫生机构及人员包含村卫生室。

Note：Health agency and personnel includes village clinic as of 2016.

19-3 各类卫生机构、床位、人员数(2020年底)

NUMBER OF HEALTH INSTITUTIONS, BEDS AND EMPLOYED PERSONS (END OF 2020)

项　目	Item	机构数（个）Health Institutions (unit)	床位数（张）Beds in Health Institutions (bed)	人员数（人）Personnel (person)
总　计		**8531**	**64423**	**114244**
一、医院合计	**Sub-total of Hospitals**	**460**	**62450**	**77418**
1. 医院	Hospitals	357	55452	68929
#综合医院	General Hospitals	178	33375	44859
中医医院	Hospitals Specialized in Traditional Chinese Medicine	41	7038	8739
中西医结合医院	Hospitals of Combination of Chinese and Western Medicine	6	609	742
专科医院	Specialized Hospitals	107	12891	14287
#口腔医院	Stomatological Hospitals	7	85	704
眼科医院	Ophthalmology Hospitals	11	732	992
肿瘤医院	Tumor Hospitals	2	60	79
心血管病医院	Cardiovascular Diseases Hospitals	3	1106	1159
精神病医院	Mental Hospitals	23	4439	2479
传染病医院	Infectious Disease Hospitals	2	590	588
皮肤病医院	The Skin Disease Hospital	2	100	117
骨科医院	Orthopaedics Hospitals	6	423	349
2. 卫生院	Sanitation Stations	103	6998	8489
二、社区卫生服务中心	**Neighborhood Service Centers**	**90**	**585**	**4173**
三、门诊部	**Outpatient Service Stations**	**404**	**35**	**6510**
四、诊所	**Clinics**	**2828**		**11052**
五、卫生所、医务室、护理站	**Medical Houses Nursing Station**	**340**	**40**	**1086**
六、社区卫生服务站	**Neighborhood Service Stations**	**206**	**139**	**2950**
七、急救中心	**First Aid Centers**	**7**		**234**
八、采供血机构	**Institutions of Blood Collection and Supply**	**1**		**249**
九、妇幼保健院(所、站)	**Maternity and Child Care Centers**	**12**	**385**	**1488**
十、专科疾病防治院(所、站)	**Specialized Disease Prevention & Treatment Institutions**	**6**	**232**	**255**
十一、疾病预防控制中心(防疫站)	**Centers for Disease Control and Prevention (Epidemic Prevention Stations)**	**41**		**1095**
十二、卫生监督所	**Sanitation Control Stations**	**12**		**481**
十三、卫生监督检验所(站)	**Sanitation Control and Test Stations**			
十四、计划生育技术服务机构	**Family Planning Service Institutions**	**16**		**81**
十五、健康教育所(站、中心)	**Health Education Stations**			
十六、其它卫生机构	**Other Health Institutions**	**35**	**557**	**1294**
十七、村卫生室	**Village clinic**	**4073**		**5878**

注：床位数指实有床位数。

Note： The number of beds refers to the number of beds actually available.

# 卫生技术人员 Medical and Technical Personnel				
	# 医生 Doctors	注册护士 Registered Nurses	药剂人员 Pharmacists	检验人员 Laboratory Technicians
94854	**39708**	**42760**	**4534**	**2980**
65991	**23993**	**32617**	**3547**	**2211**
58650	20993	29915	2970	1891
38728	14005	19806	1811	1174
7559	2885	3553	535	222
636	238	273	67	25
11485	3796	6126	544	467
573	264	270	6	10
652	230	364	26	21
65	22	26	8	8
974	342	503	41	28
2173	470	1519	85	46
505	169	258	27	29
87	31	39	8	9
269	106	123	12	11
7341	3000	2702	577	320
3448	**1557**	**1309**	**294**	**118**
5523	**2744**	**2324**	**200**	**122**
10777	**6483**	**4084**	**148**	**15**
1038	**606**	**383**	**13**	**2**
2515	**1241**	**942**	**220**	**47**
158	**63**	**88**	**1**	**5**
183	**49**	**79**	**1**	**53**
1189	**461**	**479**	**62**	**102**
187	**82**	**62**	**15**	**13**
782	**417**	**49**	**12**	**89**
373				
22	**11**	**3**		
742	**186**	**230**	**21**	**203**
1926	**1815**	**111**		

19-4 分市、区各类卫生机构数（2020年底）

NUMBER OF HEALTH INSTITUTIONS IN VARIOUS TYPES OF CITIES AND DISTRICTS (END OF 2020)

市、区名称	Region	机构数（个）Number of institutions (unit)	医院小计 Sub-total of Hospitals	#医院 Hospitals	#卫生院 Sanitation Stations
全　市	**Whole Municipality**	**8531**	**460**	**357**	**103**
市南区	Shinan District	440	33	33	
市北区	Shibei District	821	70	70	
李沧区	Licang District	524	44	44	
崂山区	Laoshan District	487	26	24	2
西海岸新区	West Coast New Area	1338	61	45	16
城阳区	Chengyang District	827	35	30	5
即墨区	Jimo District	1101	55	34	21
胶州市	Jiaozhou	997	36	22	14
平度市	Pingdu	1171	55	26	29
莱西市	Laixi	825	45	29	16

19-4 续表

Continued

市、区名称	Region	采供血机构 Institutions of Blood Collection and Supply	妇幼保健院（所、站）Maternity and Child Care Centers	专科疾病防治院（所、站）Specialized Disease Prevention & Treatment Institutions
全　市	**Whole Municipality**	**1**	**12**	
市南区	Shinan District	1	1	
市北区	Shibei District		2	
李沧区	Licang District		1	
崂山区	Laoshan District		1	
西海岸新区	West Coast New Area		2	
城阳区	Chengyang District		1	
即墨区	Jimo District		1	
胶州市	Jiaozhou		1	
平度市	Pingdu		1	
莱西市	Laixi		1	

社区卫生服务中心 Neighborhood Service Centers	社区卫生服务站 Neighborhood Service Stations	门诊部 Outpatient Service Stations	诊所、卫生所、医务室、护理站 Clinics Medical Houses	急救中心 First Aid Centers
90	**206**	**404**	**3168**	**7**
11	27	48	309	
25	59	75	582	1
15	45	37	380	
3	30	33	248	
15	14	71	492	1
12	5	68	289	1
2	20	25	305	1
4	0	22	236	1
1	0	22	243	1
2	6	3	84	1

疾病预防控制中心（防疫站） Centers for Disease Control and Prevention (Epidemic Prevention Stations)	卫生监督所 Sanitation Control Stations	村卫生室 Village health room	计划生育技术服务机构 Family Planning Service Institutions	其他卫生机构 Other Health Institutions
41	**12**	**4073**	**16**	**35**
1	1			7
2	2			3
1	1			
1	1	137		7
1	1	672		6
9	1	402		4
23	1	648	16	3
1	1	692		3
1	1	843		1
1	2	679		1

19-5 分市、区各类卫生床位数（2020 年底）

NUMBER OF SANITARY BEDS IN VARIOUS TYPES OF CITIES AND DISTRICTS (END OF 2020)

市、区名称	Region	床位数（张） Beds in Health Institutions (bed)	医院小计 Sub-total of Hospitals
全　市	**Whole Municipality**	**64423**	**62450**
市南区	Shinan District	6687	6081
市北区	Shibei District	13792	13748
李沧区	Licang District	4476	4438
崂山区	Laoshan District	2576	2516
西海岸新区	West Coast New Area	10555	9904
城阳区	Chengyang District	4106	4106
即墨区	Jimo District	5457	5358
胶州市	Jiaozhou	5628	5456
平度市	Pingdu	6643	6420
莱西市	Laixi	4503	4423

19-6 分市、区各类卫生人员数（2020 年底）

NUMBER OF HEALTH PERSONNEL BY CITY AND DISTRICT (END OF 2020)

市、区名称	Region	人员数（人） Personnel (person)	# 卫生技术人员 #Medical and Technical Personnel
全　市	**Whole Municipality**	**114244**	**94854**
市南区	Shinan District	14190	10222
市北区	Shibei District	24602	22918
李沧区	Licang District	8583	7530
崂山区	Laoshan District	6839	5601
西海岸新区	West Coast New Area	17949	14767
城阳区	Chengyang District	9016	7131
即墨区	Jimo District	9274	7506
胶州市	Jiaozhou	8436	6849
平度市	Pingdu	9011	7246
莱西市	Laixi	6344	5084

# 医院 Hospitals	# 卫生院 Sanitation Stations	门诊部 Outpatient Service Stations	妇幼保健院（所、站） Maternity and Child Care Centers	专科疾病防治院（所、站） Specialized Disease Centers
55452	**6998**	**35**	**385**	**232**
6081		9		
13748		6		
4438				
2489	27			
8252	1652	2	100	114
3884	222			
4404	954	13	40	
4392	1064		105	
4334	2086	5	100	118
3430	993		40	

# 医生 #Doctors	注册护士 Registered Nurses	药剂人员 Pharmacists	检验人员 Laboratory Technicians	其他人员 Other Personnel
39708	**42760**	**4534**	**2980**	**5482**
4673	5519	587	374	909
9140	9548	1029	682	1379
3317	3504	345	200	353
2469	2503	209	184	220
5957	6829	699	456	1048
2938	3205	375	239	388
3264	3098	404	234	309
2859	3149	295	205	339
3041	3277	332	232	298
2050	2128	259	174	239

19-7 提供住宿的社会服务机构单位情况(2020年)
SITUATION OF SOCIAL SERVICE INSTITUTIONS PROVIDING ACCOMMODATION (2020)

市、区名称	Region	单位数(个) Number of Institutions (unit)	年末职工人数(人) Number of Staff and Workers at Year-end (person)	年末床位数(张) Number of Beds at Year-end (bed)
全 市	**Whole Municipality**	**275**	**5879**	**43919**
市本级	Municipal Level	3	169	1070
市南区	Shinan District	25	967	3944
市北区	Shibei District	63	1372	9105
李沧区	Licang District	37	939	4461
崂山区	Laoshan District	15	364	2689
西海岸新区	West Coast New Area	29	547	4636
城阳区	Chengyang District	23	348	4718
即墨区	Jimo District	15	276	1946
胶州市	Jiaozhou	22	361	4985
平度市	Pingdu	28	192	2686
莱西市	Laixi	15	344	3679

19-8 社会救济情况(2020年)
BASIC STATISTICS ON SOCIAL RELIEF (2020)

市、区名称	Region	城镇居民最低生活保障人数(人) Number of Persons Receiving Minimum Living Allowance in Urban Area (Person)	城镇居民最低生活保障家庭数(户) Number of Households Receiving Minimum Living Allowance in Urban Area (household)	城镇低保资金支出(万元) Urban low-security capital expenditure (10 000 yuan)
全 市	**Whole Municipality**	**18919**	**13034**	**18335**
市南区	Shinan District	3047	2201	3066.4
市北区	Shibei District	11492	7743	11334.2
李沧区	Licang District	1789	1200	1731
崂山区	Laoshan District	113	59	97.2
西海岸新区	West Coast New Area	729	551	573.7
城阳区	Chengyang District	207	143	200.5
即墨区	Jimo District	524	376	505.1
胶州市	Jiaozhou	528	396	444.5
平度市	Pingdu	325	234	264.8
莱西市	Laixi	165	131	117.6

年末在院人数（人） Residences at Year-end (person)	老年人 Senior Citizens	青壮年 Young and middle-aged	少年儿童 Youth
21341	**20742**	**344**	**186**
581	85	263	185
1591	1591		
6482	6482		
2498	2482	16	
776	729	47	
2087	2087		
1895	1895		
1051	1032	18	1
1606	1606		
1465	1449		
1309	1304		

农村居民最低生活保障人数（人） Number of Persons Receiving Minimum living Allowance in Rural Area (person)	农村居民最低生活保障家庭数（户） Number of Households Receiving Minimum Living Allowance in Rural Area (household)	农村低保资金支出（万元） Rural low-security capital expenditure (10 000 yuan)
69713	**46654**	**48869**
1792	939	1351.8
12641	8694	8272.4
3244	2094	2820.1
16937	11875	15324.7
10932	7195	6543.1
18451	11955	11436.8
5716	3902	3120.1

19-9 分市、区婚姻登记情况(2020年)

BASIC STATISTICS ON MARRIAGE REGISTRATION BY REGION (2020)

市、区名称	Region	准予登记结婚 Registered Marriages		
		合计(对) Total (couple)	初婚(人) First Marriages (person)	恢复结婚(对) Resumed Marriages (couple)
全　市	**Whole Municipality**	**48748**	**67336**	**97**
市本级	Municipal Level	84	109	2
市南区	Shinan District	3967	5650	1
市北区	Shibei District	5121	6426	2
李沧区	Licang District	2790	3592	1
崂山区	Laoshan District	2649	4186	
西海岸新区	West Coast New Area	9220	12034	16
城阳区	Chengyang District	4123	5932	
即墨区	Jimo District	5978	9205	18
胶州市	Jiaozhou	4495	6224	
平度市	Pingdu	6848	9300	57
莱西市	Laixi	3473	4678	

再婚（人）Remarriages (person)		准予登记离婚（对）Registered Divorces (couple)	涉外婚姻登记（对）Registered Marriages with Foreigner (couple)
男 Male	女 Female		
14834	**15326**	**24219**	**84**
31	28	21	84
1185	1099	2203	
1960	1856	3461	
1022	966	1865	
582	530	941	
3145	3261	5019	
1156	1158	1954	
1306	1445	1929	
1336	1430	2179	
2038	2358	2968	
1073	1195	1679	

19-10 律师、公证、调解、社会治安基本情况（2000-2020 年）

BASIC STATISTICS ON LAWYERS, NOTARIZATION, MEDIATION AND SOCIAL ORDER (2000-2020)

项　目	Item	单位	Unit	2000 年	2005 年	2009 年	2010 年	2011 年
一、律师工作	**Lawyers**							
律师事务所	Law Offices	个	unit	76	116	203	222	247
律师工作者	Lawyers	人	person	1439	1941	3144	2487	2801
专职	Full-time Lawyers	人	person	971	1542	1934	2377	2643
兼职（含特邀）	Part-time Lawyers	人	person	150	73	86	94	105
请常年法律顾问单位	Units with Permanent Legal Advisors	个	unit	2508	3564	4457	4779	5180
全年办理民事代理	Agent of Civil Gases	件	case	5571	11104	29025	26935	27702
刑事辩护	Defender of Criminal Cases	件	case	1755	3003	3758	3964	4535
非诉讼事件	Agent of Non-litigious Legal Affairs	件	case	5251	6501	5897	4274	3576
解答法律询问	Agent of Legal Advisory Services	件	case	58385	27880	30123	21102	42428
代写法律事务文书	Agent of Legal Documents Written on Behalf of Clients	件	case	9335	8595	6015	6210	6762
二、公证工作	**Notarization**							
公证处	Notary Offices	个	unit	15	15	13	13	13
公证人员	Notarial Personnel	人	person	152	196	214	214	221
公证员	Notaries	人	person	106	112	118	117	119
办理公证文书	Notarized Documents	件	case	120849	105787	97019	94077	88506
三、人民调解	**People's Mediation**							
人民调解委员会	People's Mediation Committees	个	unit	9750	11480	9643	8014	8486
调解人员	Mediators	人	person	34714	46735	32675	27820	28094
调解民间纠纷	Civil Disputes Mediated	件	case	18501	13658	14660	20550	22882
四、社会治安	**Social Order**							
交通事故发生次数	Traffic Accidents	次	time	15601	7051	2570	2313	2164
死亡人数	Deaths	人	person	1371	776	402	393	374
受伤人数	Injuries	人	person	8620	6639	2943	2504	2240
经济损失	Losses	万元	10000 yuan	4815.70	2208.20	854.80	811.27	861.05
火灾发生次数	Fire Accidents	次	time	3088	1948	773	683	369
死亡人数	Deaths	人	person	10	3	5	9	1
受伤人数	Injuries	人	person	43	3		4	2
经济损失	Losses	万元	10000 yuan	1531.06	550.40	865.50	5566.11	598.20

2012 年	2013 年	2014 年	2015 年	2016 年	2017 年	2018 年	2019 年	2020 年
266	285	322	337	355	371	394	427	458
3130	3143	3637	3896	4260	4839	5451	5960	6470
2944	2980	3443	3728	4134	4578	5179		5911
107	93	110	112	123	127	129		146
5228	5374	5647	6101	6294	6952			7702
30586	31147	36317	39640	42216	47679	63277	75116	78940
4935	4858	5370	5107	4560	4936	7490	8372	6205
4251	4133	4833	4900	4624	5386	8486	9795	14569
45388	53775	33717	34003	40884	55320			
6388	7376	5961	6272	7326	7112			
13	13	13	12	12	12	12	12	14
225	244	249	242	250	264	265	256	294
118	113	119	129	125	127	125	121	129
87703	99852	100553	96085	104423	105200	88619	88370	71102
8426	8448	8027	7708	7861	7413	7366	7098	6416
27421	27035	25646	25222	26318	23918	24761	24366	23396
23999	19525	23737	23552	30084		29989	26880	31960
1951	1896	1857	1814	1759	1847	1825	1787	1751
343	333	321	313	308	324	319	315	311
1913	1840	1796	1785	1770	1828	1814	1782	1750
652.10	609.80	561.80	509.1	506.6	528.7	573.8	545.7	533.6
366	742	1170	1001	1654	1458	1269	704	
6	7	12	10	8	13	2	8	
2	11	9	3	10	9	6	7	
601.90	2348.10	1725.50	1491.0	1433.2	2739.7	3023.2	1208.2	

19-11 分区、市殡葬服务情况(2020年)

BASIC STATISTICS ON FUNERAL SERVICES (2020)

区、市名称	Region	单位数（个） Number of Institutions (unit)	年末职工人数（人） Number of Staff and Workers at Year-end (person)	火化炉数（台） Number of Cremation Furnaces (unit)	处理遗体数（具） Number of Remains Cremated (body)
全 市	**Whole Municipality**	**10**	**231**	**46**	**66921**
市本级	Municipal Level	1	43	10	13852
市南区	Shinan District				
市北区	Shibei District				
李沧区	Licang District				
崂山区	Laoshan District				
西海岸新区	West Coast New Area	2	56	6	9995
城阳区	Chengyang District	1	15	5	7111
即墨区	Jimo District	1	10	7	9918
胶州市	Jiaozhou	1	8	5	7309
平度市	Pingdu	2	31	7	12002
莱西市	Laixi	2	68	6	6734

19-11 续表
Continued

区、市名称	Region	穴位数（个）Number of Graves (uni)	本年销售穴位数 Number of Graves Saled in the Year	安葬数（具）Number of Remains Buried (body)	本年安葬数 Number of Remains Buried in the Year
全　市	**Whole Municipality**	**71199**	**615**	**38096**	**9530**
市本级	Municipal Level	21206	148	18329	428
市南区	Shinan District				
市北区	Shibei District				
李沧区	Licang District				
崂山区	Laoshan District				
西海岸新区	West Coast New Area	45622	361	16155	8996
城阳区	Chengyang District				
即墨区	Jimo District				
胶州市	Jiaozhou				
平度市	Pingdu	1910	73	1944	73
莱西市	Laixi	2461	33	1668	33

主要统计指标解释

卫生机构　按类别分为医院、社区卫生服务中心（站）、卫生院、门诊部（诊所、医务室、村卫生室）、急救中心（站）、采供血机构、妇幼保健院（所、站）、专科疾病防治院（所、站）、疾病预防控制中心（防疫站）、卫生监督所、卫生监督检验（监测、检测）所（站）、医学科学研究机构、医学教育机构、健康教育所（站）、其他卫生机构和社会团体 16 大类。

医疗卫生机构　包括医院、基层医疗卫生机构、专业公共卫生机构、其他医疗卫生机构。

（1）医院包括综合医院、中医医院、中西医结合医院、民族医院、各类专科医院和护理院，不包括专科疾病防治院、妇幼保健院和疗养院，包括医学院校附属医院。

（2）基层医疗卫生机构包括社区卫生服务中心（站）、乡镇（街道）卫生院、村卫生室、门诊部、诊所（医务室）。

（3）专业公共卫生机构包括疾病预防控制中心、专科疾病防治机构、妇幼保健机构（含妇幼保健计划生育服务中心）、健康教育机构、急救中心（站）、采供血机构、卫生监督机构、取得《医疗机构执业许可证》或《计划生育技术服务许可证》的计划生育技术服务机构。

（4）其他医疗卫生机构包括疗养院、临床检验中心、医学科研机构、医学在职教育机构、卫生监督（监测、检测）机构、医学考试中心、农村改水中心、人才交流中心、统计信息中心等卫生事业单位。

医院　包括综合医院、中医医院、中西医结合医院、民族医院、各类专科医院和护理院，不包括专科疾病防治院、妇幼保健院和疗养院，包括医学院校附属医院。

执业（助理）医师　指在医疗卫生机构中取得医师执业证书且实际从事医疗、妇幼保健、疾病防治等工作的执业医师和执业助理医师。

卫生技术人员　包括医疗卫生机构中执业医师、执业助理医师、注册护士、药师（士）、检验及影像技师（士）、卫生监督员和见习医（药、护、技）等卫生专业人员。

社会福利事业单位　指集中收养社会孤老、残、幼的机构，包括由民政部门管理的社会福利院、儿童福利院、精神病人福利院和城镇集体举办的福利院及农村集体举办的敬老院和具有收养能力的社区服务中心等。

Explanatory Notes on Main Statistical Indicators

Health Agency　according to categories, it is divided into hospitals, community health service centers (stations), health centers, outpatient departments (clinics, infirmaries, village clinics), emergency centers (stations), blood collection and supply institutions, maternal and child health care centers (stations, stations), and specialties Disease prevention and control institutes (stations, stations), disease prevention and control centers (epidemic prevention stations), sanitary supervision institutes, sanitary supervision and inspection (monitoring, testing) institutes (stations), medical scientific research institutes, medical education institutes, health education institutes (stations) , 16 categories of other health institutions and social organizations.

Medical and Health Institutions　including hospitals, primary medical and health institutions, professional public health institutions, and other medical and health institutions.

(1) Hospitals include general hospitals, hospitals of traditional Chinese medicine, hospitals of integrated traditional Chinese and western medicine, ethnic hospitals, various specialized hospitals and nursing homes, excluding specialized disease prevention and treatment hospitals, maternal and child health care hospitals, and nursing homes, including hospitals affiliated to medical schools.

(2) Primary medical and health institutions include community health service centers (stations), township (street) health centers, village clinics, outpatient departments, and clinics (medical offices).

(3) Professional public health institutions include disease prevention and control centers, specialized disease prevention institutions, maternal and child health institutions (including maternal and child health and family planning service centers), health education institutions, emergency centers (stations), blood collection and supply institutions, health supervision institutions, and Family planning technical service organizations with "Medical Institution Practicing License" or "Family Planning Technical Service License".

(4) Other medical and health institutions include nursing homes, clinical testing centers, medical research institutions, medical on-the-job education institutions, health supervision (monitoring, testing) institutions, medical examination centers, rural water reform centers, talent exchange centers, statistical information centers, etc. Institutions.

Hospitals including general hospitals, traditional Chinese medicine hospitals, integrated traditional Chinese and western medicine hospitals, ethnic hospitals, various specialized hospitals and nursing homes, excluding specialized disease prevention and treatment hospitals, maternal and child health care hospitals, and nursing homes, including hospitals affiliated to medical schools.

Practicing (Assistant) Physician refers to the practicing doctors and assistant practicing doctors who have obtained the doctor's practice certificate in medical and health institutions and are actually engaged in medical treatment, maternal and child health care, disease prevention and treatment, etc.

Health Technician including health professionals such as practicing physicians, practicing assistant physicians, registered nurses, pharmacists (persons), laboratory and imaging technologists (persons), health supervisors, and trainee doctors (medicine, nursing, technology) in medical and health institutions.

Social Welfare Institutions refers to institutions that collectively adopt social orphans, the disabled, and children, including social welfare homes, children's welfare homes, mentally ill welfare homes managed by the civil affairs department, welfare homes organized by urban collectives, nursing homes organized by rural collectives, and community services capable of adopting Central, etc.

附　录

APPENDIX

2020 年省内各市主要经济指标对比情况
MAJOR ECONOMIC INDICATORS ON CITIES OF THE PROVINCE (2020)

指标 Indicator	单位 Unit	全省 Whole province	青岛市 Qingdao	济南市 Jinan	淄博市 Zibo	枣庄市 Zaozhuang	东营市 Dongying
全市生产总值 (GDP)	亿元 (100 million yuan)	73129.0	12400.6	10140.9	3673.5	1733.2	2981.2
同比增长 Year-on- year Growth	%	3.6	3.7	4.9	2.5	3.0	3.8
规模以上工业增加值同比增长 Year-on- year Growth of Industrial Value Added on Regulations	%	5.0	5.5	12.2	3.6	1.4	6.3
固定资产投资同比增长 Year-on- year Growth of Investment Fixed Assets	%	3.6	3.2	4.0	7.5	3.2	8.9
货物进出口总额 Imports and Exports	亿元 (100 million yuan)	22009.4	6407.0	1382.7	887.7	263.8	1344.3
同比增长 Year-on- year Growth	%	7.5	8.2	22.9	0.1	80.2	-19.0
#货物出口 Exports	亿元 (100 million yuan)	13054.8	3876.8	755.0	489.2	249.8	455.3
同比增长 Year-on- year Growth	%	17.3	13.7	17.2	17.3	79.6	33.0
货物进口 Imports	亿元 (100 million yuan)	8954.6	2530.2	627.6	398.5	14.0	889.0
同比增长 Year-on- year Growth	%	-4.1	0.7	30.7	-15.2	91.7	-32.5
社会消费品零售总额同比增长 Year-on- year Growth of Total Retail Sales of Consumer Goods	%	0.0	1.5	1.1	-1.8	-2.6	-1.8
一般公共预算收入 General Public Budget Revenue	亿元 (100 million yuan)	6559.9	1253.8	906.1	321.5	140.8	249.3
同比增长 Year-on- year Growth	%	0.5	1.0	3.6	-12.8	-4.4	1.7
全体居民人均可支配收入 Disposable income per capita of all residents	元 (yuan)	32886	47156	43056	38932	27379	42204
同比增长 Year-on- year Growth	%	4.1	3.7	3.8	3.7	4.1	3.9
城镇居民人均可支配收入 Per Capita Disposable Income of Urban Residents	元 (yuan)	43726	55905	53329	46415	35098	52684
同比增长 Year-on- year Growth	%	3.3	2.6	2.7	2.6	3.1	3.0
农村居民人均可支配收入 Per Capita Disposable Income of Rural Residents	元 (yuan)	18753	23656	20432	20891	17690	20003
同比增长 Year-on- year Growth	%	5.5	4.8	5.0	4.9	5.6	5.2

烟台市 Yantai	潍坊市 Weifang	济宁市 Jining	泰安市 Taian	威海市 Weihai	日照市 Rizhao	临沂市 Linyi	德州市 Dezhou	聊城市 Liaocheng	滨州市 Binzhou	菏泽市 Heze
7816.4	5872.2	4494.3	2766.5	3017.8	2006.4	4805.3	3079.0	2316.8	2508.1	3483.1
3.6	3.6	3.6	3.5	3.0	3.8	3.9	3.6	2.8	3.7	3.9
7.7	8.3	5.9	5.4	4.6	9.9	7.8	5.5	3.4	3.6	3.4
2.9	4.5	3.2	2.9	2.9	3.2	4.0	−2.9	6.8	7.8	7.5
3214.9	1903.9	545.1	211.9	1614.6	1023.9	1167.2	386.9	404.2	817.5	433.8
10.7	6.4	18.3	24.8	15.1	−2.8	39.9	11.9	−1.0	−6.6	−10.6
1963.1	1215.6	386.1	145.9	1165.8	343.5	992.2	247.2	227.4	327.4	214.3
13.4	7.8	35.9	10.4	26.6	−15.5	46.2	21.6	10.2	5.1	21.9
1251.8	688.3	159.0	66.0	448.8	680.4	175.0	139.6	176.8	490.1	219.4
6.7	3.9	−9.9	75.5	−7.0	5.1	12.5	−2.0	−12.4	−13.1	−29.0
−0.2	0.1	−1.2	−3.0	0.3	−3.3	0.2	0.0	−3.2	1.1	1.2
610.1	573.9	411.8	229.2	252.4	176.3	349.8	208.5	202.0	252.8	237.9
2.5	0.5	1.7	2.0	1.0	3.5	6.0	1.1	2.7	4.0	7.2
39306	33919	29261	30937	41137	28695	28887	23626	22488	29718	21741
4.0	4.3	4.3	4.2	3.9	4.1	4.6	4.5	4.1	4.2	5.2
49434	43085	38368	38901	50424	36752	39466	29594	30036	38582	29365
3.0	3.4	3.3	3.2	2.8	2.9	4.1	3.7	2.8	3.2	3.7
22305	21651	18653	19682	23351	18274	15918	16996	15718	18496	15107
5.1	6.3	5.7	5.7	5.3	5.6	6.3	6.0	6.1	5.8	6.6

2020年十五个副省级城市主要经济指标对比表
MAJOR ECONOMIC INDICATORS ON CITIES UNDER PROVINCIAL LEVELS (2020)

指标 Indicator	单位 Unit	青岛 Qingdao	沈阳 Shenyang	大连 Dalian	长春 Changchun	哈尔滨 Haerbin
全市生产总值 (GDP)	亿元 (100 million yuan)	12400.6	6571.6	7030.4	6638.0	5183.8
同比增长 Year-on- year Growth	%	3.7	0.8	0.9	3.6	0.6
第一产业 Primary Industry	亿元 (100 million yuan)	425.4	303.6	459.2	533.8	615.8
同比增长 Year-on- year Growth	%	2.6	2.9	3.2	-2.4	2.1
第二产业 Secondary Industry	亿元 (100 million yuan)	4361.6	2160.4	2815.2	2758.1	1144.5
同比增长 Year-on- year Growth	%	3.0	2.9	4.3	8.0	2.3
第三产业 Tertiary Industry	亿元 (100 million yuan)	7613.6	4107.6	3756.0	3346.1	3423.5
同比增长 Year-on- year Growth	%	4.1	-0.6	-2.5	0.3	-0.4
三产占比 Three-yield ratio	%	61.4	62.5	53.4	50.4	66.0
规模以上工业增加值同比增长 Year-on- year Growth of Industrial Value Added on Regulations	%	5.5	2.8	3.8	10.4	4.2
固定资产投资同比增长 Year-on- year Growth of Investment Fixed Assets	%	3.2	4.1	0.1	8.8	2.8
社会消费品零售总额 Total Retail Sales of Consumer Goods	亿元 (100 million yuan)	5203.5	3637.6	1828.0	-	-
同比增长 Year-on- year Growth	%	1.5	-5.4	-11.5	-6.5	-11.3
货物进出口总额 Imports and Exports	亿元 (100 million yuan)	6407.0	1028.1	3854.2	1027.6	225.9
同比增长 Year-on- year Growth	%	8.2	-4.2	-11.7	3.0	1.5
#货物出口 Exports	亿元 (100 million yuan)	3876.8	274.4	1672.6	135.4	136.9
同比增长 Year-on- year Growth	%	13.7	-13.2	-13.8	-9.3	14.1
货物进口 Imports	亿元 (100 million yuan)	2530.2	753.7	2181.6	892.2	119.0
同比增长 Year-on- year Growth	%	0.7	-0.4	-10.0	5.2	-9.9
一般公共预算收入 General Public Budget Revenue	亿元 (100 million yuan)	1253.8	736.1	702.7	440.4	339.6
同比增长 Year-on- year Growth	%	1.0	0.8	1.4	1.5	-8.4
城镇居民人均可支配收入 Per Capita Disposable Income of Urban Residents	元 (yuan)	55905	47413	47380	40001	39791
同比增长 Year-on- year Growth	%	2.6	1.3	2.0	5.7	-0.5
农村居民人均可支配收入 Per Capita Disposable Income of Rural Residents	元 (yuan)	23656	19598	21558	-	19631
同比增长 Year-on- year Growth	%	4.8	8.1	7.9	-	7.6
居民消费价格指数 Consumer Price Index	上年同期=100 Preceding Year=100	102.4	102.3	102.1	101.9	101.4

注：部分城市数据未公布。
Note: Some of the urban income data has not been finalized.

南京 Nanjing	杭州 Hangzhou	宁波 Ningbo	厦门 Xiamen	济南 Jinan	武汉 Wuhan	广州 Guangzhou	深圳 Shenzhen	成都 Chengdu	西安 Xian
14818.0	16106.0	12408.7	6384.0	10140.9	15616.1	25019.1	27670.2	17716.7	10020.4
4.6	3.9	3.3	5.7	4.9	−4.7	2.7	3.1	4.0	5.2
296.8	326.0	338.4	28.9	361.7	402.2	288.1	25.8	655.2	312.8
0.9	−1.1	2.1	2.5	2.2	−3.8	9.8	−3.1	3.3	3.0
5214.4	4821.0	5693.9	2519.8	3530.7	5557.5	6590.4	10454.0	5418.5	3328.3
5.6	2.3	3.0	6.1	7.0	−7.3	3.3	1.9	4.8	7.4
9306.8	10959.0	6376.4	3835.3	6248.6	9656.4	18140.6	17190.4	11643.0	6379.4
4.1	5.0	3.6	5.5	3.7	−3.1	2.3	3.9	3.6	4.2
62.8	68.0	51.4	60.1	61.6	61.8	72.5	62.1	65.7	63.7
6.5	3.8	5.2	6.0	12.2	−6.9	2.5	2.0	5.0	7.0
6.6	6.8	5.5	8.8	4.0	−11.8	10.0	8.2	9.9	12.8
7203.0	5973.0	4238.3	2293.9	4469.1	6149.8	9218.7	8664.8	8118.5	4989.3
0.9	−3.5	−0.7	1.6	1.1	−20.9	−3.5	−5.2	−2.3	−2.9
5340.2	5934.2	9786.9	6915.8	1382.7	2704.3	9530.1	30502.5	7154.2	3473.8
10.6	5.9	6.7	7.8	23.0	10.8	−4.8	2.4	22.4	7.2
3398.9	3693.2	6407.0	3572.92	755.0	1421.7	5427.7	16972.7	4106.8	1776.0
13.0	2.1	7.3	1.2	17.2	4.3	3.2	1.5	23.7	2.6
1941.3	2240.9	3379.9	3342.9	627.6	1282.6	4102.4	13529.9	3047.4	1697.9
6.6	12.9	5.6	16.0	30.7	19.0	−13.6	3.6	20.7	12.3
1637.7	2093.0	1510.8	783.9	906.1	1564.1	1721.6	3857.4	1520.4	724.1
3.7	6.5	2.9	2.0	3.6	−21.3	1.4	2.2	2.5	3.1
67553	68666	68008	61331	53329	50362	68304	64878	48593	43713
4.9	3.9	4.8	3.9	2.7	−2.6	5.0	3.8	5.9	4.5
29621	38700	39132	26612	20432	24057	31266	–	26432	15749
7.2	6.7	6.8	7.3	5.0	−2.9	8.3	–	8.5	8.0
102.4	102.1	101.9	102.5	102.4	102.4	102.6	102.3	102.5	102.1

2020 年副省级城市之外部分城市主要经济指标情况

THE MAIN ECONOMIC INDICATORS OF SOME OTHER CITIES THAN THE SUB-PROVINCIAL CITY FOR (2020)

指标 Indicator	单位 Unit	北京 Beijing	天津 Tianjin	上海 Shanghai	重庆 Chongqing	苏州 Suzhou	无锡 Wuxi
全市生产总值（GDP）	亿元 (100 million yuan)	36102.6	14083.7	38700.6	25002.8	20170.5	12370.5
同比增长 Year-on-year growth	%	1.2	1.5	1.7	3.9	3.4	3.7
#第一产业 Primary Industry	亿元 (100 million yuan)	107.6	210.2	103.6	1803.3	196.4	128.1
同比增长 Year-on-year growth	%	-8.5	-0.6	-8.2	4.7	-2.0	1.6
第二产业 Secondary Industry	亿元 (100 million yuan)	5716.4	4804.1	10289.5	9992.2	9385.6	5751.2
同比增长 Year-on-year growth	%	2.1	1.6	1.3	4.9	3.4	4.3
第三产业 Tertiary Industry	亿元 (100 million yuan)	30278.6	9069.5	28307.5	13207.3	10588.5	6491.2
同比增长 Year-on-year growth	%	1.0	1.4	1.8	2.9	3.5	3.2
第三产业增加值占 GDP 比重 Proportion taken by the added value in GDP for the Tertiary Industry	%	83.8	64.4	73.1	52.8	52.5	52.5
规模以上工业增加值同比增长 YOY Growth of Industrial Added Value above Designated Size	%	2.3	1.6	1.7	5.8	6.0	6.6
固定资产投资同比增长 YOY Growth of Investment in Fixed Assets	%	2.2	3.0	10.3	3.9	6.6	6.1
社会消费品零售总额 Total Retail Sales of Consumer Goods	亿元 (100 million yuan)	13716.4	-	15932.5	11787.2	7702.0	2994.4
同比增长 Year-on-year growth	%	-8.9	-15.1	0.5	1.3	-1.4	-1.0
货物进出口总额 Imports and Exports	亿元 (100 million yuan)	23215.9	7340.7	34828.5	6513.4	22321.4	6075.6
同比增长 Year-on-year growth	%	-19.1	-0.1	2.3	12.5	1.5	-4.6
#货物出口总额 Exports	亿元 (100 million yuan)	4654.9	3075.1	13725.4	4187.5	12941.5	3547.1
同比增长 Year-on-year growth	%	-10.0	1.9	0.0	12.8	-2.2	-7.2
一般公共预算收入 General Public Budget Revenue	亿元 (100 million yuan)	5483.9	1923.1	7046.3	2094.8	2303.0	1075.7
同比增长 Year-on-year growth	%	-5.7	-10.2	-1.7	-1.9	3.7	3.8
城镇居民人均可支配收入 Per Capita Disposable Income of Urban Residents	元 (yuan)	69434	47659	76437	40006	70966	64714
同比增长 Year-on-year growth	%	2.5	3.3	3.8	5.4	3.4	4.5
农村居民人均可支配收入 Per Capita Disposable Income of Rural Residents	元 (yuan)	-	25691	34911	16361	37563	35750
同比增长 Year-on-year growth	%	-	3.6	5.2	8.1	6.9	6.5
居民消费价格指数 Consumer Price Index	%	101.7	102.0	101.7	102.3	102.2	102.3

中国统计出版社有限公司最新图书简目

(仅供参考,以实际出版为准)

统计资料

中国统计年鉴　中国统计摘要　中国第三产业统计年鉴
中国第三次全国农业普查综合资料　国际统计年鉴　金砖国家联合统计手册
中国-东盟国家统计手册　中国农村统计年鉴　中国县域统计年鉴
中国农产品价格调查年鉴　中国城市统计年鉴　中国价格统计年鉴
中国贸易外经统计年鉴　中国零售和餐饮连锁企业统计年鉴　中国商品交易市场统计年鉴
大中型批发零售和住宿餐饮企业统计年鉴　中国住户调查年鉴　中国工业统计年鉴
中国环境统计年鉴　中国能源统计年鉴　中国建筑业统计年鉴
中国房地产统计年鉴　中国投资领域统计年鉴　长江经济带发展统计年鉴
中国人口和就业统计年鉴　中国劳动统计年鉴　中国社会统计年鉴
中国科技统计年鉴　中国高技术产业统计年鉴　全国企业创新调查年鉴
中国文化及相关产业统计年鉴　中国妇女儿童状况统计资料　中国青年发展状况统计年鉴
中国基本单位统计年鉴　中国教育统计年鉴　中国教育经费统计年鉴
中国民族统计年鉴　中国残疾人事业统计年鉴　中国电力统计年鉴

省级综合统计年鉴系列

北京 天津 河北 山西 内蒙古 辽宁 吉林 黑龙江 上海 江苏 浙江 安徽 福建 江西 山东 河南 湖北 湖南
广东 广西 海南 重庆 四川 贵州 云南 西藏 陕西 甘肃 青海 宁夏 新疆 新疆生产建设兵团

市(县)级综合统计年鉴系列

滨海新区 石家庄 唐山 邯郸 邢台 保定 承德 沧州 衡水 太原 大同 晋城 晋中 长治 忻州 朔州 临汾 运城
阳泉 吕梁 呼和浩特 包头 鄂尔多斯 赤峰 大连 长春 四平 延吉 延边 哈尔滨 齐齐哈尔 黑龙江垦区 浦东新区
南京 无锡 徐州 常州 苏州 南通 淮安 盐城 扬州 镇江 宿迁 江阴 丹阳 海门 张家港 通州 如东 杭州 宁波
绍兴 台州 温州 金华 嘉兴 湖州 丽水 舟山 合肥 安庆 福州 厦门 漳州 宁德 龙岩 莆田 泉州 三明 南平 思明
南昌 上饶 抚州 赣州 九江 景德镇 宁都 济南 青岛 枣庄 潍坊 聊城 郑州 洛阳 三门峡 南阳 商丘 平顶山
信阳 济源 武汉 宜昌 十堰 荆州 荆门 咸宁 黄冈 长沙 广州 东莞 惠州 深圳 汕尾 珠海 南宁 桂林 柳州
防城港 贵港 梧州 玉林 钦州 海口 三亚 儋州 成都 贵阳 毕节 黔南 昆明 文山 德宏 西安 安康 延安 汉中
渭南 商洛 榆林 银川 兰州 庆阳 乌鲁木齐

调查年鉴系列

天津 内蒙古 上海 河南 湖北 湖南 广西 重庆 四川 云南 甘肃 宁夏 南宁 桂林 贵港 昆明

统计方法应用/实用手册

Python数据分析基础（第二版）　非参数统计（第五版）　现代金融投资统计分析（第四版）
国民经济核算初级教程（第二版）　国民经济核算教程（第五版）　概率统计基础
全国统计专业技术资格考试系列考试用书：统计业务知识（第四版修订版）　统计业务知识学习指导与习题
全国统计专业技术资格考试系列考试用书：统计相关知识（第四版）　统计相关知识学习指导与习题

统计通俗读物/统计科普图书

领导干部统计知识问答（第二版）　统计公文写作及会议办理实用手册　大数据在统计工作中的应用案例汇编
中国国民经济核算知识问答（修订版）　地区生产总值核算国际比较研究　新中国统计制度方法的发展与改革

重点图书

第七次全国人口普查年鉴　第四次全国经济普查地图集　中国经济普查年鉴2018
新编英汉汉英统计大词典　中国国民经济核算体系2016　国民经济行业分类注释
挑大学选专业2020—考研择校指南　挑大学选专业2020—高考志愿填报指南　中华医学统计百科全书

发行部电话：（010）63376907　63376908　63376909　同楫行书店电话：（010）68783171　68783172
地址：北京市丰台区西三环南路甲6号　邮政编码：100073　网址：http://www.zgtjcbs.com